OXFORD STUDIES IN
SOCIAL AND LEGAL HISTORY

OXFORD STUDIES
IN SOCIAL AND LEGAL
HISTORY

EDITED BY THE LATE

SIR PAUL VINOGRADOFF

VOL. IX

THE SOCIAL STRUCTURE OF
MEDIEVAL EAST ANGLIA

By DAVID C. DOUGLAS

LECTURER IN MEDIEVAL HISTORY TO THE UNIVERSITY OF GLASGOW

OCTAGON BOOKS

A DIVISION OF FARRAR, STRAUS AND GIROUX

New York   1974

Originally published in 1927 by the Clarendon Press

Reprinted 1974
by special arrangement with Oxford University Press, Inc.

OCTAGON BOOKS
A DIVISION OF FARRAR, STRAUS & GIROUX, INC.
19 Union Square West
New York, N. Y. 10003

Library of Congress Cataloging in Publication Data

Douglas, David Charles, 1898-
    The social structure of medieval East Anglia.

    Reprint of the 1927 ed. published by the Clarendon Press, Oxford, which was issued as v. 9 of Oxford studies in social and legal history.

    Includes bibliographical references.
    1. East Anglia. 2. Land tenure—Great Britain—History. I. Title. II. Series: Oxford studies in social and legal history, v. 9.

HD599.E27D68   333.3'23'09426   73-22288
ISBN 0-374-96168-9

Printed in USA by
Thomson-Shore,Inc.
Dexter, Michigan

PREFACE

THIS volume was planned and written under the supervision of the late lamented Sir Paul Vinogradoff, who directed the series of Oxford Studies in Social and Legal History from its inception in 1909 to the date of his death (19 December 1925). Nine volumes, containing sixteen substantial and valuable monographs, bear witness to the wide range of his studies in these branches of history, and to the high standard of scholarship which was inspired by his precepts and example in those who studied under him. It would be presumptuous to attempt, within the narrow limits of a preface, any appreciation of Vinogradoff's merits as an historian and a jurist. They have been worthily assessed by Professor F. M. Powicke in the *English Historical Review* (1926), by Professor W. S. Holdsworth in the *Proceedings of the British Academy* (1926), and by Professor de Zulueta in the *Law Quarterly Review* (1926). But in this place it is permissible to regret that death has cheated us of all but a fragment of the third volume of his *Historical Jurisprudence*, a work which, even in its unfinished state, is the most imposing monument of an intellect remarkable alike for its massiveness and its versatility. The Jurisprudence, Vinogradoff's last great undertaking, was published at the Clarendon Press, which had previously produced what we may call, in the original sense of the word, his masterpiece, *Villeinage in England*, and also the work on *English*

Society in the Twelfth Century, which was the firstfruit
of his labours in his Oxford Seminar.

Mr. Douglas has worked on a plan which was
perhaps suggested by a study of *English Society*. His
business has been to survey the rural life of East
Anglia in the twelfth and thirteenth centuries, com-
paring the evidence of Domesday Book with that of
thirteenth-century extents, and using the charter
materials of the twelfth century as clues in tracing the
process of development from the state of things revealed in Domesday to that revealed in the extents.
The survey is based upon a large mass of documentary
material, some of which Mr. Douglas has printed or
has analysed for the first time. Naturally he has
taken especial pains to test the theories of other in-
vestigators in the light of his new material. His
second chapter, for example, opens with a criticism of
Dr. H. L. Gray, who would reduce to a minimum the
effects of Scandinavian immigration on East Anglian
agriculture ; while towards the end of the chapter
some suggestions made by the late W. J. Corbett, by
Mr. G. T. Turner, and by Mr. J. C. Tingey are shown
to be compatible with the conclusions of Mr. Douglas
himself. His own conclusions have a substantial value
—especially the proof that the normal *tenementum* in
the East Anglian village was the *manloth* or bovate of
12½ acres of arable, with a toftland and a share in the
common meadow as appurtenances. In the sixteenth
century such holdings were not composed of scattered
acre-strips, but were compact blocks, because of the
prevalence of sheep-rearing. Mr. Douglas thinks that
this state of things can be traced back into the twelfth
century, since sheep-farming was already usual then,

and the virgate is a rare and anomalous apparition in East Anglian fields. However this may be, the commutation of customary services had gone so far in East Anglia by the thirteenth century that we may take for granted an abundance of coined money which is only to be explained by a brisk production of marketable produce. Side by side with a progressive system of agriculture we find in East Anglia some interesting survivals—notably the leets of north-west Norfolk, and the sokes which, unlike those of Bury St. Edmunds, were not private hundreds, but much more straggling areas. Mr. Douglas discusses the origins of these jurisdictions. He also illustrates the vitality of the soke-courts from charters in which the whole soke appear collectively as witnesses. Less significant perhaps are the cases in which he finds the householders of a township, or the congregation of a parish invited to fulfil this office. The most valuable assistance that he provides for other students working in his own or adjacent territory, is the appendix of sixtỷ-five East Anglian charters. This collection will be welcome for purposes of comparison to all who make use of Farrer's *Yorkshire Charters* or of the *Danelaw Charters* of Professor Stenton. It goes without saying that this valuable essay leaves unanswered many important questions that will naturally suggest themselves to curious readers. That is the fault of the evidence, not of Mr. Douglas, who has shown great discretion in fastening upon problems that are of interest in themselves, and are capable of being answered, at least in some measure, from his documents.

H. W. C. DAVIS.

PREFATORY NOTE

THIS essay was begun in connexion with the tenure by me of the Research Scholarship in Medieval History and Thought offered by the General Board of the Faculties of the University of Oxford in 1922.

It is hoped that the conclusions reached in the pages which follow are based upon a comprehensive study of the available material. Whilst they were in proof, however, a document came under the author's notice as having a considerable historical significance. This is a feudal survey drawn up by Abbot Baldwin of Bury St. Edmunds before the close of the eleventh century. None of the general conclusions of this essay need to be modified as the result of this discovery. But it is believed that this text may constitute an important addition to the literature of Domesday Book, and as such may have a wide bearing upon East Anglian social history. It is, however, too long to be included among the documents printed at the end of this volume, and I am at present editing it for separate publication.

Whilst I must hold myself responsible for the opinions expressed in these pages, I would like to thank all those scholars who have been good enough to help me with their criticism and advice. Among them my chief debt is to the late editor of this Series, who originally suggested the subject of this essay to me, and up to his death found time to supervise my work with that sympathy and interest known to all those who had the great privilege of being his pupils. My recollections of his constant kindness I share with many others: my own personal debt of gratitude to him can never be repaid or even adequately expressed. Mr. J. E. A. Jolliffe, of Keble College, I would thank for much very helpful criticism. Finally, my indebtedness to Professor Stenton's published work will be apparent to any one who reads these pages, but I should like here gratefully to acknowledge the help which he has always been ready to give. In particular my thanks are due to him for most generously allowing me access to his transcripts of charters, for calling my attention to many documents which would otherwise have escaped my notice, and for allowing me to benefit in so many ways by his unsurpassed knowledge of English twelfth-century material.

D. C. D.

THE UNIVERSITY OF GLASGOW
1926

CONTENTS

ABBREVIATIONS

A discussion of the main manuscript sources for this study will be found in Chapter I. Unless otherwise stated all references to MSS. are to collections in the British Museum.

The following abbreviations have also been used in the foot-notes:

Birch, *Cart. Sax.*   Birch, *Cartularium Saxonicum*.

D. B.   *Domesday Book*. (References are all to the Record Commission edition of 1783, &c.)

D. C.   *Danelaw Charters*, ed. F. W. Stenton. (Documents illustrative of the Social and Economic History of the Danelaw. British Academy Records of Social and Economic History, vol. v.)

Dugdale, *Monasticon*.   Dugdale, *Monasticon Anglicanum*, ed. 1817, &c.

E. H. R.   *English Historical Review*.

H. R.   *Hundred Rolls*, ed. Record Commission.

Kemble, *C. D.*   Kemble, *Codex Diplomaticus aevi Saxonici*.

Maitland, *D. B. B.*   Maitland, *Domesday Book and Beyond*.

O. S. L. S.   Oxford Studies in Social and Legal History.

R. C.   *Ramsey Cartulary* (Rolls Series).

R. H. S.   Royal Historical Society.

Thorpe, *Diplomatarium*.   Thorpe, *Diplomatarium Anglicum aevi Saxonici*.

V. C. H.   *Victoria County History*.

Y. C.   *Early Yorkshire Charters*, ed. Farrer.

CHAPTER I

INTRODUCTION

THE social history of East Anglia between the Norman
Conquest and the end of the thirteenth century has a peculiar
interest and a general importance. In the period immediately subsequent to Domesday the dominant factor which
has to be considered in the development of English social
organization is the broad distinction made in that record
between the Danish districts and those of the South and
West.[1] But the conditions revealed in the East Anglian
Domesday cannot strictly be placed in either of these categories,[2] though in particular details they present affinities to
each, and any estimate of the importance of Danish influence
on English medieval social arrangements and of its duration
must thus take account of the structure of this district. On
the other hand, from the paucity of direct evidence of the
pre-Conquest period for the East of England, the conditions
prevailing therein in the eleventh and twelfth centuries have
a retrospective significance.[3] All discussions, therefore, of the
early history of lordship in England must give due weight to
the exceptional character of the East Anglian Survey, where
the proportion of free peasants is far higher than in any other
county except Lincolnshire,[4] and the obligations to which

[1] Cf. Stenton, *Danelaw Charters* (*British Academy Sources of Social
and Economic History*, vol. v), p. 1.
[2] For a general discussion of the peculiarities of the East Anglian
Domesday cf. Maitland, *Domesday Book and Beyond*; Vinogradoff,
English Society in the Eleventh Century; Round, *Feudal England*.
For a more particular treatment see *V. C. H. Norfolk*, vol. ii, pp. 1–37
(Johnson), and *Suffolk*, vol. i, pp. 357–411 (Lees).
[3] Cf. the treatment of these conditions by Maitland and the late
Professor Vinogradoff, and the remarks of Professor Stenton in the
Introduction to the edition of Gilbertine charters published for the
Lincoln Record Society.
[4] Cf. the maps made by Seebohm, *English Village Community*, p. 85.

these are subject are not embraced in any rigid manorial scheme but are personal in their nature, irregular in their incidence, and heterogeneous in their scope.[1] All the more recent work on early English social history tends to show that an examination of the local conditions prevailing in different parts of the country is essential before further wide generalizations can be made. Such studies, therefore, have more than a merely topographical interest; and from the peculiar character of the East Anglian arrangements it might be hoped that their investigation would contribute to the interpretation of the forces governing medieval social development in England.

The amalgamation of Norfolk and Suffolk into one district is no mere matter of geographical propinquity, but the result of the earlier history of both counties. It is probable, indeed, both on historical[2] and archaeological[3] grounds, that no broad race distinction marked off the district at the time of the settlement, but the individual character of East Anglia is made clear from the seventh century onwards.[4] In later days the unity between the two shires is very pronounced, and is symbolized by their subjection to a common bishop and a common earl,[5] both of which have their origin in pre-Conquest arrangements of an early date. In the eleventh century, both before and after the Conquest, writs were often addressed to the magnates of Norfolk and Suffolk jointly,[6] and it seems probable that in the twelfth century the two shire courts often met together. Between 1114 and 1116 a grant of land was made by the son of 'Godric dapifer' the Domesday tenant to St. Benet of Hulme,[7] 'coram duobus comitatibus uidelicet Norfolchie et Suffolchie', and the close connexion of the two counties appears in many other post-Domesday documents.

[1] Maitland, *D. B. B.*, pp. 66 seq.
[2] Chadwick, *Origin of the English Nation*, pp. 54–89.
[3] Fox, *Archaeology of the Cambridge Region*, pp. 285 seq.
[4] The importance of East Anglia is first emphasized in the elevation of Redwald as Bretwalda.
[5] Round, *V. C. H. Essex*, vol. i, p. 333.
[6] Thorpe, *Diplomatarium, passim*.
[7] Cott. Galba E. ii, fol. 54. See Appendix I, No. 40.

Of more importance, however, than these administrative arrangements is the broad line of cleavage which marks off the district from the neighbouring shires, and is pre-supposed alike in the matter[1] and in the method[2] of the East Anglian Domesday. The most cursory inspection of the eleventh-century conditions shows this. Nowhere was the failure of the manor to comprise the agricultural and tenurial arrangements of society more noticeable, and no-where in consequence were the rights involved in lordship so miscellaneous or so loosely organized. In particular the complete lack of coincidence between manor and village is a most striking feature of the East Anglian Domesday, and though it has frequently been noticed, too much stress can hardly be laid upon it. If any group of East Anglian villages were to be examined it would be found that each contained on an average four to five ' manors ' within it, and sometimes the subdivision was very much greater.[3] Furthermore, the divergence between the manor and the village was per-manent, and the fourteenth-century returns embodied in *Feudal Aids*[4] show the continued existence of the exceptional Domesday conditions. The peculiar relation borne by the manor to the village in this district will have to be considered in many connexions. It is in a sense also reflected in the arrangement of the peasant classes in the East Anglian Domesday. The widespread existence of large numbers of freemen and socmen liable to a variety of duties and often

---

[1] Vinogradoff, *English Society*, p. 94.
[2] Dr. Round has described the Little Domesday as being characterized by ' its contractual forms, its inferior workmanship, and its marvellous wealth of detail ' : *V. C. H. Essex*, vol. i, p. 334. The best discussion of the general method of the East Anglian Survey is in Round, *Feudal England*.
[3] Fincham may be taken as a good example of one of these much-divided East Anglian villages. In Fincham no less than six tenants-in-chief held lands : the Abbot of Ely, William of Warenne, Hermer de Ferrers, the Abbot of St. Edmunds, Reynold the son of Ivo, and Ralf Bainard. The two last-named had stepped into the place of a freeman and free woman of Saxon times. Under William of Warenne there were three subtenants with different estates, and there were two groups of freemen. Rights of commendation and soke were also much divided in all cases and sometimes in dispute. *D. B.*, vol. ii, fols. 130, 159, 205, 209, 212 b, and 250 b. This might be paralleled in every hundred.
[4] *Feudal Aids*, vol. iii, pp. 461 seq. ; vol. v, pp. 35 seq.

able to go with their land where they would [1] has no parallel elsewhere in England. Yet while the implications of these conditions were, as will be seen, far-reaching, they are by no means the only distinguishing characteristics of the East Anglian Domesday. Norfolk and Suffolk are 'carucated' shires like those belonging to the Danelagh proper and in this respect to be contrasted with the South and West.[2] But the carucates in this district do not break up as elsewhere into bovates, but into holdings containing irregular numbers of acres. In contrast also with the wapentake arrangements of the northern Danelagh, East Anglia is divided into hundreds of more or less equal size.[3] But the geld arrangements in which they are involved at once distinguish the district from the adjoining counties in which similar hundreds exist. In East Anglia the geld is assessed primarily not according to carucates [4] but according to a system peculiar to the district. Each village is calculated as contributing so many pence to every pound of geld furnished by the hundred and the hundred's pound is subdivided among 'leets'.[5] Such arrangements are interesting in themselves and need special examination. Nothing about them is, however, more remarkable than the manner in which they mark the unity of the district and distinguish it in different ways, alike from Lincolnshire on the North, from Cambridgeshire on the West, and from Essex on the South.

The peculiarities of this district suggest two lines of special inquiry. In the loose organization of East Anglia it might be hoped that the various stages of social developments common throughout England could perhaps be more closely examined than elsewhere. But the main purpose of an investigation

---

[1] Maitland, *D. B. B.*, p. 73 ; Vinogradoff, *English Society*, pp. 431 seq.

[2] 'The carucated north of England is the land of the Norse people, and the suggestion that it was as such contrasted with the hidated south seems a very appropriate one.' Vinogradoff, *English Society*, p. 147.

[3] Corbett, *R. H. S. Trans.*, New Series, vol. xiv.

[4] These, however, were connected with a sub-repartition on a tenurial basis. Cf. Maitland, *D. B. B.*, pp. 429 seq., but contrast Johnson, *V. C. H. Norfolk*, vol. ii, p. 8.

[5] On the whole question of the leet's geld cf. Round, *Feudal England*, pp. 98 seq., and cf. Lees, *V. C. H. Suffolk*, vol. ii, pp. 361 seq.

into the conditions prevailing in a restricted area must always be to bring them into relation with the social history of England as a whole. On the one hand it is important thus to discover to what extent the specifically Danish characteristics of the North and Midlands are to be found in East Anglia. In this respect the territorial soke, the twelve-carucated hundred, and Danish systems of land sharing form the most convenient tests of Scandinavian influence. On the other hand some estimate of the relation in which the district stood to the development of manorial and social organization in England is imperative. And in this connexion it might specially be inquired how far the conditions described in the Little Domesday itself were the result of a peculiar terminology or represented actual facts. The presence in these counties of large numbers of free peasants, for instance, has formed in the past a turning-point in a great controversy. Some scholars[1] have held that the effect of the Danish invasions on a society consisting mainly of praedial serfs from the time of the original settlements resulted in the East in the conditions to be found in eleventh-century Norfolk and Suffolk. Against this it was urged that such conditions themselves forbade the acceptance of any theory which postulated the general servitude of the mass of the English peasantry from the sixth century onwards, whether the East Anglian Domesday organization is to be viewed as the outcome of a new incursion of tribal warriors or as the result of the survival of earlier arrangements.[2] It is thus of considerable importance to ascertain how far the conditions presented in the East Anglian survey are reflected in the documents most nearly contemporary therewith, and how far, if this is the case, they remained a permanent feature of the twelfth-century social structure of Norfolk and Suffolk. The descriptive method of the Little Domesday also renders it possible to examine another aspect of the same general problem. For the inter-relation of manor and village can nowhere be watched so

---

[1] Cf. especially Seebohm, *English Village Community*, pp. 98 seq.

[2] Cf. especially the treatment of the whole question of the conditions in the East of England by Maitland (*D. B. B.*).

closely in England as in this district, and the twelfth and thirteenth centuries are the critical period in which it might be
discovered how far the loose arrangements depicted in the East
Anglian Domesday were transformed into a rigidly manorialized scheme of society. Both in relation to the problem of
Scandinavian influence on English society and the contrast
which it implies between the Danelagh and the South and
West, and with regard to the question of the development of
English seignorial organization, there seem to be indicated
certain specific lines of inquiry by which the social history of
medieval East Anglia might be made of general importance to an interpretation of the 'growth of the manor' in
England.

The documents relating to East Anglian conditions in the
earlier Middle Ages are fairly numerous and to some extent
remarkable. The starting-point of any inquiry here, as elsewhere, must be the Domesday Survey, and the description of
Norfolk and Suffolk forms therein the greater part of the
so-called Little Domesday, whose earlier date and extended
form sometimes facilitates investigation into matters concealed
by the greater compression and more ordered arrangement
of the other counties of England. The actual date of the
Little Domesday is a matter of some doubt, but the well-known
writ of William Rufus to St. Benet of Hulme [1] suggests that
the long process of compilation lasted until nearly the end of
the eleventh century. As a corollary to Domesday there
is the Inquisitio Eliensis, but, as has been shown,[2] the section
of that interesting record which refers to Essex, Norfolk, and
Suffolk was in all probability compiled from the Little
Domesday itself and is consequently of little use in supple-
menting the information of the Survey. There is also a
somewhat similar record relating to the lands of St. Edmund
contained in the twelfth-century 'Registrum Nigrum' of that
abbey which is preserved in the Cambridge University

---

[1] Cott. Galba E. ii, fol. 30. For the significance of this writ and of the
other evidence for the dating of the Little Domesday cf. Johnson, *op. cit.*,
pp. 3 seq.
[2] Round, *Feudal England*, pp. 123 seq.

Library.[1] This contains some interesting additions to the
Survey, two of which have been printed by Gage.[2] But the
real interest of this difficult text lies in the appendix thereto,
which is headed 'Hec sunt terre feudatorum hominum sancti
Edmundi et Baldwini abbatis que, cum superius inter alias
conscripte sunt, ideo nunc rescribuntur ut quantum unusquisque teneat hoc scire uolentibus facile hic pateat '.[3] A comparison of this curious record, which occupies eleven folios of
the MS., with Domesday Book suggests that the lands of
these men are to be found in the Survey in the lands of the
freemen and sokemen which the Little Domesday always
clearly distinguishes from the manorial descriptions proper.[4]

For a repetition of anything like the comprehensive surveys
comprised in Domesday we have to wait till the thirteenth
century. The 'Hundred Rolls' and the 'Placita Quo Warranto' are scanty, however, in their treatment of East Anglia.
Nor are the various Ministers' Accounts in the Public Record
Office relating to estates in the district of any special importance.[5] The main source of our later evidence is thus supplied
by the registers and extents of the great religious houses. A
large proportion of these terriers have been examined for the
purposes of this essay. The most important of these are the
records of the See of Ely, which have long been known and
valued by scholars. These are three in number, and they
date from 1222, 1256, and 1277. The first[6] and the last[7] of
these extents are in the British Museum, that of 1256 is still
preserved in the Muniment Room of the bishop in Ely.[8] As
early as 1894 Maitland remarked that 'these Ely extents
ought to be published as soon as possible ',[9] and it is much to
be hoped that this will soon be done. For these registers are

---

[1] MS. MM. 4. 19, fols. 124–41. The importance of this text in its
relation to Domesday is probably very considerable. It cannot be fully
appraised within the scope of this essay. I am at present editing it for
publication.

[2] Gage, *History of Suffolk*, pp. 100 *n.* and 387 *n.*

[3] MS. MM. 4. 19, fol. 132.   [4] Ibid., fols. 132–41.

[5] Certain of these accounts are preserved for the lands of the See of
Ely.   [6] Cott. Tib. B. ii.   [7] Cott. Claud. C. xi.

[8] The Coucher Book (Ely Muniment Room).

[9] *E. H. R.*, vol. ix, p. 418 *n.*

of quite peculiar interest, not only for their matter but because of the method in which they are drawn up. The closeness of their dates makes it possible to watch the more minute changes in the tenurial arrangements of these manors, and, what is more important, the fact that they are all arranged according to an exactly similar method makes such a comparison unusually easy. The exceptionally categorical character of their arrangement furthermore shows a remarkably well-marked distinction between the peasant classes which is emphasized by plentiful contemporary rubrics. It is thus that these documents are especially well fitted to serve as 'an illustration of the continuity of the fundamental character of the feudal village '.[1] Besides these extents there are those concerning East Anglia contained in the Ramsey Cartulary [2] which date both from the thirteenth and from the late twelfth century. Numerous documents containing extents of the lands of St. Edmunds are preserved both in the British Museum and in the Cambridge University Library,[3] and among the records of this house may be particularly mentioned the survey which Jocelyn of Brakelonda tells us was drawn up by Abbot Samson and called by him his ' Kalendar '.[4] Part of this was printed by Gage as an Introduction to his *History of Suffolk*.[5] Reference has also been made to the one terrier of the Bishop of Norwich which is in the British Museum,[6] a thirteenth-century text whose interest is by no means exhausted with its elaborate descriptions of the manor of Martham, the importance of which has recently been stressed by Mr. Hudson.[7] There is also in the British Museum a cartulary of the Priory of Binham,[8] drawn up in the fourteenth century and containing some extents. Of these, that of the

---

[1] Vinogradoff, *Villainage in England*, p. 441.   [2] Ed. Rolls Series.
[3] A complete list of these is given in *V. C. H. Suffolk*, vol. ii, pp. 56-7.
[4] ' Facta eo iubente descriptio generalis per hundredos de letis et sectis de hidagiis et foddercorn de gallinis reddendis et aliis consuetudinibus et redditibus et exitibus qui in magna parte semper celati fuerant per firmarios et omnia redegit in scriptum. . . . Hanc autem librum vocavit Kalendarium.' *Memorials of St. Edmund's Abbey* (Rolls Series), vol. i, p. 235.
[5] pp. xii–xvii.   [6] Stowe MS. 936.
[7] *R. H. S. Trans.*, 4th Series, vol. i and vol. iv, and *Norfolk Archaeological Society Trans.*, 1921.   [8] Cott. Claud. D. xiii.

manor of Binham itself merits some particular note. In the main it is of the early years of Edward II,[1] but it includes a smaller extent which purports to date from the time of the foundation of the abbey itself and is prefaced by the heading, ' Incipit tenura tenentium de Binham in prima fundatione per dominum Petrum de Valognis '.[2] Matthew Paris speaks of the Priory as being in existence in 1093,[3] and the foundation charter may be dated 1104,[4] so that if we could take the statement of the Register at its face value we would have in this record an almost unique detailed description of a manor at that period. It seems, however, impossible to do this.[5] But the extent was certainly meant to indicate what to these early fourteenth-century jurors was remote antiquity, and it seems reasonable to suppose that this retrospective document in the later Survey reflects twelfth-century conditions. The possibility must further always be entertained that these later jurors were working from an actual early text, which would account for their precise dating of the foundation extent, and in any case this text supplies another of the none too common instances where the conditions described in a later terrier can be compared with an extent of an earlier age intermediate between it and the Domesday Survey.

While for East Anglia the material supplied by the thirteenth-century registers is fairly copious and the Domesday description is unusually full, the problem for this district as for England generally is to link up the two series of records and to bridge the dark gulf which lies in between them. Our knowledge of twelfth-century conditions throughout England has for the most part to be laboriously constructed from isolated charters. And it is just here that the East Anglian evidence is of peculiar interest. Professor Stenton has shown the value of twelfth-century charters alike as direct evidence of social conditions and as offering an explanation of Domes-

---

[1] Ibid., fol. 10 b.   [2] Ibid., fol. 5, and see Appendix II, No. 3.

[3] *Vita Sancti Albani*, p. 1002.

[4] Dugdale, *Mon. Ang.*, vol. iii, p. 329 ; cf. *V. C. H. Norfolk*, vol. ii, p. 343.

[5] 40 per cent. of the personal names in this extent are of O.E. or O.N. derivation which agrees with a late twelfth-century date.

day itself.[1] In the abundance of such material East Anglia will bear comparison only with Yorkshire and the Danelagh.[2] The value of such evidence is enhanced by the fact that in the isolated grants by peasants or small land-holders, either to each other or to the church, a light is sometimes thrown on the arrangements within vills outside the ecclesiastical lands to which the post-Domesday material mostly relates. But quite apart from this, the value of such charters as evidence of the social arrangements of the twelfth century and as a commentary on the great Survey can hardly be over-estimated.

The bulk of such documents is to be found in the cartularies of the religious houses, and of these a large number contain deeds relative to East Anglia. Outside such printed sources as the Ramsey Cartulary and the Colchester Cartulary[3] there are fairly numerous unprinted texts. In the Muniment Room at Ely there is a large Cartulary[4] which is of great value in throwing light on certain early transactions relative to the lands of the abbey and the bishopric,[5] whilst in the Cambridge University Library the Registrum Nigrum of St. Edmund has been found to contain many interesting early East Anglian documents. But the majority of the East Anglian cartularies to which reference has been made are to be found in the British Museum. Of the greatest importance among these is that belonging to Castleacre Priory.[6] This text is drawn up in a late thirteenth-century hand and it contains a great number of peasant gifts. It is mainly concerned with transactions relating to small parcels of land, and the complete form in which the charters are transcribed makes it possible usually to date with some degree of accuracy the deeds contained therein. There are also a large number of charters in the Binham cartulary, some of which are of very early date. Besides these texts the valuable cartulary of St.

---

[1] Introduction to *D. C.*
[2] Especially as regards peasant charters. Cf. Stenton, *D. C.*, p. cii.
[3] Ed. Roxburghe Club.
[4] Ely Muniment Room, Liber ' M '.
[5] The abbey possessions were split up in 1109 by Henry I when the bishopric was created. The division is described in detail in an original charter in the British Museum: Harl. Ch. 43, H. 4.
[6] Harl. MS. 2110.

Benet of Hulme,[1] whose importance has recently been stressed by Professor Stenton,[2] has also been found to contain many twelfth-century documents of considerable importance. There are also a good number of early charters to be found in two fifteenth-century cartularies. The former of these is that of the Priory of Lewes[3] which possessed considerable estates in East Anglia, and in one case a comparison between the text given in the cartulary and that of the original charter[4] has testified to the accuracy with which these fifteenth-century scribes copied documents of some three hundred years earlier date. The other of these fifteenth-century registers is the curious paper cartulary of the Earls of Warwick,[5] from which have been taken the very early charters relating to the soke of Necton.

Whilst it is in these and a few less important cartularies that in the main must be sought the twelfth-century charter evidence concerning East Anglia, there are also many original deeds which are of great value in estimating the social conditions of the period. It is probable that a great many of these could be found scattered about the various libraries of the kingdom, but in the British Museum is certainly to be found the nucleus of the national collection. The value of such documents has recently been very fully shown with the publication of the twelfth-century charters of Yorkshire[6] and the Danelagh,[7] and the East Anglian documents of the same date are sufficiently numerous to make it highly desirable that a printed collection of these should be published to enlarge our knowledge of what is certainly the least contestable of all evidence of twelfth-century social conditions.

The twelfth-century charter material from East Anglia is indeed sufficiently extensive to make it possible that it might serve to illustrate what is known of the diplomatic characteristics of such documents.[8] The epistolary form from which

---

[1] Cott. MS. Galba E. ii.   [2] *E. H. R.*, vol. xxxvii, p. 225 seq.
[3] Cott. MS. Vesp. F. xv.
[4] D. of L. Misc. Books, A. 75/4, and see Appendix I, No. 24.
[5] Add. MS. 28024.   [6] Ed. Farrer.   [7] Ed. Stenton.
[8] Cf. Stenton, *Gilbertine Charters*, Introduction (Lincoln Record Society), upon which the whole of this paragraph is based.

all such deeds are ultimately derived is very marked in certain
of these charters,[1] and the pious motive which marks their
ecclesiastical origin is also very prominent and sometimes
enlarged to an extent which is unusual in twelfth-century
texts.[2] An early charter in the Hulme Register also offers an
example of the post-Conquest anathema.[3] As in the Danelagh,[4] too, there is the same tendency towards uniformity, and
the charters of all free men under the king are for the most
part couched in terms which do not vary very greatly
with the social position of the donor. There are, however,
indications that this general statement is not universally
true. There is for instance a writ[5] issued by Richard
Basset in the identical royal form, which is curious, even if we
assume that he was acting as the king's representative in his
capacity as sheriff of eleven shires,[6] and the royal 'Quare uolo
et firmiter precipio' is not unknown in the early Warenne
charters.[7] Such cases are, however, clearly exceptions to a
general unifying development of formulae coinciding here
as elsewhere with the growth of royal justice.[8]

In these East Anglian documents of the twelfth century the
confirmatory function of the charter is also illustrated with
great precision. The purpose of the charter we have been
told was to record a transaction which had already taken
place and is appropriately spoken of in the past tense. The
symbolical acts which were the essence of the transference of
possession are in fact rarely referred to in these documents,

---

[1] e. g. Add. MS. 28024, fol. 183 b, and see Appendix I, No. 59.
[2] e. g. Cott. Claud. D. xiii, fol. 173, and see Appendix I, No. 37 : 'Hanc
itaque elemosinam feci pro salute mea tam corporis et anime et pro
salute uxoris mee cuius instinctu hoc opus aggressus sum et pro remedio
animarum patris et matris et parentum eorum et ut me deus meritis
sancte Marie protegat et defendat et in presenti succurrat ad uitam
eternam perducet.'
[3] Cott. Galba E. ii, fol. 54 : 'Quicunque hanc conuencionem dissoluere
presumpserit ex auctoritate dei patris omnipotentis et Sancte Marie uirginis
et sancti Benedicti omniumque sanctorum dei et sanctorum canonum ac
nostri misterii perpetuo anathemate feriantur. Amen.' Appendix I,
No. 39.
[4] Stenton, *Gilbertine Charters*, Introduction (Lincoln Record Society),
p. xxxiii.   [5] Cott. Galba E. ii, fol. 58 b, and see Appendix I, No. 48.
[6] *D. N. B.*   [7] e. g. Harl. 2110, fols. 1–7.
[8] Stenton, *op. cit.*, p. xvi.

but the rare allusions to them are sometimes of great interest.
Occasionally it is mentioned that the gift has been made at
the altar of the church or in the presence of the full chapter
of a religious house.[1] Sometimes also, as in the Danelagh,[2]
older rites have survived in the terminology of these charters.
' Hanc conuentionem ', we read, ' sine fraude et ingenio
tenendam affidauimus ego Richardus et Willelmus frater
meus et Robertus Iordanus et Osbertus clericus de Sipedham
in manu Willelmi dapiferi in preseneia (*sic*) domini Henrici
prioris de Acra ',[3] and we have probably reference to a similar
physical act in the vaguer phrase, ' pro hac concessione est
prefatus Petrus meus affidatus '.[4] In one or two documents,
indeed, the distinction between the formal ratification of the
charter and the formal donation itself is made exceptionally
prominent. A gift of Abbot Anselm [5] of St. Benet of Hulme
to William of Curcun is witnessed in the normal way ; but
the document proceeds to relate how William had actually
received the land from Abbot Richer (1125–7), and had then
sworn fealty to the abbey. A new list of witnesses who
testify to the gift itself is then introduced by the phrase,
' Testimonio eorum qui affuerunt '. Another deed in the
Benet of Hulme [6] cartulary gives a similar dual attestation,
one part of which is described as having taken place in the
fields in which the land lay and certainly refers to a
ceremonial act ; and yet another early document, this time
in the Binham register,[7] is first attested by the prior and a
subjoined list of witnesses, and then (*deinde*) in the village of
Ingoldisthorpe where the gift was situated before all the
villagers and another quite distinct series of witnesses. The
usual order is here reversed, and the charter is therefore
couched in the present tense, but there can be little doubt

[1] Plentiful examples of this are to be found in the early charters in Cott.
Galba E. ii.
[2] Cf. Stenton, *op. cit.*, p. xxix.
[3] Cott. Nero C. iii, fol. 191, fig. 1. See Appendix I, No. 22.
[4] Harl. Ch. 50 B. 37. See Appendix I, No. 7.
[5] Cott. Galba E. ii, fol. 56. See Appendix I, No. 43.
[6] Cott. Galba E. ii, fol. 56 b. See Appendix I, No. 51.
[7] Cott. Claud. D. xiii, fol. 173. See Appendix I, No. 37.

that in this deed also we have another of the rare twelfth-
century references to a ceremony of donation at the actual
site of the gifted land.

It is thus in their attestation clauses that these East Anglian
charters are formally of most interest. In this district also
there is evidence that the function of witness was changing
throughout the century, at the close of which the vague ' hiis
testibus' tends uniformly to conceal the action of witnesses
who frequently never saw the charter to which their attestation was appended.[1] While Richard pledges his faith in the
hands of William the Steward before numerous witnesses, the
charter recording this act is itself attested by a group of
people who probably played a far less personal part in the
matter.[2] In the deeds of this district, as of those of Lincolnshire,[3]
the occasional addition of witnesses in ink different from that
of the body of the charter suggests that they had subsequently
been 'called in testimony' of a document which had already
been ratified and of whose content they were but generally informed. After a very curiously attested document, for instance,
concerning land at Nettlestead, there is added in different ink
the remark ' Hoc a nobis precipi audierunt ex baronibus
comitis Alani Alanus Aimeric et Gaufridus Aldroini anno ab
incarnatione domini MCXXXVIIII '.[4] There is, however, also to
be found in these charters an unusually copious collection of
phrases which indicate the physical presence of the witnesses
at the ratification. The best instances of this are perhaps
the remarkably numerous charters of this district attested by
groups of men belonging to the same agricultural or administrative organization. The charters witnessed by villages,
sokes, and hundreds will have to be discussed in some detail
in this essay. They are, however, noticeable in this connexion
in that they offer the best illustration of the manner in which
an attestation did in fact often imply the actual presence of
the witness. With the remark that a gift of land in Yarmouth

---

[1] Cf. Stenton, *Gilbertine Charters*, Introduction, p. xxxi.
[2] Cott. Nero C. iii, fol. 191, fig. 1.   See Appendix I, No. 22.
[3] Stenton, *D. C.*, Introduction, p. ciii.
[4] Add. Ch. 28322.   See Appendix I, No. 16.

is witnessed by ' multi seniores et iuniores de uilla '[1] the very presence of these men is strongly suggested ; with such phrases as ' coram socna . . . teste socna ',[2] ' coram capitulo de hundredo ',[3] ' omni uillata . . . teste ',[4] all doubt about the matter is removed. In one case we have a very unusual description of the ratification itself, when a donor actually instructs his reeve ' ut cartula hec in ecclesia coram tota parrochia legatur ut parrochiani omnes huius doni mei testes sint '.[5] Such amplifications are very rare in all twelfth-century documents, and their occurrence in these East Anglian texts is of interest in supplying additional evidence of a diplomatic development which has been observed elsewhere. The form and number of the twelfth-century texts relating to the Danelagh have a wide bearing on the social history of that district, and it s of considerable importance to note the similarity to them in each respect of the East Anglian charters of the same period.

The most superficial examination of the scope of East Anglian medieval social history and its bearing upon general problems, coupled with the briefest notification of the materials upon which it must be based, thus suggests features of interest. A more detailed study of such conditions falls naturally under three heads. In the first place the intimate connexion of primitive social arrangements with land-holding indicates that an examination of the tenemental organization of the district might serve to lay bare the foundation beneath its social structure. Owing to the nature of the early evidence such a study must take cognizance of the geld arrangements which were in England so closely bound up with the division of the land. Secondly, an analysis and criticism of the rents and services, by which the tenements were held, might aptly illustrate the variations of peasant tenure and status. And lastly, the relation of the jurisdictional organization, which lay at the root of all medieval government, to both of these problems might illustrate the manner in which the various

---

[1] Bodleian Library, Norfolk Charters, 602. See Appendix I, No. 25.
[2] P.R.O., D. of L., Misc. Books A. 75/4. See Appendix I, No. 24.
[3] Cott. Nero C. iii, fol. 191, fig. iv. See Appendix I, No. 23.
[4] Cott. Claud. D. xiii, fol. 121. See Appendix I, No. 36.
[5] Add. Ch. 28322. See Appendix I, No. 16.

peasant groups were held together and enable a wider view
to be taken of the general social organization of the district.
It is within these categories that the East Anglian conditions
will be examined in the pages which follow, and in each
inquiry some estimate will be attempted of the relation borne
by the district alike to the Danelagh and to the south-west,
and of the position occupied by East Anglia in the social
history of medieval England.

CHAPTER II

TENEMENTAL ORGANIZATION

THE series of extents and registers which record the arrangement and the administration of the lands of the great religious
houses, supplemented by such other evidence as we possess,
should supply a basis for the discussion of the holdings of the
East Anglian peasantry and perhaps throw a retrospective
light upon the tenemental conditions described in the Little
Domesday. The categorical nature of the Ely Registers
suggests furthermore two lines of inquiry. On the one hand,
in these documents might be found a further illustration of
medieval arrangements of holdings, and on the other hand,
some answer might be made to the question whether any such
could be termed characteristically free. These two aspects of
the problem are in a sense complementary to one another;
but in reality the difference between them is fundamental in
that it represents the dual nature of the development of
peasant holdings throughout England. The division of
tenements, if such there be, into those distinctively free and
those distinctively servile, is in its essence a matter relative to
a lord, and in the will of the lord is in truth to be found one
of the formative influences in the development of holdings.
But in the history of early tenure there is always another
development to be considered in which the distinction between
the 'free' and the 'servile' is of minor importance. The
intimate connexion between agricultural conditions and the
arrangement of tenements in primitive times is never to be
neglected, and the formation and growth of medieval peasant
holdings in England was largely the result of the exigencies
of co-operative husbandry. Account must be taken of both
factors in any consideration of the early history of land
holding in England. Differences between the free and servile

tenements may be looked for as the result of the action of the lord, who will endeavour to preserve intact the servile tenements as units of service. But the basis of the tenemental arrangements of both free and servile is to be found, in East Anglia as elsewhere, in the economic conditions created by primitive husbandry.

The medieval agriculture of East Anglia constitutes an important variety of open field farming, though it involved many exceptional practices. A land of large villages rather than isolated hamlets,[1] its agriculture was based upon the division of the holdings amongst the strips in the open fields, as was the case elsewhere. In view of the striking peculiarities of the system of tenemental arrangement in this district this fact deserves some emphasis and some illustration. The common terms associated with such methods of farming are of frequent occurrence in the early East Anglian charters, and we find continually references to such distinctive features as ' culturae ', ' linches ', and ' gore acres '.[2] The East Anglian evidence is in this respect similar to that recently published concerning Yorkshire [3] and the Danelagh,[4] which also discloses

---

[1] Cf. Maitland, *Domesday Book and Beyond*, pp. 15 seq.

[2] e. g. ' vi acras in campo de Lucheam in fine culture de Mesegrave ', Harl. 2110, fol. 22 b. ' iiii acras terre in medio culture mee ', fol. 22 b. Throughout this cartulary the cultura is the normal description in the allocation of land. Again we have reference to ' illam peciam terre que vocatur Gildengore ', fol. 10 b; and land at Rougham is located at Aluesgore, fol. 29. Reference to linches occur in Harl. 2110, fols. 9, 10 b, 11, e. g. ' Alteram acram que iacet in campis iuxta linches (Acre) ', fol. 9. Linches are mentioned also on fols. 10 b, 11.

[3] Farrer, *Yorkshire Charters, passim*.

[4] Stenton, *Danelaw Charters, passim* ; e. g. ' Tresdecim sellones in territorio de Gunnebi que abutissant super Siche inter culturam magistri Walteri de Braitof ex orientali parte et Upelangesiche ex occidentali parte ', *D. C.* 29. Cf. also reference to ' foreram meam ad Roudmor ', *D. C.* 111. Also : ' in campis de Clakesbi de feudo Godardi in diuersis locis ', *D. C.* 238. At Riby we have a gift of 2 bovates divided into 12 parcels, *D. C.* 533. These may be compared with the detailed descriptions of land in Lincolnshire in the Croyland Register (cf. Cole's transcripts, Add. MS. 5845, fol. 64 b) ; but the best example of the strength of these customs in a Danelagh vill occurs in the twelfth-century charter (*D. C.* 202) concerning land at Great Sturton, by which a lord in order to make his gifts the more acceptable to the church at Kirkstead took the following action : ' Concessi . . . totum dimidium dominii mei de Stretuna in terra arabili et totum dimidium prati dominii mei eiusdem uille. Set quia culture illius mei dominii iacent mixte inter terras hominum meorum et monachi

a picture of the open fields in those districts as the basis of the agricultural life of the villages. References to land scattered about in the open fields are common in the East Anglian documents.[1] The small gifts described in the Castleacre cartulary show everywhere the presence of the scattered strips.[2] The description of the demesne land in the Ely manors suggests that the possession of that land in severalty by the lord was even in the late thirteenth century exceptional in East Anglia,[3] and the whole extent of the manor of Barney taken in the early fourteenth century for the Priory of Binham reveals with the utmost clearness the scattered condition of the peasant tenements.[4] But whilst this is so, it is rarely possible to construct from the evidence at hand any definite picture of the sequence of strips. Usually when the position of the holdings is given in the fields the strips seem to occur in the fields quite independently of any

uolunt habitare ab aliis remoti ideo congregavi terram dominii mei et terram hominum meorum in extremitate camporum uersus Minthiges et dedi illam monachis in simul habendam dedi hominibus meis de Stretuna escambium de terra dominii mei pro parte sua terre quam habebant ad libitum eorum.'

[1] The later charters normally bring out the scattered nature of the peasant holdings, and make it clear that the appearance of East Anglian village fields must have been different in no sense from those of the rest of England. The admirable plans given by Gray, *op. cit.*, p. 320, illustrate this. Rye's transcriptions of Norfolk fines show again the same picture, and an excellent example of the continuance of the strip system in Norfolk until later days is presented in Miss Davenport's monograph on Forncett.

[2] Cf. among many other examples : ' duas acras terre mee in campis de Castleacre scilicet in West feld quarum una acra iacet inter terram Radulphi de Duntune et terram Walteri Kineman et abuttat ad unum capud super terram Hugonis Withie versus orientem et ad aliud super terram Hugonis Gerebod versus occidentem. Et alia acra terre iacet apud Repetunedele inter terram domini comitis Warenne et terram Reinerii Campellun' et unum capud abutat super terram Georgii filii Wile versus austrum et aliud abutat super terram Nicholai de Trunchet versus aquilonem.' Harl. 2110, fol. 8. Cf. also : ' iii acras et iii percatas terre in campis de Rucham duas acras scilicet iuxta Gatecroft que iacent inter terras Ricardi de Butilier et Thomae filii Agnetae et i acram in meredele dimidia roda minus inter terras predicti Thomae et Matilde quondam uxoris Henrici Reinaldi et iii percatas et dimidiam apud Hodeswell inter terras Scule et Rogeri Peko ' (Rougham), Harl. 2110, fol. 32.

[3] It is rare even on the Ely lands for the demesne to be held in severalty, and when this is so it is noted in the extents as an exceptional privilege.   [4] Cott. Claud. D. xiii, fols. 62, 75 b.

settled scheme.[1] One charter concerning land at Rougham suggests the presence of some more ordered arrangement.[2] A holding is there divided into eleven parcels, the position of which is in nine cases carefully described. In all of these nine cases this tenement adjoins on one side the holding of the same neighbour whilst on the other side the tenants vary. It is possible that this description may be explained by a late division of the holding into two parts, but it is none the less curious and illustrates very clearly the scattered nature of the small holdings. But such evidence is of course insufficient to serve as the proof of any settled rota in an East Anglian village, and the position of the strip holdings in the fields seems as a rule to have been very confused in the twelfth and thirteenth centuries.

Such evidence as has been cited is for the most part important as showing the exceptional conditions of East Anglian field arrangements, but in view of such peculiarities as will later have to be considered, it is well to insist at the start very strongly on the presence and the importance of the system of intermixed strips in the fields of East Anglian villages in the twelfth and thirteenth centuries, and on the consequent scattered condition of the peasant holdings of the district. And these arrangements were in East Anglia, as elsewhere, dependent upon the fundamental notion of share-land.[3] The early evidence of open field husbandry is largely contained in references to ' gedalleland ', both in the relevant tenth-century charters and in the famous passage in King Ine's laws,[4] and it is therefore of some interest to note traces of similar terminology in the post-Domesday East Anglian documents. In this sense it is probable that there is some significance in such allusions as that to ' duas acras de delelond '[5] which occurs in a charter concerning land at Acre.

[1] Cf. Stenton, *D. C.*, Introduction, pp. xix seq.
[2] Harl. 2110, fol. 31 b.   See Appendix I, No. 29.
[3] Vinogradoff, *English Society.*
[4] The pre-Conquest evidence for the system is summarized by Gray, *English Field Systems*, pp. 55 seq., and is discussed very fully in Vinogradoff, *English Society.*
[5] Harl. 2110, fol. 102.

At Salhouse, also, the Bishop of Norwich's register speaks of a 'deleacre',[1] and in the Binham cartulary land at Dersingham is described as divided up into 'dels', which are named furlongs.[2] A twelfth-century charter from Suffolk[3] uses the word in a very curious manner, suggesting the original intimate relation of the furlong to the shareland of the village; and in this connexion the frequent occurrence of the term as a suffix in field names[4] is not without importance. Again, the full significance of these relics of land division only appears with the consideration of the arrangements peculiar to East Anglia, but even the sporadic appearance of such terms affords an illustration in this district of the manner in which the underlying conception of land sharing was latent in all open field husbandry.

But whilst a general view of the East Anglian peasant tenements supplies an illustration of the general principles latent in early land division and their survival in later terminology, it is certain that the tenemental organization of the district had individual characteristics and was based upon arrangements of co-operative husbandry peculiar to itself. Dr. Gray has recently examined a great deal of the later evidence of the agricultural systems employed in this district,[5] and his researches have proved that very remarkable conditions prevailed in East Anglia in the sixteenth century. Under the Tudors there is evidence of the prevalence of a three-course rotation of crops which existed in the absence of anything like a normal three-field system.[6] The fields of the East Anglian townships in the Elizabethan extents vary in size and number and seem to bear no relation to any ordered scheme of husbandry;[7] and even when a village has the regular number of fields to enable a two- or three-course agricultural system to be practised upon them, there are unmistakable signs that none of these ever lay fallow in its

---

[1] Stowe 936, fol. 35 b.   [2] Cott. Claud. D. xiii, fols. 155 seq.
[3] Harl. Charters, 54 H. 5.   See Appendix I, No. 13.
[4] Vide e. g. the instances in note 2, p. 19.
[5] Gray, *English Field Systems*, Harvard Historical Studies, No. xxii. pp. 304–54.
[6] Gray, *op. cit.*, p. 333.   [7] Gray, *op. cit.*, pp. 313–14.

entirety at any given time.[1]   These conditions existed in the
unenclosed fields where a strip system of agriculture still
prevailed.   In the sixteenth century, instead, it appears that
a tenant's arable acres were likely to be concentrated in a particular field of the township and not divided, as in the
Midlands, in more or less equal proportion amongst the village
fields in the manner which a two- or three-field system of
farming renders essential.[2]   Throughout in East Anglia the
unit of husbandry is rather the 'tenementum' or peasant
holding, which sometimes in the sixteenth century remains
intact and sometimes by that date has become disintegrated.
It consists of strips not divided among the fields but lying in
a particular section of the arable land of the township.   Even
when such 'tenementa' can no longer be seen as working
units, the position of the arable holdings of the peasants is
described, not in relation to the fields but according to their
position in the 'tenementa' which had once been complete
entities.[3]   In short, in East Anglia at the close of the Middle
Ages the open fields of the villages played no important part
in the system of crop rotation, and in their place, arranged
independently of them, we can see the agricultural unit of the
village existing in the 'tenementum'.

These remarkable conditions can only be explained with
reference to the earlier history of the district, and the nature
of the medieval peasant tenements in East Anglia is thus of
peculiar importance.   Dr. Gray has discussed the evidence
for the earlier existence of the sixteenth-century conditions
which he has established.   But he has confined his attention
to the accounts of peasant holdings given in the Ramsey
Cartulary and the Bishop of Norwich's extent of his manor

----

[1] Gray, *op. cit.*, p. 314.   The case of sixteenth-century Castleacre is of
special interest in that we have abundant charters of the thirteenth century
relating to this village preserved in the Castleacre Cartulary.   These
show the scattered nature of the peasant tenements, but contain no
indication of any equal or proportionate division of the holdings between
the fields.

[2] Gray, *op. cit.*, pp. 313–23.   Again the case of Castleacre is of interest
by comparison with the earlier Cartulary.

[3] Cf. especially the account of Wymondham of the beginning of the
sixteenth century.   Gray, *op. cit.*, pp. 339 seq.

of Martham.[1] These it will be necessary to discuss in some detail. At once, however, it may be suggested that other East Anglian evidence in the earlier records shows that conditions then prevailed in the district similar to those apparent in the sixteenth century. In particular the most cursory glance at an extent of the manor of Barney[2] affords an opportunity of examining the system in its earlier stages. This extent was made for the Prior of Binham in 1334.[3] At that date most of the holdings, both free and servile, are described as belonging to 'tenementa', and in a large section of the extent the smaller holdings are definitely arranged according to these 'tenementa' which can thus be seen in their compact form.[4] The latter section of the description[5] shows at once the scattered nature of these peasant holdings and the absence of any fundamental field division. In the numerous grants by peasants in the Castleacre Cartulary the elaborate description of the small holdings conveyed, coupled with the complete absence of any description of their position and division in the various fields, is very remarkable.[6] And whilst the allocation of strips in named furlongs or precincts makes it impossible to locate the actual distribution of the holdings, nevertheless, in view of the later evidence, the omission of any reference to the fields in the description of these tenements is highly significant. In extents of Banham and Bradcar[7] drawn up in the fourteenth century there are traces of arrangements based upon 'tenementa' similar to those at Barney, and such clearly was also the case in the Binham manor of Salhouse.[8] Such conditions were, in fact, common throughout East Anglia. Thus it is well to notice that the most cursory conspectus of the East Anglian material suggests that the peculiar conditions of the sixteenth century were in existence in the district in medieval times.

[1] Gray, *op. cit.*. pp. 335 seq. and 345-6. These are the only important pieces of evidence before the fifteenth century which are considered.
[2] Cott. Claud. D. xiii, fols. 62-75 b.
[3] Cott. Claud. D. xiii, fol. 62.   [4] Cott. Claud. D. xiii, fols. 62-76.
[5] Cott. Claud. D. xiii, fols. 66 seq.
[6] The charters given in Appendix I are quite typical of the descriptional method used.
[7] Hudson in *R. H. S. Trans.*   [8] Cott. Claud. D. xiii, fols. 110 b-19.

In one important particular, however, it may be noticed how the divergence between the Midland systems and those of East Anglia is brought out with especial clarity by a piece of negative evidence. The extreme rarity of the virgate and bovate in all medieval East Anglian documents is worthy of note. There is, indeed, one solitary exception to this general rule. In the Ely extents the virgate occurs with great frequency, and is used to describe the full holding of the 'operarius'. It is also described as a 'plena terra', and it varies very greatly in size. At Terrington[1] it contains 80 acres; there are instances of 20 acres;[2] the traditional 30 acres is not unknown;[3] and there are also reckonings of 16, 24, and 48 acres.[4] But with this important exception the virgate is almost unknown in East Anglian medieval documents. The register of the Bishop of Norwich does not contain the word.[5] The fourteenth-century extents of Binham Priory do not mention any such unit.[6] In the thirteenth century all trace of a virgate arrangement is absent from chief manors of the abbot of Ramsey in Norfolk.[7] In the still earlier documents the word is extremely uncommon. The earlier charters in the cartularies of Castleacre[8] and of St. Benet of Hulme[9] do not refer to virgates, and the same is true of the twelfth-century documents of the Binham Register. The twelfth-century extents of the East Anglian land of the abbey of Ramsey do not mention the term[10] save in the case of one very exceptional manor.[11] Finally, in the whole Domes-

---

[1] Cott. Claud. C. xi, fol. 175 b.

[2] e. g. Pulham, Cott. Claud. C. xi, fol. 207; Feltwell, fol. 247 b; Wetheringsett, fol. 295; Barking, fol. 287 b; Hitcham, fol. 278 b; Rattlesden, fol. 271.

[3] Walpole, Cott. Claud. C. xi, fol. 186, and Hartest, fol. 264.

[4] 16 acres at Shipdham, ibid., fol. 236; 24 at Glemsford, fol. 256; and 48 at Bridgham and Northwold, fols. 242 and 252. At Dereham the full land contained 24 acres, ibid., fol. 220 b.

[5] Stowe MSS. 936.

[6] Cott. Claud. D. xiii. The absence of the word in the 'foundation' extent of Binham itself is also noticeable.

[7] R. C., passim. Of the exceptional character of the late list of manors of R. C., vol. iii, p. 213, cf. Gray, op. cit., p. 347 n.

[8] Harl. 2110.

[9] Cott. Galba E. ii. Cf. especially the charters of the Abbots, fols. 54 seq.   [10] R. C., vol. iii.

[11] On the exceptional nature of the Walsoken arrangements see Gray, op. cit., p. 347.

day of Norfolk it only occurs once,[1] and in the Suffolk Survey its very rare use is always in the more primitive sense of a yard measure.[2] Before the thirteenth century, in fact, the virgate and bovate may be regarded as exotic in East Anglia.

The absence of the virgate in East Anglian documents of the Middle Age is but another illustration of the insignificant part played by the fields of the villages in the co-operative agriculture of the district. The concentration of the 'tenementa' in particular fields and the manner in which 'tenementa' are regarded as the units of village husbandry are facts of the utmost importance in East Anglian social arrangements; and it is hoped in the pages which follow to show the widespread prevalence and peculiar characteristics of these 'tenementa', their relation to the organization of husbandry, and their significance in relation to the earlier history of the district. A superficial examination of these arrangements is, however, of itself sufficient to suggest the existence in scattered East Anglian manors in the Middle Ages of a system of agriculture similar to that which Dr. Gray has so copiously illustrated from sixteenth-century documents.

The explanation of these curious conditions which are thus common to both the thirteenth and the sixteenth centuries in East Anglia has been sought in two directions. In the first place, the wide extent of sheep-farming in the district undoubtedly, as Dr. Gray points out,[3] influenced the arrangement of holdings. The knowledge of the value of a private fold for manuring purposes was clearly recognized in East Anglia as early as the time of Domesday,[4] and it is implied in the phraseology of a famous Norfolk charter of Edward the Confessor.[5] The Ely registers show that similar conditions prevailed in certain parts of the district[6] in the thirteenth century. And the use of wattles for the purpose of making private folds out of fallow arable holdings themselves in some of the Ely manors suggests that the individual tenants manured

---

[1] *V. C. H. Norfolk*, vol. ii, pp. 1 seq.
[2] *V. C. H. Suffolk*, vol. i, p. 357.   [3] Gray, *op. cit.*, pp. 341 seq.
[4] *V. C. H. Norfolk*, vol. ii, pp. 23 seq.   [5] Kemble, *C. D.*, dcccliii.
[6] Cf. Gray, *op. cit.*, p. 341. On the prevalence of fold-soke in the Ely manors cf. *infra*, pp. 77–9.

their own strips during the fallow year individually, and that, in consequence, whilst a strip system was in existence and a three-course agricultural system prevailed, nevertheless husbandry tended to follow a more particularist scheme here than elsewhere as the 'tenementa' themselves became the units by which the rotation was worked.

This ingenious explanation undoubtedly contains elements of truth, and the practice of sheep-farming with the implications involved in the East Anglian methods undoubtedly stabilized the peculiar organization of holdings and perhaps contributed to its formation. But the strip system itself and the elaborate arrangements involved in co-operative agriculture are too complicated in East Anglia, as elsewhere, to be explained by such a factor alone. Consequently Dr. Gray was led to look to the earlier history of the district for a solution to the problem. His theory of origins and his explanation of the nature of these curious tenemental conditions is based upon the assumption of the primitive existence in East Anglia of an original ' iugum ' analogous to that known in Kent.[1] This speedily broke up, and at the critical point in its disintegration the invasion of the Danes took place. The newcomers in their settlement created the small manors of the district and at the same time also arrested the disintegration of the ' iuga ', with the result that there were formed the ' tenementa ' which are so prominent a feature of the agricultural arrangements of later days.

Now such a theory is confessedly open to the charge of being based upon pure assumption.[2] There is no record of the primitive ' iugum ', and speculation about a unit of which there is no evidence and which was certainly ' forgotten ' at the time when the earliest system which we know was created, though interesting as contributing to a possible theory of origins, is hardly conclusive. With the second part of the theory, however, we are more directly concerned. The hypothesis that the ' tenementa ' which formed the basis of the later field arrangements are of Danish origin is, it will be

---

[1] Gray, *op. cit.*, pp. 351 seq.   [2] Gray, *op. cit.*, pp. 351-2.

suggested, capable of proof. But it will be claimed that the holdings which the Danes created were the result of no mere arrest in the disintegration of a forgotten ' iugum ', but that they were based upon definite principles of land sharing. These, like all other such systems, were ultimately dependent upon the common plough, and they thus fitted in naturally with the earlier strip system which probably preceded them. An analysis of the tenemental arrangements of a series of East Anglian manors will, it is hoped, serve to prove the widespread prevalence of what may be termed the ' tenementum ' system in this district and also to illustrate the principles upon which it was constructed. And the result of such an analysis will be to suggest that it is to Scandinavian influence and Scandinavian land arrangements that we have to attribute the marked dissimilarity of the tenemental organization of East Anglia from that of the Midlands, and to indicate more clearly the wide extent in the Middle Ages of the individual characteristics of the agricultural system of Norfolk and Suffolk.

The Scandinavian influence upon the agricultural arrangements of the district has clearly left a permanent mark upon its field nomenclature.[1] Whilst arguments from such terminology unless backed by an expert analysis of all the available material are notoriously dangerous, nevertheless the widespread appearance in the medieval documents of the features of open field husbandry under names which are clearly of Danish or Norse derivation is of itself significant. A few examples of this may be given. The ' cultura ' is not only the furlong common to the Midlands and the South [2] but is also more commonly the ' wong', its Danish counterpart.[3] The

---

[1] It is not necessary to limit this influence to the pre-Conquest days. It is probable that Norse influence and Norse immigration is a fact to be reckoned with even in the twelfth century. Kings Lynn was a centre for the Norse trade as early as the twelfth century.

[2] Cf. Maitland, *D. B. B.*, p. 360. Among the many examples of this use may be cited the extent of Binham, Cott. Claud. D. xiii, fol. 4, and Dersingham, fol. 155.

[3] This is the normal term in the Danelagh proper, e. g. ' Unam culturam que vocatur Milnewang', *D. C.* 513; 'iuxta culturam que vocatur Widalewang', *D. C.* 528; ' culturam meam que appellatur Muchwanga',

'wong' is, in fact, a very common term, which is widespread through the East Anglian records. It occurs in the description of the demesne at Bridgham, Shipdham, and Dereham.[1] It is used in the account of the arable at Binham,[2] Ingoldisthorpe,[3] and Martham,[4] and it makes a constant appearance in the early charters.[5] Many other terms of Scandinavian origin might be found among the field names of the district. Prominent among these would probably be the 'gate'[6] which implies 'street', and the 'ing' which designates 'meadow',[7] and the combination of these with other Norse terms is sometimes very striking.[8] The study of the field-names and place-names

D. C. 529; 'dimidiam acram in Luckywang interritorio de Kelum', *D. C.* 366. Cf. Legeshouwong, *Gilbertine Charters*, Sixle Series, 29 (Lincoln Record Society).

[1] At Bridgham the term is the normal designation for the location of the demesne land, which is said to lie among other places in: Middelstiwong, Gosedelsedewong, Langewong, Horsewong, Wodegatewong, Grenegatewong, Milnewong, Postgatewong, Euethunesdelewong, Hollowewang, Salteregatewong, Krossewong, Thornewong, Ledernegatewong, Furnedikewong. Cott. Claud. C. xi, fol. 240 b. Similar evidence may be taken from the description of the demesne of Shipdham, ibid., fol. 227, and at Dereham, ibid., fol. 213.

[2] 'Wong' alternates with 'furlong' in the description of the land of this manor, and we find e. g. Cosegravewong, Twentyakerwong, fol. 4.

[3] e. g. 'culturam que vocatur Brodwong et continet xviii acras', Cott. Claud. D. xiii, fol. 172 b.

[4] Cf. the wong at Martham, vide *R. H. S. Trans.*, 4th Series, vol. i, p. 37.

[5] e. g. at Wathstead, 'cultura que vocatur Wodewong', Cott. Galba E. ii, fol. 80 b; at Massingham, 'in terra de Bromwong', Harl. 2110, fol. 10 b; at Creak, 'terra que vocatur Hadewisewong', ibid., fol. 49 b; and at Wesenham, 'vi acras super Scorlewong', ibid., fol. 36. At Thorpland, 'tres acras et dimidiam in villa Torplandie ei et heredibus suis tenendas de me et heredibus meis . . . scilicet duas acras de Lahglanda et acram et dimidiam ad Murledewang', Harl. Charters 57, A. 12. Cf. Harl. Charters 47, H. 45 (Appendix I, No. 4).

[6] Of the uses of 'gate' cf. Bugge, *R. H. S. Trans.*, 4th Series, vol. iv. Instances are very frequent. They may be found, e. g., in the Castleacre cartulary, Harl. 2110: at Rougham, fol. 30; at Lecheham, fol. 34; at Creak, fol. 48; and at Rudham, fol. 40. Cf. also the phrase 'illa via regia vocata Pottergate', Cott. Claud. D. xiii, fol. 21 b.

[7] For *ing* cf. Bugge, *op. cit.*

[8] A curious example of this is to be found in an orginal charter concerning land at Edgefield, Harl. Charters 44, A. 18 (cf. Appendix I, No. 1), where in a description of land there occurs the purely Danish term of Adelingesdele, both *ing* and *adel* being common in the formation of Danish place-names, and occurring once in a similar conjunction in a Lincolnshire charter. Professor Bugge, *op. cit.*, discusses both these terms and their meaning. The word *adel* is very frequently found in names indicating

of East Anglia does not fall within the more modest scope of this essay, but it is probable that many indications of the wide extent of Danish influence would be found on an exhaustive examination.[1]

But a more immediately interesting and important example of the application of Danish terminology to the field arrangements of the district is to be found in the extents of certain manors belonging to the See of Ely in the north-west corner of Norfolk. In the 1277 account of Walpole there is thrice mentioned a ' tenmanlond '. This is reproduced in the 1222 survey as a ' tenmanloth '—a word of Danish extraction representing the ' hlot ' or share of ten men and containing 120 acres.[2] The late Professor Vinogradoff has pointed out [3] the connexion of this terminology with the manloth arrangement which appears in a tenth-century Southwell charter [4] and its

---

parts of the Danish village, e. g. ' adel staede ', ' the chief street between the houses ' ; ' adel bol ', ' manor house '. For the importance of the ' dele ' vide *supra*, and see Stenton, *D. C.*, Introduction, p. xlv, and *D. C.* 169. The same word appears in Yorkshire in connexion with the wong, and we hear of wandales or wangdales ; cf. Farrar, *Y. C.*, Introduction, vol. ii, p. vii.

[1] This may be expected with the forthcoming general survey of place-names under the direction of Prof. Mawer and Prof. Stenton.

[2] These important entries in the Ely Surveys run as follows :
1222 (Cott. Tib. B. ii).
De libere tenentibus.
Willelmus Franceis et Thomas de Northwold tenent dimidiam tenmanloth scilicet sexaginta acras. ibid.
De Consuetudinariis.
Galfridus de Gatestone et participes tenent unam tenmanloth scilicet sexies viginti acras terre. fol. 167 b.
Willelmus filius Christiane et participes unam tenmanloth scilicet sexies viginti acras. ibid.
1277 (Cott. Claud. C. xi).
De militibus et Libere tenentibus.
Iacobus le Franceis et Thomas de Northwaude tenent dimidiam tenmanlond scilicet sexaginta acras terre et quinquaginta et duas acras ex altera parte. fol. 185.
De Consuetudinariis et Censuariis.
Alanus et Mattheus Iohannes et Radulphus Petrus et Galfridus de Castlestowe et eorum participes tenent unam tenmanlond scilicet sexies viginti acras terre. fol. 185.
Petrus et Walterus filius Willelmi filii Christiane et eorum participes tenent unam tenmanlond scilicet sexies viginti acras. fol. 186.

[3] *Villainage in England*, p. 255 ; *English Society*, pp. 103, 281.

[4] *Cart. Sax.* 1348 (Birch), and see Vinogradoff, *English Society*.

relation to the familiar 'gedalleland' of Ine's laws.[1] He also suggests that the manloth in these manors is to be found in the toftland which appears here as a holding whose average size is about 12 acres. The toftlands in these manors represent the 'tenementa' which have been noted so often elsewhere as the distinguishing mark of East Anglian agricultural organization, and the importance of the phraseology of these extents in discussing the origin and character of the 'tenementum' is thus clear.

It is therefore interesting to note that the terminology was in Walpole no creation of the Ely scribes. In the fifteenth-century cartulary of the Priory of Lewes[2] there occurs a charter which may be dated not later than 1244 and which concerns land at Walpole. In it the grantor gives 'sextam partem unius tunmanloth'. This third form of the word raises the question which of the two Ely readings is the correct one, but in view of external evidence there can be no doubt that the earlier reading of 'tenmanloth' is to be preferred.[3] Nor is the post-Domesday 'manloth' confined to East Anglia, for a twelfth-century Lincolnshire charter speaks of a gift at Killingholme as including 'mansuram que fuit Arnewi qui dicitur Maneslot',[4] and Professor Stenton has also noticed[5] the word in two other Lincolnshire charters. The one speaks of 'unam terram ... que vocatur manneslot'. The other more significantly applies the term to a bovate in Wrangle—'scilicet illam manuesloc quam Alnadus filius Leuerun tenuit'.

The terminological problems raised by the Walpole extent are certainly of great importance in a discussion of the principles involved in the later peculiar East Anglian field system. But whilst the toftland in this corner of Norfolk certainly represents the 'tenementum' elsewhere, the significance of the phraseology of the extent in indicating a Danish

---

[1] *Ine Laws* (Liebermann), clause xlii. Cf. also Cart. Sax. 1130, and see Vinogradoff, *op. cit.*, p. 281.

[2] Cott. Vesp. F. xv, fol. 284 b, and see Appendix I, No. 54. For another independent reference to the Walpole tenmanloths cf. the charter of King Stephen calendared by Round, *Documents preserved in France*, p. 512.　　　　[3] Cf. Vinogradoff, *English Society*, p. 281.

[4] *D. C.* 297.　　　　[5] Cf. Stenton, *D. C.*, Introduction, p. xxi *n.*

origin for it is largely dependent upon the suggested connexion of the toftland with the tenmanloth.   Though the
word toft is Danish in derivation,[1] it must be remembered that
its normal use in the parlance of medieval England was to
designate a small and usually an enclosed holding outside the
normal tenements in the fields.[2]   Sometimes it contained the
dwelling of the villein, but more usually it denoted the holdings
of the miscellaneous class of *cotarii, coterelli, anilepimen* [3] and
the like, who existed to supply the surplus labour which
became so necessary in the later development of the manorial
economy in England.   In these Ely manors the toftland on
the other hand is the fundamental holding in the fields.   It
contains acres of arable, and its holders contribute ploughing
services in the common agriculture of the manor.   The connexion of the toft and the manloth in the Danish sense is
dependent upon some such use of the term, and it is thus of
some moment to discover in what sense it was employed in
the twelfth-century charters of the Danish districts.

Unfortunately in these charters the word is used to denote
many different things.   Primarily in the twelfth-century
documents the term seems to have denoted, with what seems
to have been its original meaning, a dwelling with its
appurtenances.   A Yorkshire deed grants a toft for instance

---

[1] *Oxford English Dictionary*, ' Toft '.   Lindkvist, *Middle English
Place Names*, pp. 208–25.
[2] Cf. Nasse, *Zur Geschichte der mittelalterlichen Felagemeinschaft
in England.*
[3] The ' anilepimen ' are a distinct feature of the Ely extents.   They
occur through the Surveys, e. g. at Pulham, Cott. Claud C. xi, fol. 220 ;
at Bridgham, fol. 252 ; at Feltwell, fol. 255 ; at Terrington, fol. 191 b ;
at Dereham, fol. 232 b ; at Walton, fol. 207.   Their position in the manorial
economy is very clearly indicated in the Court Roll of Littleport.   Selden
Society, *The Court Baron*, pp. 146–7 : ' (Iuratores presentant) quod
extranei adventicii qui mansiones suas conducant de variis et nichil tenent
de domino communiant in marisco cum bestiis suis et alia proficua
capiunt in communa et *illi vocantur undersettles.*   Quesiti quo waranto
utuntur illa communa dicunt quod quilibet undersettle metet dimidiam
acram bladi in autumpno et ligabit et siccabit sine cibo *sicut quilibet
Anelepyman et Anelepywyman et hoc per terrarium.*'   On the nature of
the process cf. Vinogradoff, *Villainage*, p. 213 ; and on the term vide
Maitland, *Court Baron* (Selden Society), p. 112 n. : ' What is anelepyman ?   This term seems to mean a man who is single or sole in the
sense of being unmarried, and in the context it probably points to one
who is no householder—no husband.'

on the express understanding that no land shall be occupied with it.[1] But whilst the toft is often the dwelling in its simple unrestricted sense, it usually contains a small garden or enclosure. A man will have a few acres ' before his door ' [2] or a toft will be given ' cum edificiis et arboribus inventis '.[3] And by an extension frequently the toft was used in the charters to designate the enclosure quite apart from the dwelling. A Lincolnshire charter will, for instance, describe a gift as containing among other things ' unam toftam scilicet meam partem de mare que iacet iuxta domum Iohannis presbiteri '.[4] And this meaning of the word must be understood in the many cases where mention is made of divided tofts [5] or where a large toft is split up to make smaller tofts.[6] In these twelfth-century charters the term is used very frequently and perhaps usually in exactly the sense employed normally by the thirteenth-century extents, so that the man who holds a toft and nothing else belongs to that category of minor tenants in the manor who had no share in the common fields, but who supplied the ever increasing demand for surplus labour. And it is clear that in very many cases in these charters the term is applied to small holdings outside the arable arrangements of the villages and with the meaning normally given to it by later Midland usage.[7]

[1] *Y. C.* 163.

[2] e.g. among many instances, ' unam peciam terre que iacet ante portam eiusdem mansionis ', Harl. 2110, fol. 44 ; ' dimidiam acram terre, illam scilicet que iacet ad portam Eduard' versus domum Willelmi de Rochdale ', Harl. Charters 52, E. 21.

[3] Cf. *D. C.* 170.　　　　　　　　　　　　　　　　[4] *D. C.* 247.

[5] Stowe MSS. 936, fol. 1. Cf. Hudson, *op. cit.* e.g. ' septem toftis et dimidio ', *Gilbertine Charters*, Catley Series, 2 (Lincoln Record Society). ' Confirmaui medietatem tofti mei . . . illam scilicet medietatem que iacet iuxta toftum quod Rogerus Flod tenuit ', *D. C.* 402. ' Unam percatam terre arabilis in tofto quod fuit Ranulfo Coco ', *D. C.* 44. ' Tres partes illius tofti in Houtuna versus orientem quod Robertus Putrel dedit nobis salva nobis quarta parte eiusdem tofti versus occidentalem ', *D. C.* 55. Cf. also ' Medietatem tofti mei ', *Y. C.* 1092 ; ' unum dimidium toftum ', *Y. C.* 1579. The same usage is clearly implied in such passages as ' unum toftum continentem in se unam acram terre ', *Y. C.* 58 ; or ' duo tofta in Franleia in se duas acras continentia ', *Y. C.* 59.

[6] *Gilbertine Charters*, Ormesby Series, 28 (Lincoln Record Society), ' cum tofto qui est pars quarta domenii tofti '.

[7] *Supra*, p. 31, note 3. An exact parallel to the ' extranei adventicii '

But whilst this is so it does seem possible occasionally to see a unity in the toft,[1] and what is more important to connect it in the twelfth century with the holdings in the fields. In the Danelagh charters the miscellaneous gifts of land usually contain tofts roughly corresponding to the number of bovates given with them.[2] And as regards Yorkshire the evidence is similar. Whatever be the exact meaning to be assigned to the term, such phrases as ' cum omnibus toftis ad predictas bovatas terre pertinentibus '[3] which are scattered through the Yorkshire charters can hardly be explained away as merely the formal flourishes of over-zealous scribes. When a man grants ' unam bovatam terre in Ocheton cum tofto quam scilicet bovatam pater meus prius eis dedit '[4] it is probable that the bovate and the toft went together as the component parts of the same share-holding in the fields. Such passages depend for their significance largely on their frequency, but the connexion of the bovate with its toft appears fairly clearly when a gift is described as containing ' unam bovatam in Normannebi xv acrarum per perticatam xxti pedum et unam acram pro tofta eiusdem bovate eiusdem terre '.[5] In these cases the interrelation of the toft with the arable holdings is closer than when the term is applied to those miscellaneous holdings of casual labourers, but still it must be noted that the toft itself has not necessarily yet left the category of dependent holdings outside the main scheme of village husbandry.

In still earlier documents the evidence concerning the toft is scanty. In Domesday Book the word is rare and almost exclusively confined to Lincolnshire, though there is a Yorkshire reference to ' iii toftas ad geldum '.[6] And whilst the word is in general used in the same loose sense as in the

---

of the Court Roll is to be found in the charter which speaks of ' toftum quem Willelmus le neucumene tenuit et toftum unius cottarii qui est extra uillam ', D. C. 420. In the Ely extents the toft-holders are frequently of this common type, e. g. at Glemsford and at Rattlesden in 1222, Cott. Tib. B. ii, fol. 199 b and fol. 180.

[1] e. g. ' Toftum unum xii perticarum in latitudine et longitudine quantum tofta aliorum hominum ', Y. C. 891.

[2] D. C., Introduction, pp. xxv. seq.

[3] Y. C. 1261.   [4] Y. C. 1066.   [5] Y. C. 745

[6] D. B., vol. i, fol. 327.

twelfth-century charters there is a tendency for the number
of tofts described to coincide with the number of their socmen
holders.[1] In Lincolnshire a contrast is occasionally made
between socmen holding tofts and socmen holding bovates.[2]
The interest of this arrangement lies in its permanence, which
receives a striking illustration at the other end of the
medieval period in an extent made for Croyland Abbey.[3]
At Wellingborough it appears that in 1284 there was still
a class of tenants known as toft sokenmen, each of whom held
' unam toftam in sokna '.   And it is hard to believe that this
class which appears on occasion so prominently in Danelagh documents in the Middle Ages was merely recruited
from the demand for casual labour, and that the tofts which
were the tenemental badge of these men did not represent
some share in customary land of the village.   In any case it is
worthy of note that in the one pre-Conquest reference to tofts
in East Anglia, a charter concerning land at Suffolk in the
eleventh century, the toft appears to be used to indicate the
full holding of the ' landsettler ',[4] whereby its connexion with
the arable holdings is again suggested.

In general, however, it is impossible to advance any theory
of the widespread use of the toft as representing in the
Danish sense of a man's ' hlot ' or share in the fields from the
Danelagh evidence available from the period prior to the
thirteenth century.   In the early documents it is never wholly
clear how far we are not still dealing with a subordinate holding
outside the main tenemental divisions of the arable.   Nevertheless, sometimes traces can possibly be seen, in the Danish
districts, of foreign systems of land-sharing wherein the toft
would play a prominent part.   Once, for instance, in a Lincolnshire charter the normal method of description is reversed,

---

[1] e. g. ' ii socmannos de ii toftis—x socmannos de x toftis ', _D. B._ vol. i,
fol. 365 b ; ' ii socmannos de duobus toftis ', ibid., fol. 364 ; ' unum
sochmannum de i tofta ', ibid., fol. 362 b.   Cf. also fols. 360 b, 358.

[2] Stenton, _D. C._, Introduction, p. xxxvi, quoting _D. B._, vol. i, fol. 365 b ;
and cf. also fols. 362 b, 356, 358.

[3] Add. MSS. 5845, fols. 161–7.

[4] Kemble, _C. D._ dccccvii ; Birch, _Cart. Sax._ 1014 : ' And ic mine
landsethlen here toftes to owen aihte and alle mine men fre.'

and we hear of a bovate being appurtenant to a toft.[1] This
is an exceptional usage, but the implied suggestion that the
toft is here the determining factor in the allotment of holdings
tempts speculation as to whether such systems as that of the
'solskift' of Denmark have perhaps found an illustration in
some of these English documents relating to the toft. For the
characteristics of the 'solskift' system were simply that 'in it
the toft appears as the mother of the holding in the fields and
the strips follow the order of the housetofts in the village
according to the course of the sun '.[2] Unfortunately we have
no detailed description of the sequence of strips in any
Danelagh or East Anglian village in the Middle Ages,[3] so
that any sort of detailed comparison between the order of the
strips and that of the house-tofts is impossible. From another
point of view, however, it is perhaps possible to see traces of
this or a similar system of Scandinavian land division in the

[1] Stenton, *D. C.* 492 ; and cf. Introduction, p. xxxvi.
[2] Vinogradoff, *Growth of the Manor*, p. 265, where the various systems
connected with the primitive Danish toft are discussed.
[3] For the Danelagh absence of evidence cf. Stenton, *D. C.*, p. xxxvi.
With regard to East Anglia we are also left with a complete lack of
detailed testimony. It is perhaps of interest to note how in the Rougham
holding (Appendix I, No. 29) the toft adjoins the toft of the tenant whose
strips always appear to adjoin those of the original holder itself. But
this, as has been seen, is capable of another explanation, and in general
the evidence is too vague to serve as the basis of any theory. Perhaps
some significance may be seen in such passages as : 'duas bovatas terre
de duabus carucatis maritagii matris mei in Rychtona quas teneo de
Radulfo de Nevill et que iacent propinquiores soli cum tofto duarum
acrarum propinquiori tofto Serlonis fabri versus occidentem,' *Y. C.* 1210.
The position of the toft in relation to the other tofts of the village is often
carefully described : 'unum toftum . . . iacens inter toftum quod Gilebertus
filius Amfridi tenet de Sancto Johanne et toftum quod domina Sarra de
Ragnildtorp tenet de me,' *Y. C.* 1102. 'Duas bovatas terre in Kirkeby
Crandala que scilicet iacent exteriores versus occidentem de decem
bovatis quas habui in eadem villa cum uno tofto latitudinis quatuor
perticarum et longitudinis decem perticarum quod scilicet iacet proximum
a parte orientali tofto quod Rogerus Colpauche tenuit in eadem villa,'
Y. C. 1080. A Norfolk toft is described as : 'tofta quod tenuit de me et
patre meo in Westgate quod iacet inter toftam Walteri Tufard et quod
fuit Petri et toftam quod fuit Petri Balkedrie,' Harl. 2110, fol. 11. Cf.
also : 'unum toftum in Buctona iuxta terram magistri Gilberti Silver versus
occidentalem,' *Y. C.* 1162 ; 'illud videlicet toftum quod . . . iacet inter
terram A. . . . et terram R. cum tota longitudine et latitudine,' *Gilbertine
Charters*, Ormesby Series, 28 (Lincoln Record Society). But the most that
can be said of the evidence of the relation of the order of the strips to that
of the house-tofts is that the scanty evidence affords material for speculation.

curious terminology of two Lincolnshire documents.[1]   In one
of these charters [2] a gift is made of a selion of land in ' Braac de
Tittona'.   This selion is further said to lie in ' Northschifting '
in which its exact position is further discussed.   The phraseology of the other charter [3] is yet more curious.   Here in connexion with the allocation of a share of meadow in ' Folcringtoft' reference is made to 'terram que fuit Hospitalium in
Huteredploghland in Middelschifting'.   Whilst such evidence
is of course far too fragmentary to form the basis of any wide
generalization, it may be possible to see in the curious terminology of these charters an analogy to the Danish terms used
to denote the original stinting of the arable which became
inevitable with the growth of population and the development of intensive agriculture.[4]   When such arrangements can
be observed in their indigenous entirety, it is the toft like the
' bol ' which tends to determine the ideal and fundamental
holding upon which all the other tenements are based.   In the
reference to the 'schifting' which thus makes its transitory
appearance in these charters there are possibly traces of a
system of tenure common alike to Sweden and Denmark.   And
the phraseology of these documents thus perhaps also serves to
supply a new link between the manloth of Lincolnshire and the
curious arrangement of husbandry organization seen in the toft
and tenmanloth description of the tenemental units in the north-
west corner of Norfolk, and to illustrate the possibly intimate
connexion of these with Scandinavian systems of land-sharing.[5]

It would be very easy to push such terminological considerations too far.   What, however, may be stressed is that
the ' tenementum ' arrangement of later Norfolk Surveys
appears in thirteenth-century Walpole under the nomenclature

---

[1] I am indebted to Professor Stenton for most kindly drawing my
attention to these charters.

[2] Rylands Library, *Registrum Eboracense*, vol. ii, fol. 398.   See
Appendix I, No. 64.

[3] Rylands Library, *Registrum Eboracense*, vol. ii, fol. 349 b.   See
Appendix I, No. 65.

[4] Vinogradoff, *Historical Jurisprudence*, vol. i, pp. 335-7.

[5] There is a real similarity between the Walpole extents and the
conditions described in the *Lunds Domkyrkas Nekrologium*, where
'mansus' seems very generally to take the place of ' toft '.

of ' toftland ' and ' tenmanloth '.   In the north-west corner of
Norfolk, that is to say, the peculiar ' tenementum ' which
formed the basis of later East Anglian field arrangements is
represented in the Middle Ages in these manors by the
' toftland '.   It contains an average of about 12 acres of arable
land,[1] and very possibly from the phraseology of the extents
it can be taken as forming part of a Scandinavian system of
land-sharing which is also suggested by other contemporary
Danelagh documents.

The significance of the arrangements of the manor of
Martham in the thirteenth century has recently been discussed
at some length.[2]   There the ' tenementum ' of later days
takes the form of an ' eruing ' of 12 acres.[3]   This is as a rule
concentrated in one part of the fields of the township, and the
Rev. W. Hudson has argued very strongly for its pre-Domes-
day origin.[4]   It is the basis of the services and the land
division of the manor.   At Wimbotsham on the Ramsey lands
the same term occurs as representing the typical peasant holding
in a twelfth-century extent.[5]   Here it contains 12 acres.   Again
it is the fundamental holding of the manor, supplying an
illustration of the existence of the sixteenth-century arrangements ' within a generation or two of the Conquest '.[2]   Again
referring to the Norwich Register, similar ' tenementa '
occurring as the foundation of the manorial organization may
be found at Hindringham and Hindolveston.[6]   In these manors
this holding is called a ' landsettagium ', and contains in the
former village 14 acres and in the latter 18 acres.

Referring again to the Ely manors, it is possible to see there
also the existence of ' tenementa ' of a similar nature in spite of
the descriptional method of the extents, and of the exceptional
virgate which therein appears as synonymous with the ' plena
terra '.   As an example of these curious conditions which

---

[1] Cott. Claud. C. xi, ff. 192, 196, 202.   The actual figures are: at
Tyrington, 15 acres ; at Walpole, 10 acres ; and at Walton, 12 acres.
[2] Gray, *op. cit.*, pp. 335 seq.; Hudson, *R. H. S. Trans.*, 4th Series,
vols. i and iv.
[3] Hudson, *R. H. S. Trans.*, 4th Series, vol. i, pp. 35 seq.
[4] Hudson, *op. cit.*, vol. iv, pp. 1 seq. ; cf. vol. i, pp. 48 seq
[5] *R. C.*, vol. iii, p. 285 ; cf. Hudson, *op. cit.*, vol. i, p. 51.
[6] Hudson, *op. cit.*, vol. i, p. 51.

underlie the Ely description the Surveys of Bridgham and
Northwold may be selected.   At Northwold in 1222, for
instance, the juratores recorded a tenement of some prominence
in the following terms :

'Walterus de Witendon, Philippus Bering, Willelmus,
Johannes Robertus, Radulfus et Sal' Lune tenent unum molendinum et septuaginta et duas acras.' [1]

The essential unity of this tenement appears in a comparison
with the Survey of 1277.   In the later extent there is still the
mill, and the acreage is still ' sexaginta et duodecim acras ',
but the tenantry has increased and now comprises no less than
ten persons with their ' participes '.[2]   The strong tendency of
the holding to remain intact suggests analogy with the
' tenmanloth' entries of Walpole, and the number of the acres
involved—72—is itself curious.   Turn now to Bridgham.   In
the Coucher Book of 1256[3] there occurs a holding which
among the freeholders of that manor is quite exceptional in
size.   It contains 72 acres, and in the 1277 Survey again
makes its appearance.[4]   The 1222 extent offers a further
instance of this type of tenement.   Amongst a series of quite
small freeholdings held at a uniform money rent, two tenements stand out as being exceptional, both as regards their
size and the services attached to them.   They form two consecutive entries which are worth quoting :

[1] Cott. Tib. B. ii, fol. 125.
[2] The tenantry of this holding are described as follows : ' Walterus de
Witendon et Osbertus filius Philippi et fratres sui Robertus Bering Warinus
filius Willelmi Johannes le prest et Robertus frater eius, Hugo filius
Radulphi et Hugo filius Lune et eorum participes,' Cott. Claud. C. xi,
fol. 251 b.
[3] The holding is peculiar.   It is recorded among those of the free-
tenants of the manor : ' Willelmus de Blicking tenet sexaginta et duodecim
acras pro sex solidis per annum equaliter.   Et arabit cum una caruca
integra per sex dies ad cibum domini scilicet quolibet die quattor
panes ordei et siliginis.   Et sciendum quod de quarterio debet fieri
quarterviginti et duodecim panes.   Et inveniet ad quemlibet trium precarium autumpni unum hominem ad cibum suum bis in die.   Et ad
magnam precariam autumpni inveniet quinque homines metentes ad
cibum suum semel in anno.   Et carriabit bladum domini in autumpno
per unum diem integrum ad cibum domini dimidium sine cibo.   Et
debet sectam curie et habet faldam.' Coucher Book, fol. 147.
[4] Cott. Claud. C. xi, fol. 249.

' Hugo le Goiz tenet septuaginta et duas acras pro quattuor solidis et quattuor denariis equaliter et arabit pro sex dies cum cibo ut supradictum, et tres precarias in autumpno cum cibo bis in die, et inveniet quinque homines metentes per unum diem cum cibo semel et carriabit bladum domini per unam diem ut supra. Bartholemeus capellanus tenet septuaginta duas acras pro sex solidis equaliter et cetera sicut Hugo Guiz.' [1]

It seems clear that in these cases we are dealing with a unit of some kind, or at least with a series of holdings built up in these manors according to a common principle ; and this is the more remarkable in that Bridgham and Northwold are distinct manors in separate hundreds. But a further analysis of the tenements in these manors reveals a still more striking similarity. In the 1277 survey of Bridgham the description of the holdings of the *censuarii* shows that the type tenement among these contained 12 acres, and that the majority of the holdings consisted of 24 acres.[2] Referring back to Northwold, an even greater uniformity may be found. In 1222 the acreage figures of the free and customary tenants are as follows : 120, 120, 24, 48, 96, 72, 48, 48, 24, 48.[3] Thus, though the 12-acre holding here does not occur, every one of the tenements contains an acreage of some multiple of 12 acres. Such an arrangement cannot conceivably have been the result of coincidence. Nor is it likely that the 48-acre virgate common to both manors served as the basis of these holdings. The artificiality of the virgate over the whole district is a very strong argument against its use here as a primitive holding, and the figures themselves render this conclusive. Two possibilities therefore remain. It might perhaps appear possible that we have here to deal with the subdivisions of a regular ploughland, but again a glance at the figures shows this to be in the highest degree unlikely. But the only explanation in fact which will explain these conditions is that these curiously uniform holdings are made up of varying numbers of smaller tenements. Bridgham is just

[1] Cott. Tib. B. ii, fol. 181.
[2] Cott. Claud. C. xi, fol. 242 ; cf. Cott. Tib. B. ii, fol. 181.
[3] Cott. Tib. B. ii, fol. 124 b.

one of those manors where the widespread use of private
folds strongly suggests such an arrangement as that involved
in the ' tenementum ' of later times.[1] From every point of view,
in fact, it seems that in these two manors we have to reckon
with a ' tenementum ' of 12 acres analogous to the sixteenth-
century units, a unit fitting in with the sheep-farming practices
of these manors and forming part of the same scheme of
tenure which is to be found in the toft, the eruing, and the
landsettagium of the other East Anglian manors which have
been examined.

Bridgham and Northwold are in the south of Norfolk and
belonged to the Bishop of Ely.   Brancaster is in the extreme
north of the county and was part of the fief of the Abbot of
Ramsey.   That exceptional conditions prevailed there has
already been noted,[2] but in the light of the Ely evidence the
facts are sufficiently striking to merit a re-emphasis.   Two
extents were taken of this manor, one in the thirteenth century
and one in the twelfth.   In the thirteenth century[3] by far the
largest class of the tenantry held a uniform holding of 12
acres, and there were a certain number of 24-acre holdings.
The twelfth-century extent[4] supplies evidence that is strikingly
similar to this.   The 12-acre holding occurs again ; it is even
more distinctively the typical holding of the manor, though
there are a few tenements of 24 acres which seem to be
derived from it.   Further, the tenement itself is almost always
described as containing 'duodecim acras de landsettagio ',[5]
which at once recalls the similar phraseology used in describing
the primitive holdings at Hindringham and Hindolveston.
It is certainly quite clear that at Brancaster even in the
thirteenth century the fundamental holding was still the
12-acre unit.   Even at that date the men of the manor seem
to know very little of more normal systems.   ' Nescitur ', say
the juratores of Brancaster, ' quot virgatae faciunt hidam nec
quot acrae faciant virgatam.'[6]   They do not know because

[1] Cf. Gray, *op. cit.*, p. 341 and note.   Vide *infra*.
[2] Cf. Gray, *op. cit.*, pp. 345, 346.
[3] *R. C.*, vol. i, pp. 412, 413.
[4] *R. C.*, vol. iii, pp. 261–5.
[5] *R. C.*, vol. iii, p. 262.
[6] *R. C.*, vol. i, p. 413.

they do not need to know; their manor is still organized upon a basis of 12-acre share holdings. These clearly represent the ' tenementa ' of later days; they can be traced back to the twelfth century; and even then they bear—and are said to bear—the appearance of antiquity.

In the adjoining hundred to that in which lay Brancaster was the other large Norfolk manor of the Abbot of Ramsey-Ringstead. Here also the hide and the virgate common in his other estates were unknown. The peasant opinion on the matter is again unmistakable. ' Non sunt ibi hydae vel virgatae terrae '[1] is the conclusion of the extent. The basis upon which the agricultural arrangements of the vill were organized is not, however, clear. In the thirteenth century there are indications of a 14-acre and of a 10-acre unit.[2] In the twelfth century traces appear of what looks like a primitive holding of 8 acres.[3] These vague statements can, perhaps, hardly be pressed. Two points, however, about the Ring-stead extents deserve note. On the one hand the somewhat uncommon ' landsettagium '[4] appears again with great prominence. On the other hand the absence of the virgate is once more emphasized. In both of these ways does the Ringstead Survey suggest analogy with the remarkable arrangements prevailing at Brancaster.

Similar conditions are moreover indicated in the Register of the Bishop of Norwich.[5] And whilst the primitive organization of Martham, with the field arrangements of later days, has already received very full attention, the exceptional character of the arrangements recorded in the Register is not confined to those extents which contain instances of archaic terminology. For instance, at Newton there are distinct traces of an exceptional system of land division which bears a close relation to that already observed upon the Ramsey and Ely estates. The Newton extent[6] contains no reference to a virgate or to any unit which is similar to it. Instead, the Survey begins with the very detailed description of a series of

---

[1] *R. C.*, vol. i, p. 405.
[2] *R. C.*, vol. i, pp. 404–11.
[3] *R. C.*, vol. iii, pp. 266–9.
[4] e.g. *R. C.*, vol. iii, p. 268.
[5] Stowe 936.
[6] Ibid., fols. 15 b, 32.

holdings each usually held by more than one person.[1] These
tenements which are given such prominence in the extent
each contain 13 acres of arable and 1 acre of meadow. They
are carefully distinguished from any additional land that may
have been acquired by their tenants, and their fundamental
nature is alike shown in their ' collective ' character as in the
fact that, even when they have broken up, their essential unity
seems to be recognized. In this way they bear the appearance
of antiquity, and in any case they offer the only principle of
unified arrangement in the manor. Though an absolutely
exact equation can seldom be established, these tenements
certainly seemed to have formed the basis of many of the
other holdings in the manor. For instance, when we find later
in the extent six holdings each containing 7 acres of arable
and 1 acre of meadow, and one with $6\frac{1}{2}$ acres of arable and
$\frac{1}{2}$ acre of meadow, it seems reasonable to suppose that these
were formed out of tenements similar to those described with
such emphasis at the beginning of the survey.[2] Still more is
this the case when in another place the holding of $6\frac{1}{2}$ acres
and $\frac{1}{2}$ acre of meadow is attached to the tenure of ' half
a messuage '.[3] Again, the prominence given in the extent to
sheep-farming and the stated use of private folds confirms the
evidence of the extent itself, that in this striking holding at
Newton, which appears as the determining factor in the
formation of the holdings of the manor, we have to deal with
a holding different from the normal virgate and probably not
evenly divided among the fields. This again presents a remarkable similarity not only to the holdings known in Norfolk
in Tudor times but to the analogous toftlands of Walpole and
to the 12-acre tenements at Brancaster.

---

[1] Ibid., fol. 15 b.   [2] Ibid., fol. 19 b.

[3] Ibid. This and the subsequent entry contain points of interest.
' Clemens tenet medietatem unius messuagii quod fuit Fulconis et aliam
terram tenet videlicet vi acras et dimidiam acram prati.   Edmundus
Wigg tenet alteram medietatem messuagii quod Clemens tenet et facit in
omnibus pro parte sua sicut Clemens pro sua medietate.' Is it possible
that the ' messuagium ', which certainly in Clement's case went with the
full share holding in the fields, was in this extent a crude Latin translation
of ' toft '—the word being used in the sense adopted in the Walpole
extents ?

In yet another hundred of Norfolk lay the manor of Binham. An extent was taken thereof in the early fourteenth century. In it the tenantry are rigidly divided into categories in the following order :

> Tenentes mollond'.
>
> Tenentes duodecim acras terre.
>
> Tenentes viginti quattuor acras terre.
>
> Tenentes sex acras terre.
>
> Tenentes croftas.[1]

Here again there is to be noted the absence of anything suggesting a virgate arrangement, and also the presence of the 12-acre unit which appears as the determining factor in the grouping of the tenements. Further, this was no new arrangement devised in Binham to meet the requirements of the fourteenth century. In the curious section of this extent, which is described as giving the conditions in the manor at the time of the foundation of the priory, whatever may be its precise date, we have at least an opportunity of seeing what these later jurors considered to have been the conditions prevailing in the manor in a past that was already remote.[2] It is therefore of interest to note that here once again the tenantry are divided into the same groups and that still the 12-acre tenements seem to lie at the basis of the arrangement of the shares in the fields. Again, this is a holding extremely like the 'tenementum' of the Elizabethan surveys[3] and apparently akin to the tofts and the landsettagia of the other extents. And the fact of its existence in a twelfth-century extent is of considerable importance. Further, by comparison with the Walpole extent it is significant to note that in the elaborate description of the meadow at Binham there occur the names ' Onemannesdel, Twomannesdel, Nynnemannesdel, and Threemannesdel '.[4] This phraseology is related both to the descriptions of the deleland of the charters and also to the division of the arable into tenmanloths in the Ely Surveys.

---

[1] Cott. Claud. D. xiii, fol. 7.   [2] Vide *supra*, pp. 8–9.

[3] The absence of any approach to a field distribution in the description of the demesne and the presence of sheep-farming in this manor also point in the same direction.

[4] Cott. Claud. D. xiii, fol. 4 b.

And in general it may be said that the description of Binham supplies very strikingly a new illustration of the peculiar East Anglian field arrangements. The holdings are therein arranged apart from any virgate scheme, and they help to carry back to the twelfth century the field organization which has been noted as peculiar to the district in the sixteenth, and this in a manner which suggests very strongly their still higher antiquity.

One more example of these tenemental arrangements in medieval East Anglia may be given—this time from Suffolk. Lawshall was a manor of the Abbey of Ramsey and is frequently mentioned in the cartulary of that house. In the general list of hidages (which as we have seen cannot be taken as a reliable guide to the field systems of East Anglia),[1] the figures given are of such a kind to suggest that this assessment in hides and virgates was a highly artificial one. There we are told that in this manor fifty acres make a virgate and that three virgates make a hide.[2] The fictional character of this assessment is brought out very clearly in the rolls of the Broughton honour court for 1258. One Sewal of Hanningfield states that he will appear when required to answer to the charge that he does not pay fully for the two hides which he holds at Lawshall. But the writer of the roll finds it necessary to add : ' Memorandum quod hida ibi non continet nisi solummodo duas virgatas et unum quarterium terre.'[3] Clearly there is a discrepancy between the two accounts. What, however, is clear from both is that these hides and virgates in Lawshall are very artificial units. The key to the puzzle is contained in the bailiff's account of the

---

[1] Vide *supra*, p. 24, n. 7.
[2] *R. C.* iii, p. 213 :

> Laushulle.
> Decem hidae.
> Quinquaginta acrae faciunt virgatam.
> Tres virgatae hidam.

The presence of the hide in this Suffolk manor is a new indication of the artificiality of this reckoning, which is suggested by the unnatural nature of the equations. This inaccuracy can be seen clearly in the case of Brancaster and Ringstead, when an extent exists to check the ' hidages '.
[3] Selden Society, vol. ii, p. 56.

manor in 1393.[1] In this the lands of the manor are divided
in the following manner :

48 tenants each hold 12½ acres	600 acres.
8 tenants each hold 10 acres	80 acres.
9 tenants each hold 5 acres	45 acres.[2]

The 12½-acre unit is clearly the fundamental unit in the
manor and explains the curious remarks of the earlier
cartulary and roll. It is true that such a unit is called a
' quarterium ', and some explanation may be given for the
term.[3] Taken in connexion with the exceptional and contradictory estimates of hides and virgates, however, it can hardly
be doubted that throughout the thirteenth century it was the
holding upon which the lands of the manor were organized,
and that here we have another example of the basic ' tenementum ' which in this sense is strictly analogous to the units
mentioned at Brancaster and Ringstead, which under the
names of landsettagium, toftland, and eruing appear in so
many scattered manors in medieval East Anglia.

Widespread throughout East Anglia in the Middle Ages,
it has thus been possible to see the application of a system of
tenemental organization which is peculiar to the district.
This is guided by the same economic principles as those
which can be seen at work in the sixteenth century, when the
' tenementum ' takes the place of the fields as the unit through
which a three-course system of husbandry is worked ; and its
distinguishing mark under the Tudors is the concentration of
the strips in one section of the arable land of the township.
It now seems certain that we can carry back this organization
to medieval times, and that we may see the ' tenementum ' and
the field organization implied in it in the twelfth- and thirteenth-century extents.

And if this conclusion approaches the truth, it is clear that

---

[1] *Suffolk Institute of Archaeology, Trans.*, vol. xiv, pp. 111 seq., wherein
Mr. Saunders discusses this roll.   [2] Ibid., p. 113.
[3] Vide *infra*. Either we have to deal in this case with a late artificial
application of an alien terminology, which seems the most probable
solution ; or, on the other hand, it is perhaps just possible that the word
here is viewed in relation to the Domesday geld, and is a very literal
' farthing land '.

the virgate, which makes its very exceptional appearance in the Ely extents and in one late and hasty list of Ramsey hidages, must be regarded as an artificial and exotic unit of late origin in this district. The negative evidence from outside these manors may be regarded as conclusive on this point,[1] and it can hardly be doubted that the Ely virgate was the result of a late seignorial rearrangement. Its relation to the older tenements is also fairly clear. At Bridgham and Northwold the presence of a 48-acre 'plena terra' or virgate has been noticed, together with the strong probability that it was based upon a 12-acre holding. At Binham and Brancaster we have seen combinations of the 12-acre holdings to make up tenements of 24 and 48 acres, and it is probable that a similar connexion is to be found on the Ely lands between the virgate and the earlier unit. In fact, there is every indication that we are dealing with a reorganization of the servile holdings upon a new basis, in which the 'tenementa' seem to have been combined together for the purpose of the regulation of services and rents.[2] But even after such reorganization had taken place, it is clear from the sheep-farming practices on the Ely manors that the virgate on those lands could not have meant anything like the unit involved in and dependent on the two- or three-field systems of the Midlands. The great ecclesiastical lordships undoubtedly reorganized their estates from time to time, and sometimes in so doing adopted the terminology which they found on their other manors, with the result for instance that a 'virgate' appears in a hasty list in the Ramsey Cartulary in manors, which, from the recorded evidence of the same Cartulary, knew it not, and in the Ely manors a fictional virgate is evolved as an artificial unit varying in size. Ultimately the new system, like the old, was based upon the common plough, though still distinct from the Midland field systems.[3] The virgate of the Ely

---

[1] Vide *supra*.

[2] Possible traces of this may perhaps be seen in the activities of Abbot Aldwine at Ramsey (*R.C.*, *passim*) and of Bishop Nigel of Ely (*Liber Niger Scaccarii*, ed. Hearne, and cf. *Anglia Sacra*, vol. i, pp. 618–30).

[3] The making of a manor, which the *D. B.* of East Anglia so frequently

extents is therefore a confusing term. It is not to be taken as implying what was meant by the virgate of the Midlands, and it cannot be regarded as a primitive holding. Rather it was the result of an agglomeration of older and smaller holdings which have been observed scattered about among these East Anglian manors and appearing under different names whilst possessing the same characteristics.

The exceptional nature of the Ely terminology and the obviously suspicious character of the virgate in a land where it was otherwise unknown cannot be too strongly emphasized. Even in those manors the more characteristic tenement can be discovered, and in general in East Anglia from the foregoing Survey it seems clear that the individual characteristics of sixteenth-century conditions can be clearly seen to be the dominant feature of the medieval arrangement of holdings. This type of organization is not confined to one hundred of the county or to one ecclesiastical fief, but it makes its appearance in widely different parts of East Anglia and on the lands of different lords. It shows certain variations of detail, but its common characteristics are so marked and so much in accordance with those described in the more detailed evidence of later times, as to leave no doubt as to the prevalence in East Anglia in the Middle Ages also of a tenemental system based on a peculiar system of co-operative husbandry.

But it is probable that the medieval evidence does more than testify to the prevalence of these conditions. It has been suggested that there can be seen therein the principles which underlie these complicated arrangements and throw some light on their origin. And it will be suggested that in the formation of this system Danish influence played the predominant part and was not confined to the arrest of dis-

records, would result in a diminution of the area of the tenants' lands, which, shrunken in size, would now be responsible for the cultivation of the demesne that have been carved out of them. This probably happened at Martham. On this point cf. Tingey, *Norfolk Archaeology*, vol. xxi. There are indications in East Anglia that the ploughland in the thirteenth century was the 'full land' and not some larger unit. Cf. *R. H. S. Trans.*, 4th Series, vol. i, p. 51.

integration. Rather in the later organization of tenements can be seen traces of Scandinavian systems of land-sharing.

In this respect the terms under which the 'tenementum' is described are of some importance. Often the unit is un-named. But the names which in different manors it assumed are always curious : In Martham the eruing, at Walpole the toftland, at Hindringham and Hindolveston the landsettagium. As has been seen there is some reason for believing that the toft is occasionally the determinant factor in Danish allo-cations of share land. The eruing is clearly in the thirteenth century an archaic word and testifies to pre-Conquest arrange-ments.[1] Again, the landsettagium is also suggestive of primi-tive conditions.[2] Though never common, the word can be found in several East Anglian documents. Apart from the Norwich Register, a gift at Potter Heigham and Ludham to St. Benet of Hulme is described as ' terras landsettorum et terras leuicias et socmannos '.[3] Spelman noticed the appearance of the word in the 'Old Custumal of Lewes' on Norfolk lands,[4] and the word also occurs in the foundation charter of Wymondham monastery[5] and in a charter from the same house conferring land at Southwood.[6] Before the Conquest a manumission to landsettlers holding tofts in Suffolk has already been noticed.[7] In many of the later documents, how-ever, the word is used definitely to indicate servile conditions as opposed to free.[8] But it seems probable that as in the

---

[1] Cf. Hudson, *op. cit.*, vol. i, p. 36.
[2] Cf. Hudson, *op. cit.*, p. 50.   [3] Cott. Galba E. ii, fol. 33.
[4] *Henrici Spellman Glossarium*, p. 349, ed. 1664.
[5] Dugdale, *Monasticon*, vol. iii, p. 330.
[6] Cott. Titus C. viii, fol. 22.
[7] Kemble, *C. D.*, dccccvii, et vide *supra*.
[8] In the Ramsey Cartulary throughout the word usually implies servility, though the services are not heavy in one case where they are described (*R. C.* iii. 269). Land may thus be described as lying ' tam in libero tenemento quam in lancettagio' (vol. i, p. 411). Lansettage holdings follow the rules for the transmission of villein tenements in the courts (e. g. vol. i, p. 424). On the other hand, the more primitive distinction between land held in landsettage and that in demesne is frequently made (e. g. vol. iii, p. 263). For the rest it is worthy of note that the word only once occurs in the whole cartulary outside the Norfolk and Suffolk lands (*R. C.*, vol. iii, p. 260). For the use of the term at Hindolveston cf. *Nor-folk Archaeology*, vol. xx, p. 192. In the Wymondham foundation charter

case of 'villanus' the word has acquired its base meaning as the result of later corruption. Primarily of course it signifies merely 'an occupier, a man sitting on land'.[1] It would be in the highest degree unwise to push the statements of the later surveyors too far. The juratores of the late thirteenth century were not etymologists, and whilst they were quite certain that the system which they described was different from that which prevailed elsewhere, they were at a loss to find any uniform terms to apply to them. What may be stressed in connexion with these terms, however, is the fundamental similarity of their connotation. All are derived from the connexion of the tenement with common husbandry. All are derived from the necessities of primitive agriculture. And, what is more important, all suggest, in the thirteenth century, remote antiquity.

With this in mind it is well to recall the scattered strips which, however placed in the field, went to make up an East Anglian tenement. Such a system of itself indicates very strongly that its origin is to be found, in common with all other systems similar to it in this respect, in the allocation of tenements to sharers of the land, and this according to some definite plan.[2] The notions of land division held by the invading Danes were different in detail but not in essence[3] from those which they must have found in England, and there is no reason to suppose that if, as is probable, they rearranged the tenemental organization of the conquered districts, they should not do so, like their predecessors, according to fixed proportions. Consequently, for the purposes of discovering the origin and the primitive nature of these 'tenementa', an examination of their size is far more important than the criticism of the names under which they appear. Nor does such an examination fail to produce some-

the word is also used in contrast to the 'liberi homines', and the same is true of the Southwood charter.
  [1] Vinogradoff, *Villainage in England*, p. 146.
  [2] Cf. Vinogradoff, *English Society*: 'the English open-field settlements were primarily communities of shareholders whose shares had been apportioned according to fixed proportions' (p. 282).
  [3] Cf. Vinogradoff, *op. cit.*, p. 478.

what remarkable results. But since conclusions will be drawn from the acreage of these tenements it is well at once to state that in the thirteenth century no absolute uniformity can be seen in them, and it is in the highest degree unlikely that any such ever existed. With this qualification, however, it is interesting to note the extent of the holdings which have been discussed. Their acreage it will be recalled is as follows : 15,[1] 10,[2] 12,[3] 12,[4] 10,[5] 18,[6] 14,[7] 12,[8] 12,[9] 13,[10] 12,[11] 12,[12] 12½.[13] Now a glance at these figures suggests that these tenements have been formed according to some common principle, widely scattered as they are through East Anglia. They occur at the earliest at a period of two centuries from their original formation, whatever the actual extent of Danish influence may have been, and in view of the changes and the drastic reorganization which had occurred in the district it is to be expected that such holdings occurring in the later documents should have deflected somewhat their original prototype if such there was. In view of this it seems fairly clear that the norm to which these holdings tend is a unit of some 12 or 13 acres. And the explanation of these tenements which is here put forward is that all are derived from a single primitive holding, and that this was a Danish bovate whose normal size was 12½ acres, that is to say, 50 roods and 25 half-acre strips. Further, this represented a unit of husbandry based upon the contribution of one ox to the common plough, and was itself the 'manloth' and the foundation of a Scandinavian system of land-sharing.

If this is correct, then the independent testimony of these scattered East Anglian manors goes very far to support the theory of the carucate and the bovate put forward by Mr. Turner in 1913. In his Introduction to the *Feet of Fines for Huntingdonshire* he remarks justly that no good evidence has ever been put forward to show that the carucate at the

---

[1] Terrington. [2] Walpole. [3] Walton. [4] Martham.
[5] Wimbotsham. [6] Hindolveston. [7] Hindringham.
[8] Bridgham. [9] Northwold. [10] Newton.
[11] Brancaster. The Ringstead unit seems to vary between 14 acres and 8 acres, and therefore does not alter the general trend of the figures.
[12] Binham. [13] Lawshall.

time of Domesday contained 120 acres.[1] Further, Mr. Turner has suggested that the bovate was the original customary holding of a peasant who contributes an ox to one of the teams of a village community, and that the carucate is the natural derivative from the smaller holding.[2]

It is easy to see how directly the Lincolnshire evidence of the possible equation of the bovate and the manloth bears upon this; and the references to the tenmanloth in the Walpole extent and in the Lewes charter would suggest the prevalence of similar ideas in north-west Norfolk. In the twelfth-century Lincolnshire charters there is nothing to imply that ' so considerable a tenement as the carucate had ever been common among the peasant population '.[3] The word is not only of rare occurrence in the charters, but it seems to have been avoided in cases where it would certainly have been used had it been a common method of reckoning the extent of land.[4] In Yorkshire also there seems no reason for attributing to the carucate any fundamental function in the original allocation of land. The appearance of the hide in a Yorkshire land-book of the tenth century has been adduced as very strong evidence of the late introduction of the carucate system,[5] though there are indications that curious rents based on the working plough go back in Deira to the time of Athelstan.[6]

---

[1] Turner, *op. cit.*, p. lxxxiii. Mr. Turner establishes the strong probability of a normal Danish carucate of 100 acres.

[2] Turner, *op. cit.*, pp. lxxxiii-xciv.   [3] Stenton, *D. C.*, p. xx.

[4] Large estates are reckoned in ' culturae' or in large numbers of bovates. Stenton, *op. cit.*, pp. xx and lvii.

[5] Stenton, *Oxford Social and Legal Studies*, vol. ii, p. 86.

[6] *Y. C.* 99. A charter of Stephen confirms the privileges of the church of St. John of Beverley, which it alleges were conferred by Athelstan. Among these was the receipt of thraves at the rate of four from each plough and ploughshare throughout the East Riding: ' travas quoque suas per totam Austriding iiii ad cultrum et vomerem.' The *Chronica Monasterii de Melsa* notes this rent and ascribes it to Athelstan (ii. 236). It brings the term carucate into the discussion. After mentioning the privileges of Athelstan it continues : ' Inter quae etiam eidem ecclesie per totum Estridingum videlicet a regione illa quae clauditur ex uno latere flumine Derwent ex altero flumine Humbriae et ex tertio latere mari septentrionali vel orientali quae quidem provincia antiquitus Deira vocabatur de unaquaque carucata terrae id est ad cultrum et vomerem quattuor travas de suis frugibus assignavit.' The charter itself is only preserved in a rhyming version of a century after the death of Athelstan, and ' was not exemplified in the later inspeximus of 1310 '. On the whole

The phraseology of the twelfth-century Yorkshire charters is in this respect similar to that of those of Lincolnshire, and in the latter county it is abundantly clear that the bovate was of a 'fundamental character'[1] and that it was in the twelfth century still the typical peasant holding.

The East Anglian Domesday evidence points the same way, though it is in many respects peculiar. For whilst the carucate is itself the mark of the Danish districts in Domesday, in East Anglia it plays a somewhat peculiar role. Not only does the carucate in this district split in the Survey at once into holdings of irregular numbers of acres, but there is a further peculiarity in its use. Throughout the carucated districts this unit forms part of a system of assessment similar to the hide valuation of the south and west, though it was very probably 'a more modern attempt to make use of agrarian terms for the purposes of estimation'.[2] Yet in East Anglia the problem of the carucate is complicated by the fact that there was at the same time in use in Norfolk and Suffolk a wholly different scheme of assessment which was based upon an arrangement by which each village paid so many pence for every pound contributed by the hundred; and possibly also a further method of valuation is to be found in the peculiar description of the superficial area or shape of the villages.[3] But whilst these exceptional conditions must be given full weight and deserve a special exposition, it remains true that all early East Anglian evidence confirms that of

it seems that this tradition, interesting as it is, is hardly of sufficient weight to put against the contrary testimony of the Elmet document. The whole question of the documents involved is discussed by Farrer, *Y. C.*, vol. i, pp. 95–6. There are traces also of rents based upon the working plough in the St. Benet of Hulme Cartulary. Cf. the very curious charter in Cott. MS. Galba E. ii, fol. 56 b. Cf. Appendix I, No. 46.

[1] Stenton, *D. C.*, Introduction.

[2] Vinogradoff, *English Society*, p. 148.

[3] Cf. Vinogradoff, *English Society*, pp. 145, 301 ; Maitland, *D. B. B.*, 429–31. It is possible, thinks Maitland, that whilst the main geld contribution is reckoned according to the pence paid by the vill to the pound of the hundred, the carucates represent a tenurial liability. The superficial 'league' measurement and its relation to the geld is as yet an unsolved problem ; cf. *V. C. H. Suffolk*, vol. i, p. 363. On the whole subject of East Anglian geld arrangements cf. Round, *Feudal England*, pp. 98 seq.

Lincolnshire in denying to the carucate any position as the typical peasant holding. In the charters of the period immediately after Domesday it does occur, but its use is very rare, as is the case also in the later extents. The cartularies both of Castleacre and St. Benet of Hulme may be taken as good examples of the rarity of the word in twelfth-century parlance and as illustrative of the improbability that it ever was a typical peasant holding in this district.[1] An examination of Domesday tends moreover to confirm this. Even allowing for the inaccuracies which are to be expected in the Survey, it is remarkable that throughout Suffolk the proportion of households to carucates was on the average 10 to 1,[2] and that ' if in Norfolk we divide the recorded population by the number of carucates we shall get 11 as our quotient '.[3] That is so very different from what is recorded elsewhere that even allowing for the peculiar difficulties latent in the East Anglian Domesday figures [4] it militates very strongly against the supposition that the carucate could ever have been regarded as the typical peasant holding. The general tenor of the East Anglian evidence, supported by that from Lincolnshire, goes far to confirm the suggestion that the carucate in these districts was in any primitive system of land-sharing itself a derivative holding from a smaller peasant tenement, and the most likely place to look for such a tenement is in the unit which contribted one ox to one of the ploughs of the township. The application of a new term to describe eight of such holdings was a subsequent development, and, as has been pointed out, the element of the lord's demesne renders it impossible to see in this a basic area of the land

[1] The whole tenor of the Castleacre cartulary suggests a small peasant holding. For the absence of the fundamental carucate in the St. Benet of Hulme cartulary the charters of the early abbots, Cott. Galba E. ii, fols. 54 seq., are especially noteworthy.

[2] *V. C. H. Suffolk*, vol. i, p. 360. Miss Lees' table is of special interest in this connexion.

[3] Maitland, *D. B. B.*, p. 430.

[4] The dangers of relying too much upon the Domesday figures have been well shown by Dr. Round, who points out how often the D. B. statistics break down when they offer a check upon themselves. The peculiar difficulties of the East Anglian evidence are discussed later. Vide *infra*, pp. 121 seq. Much reduplication is to be expected.

which one plough could till in one year. It is the smaller peasant holding which is at the root of such arrangements. And such a unit, at once manloth and bovate, is claimed to be at the back of these curious 'tenementa' centring round $12\frac{1}{2}$ acres which make their appearance in the twelfth- and thirteenth-century extents and play a peculiar part in East Anglian husbandry till the days of the Tudors.

A somewhat more detailed examination of these figures tends, moreover, strongly to confirm this theory. The strongest argument for the $12\frac{1}{2}$-acre bovate and the 100-acre carucate of the Midland and Northern districts is that 'it offers a more coherent explanation of the fiscal system of Northern England '.[1] Here it is suggested that the evidence of this primitive share-holding of the extents which represents a manloth or a bovate and centres in size round $12\frac{1}{2}$ acres offers the only possible explanation of the unique fiscal arrangements of the East Anglian Domesday.[2] It will be remembered how the geld of Norfolk and Suffolk was assessed on the principle that for every pound that the hundred pays the vills pay so many pence. It is hardly likely that such units were originally created out of all relation to the geld capabilities of the tenements which they contained, or that the preliminary calculation of such geld capabilities would be made without reference to the agrarian units. And it is claimed that the most likely course for primitive assessors to adopt was to use the manloth or bovate—the typical peasant holding—as their unit, and to base their statistics upon a reckoning which gave to it the 50 roods or $12\frac{1}{2}$ acres which was its normal size. In this way were the East Anglian hundreds originally formed for geld purposes, and were calculated to contain a certain number of geld-paying units

[1] Turner, *op. cit.*, p. lxxxiii.

[2] The probability that Mr. Turner's conclusions of the Northern carucate can be applied to the East Anglian Domesday has been pointed out by Mr. Tingey, *Norfolk Archaeology*, vol. xxi, part 2, where he discusses the probable presence of a $12\frac{1}{2}$ acre farthing unit as the key to the Domesday assessment. Here it is hoped that the application to this of the scattered evidence of numerous later extents may give this a sounder basis, and also that it may lead to the inclusion of the leet scheme into the general organization in a more fundamental way.

which were in turn estimated according to the normal share-holdings of the peasants in the fields, however artificial the later assessment became.[1]   Now apply this to the parallel system which also makes its unique appearance in East Anglian Domesday.   There the hundred is not only a unit ideally composed of a certain number of carucates and bovates.   It was also the unit which paid one pound to the geld.   Here again we surely have to deal in the first place with a rough reckoning of geld capabilities, before the formation of the district of a given size as such a unit, and it is suggested that the unit adopted was that which paid one farthing to the geld.   Now the strength of such a theory, based as it is on the $12\frac{1}{2}$-acre geld bovate, lies in the truly remarkable results to which its application leads.   For if, as is probable, the East Anglian hundred is the long hundred of 120 carucates, a complete equation between the two assessment methods is established.   From the purely fiscal point of view we have to deal with a pound-paying unit consisting of 960 farthing units. But this finds its exact equivalent in the assessment according to estimated agrarian units, for according to this latter arrangement we have a unit of 120 carucates, or 960 bovates or man-loths of $12\frac{1}{2}$ acres each.   The manloth thus appears as the basic farthing unit of the fiscal assessment.   And the highly peculiar construction of the East Anglian geld system of the eleventh century can be explained by the very striking tenurial arrangements of later days, which in turn derive from a typical peasant holding which lies behind the Domesday statistics.

This explanation seems to be the only one which will account for the geld arrangements of the East Anglian Domesday.   It rests upon recorded evidence concerning manors widely scattered through the district, and it is bound up with the peculiar tenemental organization of the district.   But this is not all.   It receives support also from an examination of the most individual of all the East Anglian fiscal institutions of Domesday.   Not only was the pound owed by the hundred

---

[1] On this see Round, *Feudal England*, pp. 98 seq.

and subdivided among the various vills, but also it was partitioned among leets, each of which contributed a given sum in shillings and pence to every pound paid by the hundred.[1] It will be shown hereafter that the leet was no mere artificial fiscal division.[2] From the point of view of the tax, however, it may here be seen that the suggestion of the intimate relation borne by the $12\frac{1}{2}$-acre unit of the extents to the Domesday geld throws considerable light upon the leet itself. The typical leet has been held to contribute to the geld in the assessment one ora or one shilling and eight pence.[3] Taking these farthing bovates as the basis of calculation this would give a leet of 80 bovates or 10 carucates. Such a unit containing thus a round number of carucates is highly probable. But this is not all. The evidence for the ora leets comes mainly from Suffolk.[4] The Norfolk leet statistics show considerably more variation. The figures are given in full in the Norfolk Victoria County History.[5] Briefly they may be summarized thus : Of the thirty-two hundreds of the county only three [6] show certain evidence of a uniform ' ora ' arrangement. In five more [7] the reckoning of a leet to the ora is to be seen in more than one leet in the hundred, though in the whole hundred there is no uniformity and other reckonings are adopted. In nine hundreds,[8] however, an assessment reckoning the leet at two shillings (or sometimes perhaps at one shilling) is so prominent as to make it certain that it was the guiding principle upon which the leets were arranged, and in three of these [9] by the two-shilling assessment a wholly extraordinary uniformity is obtained. In addition to these, in the hundreds of Henstead and West Flegg the two-shilling assessment predominates, but the ora unit is also introduced. In the rest of the county some other principle of assessment was

---

[1] Round, *op. cit.*; cf. *V. C. H. Suffolk*, vol. i, pp. 360 seq.
[2] Vide, *infra*, pp. 191 seq.   [3] *V. C. H. Suffolk, loc. cit.*
[4] Cf. the tables concerning the leets, *V. C. H. Suffolk*, pp. 412–16.
[5] *V. C. H. Norfolk*, vol. ii, pp. 204–11.   [6] Blofield, Forehoe, Launditch.
[7] Wayland, South Erpingham, Loddon, Eynesford, Taverham.
[8] Freebridge, Clackclose, Smethden, North Grenehoe, East Flegg, Diss, Holt, Walsham, Gallow.
[9] Freebridge, Clackclose, Walsham. The two former of these give a beautiful symmetry on this assessment.

adopted. The object of these remarks is in no way to deny the prevalence or even the predominance of the ora leet in the two counties taking them as a whole, but merely to point out that in Norfolk some other scheme based upon a two-shilling unit was frequently adopted, where it is the most usual valuation and in some cases gives a startling uniformity in its results. The importance of this becomes clear if a reference is again made to the suggested farthing unit, the 12½-acre manloth or bovate of the extents. For the two-shilling leet assessment would give an entity of 96 bovates or 12 carucates, and an identity would thus be established between the East Anglian leet and the 12-carucated hundreds of Lincolnshire. Not only that is to say does this unit of the later extents explain the carucate arrangement of East Anglia, but also, viewed as representing a bovate or manloth assessed at 12½ acres, which was its normal size, it goes far to solve the problem of the Domesday leet by bringing that system into line with the Danish arrangements which appear more prominently in Lincolnshire.

It is not of course suggested that there was ever any absolute uniformity in the actual agrarian tenements, but the remarkable analogy which is presented between the field holdings in the extents and the elaborate geld system of the East Anglian Domesday indicates very strongly that the later tenements are derived from Danish systems of land-sharing. Before leaving them, however, it may be well to notice certain implications that are involved in this theory. Primarily it reacts upon any view of the carucate of the East Anglian Domesday. Here, as elsewhere, in East Anglia the carucate will normally contain 100 and not 120 acres. And, what is more important, it must be regarded as itself a derivative holding from the smaller fundamental holding of bovate or manloth and not the original basis of the shares in the fields.[1] Again, this comparison of the two sets of records also reflects upon the problem of the East Anglian hundred. The suggested presence of a farthing unit in the manloth

---

[1] Nor is it inconceivable that this may perhaps have some bearing upon the larger problems connected with the early hide.

as the original basis of the geld assessments does not detract from the artificiality of the repartition of the Domesday geld. But it may be urged that these hundreds were originally formed according to a computed number of geld-paying units within them, and that these calculations were based upon the typical peasant holding, the manloth, whose normal size was conceived to be $12\frac{1}{2}$ acres. These units preceded the construction of the hundreds in East Anglia. And the geld arrangement in which the East Anglian hundred plays so peculiar a part still reflects the method of its construction. But the most important implication of this view of East Anglian tenemental conditions is the new light which it sheds on the leet. With the distinct probability of an identity existing between the 12-carucate hundred and the leet as it appears in certain parts of Norfolk, the suggestion that the leets were originally hundreds[1] themselves prior to the formation of the Domesday hundreds is very considerably strengthened. Here also must be noticed another equation which has been raised by these figures and which points in the same direction. If these leets are on occasion 12-carucated units, we have an ideal geld acreage of 1,200 acres. This fits in rather strikingly with the 120-acre tenmanloth of the Walpole extents and the Lewes charter, and makes the leet appear as a hundred consisting of ten tenmanloths.[2] Here, however, it must be noticed that there is a slight discrepancy between this and the former assessments which have been noticed, since the manloth unit would by this consist of 12 acres and not of the $12\frac{1}{2}$ acres which has been claimed to represent the normal fundamental holding. But, as in the tenmanloth of the thirteenth century, we are dealing with a system which was already becoming archaic, and the schemes of original partition of the deleland had long since been forgotten, it may be sug-

---

[1] On this cf. Corbett, *R. H. S. Transactions*, New Series, vol. xiv, p. 187. The possibility of the relation to the leet of the reduction in the 'hidages' of East Anglia between the Tribal Hidage and Domesday must be borne in mind.

[2] Vinogradoff, *English Society*, p. 163. The reference to the word in the Lewes charter is corroborative evidence of its common use in Walpole.

gested (without pressing unduly this new equation in its relationship with the one which has earlier been insisted upon) that the slightness of the discrepancy seems perhaps on the whole more remarkable than the lapse from perfect accuracy.[1] And whatever difficulties stand in the way of a complete identification, it may be urged that here, too, there seem to be traces of a reckoning based upon the typical peasant holding as it is disclosed in the later extents. But quite apart from this, the argument which has been put forward of the relationship of the ' tenementa ' with the Domesday geld removes the leet from its position of isolation and brings it into line with the normal arrangements of the Danish districts.

From many points of view, therefore, the tenemental arrangement of medieval East Anglia viewed in relation to the husbandry organization of the district thus discloses features of interest. In the sixteenth century these have been shown to be peculiar in that the crop rotation was worked by means of units or ' tenementa ' and not by means of any regular field system. It can, however, be clearly shown that such arrangements were widespread throughout the district in medieval times also, and it is probable such organization was stabilized by peculiar sheep-farming practices. The contrast between the tenemental system of Norfolk and Suffolk with that of the Midlands may certainly be carried into medieval times. But the medieval records also suggest that these holdings, which are the basis of the manorial economy, show signs, both from their relation to other later systems of reorganization and from the terms under which they are sometimes described, of being the result of primitive divisions of shareland according to fixed proportions. In this they conform to what is known of the origin of all other schemes which are based upon a strip system. Lastly, a comparison of the nomenclature and of the size of these tenementa with Domesday geld statistics brings out their intimate connexion, and goes far to explain the peculiar geld arrangements of eleventh-

---

[1] The fluctuating size of the customary acre must be taken into consideration in these translations of earlier holdings into later measurements.

century Norfolk and Suffolk ; it thus points to the primitive origin of these holdings, which were later to be the distinguishing mark of the tenemental arrangements of East Anglia.

This continuity of the tenurial arrangements of the district from the Danish times throughout the Middle Ages thus represents the close connexion of these peasant holdings with the husbandry organization of the district. From a wholly different point of view, however, the East Anglian peasant holdings are also peculiar. Throughout, in the records of Norfolk and Suffolk, we have to deal with a great amount of confusion, and it is clear that any primitive scheme that existed is concealed in the later records under the utmost irregularity of tenure. The miscellaneous holdings of the freemen and socmen in Domesday, assessed as they are in odd numbers of acres, appear throughout the period in the free tenements. The Domesday conditions are paralleled in the early charters, which again reveal the utmost irregularity amongst the holdings of the smaller free peasants.[1] In general we have to reckon with a great deal of disintegration, and though in some cases this has not broken the continuity between the later holdings and primitive arrangements, yet it does remain the most prominent feature of the tenurial development of East Anglia. And in the contrast which may be seen in this respect between the free and servile tenements lies a very striking example of the operation of the other force which has been described as the second formative influence in the growth of medieval peasant holdings in England. The strength of the influence of the lord's will in the creation of peasant tenements finds paradoxically a unique illustration in East Anglia. This influence, always exercised to preserve intact the holdings of the tenants, has been shown at work in the formation of certain servile holdings. It might therefore be suggested that the miscellaneous character of the free holdings which is so marked in this district, and which in the thirteenth century presents a contrast to the servile tenements nowhere to be found in the south and west, is to be attributed to a disintegration which seignorial pressure in Norfolk and Suffolk has

[1] The Castleacre cartulary is particularly good evidence in this respect.

been powerless to check. The available materials offer a good opportunity for the examination of an economic development which is in many respects confined to East Anglia, and which helps to explain many of the peculiarities of the social structure of the district from the time of Domesday.

In particular the Ely extents afford an opportunity for such an examination. By their categorical nature they are excellent evidence of the types of tenements prevailing among the different classes of the peasantry. Primarily they serve to bring into prominence the important distinction to which allusion has been made. Whilst among the servile classes regular holdings are to be found, the description of the free and rent-paying tenants reveals the utmost irregularity. Among these the carucate is very rare, and the virgate as a free tenement is confined to two manors. Nowhere are these holdings at all typical. On the one hand, that is to say, the free holdings vary very greatly in size, and on the other hand they are assessed not in virgates, bovates, and the like, but in irregular numbers of acres.[1] This is in marked contrast with the conditions prevailing for instance in such surveys as that of Worcester,[2] and also with later Danelagh arrangements which to a great extent preserved the bovate as the typical peasant free tenement.[3] In these East Anglian manors of the See of Ely the freeholder is usually described as holding an irregular number of acres, and the diversity of tenements is so great as to render it impossible, in general, to connect these in any uniform manner with the traditional open field arrangements of the south and west.

But besides bringing out the contrast between the free and

---

[1] An example of this might be taken from almost any manor on the Ely lands. Pulham in 1222 may serve as an example, where we have holdings among the free tenants of 35, $1\frac{1}{2}$, $12\frac{1}{2}$, 22, $10\frac{1}{4}$, and the like: Cott. Tib. B. ii, fol. 184 b.

[2] Ed. Camden Society. The holdings of the free tenants are normally expressed in the common field measurements, and though there are both large and small free tenements yet within the manors themselves the variations do not appear to have been nearly so great. For instance, in the manor of 'Grimaleh' the free tenements are all of half a virgate or under (p. 44 a), whilst at Blakewell, where there is a half-hide holding, there is not a free holding under half a virgate (p. 64 b).

[3] Vide *supra*, and Stenton, *D. C.*, Introduction, *passim.*

servile holdings, the Ely registers from their date make
possible a comparison which throws much light on the history
of individual holdings during fifty years of the thirteenth
century. They reveal a process of disintegration, the
rapidity of which is wholly surprising. In Pulham, for
instance, in 1222 both Richard Ketelshaw and Richard Lord
held unusually large tenements.[1] In 1277 the holding of the
former remains unchanged. Not so the tenement of Richard
Lord, for we read that 'de terra que fuit Ricardi Lord' no
fewer than twenty-four people now have shares.[2] The extent
of Bridgham offers an even more remarkable illustration of
the process. The whole holding of 'Radulphus clericus' in
1222 can be accounted for in the holdings of Walter of
Burkenham and William of Hakeford in 1277.[3] And whilst
the holdings of the free tenants were thus disintegrating,

[1] Cott. Tib. B. ii, fol. 184 b.
[2] Cott. Claud. C. xi, fol. 210 b. It is probable that we have here an
example of what must have been a common feature of the disintegration
of tenements. Among the 1277 holders there are two sons of the original
Richard Lord. These hold only tiny tenements. The holding has not
split up for lack of heirs, and the statement that in 1277 the bishop
himself holds the 'capitale mesuagium' of the tenement suggests that
for some reason the holding has escheated to the bishop and been once
again let out to new tenants.
[3] In 1222 we read : 'Radulfus clericus tenet de terra Uluin viginti
acras pro viginti denariis equaliter. Idem tenet unam acram de dominico
per firmarios pro duobus denariis equaliter. Idem tenet quattuor acras
pro quattuor denariis equaliter. Idem tenet de novo sexdecim acras pro
duobus solidis et octo denariis equaliter.' Cott. Tib. B. ii, fol. 181. In
1277 the holding is accounted for in the following entries : (1) 'Walterus
de Burkenham tenet viginti acras de terre Wlwine que fuerunt Radulfi
clerici.' Cott. Claud. C. xi, fol. 241. (2) 'Willelmus de Hakford tenet
unam acram terre que fuerunt Radulfi clerici pro duobus denariis per
annum equaliter.' Ibid., fol. 241 b. (3) 'Idem tenet quattuor acras que
fuerunt eiusdem Radulfi pro quattuor denariis.' Ibid. (4) 'Idem tenet
octo acras et dimidiam que fuerunt eiusdem Radulfi pro octodecim
denariis equaliter.' Ibid. (5) 'Idem tenet sexdecim acras que fuerunt
eiusdem Radulfi pro duobus solidis et octo denariis equaliter.' Ibid.
Several points may here be noted. The original holding was by no means
a compact one. It was built up by a prosperous freeman, probably not
all at the same time, and itself shows how a capitalist system was beginning to play havoc with the older normal holdings of the free tenants.
On his death the tenement at once breaks up into its component parts,
which are acquired by two tenants in unequal shares. The whole
tenement thus can be accounted for fifty-five years later. Its subdivisions
remain the same, and, what is more remarkable, the moneys owed from
these subdivisions when they are given in the later Survey are the same
as those of 1222.

with equal rapidity were new holdings being built up. Again Bridgham offers a good example of this development, which can for instance be seen very clearly in the description of the holding of Walter Burkenham in 1277 :

'Walterus de Burkenham tenet viginti acras de terra Wlwine que fuerunt Radulfi clerici. Et viginti et unam acras que fuerunt Willelmi filii Iohannis de Brandon. Et quattuor acras terre que fuerunt Ricardi clerici. Et sex acras terre que fuerunt Roberti Mareschalli. Et duas acras que fuerunt Hugonis de Rudham. Et quinque acras que fuerunt de terra Bartholomei capellani. Et viginti et octo acras que fuerunt Christiane Wilwine.'[1]

All these isolated tenements with the exception of the last named can be identified in the earlier Survey,[2] and we thus have a complete illustration of the manner in which a prosperous peasant could in the thirteenth century build up

---

[1] Cott. Claud. C. xi, fol. 241.

[2] Cott. Tib. B. ii, fols. 181, 181 b. Another most curious instance of disintegration upon the Ely lands may be given. This comes from the Pulham extent, and this time from a servile category of tenants called 'Leudimen'. The result of a comparison can perhaps best be set out in parallel columns :

1222	1277
Adam Kiggel tenet septem acras pro duobus solidis et quattuor denariis equaliter. Item tenet duas acras pro sex denariis equaliter . . . Item tenet unam acram.—Cott. Tib. B. ii, fol. 187.	Willelmus Kiggel tenet quinque acras et dimidiam pro viginti tribus denariis et obolo per annum. Idem tenet duas acras pro sex denariis equaliter . . . Idem tenet unam acram.—Cott. Claud. C. xi, fol. 206 b. De Consuetudinariis. Ricardus et Willelmus filii Willelmi . . . tenent unam acram et dimidiam que fuit Willelmi Kegel pro quattuor denariis equaliter et obolo ad festum Sancti Andree.—Cott. Claud. C. xi, fol. 204.

Here even the parcels have changed. The whole 1222 tenement is, however, to be accounted for in the entries of fifty-five years later, and though the money rent liable is divided quite differently its total— 2s. 10d.—remains the same. The one force, in short, which has succeeded in preserving any semblance of unity in the tenement is the lord's will in regard to service and rent. If this disintegration was taking place thus rapidly among the servile tenants, how much more is it to be expected in the case of the freeholders over whom the lord has of necessity less power?

within fifty years a substantial estate for himself. Such development could be seen on nearly every page of the Ely Surveys, the comparison between which affords an opportunity of watching in detail the fluctuation in the land of obscure families throughout half a century.

But outside the Ely lands also there is ample evidence for the exceptional rapidity of this process in East Anglia. The court rolls for instance of the manor of Hindolveston[1] show that there the peasantry were constantly alienating small parcels of land to an extent which was wholly remarkable. The same disintegration is prominent also in the Binham Survey.[2] Everywhere in short in the thirteenth century we can watch the constant transference of land from one peasant holder to another. This in the manors marks off more and more sharply the free tenant from his unfree companions by making ever more apparent the contrast between the heterogeneous holdings of the former and the more regularly formed tenements of the latter, and tends to obscure very effectively all organized schemes of original holdings.

This disintegrating movement which is so closely dependent upon the weakness of the power of the lord in this district can be very clearly seen in the earlier documents. We can watch the constant breaking up and re-formation of the peasant holdings in the twelfth-century charters of the religious houses. There the extent to which small holdings are being bought, sold, and given away is wholly remarkable. The cartulary of Castleacre Priory is full of minute gifts of quite humble people to the church for the good of their souls.[3] In this

---

[1] Hudson, *op. cit.*, p. 31.

[2] e.g. one John Pilate is recorded as holding from the bishop a messuage and a rood of land (Cott. Claud. D. xiii, fol. 10). Scattered, however, throughout the survey we read that no less than four men hold tiny tenements at a money rent from this John (fol. 10).

[3] This is to be seen throughout the Survey. In Acre itself, for example, the gifts to the monks are when specified of the following sizes : 2 acres, 17 acres, 1 acre, 12 acres, 1 acre, 2 acres, $\frac{1}{2}$ acre, $1\frac{1}{2}$ acres, 5 acres and a rood, 5 'perticatas', 3 acres and 3 'perticatas', $6\frac{1}{2}$ acres, 9 acres, 3 acres, 17 acres, 12 acres in very small parcels, 1 acre (Harl. 2110, fols. 8–12 b). A lord will sanction on occasion the gifts and the sales of his men ; e. g. at Massingham, says Robert 'filius Bruisii', 'Concedo totam terram quam homines mei dederunt ipsis monachis et totam terram quam ipsi

very striking register it is impossible not to be struck with
the number of donors whose names suggest Anglo-Scandinavian ancestry,[1] and the small extent of the majority of the
gifts recorded makes it quite clear that we have here to
deal in general with the alienation of sections of small
tenements by peasant proprietors. The St. Benet of Hulme
register is concerned in many cases with somewhat larger
gifts, but there are frequent instances therein of gifts of a few
acres by a peasant holder.[2] Some of these will have to be
considered in detail in other connexions.[3] Here, however,
the general importance of these early peasant charters, both
as regards their number and their character, can hardly be
over-emphasized. The extent of the transference of land was
in East Anglia even greater than that recorded in the remarkable charters of the Danelagh.[4] And the inevitable result
was the constant fluctuation of tenements and the existence
of a multitude of peasant proprietors with heterogeneous
holdings each containing an irregular amount of acreage.

There is also no need to limit these characteristics of East
Anglian society to the twelfth century, and it may well be
suggested that the very peculiar tenemental conditions of the
Norfolk and Suffolk Domesdays were due to an economic
force operating so to speak in the present as well as to past
political events. If, as seems probable, a tenemental continuity
can occasionally be found which suggests the prevalence of
ordered Danish arrangements in the pre-Conquest period, it is
clear that disintegration has by the time of the Survey been
operating in East Anglia with greater strength than elsewhere.
Nothing else will explain the miscellaneous character of the
small freeholdings at the time of the Survey. And if on
the one hand we regard the prevalence of the 'liber homo'

vendiderunt' (fol. 16). The rapidity of the process of disintegration is to
be seen when a gift to the Priory is described as 'vii acras terre cum
mesuagio . . . quas Radulphus pater meus emit a Ricardo fratre meo'
(Harl. MS. 2110, fol. 42 b).

[1] Stenton, *D. C.*, Introduction, p. cii.

[2] Again, this might be illustrated throughout the Cartulary. The
collection of East Anglian Fines in the P. R. O. amply bears out the
evidence of the cartularies in this respect. [3] Vide *infra*.

[4] Cf. Stenton, *D. C.*, Introduction, pp. xlix seq.

and the socman of the Little Domesday as due to the Danish invasions, it also seems clear that we may stress more fully than has usually been done the fact that the heterogeneous tenements which they hold were primarily the result of an economic process, the nature of which terminology of Domesday tends to hide. This, as will be seen, reacted on the whole scheme of relationship between man and lord in this district.[1] What may, however, here be emphasized is that the problem of the numberless small and irregular holdings of the East Anglian Domesday has to a great extent an economic solution. And the tenements which appear in the bewildering form presented by the Little Domesday are in the main the result of a general disruption of holdings consequent upon the absence of any strictly organized form of seignorial pressure. The testimony of Domesday thus falls into line in this respect with the very copious evidence of the twelfth and thirteenth centuries. Everywhere from the Conquest onwards, in short, there may be seen in operation a wholesale disintegration and reintegration of tenements which plays throughout the medieval period an important part in the formation of the peculiar social structure of East Anglia, and already by the time of Domesday has broken up all uniform schemes of peasant holdings.

A consideration of the peasant tenements in medieval East Anglia may thus be held to bring to light certain facts of general importance. For from both the points of view from which they have been examined there have appeared at once illustrations of the general social development of medieval England, and also peculiarities of growth whose cause must be ascribed to the individual character of the district. The peculiar arrangements of husbandry, and the tenements which in the sixteenth century they postulate, can be traced back to the twelfth and thirteenth centuries, where still the peculiar holdings are to be found and an example is to be seen of a remarkable variation of co-operative agriculture. These peculiar tenements seem also to have been the outcome of ordered tenurial arrangements resulting from the exigencies of

[1] Vide *infra*, pp. 114 seq.

primitive husbandry, and are probably ultimately to be traced to Danish schemes of land-sharing. They present analogies to Scandinavian usage, and are most strikingly reflected in the curious geld arrangements of the East Anglian Domesday, of which they provide the explanation. Such organization explains also the peculiarity of the tenemental arrangements of Norfolk and Suffolk throughout the medieval period; it was certainly stabilized by exceptional sheep-farming practices, and it remained in general the basis of the co-operative husbandry. Very rarely, however, a virgate is to be found in the later documents concerning certain manors, but the term is clearly exotic and certainly does not bear here its normal connotation; it seems to have been introduced late into the district and to have been the result of the seignorial reorganization of a few manors in the twelfth century. In this way is provided an illustration of the late arrangement of the district upon a more truly manorial basis as the organized enforcement of the will of the lord created new service units out of the older tenements which had their origin in the conditions imposed by common farming. Thus in the development of the peasant holdings of this district a clear distinction can be drawn between the two formative influences at work, which in the south and west (where seignorial pressure was stronger and more highly organized by the time of plentiful records) are inextricably blended together. Further, the absence in early times in East Anglia of the seignorial element in the construction of tenements is strikingly exemplified in the exceptional contrast between the free and the servile holdings. The cohesive force of the lord's will has here been insufficient to preserve intact the free holdings, though it has been to some extent successful with those of the servile classes. This, again, is an important aspect of the weakness of any strictly manorial system in this district, and a general tenemental disintegration, which thus had more scope here than elsewhere, seems to explain much of the tenurial confusion both of the eleventh and subsequent centuries, and to account for many of the peculiarities of the social structure of medieval East Anglia.

CHAPTER III

RENTS AND SERVICES

A CONSIDERATION of the tenemental organization of medieval East Anglia and its general significance inevitably tempts speculation as to the manner in which the tenements were held ; and the conclusions which have been reached in regard to the arrangement of holdings would suggest that the characteristics of tenure in this district would also be somewhat peculiar. The establishment of the various forms of lordship in East Anglia was in the eleventh and twelfth centuries a sporadic and irregular development, and at the same time the rapid disintegration of peasant tenements in the absence of any rigid seignorial control implied the existence of tenurial bonds varying very greatly, both in their nature and their strength. An examination of the slow consolidation of such a loosely organized society furthermore should afford some illustration of the process by which certain services and certain payments throughout England came later to be regarded as the tests of peasant status. Before the close of the thirteenth century we have been told that the separation of the manorial classes was mainly the outcome of a distinction drawn between money rent and service.[1] And it might be hoped that a survey of the peculiar conditions existing in East Anglia in earlier times would help to expose the obscure process by which such practical tests were evolved and the extent to which in the thirteenth century they were applied.

It is, however, important to bear in mind, throughout any discussion of peasant status, the distinction between the manorialized and the non-manorialized sections of this district, and to remember that the evidence of the later surveys which comes almost exclusively from the former can hardly be

[1] Vinogradoff, *Villainage*, p. 319.

generally applied. With this qualification the two Ely registers, covering as they do the critical period of the thirteenth century, are in this respect of much importance ; and it is not without significance that in the main they conform to the normal conditions prevailing in districts whose manorial organization was of greater antiquity. If we may generalize at all from these extents, the most obvious characteristic of the free tenure therein, as opposed to that of the servile classes, is that it involves in 1222 as in 1277 the payment of a money rent.[1] In the East Anglian manors of the Abbot of Ramsey also a general distinction is made between the money rent owed by the freeholders and the services due from their unfree companions.[2] And the extents of the Bishop of Norwich[3] and of the Prior of Binham[4] show precisely similar conditions. There is no doubt that on the manorialized lands of the great ecclesiastical houses in thirteenth-century East Anglia the normal rent owed by the freeholder for his tenement consisted in money payments.

It would, however, be impossible to make any very rigid classification of peasant obligation on these lines. The confusion caused in later days by the acquisition of unfree land by free tenants and free land by villeins had by the beginning of the fourteenth century introduced into the scheme of peasant classes a complicated tangle, which it needed all the ingenuity of the lawyers to unravel.[5] This alone would forbid any sweeping generalization as to the incidence of rent and service, though in more primitive times, when status depended primarily on moot- or fyrd-worthiness or on the possession of a high wergild, such considerations would have less

---

[1] This might be illustrated from any of the manors, and is as marked in one extent as the other. Cott. Tib. B. ii and Cott. Claud. C. xi.

[2] Cf. especially *R. C.*, vol. i, pp. 412 seq. (Brancaster).

[3] Stowe MS. 936, *passim*. The distinction between work and rent runs through this Norwich Survey. Cf. *R. H. S. Trans.*, 4th Ser., vol. iv, 35 *n*.

[4] Cott. Claud. D. xiii. Cf. especially the two Binham extents, where again there is the same broad contrast between a rent-paying peasantry and those whose primary duty is the performance of work.

[5] Cf. Vinogradoff, *Economic Journal*, vol. x, pp. 308 seq. Examples of the practical confusion can be found for instance in the Barney extent.

weight ; and later, when tenure and status became so inextricably intertwined, they must always have been regarded
as exceptional. But quite apart from this, no absolute distinction of classes could be made on a basis of rent and
service. In the East Anglian estates of the ecclesiastical
houses, other classes besides the free tenantry pay a money
rent, and on occasion we may find the free tenant holding by
service alone. On both the Ely and Ramsey manors there
are not a few examples of a tenure which should more
properly be called a petty serjeanty.[1] A free tenant, for
instance, will hold a small tenement ‘ quod pertinet ad mini-
sterium navigandi episcopum ’,[2] and the description of many
of the freeholdings on the scattered Ely manors shows that
their tenure was in essence similar to this.[3] The ‘ serviens ’

[1] ‘ The notion of servantship, free servantship as opposed to any form
of serfdom, seems to be the notion which brings the various serjeanties
under one class name.’ Pollock and Maitland, *Hist. Eng. Law*, vol. i,
p. 287.
[2] Cott. Tib. B. ii, fol. 86. Cf. the similar entry in an early Ramsey
extent of Walsoken : ‘ Septemdecim homines qui tenent de septemdecim
dimidiis virgatis terrae debent bis in anno invenire Domino Abbati
navem cum hominibus ; et aliis vicibus quotiens voluerit homines sine
nave.’ *R. C.*, vol. iii. 295.
[3] As a good example of this may be taken the tenure of Robert, a free
tenant of Hecham in 1277 : ‘ Robertus forestarius tenet septemdecim
acras pro quattuor solidis et octo denariis equaliter et debet sectam curie.
Et custodire omnes boscos domini preter grauam de Caldhale et hoc de
feodo. Et propter hoc habebit husbote ferbote et heybote. Et quolibet
anno contra Natalem unum lignum idoneum ad ignem. Et escaetas
omnium arborum quas dominus dederit in predictis boscis et omnes
sespetes similiter illarum arborum vel pro quolibet sespite unum denarium
de eo cui ignum datum fuerit. Et omnes arbores et ramos in predictis
boscis prostratos per tempestatem. Et pasturas omnium viarum circa predictos boscos et infra. Et habebit porcos suos in eisdem boscis in palnagio.
Et animalia sua similiter cum animalibus domini in predictis boscis. Et
insuper habebit quolibet die in quolibet adventu domini et similiter quamdiu
fuerit in manerio cibum suum cum garrifone suo et qualibet nocte fenum
et prebendam ad equum suum et unam candelam de camerario. Et hoc
de liberatione mariscalli. Idem tenet unum molendinum ventricium in
foedi firma cum secta tocius villate ad idem pertinente pro quadraginta
solidis equaliter. Et si quis inciderit in misericordia pro defectu illius
secte tunc predictus Robertus et heredes sui medietatem illius miseri-
cordiam habebunt. Et idem Robertus et heredes sui sustinebunt predictum
molendinum ad sumptus suos proprios in omnibus. Sed habebunt in
boscis predictis per visum ballivi postes axes et virgas ad idem cum
necesse fuerit si inveniri possint in dictis boscis. Et si non possint in
eisdem invenire tunc dictus Robertus et heredes sui querant illa alibi et
acquietabunt ad custus suos proprios.’ Cott. Claud. C. xi, fol. 276 b. At

is common on the Ramsey lands and his position is sometimes very clearly defined;[1] and in general the frequent
designations of 'minister',[2] 'janitor',[3] 'pincerna',[4] 'cocus',[5]
and the like[6] which occur both in the later extents and in
the attestations to the twelfth-century charters show the prevalence of a tenure by free service which was at once distinct
from a servile tenure and from the military tenures which
spread downward from that of the knight. And whilst it is
clear that on these manors in the thirteenth century services
were not a normal incident of free tenure, nevertheless they
not infrequently were added as a supplement to a money rent,
and were often performed by the freeholders as personal or
domestic duties in return for a small tenement or a small
wage.

The necessity for such qualifications itself suggests that in
these manors any practical criterion of peasant status which
rested ultimately upon the liabilities of the tenants themselves
would have to be based not only on the mere payment of
rent or service, but rather upon the nature of such payments
and the significance of such services. That such tests were
frequently applied there can be no doubt, but their application
was in general[7] so irregular from district to district and so
confusing even to the legists of their own day,[8] that a brief
statement of their operation upon a given group of manors
at distinct periods in the thirteenth century may perhaps be
of some value.

Pulham in 1222 a free tenant held 20 acres 'per servicium forestare'.
Cott. Tib. B. ii, fol. 184 b. The growth of a class of manorial officials
certainly reacted upon free tenure, and is partly responsible for the
increase of free tenements after the Conquest. It certainly frequently
created a free tenure which differed from the normal tenure by money
rent. Cf. Lipson, *Economic History*, p. 51.

[1] Especially *R. C.*, vol. ii, p. 206. In the Welsh wars of 1241 the
knights of the Abbey of Ramsey sometimes went in person and sometimes
were represented by two 'servientes'. *R. C.*, vol. iii, p. 50.

[2] Cott. Tib. B. ii, fol. 89 b.   [3] Ibid., fol. 89.

[4] Ibid., fol. 89 b.

[5] Very frequent as the designation of a witness in the early charters.
See Appendix I.

[6] e. g. 'serviens' itself. Add. Charter 15508, and in general cf. the
charters in Appendix I.

[7] Vinogradoff, *Villainage*, pp. 138 seq.

[8] Cf. Vinogradoff, *Economic Journal*, vol. x, pp. 308 seq.

Of the first importance among such exactions was the payment of merchet, which was throughout the thirteenth century widely held to be the typical servile liability. The two Ely extents are therefore of some importance as showing how far such a rule was enforced in actual practice. On these lands the normal villein paid merchet and the normal free tenant was exempt from the obligation. Further, there is certain evidence which is brought out by a comparison of the two records which suggests that on occasion the liability to merchet was regarded as a definite practical test of peasant servitude. In the description of the free tenants of Wiggenhall, for example, in 1277, in one case there is added the remark 'et est liber'.[1] Such a statement occurring in an account of men who have already been described as free is itself curious, and can only be explained with reference to the earlier extent where this man's ancestor can be identified. Here the enigmatic phrase is expanded into 'et est liber ita quod non dabit gersumam pro filia'.[2] Such definite statements are rare in the extents and illustrate an unusual definition of such rules.

More interesting, however, than the isolated phrases of the Ely jurors in this respect, is the fact that the application of the merchet test of unfree status seems occasionally to have distorted the normal categorical arrangement of peasant classes. In the 1222 extent, for instance, of the Cambridgeshire manor of Littleport, there is noted a complete absence of freeholders in the manor[3]—a condition of affairs so abnormal in such a county as to excite suspicion. Instead, the survey begins with the rubric 'De consuetudinibus censuariorum et dabunt gersumam',[4] and it is probable that the exceptional arrangement is due to the use of the merchet payment as a test of status. These men it would seem would have elsewhere been termed 'libere tenentes'. But they pay merchet; and this the jurors of Littleport hold to be incompatible with

---

[1] Cott. Claud. C. xi, fol. 204.
[2] Cott. Tib. B. ii, fol. 172 b.   Cf. Appendix II, No. 2.
[3] Cott. Tib. B. ii, fol. 95.   Cf. Maitland, E. H. R., vol. ix, pp. 417 seq.
[4] Cott. Tib. B. ii, fol. 95.

free tenure, with the result that here in 1222 we have a manor recorded as being possessed of no free tenants at all. The same considerations seem to have been applied to the classi- fication of the tenantry at Northwold. In the 1222 survey the rubric ' De libere tenentibus ' is followed by but one name.[1] Then comes the heading ' de consuetudinibus cen- suariorum '. But preceding this in a contemporary hand there is a marginal note which reads ' Iste (i. e. the one free tenant) et Hamo de Hoga, Robertus diaconus, Osbertus de Ripa Ricardus de Mundeford Walterus filius parsone non dant gersumam pro filiabus suis et habent libertatem falde '.[2] Now these names may all be found in the censuarii category, which looks as if the jurors regarded it as an exceptional circumstance for an unfree tenant not to pay merchet. Again, a comparison of the two surveys brings out the full signi- ficance of this. In the case of Richard of Mundeford we can make an identification between the two extents, for in 1277 his tenement is held by his son Thomas.[3] But Thomas in the 1277 Survey is now placed among the free tenants. Nor is this the only transformation which may be seen. For certain of the 1222 censuarii class who in the earlier survey are recorded as paying merchet also appear in the later docu- ment among the free tenants.[4] The merchet payment, that is to say, has not succeeded in preventing the reclassification. Either we are dealing with a wholesale rise of customary tenants into freeholders, which is most unlikely, or we must suppose some reason which made the jurors of 1222 decline to place these men along with the free tenants. And one can only think in view of the evidence that such a reason was connected with the merchet payment which was so heavily stressed. The jurors of 1222, it would seem, had before them a group of men very similar to each other in respect of their relations with the lord. They could not according to these jurors be free tenants because some of them paid merchet, so they were assigned to another category. But still it was clear that some of them did not pay merchet, and so a note

---

[1] Ibid., fol. 124 b.
[2] Ibid., fol. 124 b.
[3] Cott. Claud. C. xi, fol. 259.
[4] Cott. Tib. B. ii, fol. 124 b.

was made to that effect. In 1277 the jurors, however, must
have argued in exactly the opposite way, and made their
classification upon grounds of economic position rather than
of the payment of merchet which had distorted the arrangement of the earlier extent.

A detailed examination of the merchet conditions at
Northwold has seemed excusable, in that, taken in conjunction
with the other evidence, it suggests not unimportant conclusions. The general division of the tenantry on these
manors coincides with the incidence and non-incidence of the
liability to merchet, and in certain particular cases it seems
likely that it was the determining factor in the classification.
The merchet test for freedom is frequently before the jurors,
though not always applied, and, what is more significant, its
application in disputable cases seems to have been more rigid
in 1222 than in 1277. This is in fact very strongly suggested
by the evidence from both Littleport and Northwold. On
occasion it is possible to see that the normal classification of
the tenantry according to economic considerations has been
deflected in the earlier extent by the use of the merchet
criterion. And on the whole we seem justified in remarking
that when the liability to merchet failed to correspond with
the other determinants of peasant status it was but irregularly
applied, and even this in practice was declining in importance
throughout the century. Whilst in 1222 it was still sporadically used, in 1277 on these Ely lands it had almost entirely
given place to the normal economic tests which formed the
general criteria of tenant-right.

It would thus be impossible to say that the merchet payment
was ever used on these lands as a general mark and test of
servitude. Though on occasion it made its influence felt in
the formation of the peasant classes, yet in the main it gave
place to other considerations. And throughout both surveys
it is possible to find exceptions to any rule based on the
payment. At Wilburton in Cambridgeshire the free tenant
paying merchet may be noticed,[1] and he is to be found, if

---

[1] Cott. Claud. C. xi, fol. 49 b. For the whole question of freemen
paying merchet cf. Vinogradoff, *Villainage*, p. 202.

rarely, scattered through the surveys. He appears for instance at Wiggenhall in 1222 [1] and at Dereham in 1277.[2] Freedom was always measured in England according to many different scales, and the whole treatment of East Anglian merchet on these ecclesiastical lands is illustrative of this. In the manor of Binham at the beginning of the fourteenth century, for example, there were no free tenants recorded on the manor. Instead, there was a class of molmen described as paying merchet. But the jurors there evidently feel that they must qualify this statement with the later remark 'Et sciendum quod omnes isti predicti et prescripti alleviabunt sanguinem exceptis istis qui sunt de corpore liberi'.[3] Here again there is once more the interrelation of merchet and servitude, but once again also it has been insufficient to alter the predominant classification of tenants in accordance with their relation to the manorial husbandry; and the merchet test seems to have been restricted to a personal consideration. Before the time of the extents and on other lands there is no evidence concerning merchet. The twelfth-century charters and the Domesday Survey are equally silent. The Nottinghamshire instance of the socmen of Blythe,[4] however, indicates that even at that time no definite rules could be laid down, and it seems very reasonable to conclude that though the criterion of merchet liability was always in practice in the minds of East Anglian jurors, nevertheless no general rules on the subject were ever adopted or applied; the payment never became in this district the dominant influence in the arrangement of manorial classes; and even the sporadic use of the test declined in importance throughout the thirteenth century.

Frequently coupled with the merchet is the tallage,[5] which was seized upon by the later lawyers in that 'it could be made uncertain in the plainest sense of the word by being raised and lowered at the will of the lord'.[6] It is, however, very clear

---

[1] Cott. Tib. B. ii, fol. 172 b.   [2] Cott. Claud. C. xi, fol. 215 b.
[3] Cott. Claud. D. xiii, fol. 13 b.
[4] Stenton, *Northern Danelaw*, p. 24.
[5] Cf. *R. C*, vol. i, pp. 309, 314, 322, 335, 349; vol. ii, pp. 12, 15, 22; and compare Vinogradoff, *Villainage*, p. 202.
[6] Vinogradoff, *Economic Journal*, vol. x, p. 315.

that the lord was in this matter as in others bound by the
strength of manorial custom. But even with this practical
limitation it is certain that on the Ely lands, tallage, like
merchet, appears regularly as an incident of villein tenure.
The unfree shall pay the tallage; the freeholder shall be
exempt.[1] The ultimate connexion of the tallage payment
and villein status is frequently to be found also outside the
Ely lands. On the Ramsey manors it is continually appearing
among the typical villein burdens,[2] and on the manors of the
Bishop of Norwich the words ' talliabilis ' and ' villenagia ' as
applied to land seem to be used indiscriminately.[3] Taking
the East Anglian ecclesiastical lands as a whole, a general
contrast may be made between the ' auxilium ' fixed in amount
and limited to certain definite occasions which was paid by
the free tenant[4] and the tallage to which ' ad voluntatem
domini ' the unfree were subject.

Still, it would be highly rash to push this distinction too far.
The villein frequently in the Ely manors pays ' auxilium ' as
well as the tallage, and the free tenant is not wholly exempt
from the later burden.[5] The individual exceptions to the
general rule of the Ely lands are of some interest in that they
bring out the peculiar nature of the exaction. When the free
tenant does pay tallage, the nature of the obligation is in
these extents usually described with some care. One freeholder at Shipdham pays tallage ' quando ponitur per episcopatum '.[6] Eight free tenants at Glemsford[7] have a similar
burden to bear. At Feltwell, in 1277, the peculiar form of

---

[1] An analysis of the Ely manors shows the distinction holding good in
both surveys at Terrington, Walpole, Walton, Walsoken, Emneth,
Pulham, Brandon, Bridgham, Northwold, Hartest, Rattlesden, Barking,
and Wetheringsett.

[2] Vide *supra*, p. 75, note 5.

[3] ' Terra est talliabilis et villenagia '—Stowe MS. 936, fol. 18 b ; cf.
fols. 20, 29.

[4] This distinction, if considered broadly, may be said to appear on all
the extents. The auxilium is on the whole a free burden. The St.
Edmunds manumission charters reserve the auxilium to the manumitted
man, Add. MSS. 14847, fols. 26, 64 b. A twelfth-century Yorkshire
charter will speak of ' commune auxilium super omnes libere tenentes '.

[5] Cf. e. g. the later Dereham extent, Cott. Claud. D. xiii, fol. 215 b.

[6] Cott. Claud. C. xi, fol. 228.

[7] Ibid., fols. 256 seq.

the tallage paid by the freeholder is still more strongly marked, for there eight free tenants owe tallage ' quando ponitur per episcopatum per preceptum domini regis '.[1] These qualifications illustrate the real significance of tallage as a servile test—which lay for the lawyers in the fact that it could be made the most completely dependent upon the will of the lord. Tallage, furthermore, it has been aptly remarked, is ' on the boundary between personal subjection and political subordination '.[2] That is true ; but these Ely jurors have gone one stage further and separated the two aspects of tallage. In the case of the unfree it is to be imposed ' quando dominus voluerit ',[3] or ' ad voluntatem domini ' ;[4] in the case of the free it is imposed on conditions, and often only when the writ of the king has transformed the whole payment into a royal tax. The servile nature of tallage lay in its uncertainty. If this were removed, as the Ely jurors were quick to realize, there was nothing in the payment incompatible with freedom.

A comparison between the Ely surveys, furthermore, suggests that here, as in the case of merchet, a definite process of development may be seen. The exceptions to the rule of the servility of tallage are only to be found in the later extent, for there is no instance of a freeholder paying tallage on the East Anglian lands of Ely in 1222. This, of course, may be explained by the more detailed character of the later extent, but a more probable explanation is surely that the word, perhaps under French influence, was loosing its technical meaning and achieving something of the vague sense which attached to it in the France of Philippe le Bel. But in any case this increase in the incidence of tallage on the free may serve as an indication that its use as a test of status was declining in importance throughout the century ; and it is clear that the obligation to tallage, limited as it was by manorial custom and falling sporadically upon men outside the villein class, could in practice serve as no very rigid criterion of servitude on the thirteenth-century manors of the See of Ely.

[1] Ibid., fol. 247.　　[2] Vinogradoff, *Villainage in England*, p. 162.
[3] e. g. the censuales at Terrington, Cott. Claud. C. xi, fol. 175.
[4] Thus nearly all the descriptions of the villein services in the survey.

The same result is obtained with reference to what, unlike merchet or tallage, was primarily an East Anglian incident of servile tenure. The extensive practice of sheep-farming has been noted as profoundly influencing the tenemental arrangements of the district.[1] Moreover, it is quite clear that the possession of a private fold was in eleventh-century East Anglia on occasion considered as being one of the marks of freedom.[2] It is of some significance, therefore, to remark how such considerations affected the terminology of the thirteenth-century jurors. The villein tenant, here as elsewhere, has to send his beasts to the lord's fold.[3] Something nearer to the Domesday distinctions can, however, be seen in the terminology of such an extent as that of Bridgham. In that manor, in 1277, it is no uncommon thing to remark of a freeholder, 'Et debet sectam curie et habet faldam '[4]—which in the parlance of Domesday is simply 'owes soke but not foldsoke '. The right to such foldsoke remained an important part of lordship in East Anglia, and the charters as late as the fourteenth century continually speak of gifts of 'unam faldsocham ',[5] or 'dimidiam faldsocham '.[6] But that any criterion of status was ever applied on these lines seems extremely unlikely. The later free tenants are continually subject to this or kindred burdens, and the Domesday Survey itself suggests that if any such test was ever used, it was local in its application and irregular in its incidence.[7] At Hillington, for instance, in Loddon hundred, those who owe foldsoke are contrasted with those who are free.[8] The curious connexion of foldsoke with jurisdictional right which has been noticed at Bridgham, frequently appears in Domesday.[9] But on the other hand foldsoke and commendation appear elsewhere as the normal

---

[1] Vide *supra*, pp. 25 seq.
[2] Cf. Maitland, *D. B. B.*, pp. 76 seq., and cf. Johnson, *V. C. H. Norfolk*, vol. ii, p. 31.
[3] 'Omnia averia iacebunt in falda domini' is common in the Ely and Norwich extents. For peculiar sheep-farming practices cf. *supra*.
[4] Cott. Claud. C. xi, fol. 241 b.   [5] Harl. MS. 2110, fol. 22.
[6] Harl. MS. 2110, fol. 28, and cf. Cott. Vesp. F. xv, fol. 343. This latter charter may be dated 1325.
[7] Cf. Johnson, *V. C. H. Norfolk*, vol. ii, pp. 30 seq.
[8] *D. B.*, vol. ii, fol. 203 b.
[9] Cf. Johnson, *op. cit.*, and vide *infra*.

marks of the tenure of the ' liberi homines ' and socmen.[1] And
not only do these conditions vary with regard to local custom,
or as might be expected with the prevalence or absence of
intensive sheep-farming,[2] but they seem to have been widely
different on the lands of different lords.   Indeed, in the whole
of the Suffolk Domesday, foldsoke is only once mentioned [3]
outside the lands of St. Edmunds where it is extremely common,
and there it seems to have been normally incumbent upon
the freemen.   Whatever may have been the varieties of local
usage, the performance of foldsoke never seems to have been
generally applied in East Anglia as a test of peasant servitude.
    The briefest survey of the incidence of merchet, tallage, and
foldsoke in thirteenth-century East Anglia on the ecclesiastical
lands thus suggests that the obligation to none of these
burdens could be made a rigid test of freedom and servitude.
In all cases these exactions serve broadly to indicate the ranks
and classes of the peasantry within the manor, but none of
them can serve in particular cases as the absolute determinants
of status.   In these manors the real criterion to be applied
here as elsewhere [4] in the thirteenth century lies far more in
the part played by the individual peasant in the manorial
economy.   And the importance of this lies in the fact that in
East Anglia we have to deal with a society and with a development distinct from that of the south and west where, in the
thirteenth century, similar conditions prevailed.   The contrast
between the social organization presented by the East Anglian
Domesday and that revealed by documents such as the Ely
extents is a very sharp one and indicates a very rapid development.   It is thus much to be deplored that so little information
is to be obtained concerning the obligations of the servile
tenants of the district during the intermediate period.   These
extents for the most part deal only with the thirteenth-century
conditions, and all are concerned only with the rigid organized
estates of the great religious houses.   The mass of twelfth-
century charter material as regards this matter is silent.

---

[1] Cf. for example the St. Edmunds tenures of Suffolk.
[2] Cf. Johnson, *op. cit.*   [3] *D. B.*, vol. ii, fols. 356 b seq.
[4] Cf. Vinogradoff, *Villainage*, p. 310.

Consequently it would be highly rash to generalize concerning peasant liabilities during the twelfth and thirteenth centuries from these extents. East Anglia was not, until long after the thirteenth century, a manorialized country in the sense in which this designation could be applied to other parts of England, and the vill and manor in this district never become coincident and frequently acted separately.[1] In many directions it is indicated that a view of social conditions taken solely from the great ecclesiastical estates would be a one-sided one,[2] and the impossibility of checking their evidence in this particular question renders it inadvisable to attempt any wide generalizations on its strength. Nevertheless, it is important to note that on manors like those of the Bishops of Ely and Norwich conditions of peasant tenure prevailed as on the ecclesiastical lands at the same period elsewhere, and that in both cases the status of the peasant is determined primarily by his relation to the manorial husbandry.

It is thus that on these manors the performance of week work becomes of the first importance in the arrangement of classes, and this is, in fact, the most certain criterion of peasant status. A definite division can, for instance, be seen throughout the Ely manors between those who perform this duty and those who are exempt. And there are no exceptions to this rule. But the Ely records supply a very useful warning against any notion of ' uncertainty ', forming in practice the basis of the servile nature of week work.[3] The later Ely accounts of villein services often allude to ' omnes incertas operaciones ', but it seems probable that they were thus merely introducing a lawyer's phrase to emphasize the fact that these tenants were wholly the villeins of the lord. And whilst it is reasonable to conclude that the kind of service to which the villein might be put during his weekly service was a matter of very little material concern to the tenant in question, so also in quantity the amount of villein service that could be exacted

---

[1] Vide *infra*, pp. 161–7 and 209–10.

[2] In this connexion note Stenton, *D. C.*, Introduction, *passim*, and cf. Wake, ' Communitas Villae ', *E. H. R.*, vol. xxxvii, pp. 406 seq.

[3] Vinogradoff, *Economic Journal*, vol. x, pp. 308 seq.

was very rigorously specified. The week work varies from
season to season, and the terms differ from manor to manor.
Moreover, the amount of week work performed on the various
manors differs widely. At Northwold, for instance, the 'operarius' performs two days' work from Michaelmas to St. John's
day and four days from St. John's day to Michaelmas.[1] At
Walton[2] and Walpole[3] on the other hand the villein is very
heavily burdened, performing six days week work throughout the year. The conditions of the 'operarius' in the two
latter manors could very seldom be paralleled in thirteenth-
century England. But, quite apart from such exceptional
cases, the incidence and amount of week work, varying as it
did from manor to manor, seems to have been quite definitely
regulated by a manorial custom which prevented its arbitrary
regulation by the lord.[4]

Thus, though the lack of evidence forbids any discussion of
these aspects of peasant liabilities in the less highly organized
parts of East Anglia, the conditions on the manors of the
great religious houses seem to have been normal in spite of
an irregular earlier development, and the distinguishing marks
of servile tenure were here, as elsewhere, to be found in the
allocation of the duties involved in the manorial husbandry.
Week work is servile, but the 'precariae' were scattered over
all the classes of the community, though in very varying
amounts. In this the Ely registers form but another part of
a general chain of evidence which divides the tenantry on
the large ecclesiastical estates on this basis from the time of

---

[1] Cott. Claud. C. xi, p. 252. [2] Ibid., fol. 193.
[3] Ibid., fol. 186 b.
[4] The elaborate nature of the customary regulation of the week work is
well seen in the conditions prevailing at Pulham in 1222. There the
typical villein works for one day a week from Michaelmas to St. Andrew's
day, two days from St. Andrew's day to the Feast of the Purification, one
day from the Feast of the Purification to Pentecost, two days from
Pentecost to August 1st, and five days from August 1st to Michaelmas
(Cott. Tib. B. ii, fol. 187). These elaborate conditions are repeated in
the survey of fifty years later (Cott. Claud. C. xi, fol. 207); and though
there are cases of an alteration of the custom in this respect between the
dates of the two surveys (vide *infra*, p. 112) this was exceptional, and in
general the regulations remain rigid in the manors throughout the
thirteenth century.

G

the Peterborough Black Book[1] and the Ely Placitum,[2] and in general re-emphasizes to the fundamental distinction between the geneat and the gebur in Rectitudines.[3] It is in this qualified sense only that a broad separation of classes can be made on the basis of money rent and service.

But whilst this distinction, viewed in relation to its origin, probably has a special bearing upon East Anglian social history, its significance can hardly be appraised without some consideration of the importance attached to the specific exemption from this burden of week work on the highly manorialized estates. The East Anglian extents show with peculiar clearness the influence of the process of commutation in the formation of a new and intermediate class of tenants, and bring out the stress laid throughout the Middle Ages on the interconnexion of freedom with the payment of a money rent. The influence of this movement upon later social history has been very thoroughly discussed,[4] but it is by no means so clear how far the movement towards commutation was responsible for the growth of all tenures by money rent.

The categorical form of the Ely registers reveals very strikingly the existence and importance of a non-free rent-paying class which is the distinctive mark of the operation of commutation. This class is a large one and occurs on almost all the manors of the bishop.[5] Its normal position is between the ' libere tenentes ' and the ' operarii ', which thus well illustrates its mediate position.[6] More interesting is the fact, however, that this class occurs with the same regularity in 1222 as in 1277, and seems to bear in both the registers very much the same proportion to the rest of the manorial inhabitants. There

---

[1] *Chronicon Petroburgense*, ed. Camden Society, pp. 157-83. Cf. Stenton, *Northern Danelaw, passim*.

[2] Ed. Hamilton. Cf. Maitland on the services there described as belonging to the socmen (*D. B. B.*, p. 77). This record seems to point rather to ' boon-days than to continuous week work '.

[3] Liebermann, *Gesetze*, p. 444.

[4] Cf. especially Vinogradoff, *Villainage*, pp. 178 seq., and Lipson, *Economic History*, pp. 77 seq.

[5] Wiggenhall is the chief exception, and, as will be shown (*infra*, pp. 119-21) for special reasons.

[6] In this respect the extents of Walpole (cf. Appendix II) are the only important exceptions.

seems little reason to suppose any widespread increase in this category of tenants during this part of the thirteenth century. The normal name for these tenants is ' censuales ' or ' consuetudinarii censuales ', and the contrast between them and the other class of working customary tenants is sometimes very clearly shown.[1] Sometimes, too, they appear under the name of ' molmen '.[2] Alike in fact from its general position in the manors and from its characteristics, there can be little doubt that this large class of rent-paying tenants, distinct both from the free tenant and from the ' operarius ', is in essentials the same as the molman class elsewhere,[3] and is primarily recruited from villeins whose labour services have been commuted into money payments.

This category of tenants appears also outside the Ely lands. At fourteenth-century Salhouse, for instance, there appear ' tenentes terram nativam mollond et custumariam '.[4] At Binham, at the beginning of the fourteenth century, a molmen class is very prominent.[5] The interest, however, of the evidence outside the Ely extents concerning this class is that it shows its scattered existence at an early date.[6] Throughout the Ramsey lands there is record of a commutation which was in operation throughout the twelfth century,[7] and this includes the East Anglian manors. At Brancaster in the twelfth century there can be found several instances of commutation, and the existence of a large non-free rent-paying

---

[1] This is brought out with especial clearness at Bridgham in 1222, where an opposition is made between the category of ' de consuetudinariis et censuariis ' and that of ' de consuetudinariis et operariis ' (Cott. Tib. B. ii, fols. 182 seq). The interest of this is increased by the similar distinction made in the summary of the later extent between ' molmen ' and ' operarii ' (Cott. Claud. C. xi, fol. 245 b).

[2] See previous note, and compare also extent of Shipdham in later register, where the class is called indifferently by the two terms (Cott. Claud. C. xi, fol. 239 b).

[3] Cf. Vinogradoff, *E. H. R.*, vol. i, p. 734, and see also *Villainage in England*, pp. 183 seq.

[4] Cott. Claud. D. xiii, fol. 111.   [5] Ibid., fol. 10 b.

[6] Cf. Round, *E. H. R.*, vol. ii, p. 103, who points out the existence of the molmen tenure on the morrow of the Conquest; and Lipson, who quotes the *V. C. H. Middlesex*, vol. ii, p. 73, for an example of definite commutation as early as 1110.

[7] e. g. at Holywell, Ellington, Barton (*R. C.*, vol. iii, pp. 281, 259, and 274).

class is very noticeable.[1] On the evidence of the extents
alone it is in fact necessary to allow for much commutation in
East Anglia by the end of the twelfth century.

The characteristics as well as the incidence of commutation
present in East Anglia the same appearance as elsewhere.
The process is usually emphatically confined to week work,
and the normal liabilities of the ' censuales ' include the performance of ' precariae '. This applies equally to the Ely lands
and also to the other manors. The importance, for instance,
of the boon-services in the tenure of the ' censuarii ' at Walpole
is very striking.[2] The very extensive services of the same
class at Bridgham in 1222, which may be regarded as typical
in this respect of the Ely manors, again shows a very definite
limitation of the commutation to the week work. At fourteenth-century Binham the molmen have to labour on certain
boon-days,[3] and at twelfth-century Brancaster the distinction
between the commuted week work and the uncommuted
' precariae ' is made equally clear.[4] The tendency for elaborate
arrangements as to the provision of food on the boon-days [5]
shows how essential their preservation was to the manorial
arrangements, and of itself explains why the ' precariae ' were
the last part of the villeins' services to be commuted. In this
respect these extents are interesting in connexion with the
records of Hutton in Essex.[6] At the time of the Ely records
there was no commutation on this manor, and when a quarter of
a century afterwards commutation does appear, the ' precariae '
as well as the week work are involved. In this Hutton was
highly peculiar, but the Ely evidence, taken in conjunction
with that from this manor and with the Forncett material,[7]
affords yet another illustration of the extent to which the

---

[1] There was only one free tenant at twelfth-century Brancaster, but
there were many tenants paying a money rent in lieu of services. *R. C.*,
vol. iii, pp. 261–5.

[2] Vide Appendix II, 1.   [3] Cott. Claud. D. xiii, fol. 10 b.

[4] The ' aratio ' which is so frequently excepted from the commutation
can only be the ploughing boon-works. *R. C.*, vol. iii, pp. 261 seq.

[5] These considerations run all through the East Anglian extents.
Cf. Vinogradoff, *Villainage*, p. 174.

[6] Feiling, *E. H. R.*, vol. xxvi, pp. 333 seq.

[7] Davenport, *Economic History of a Norfolk Manor.*

movement towards commutation was in the eastern counties largely dictated by local conditions and very irregular in its development. Many varieties of the tenure are to be noted on the Ely lands, and we must always distinguish between a permanent commutation and a commutation which consisted of independent yearly arrangements permanently binding upon neither party.[1] This distinction, however, these extents are not concerned to bring out. But they do show with great clarity how the process of commutation must often have been started by the lord and have operated in his favour.[2] And, in view of later legal distinctions, it is perhaps worthy of note that the merchet payment seems here to have invariably remained as an incidence of the tenure of the villein whose services have been commuted.[3] This is emphatically insisted upon both in the Ely and the Binham records, and again represents on these manors a normal feature of the class throughout England.

In some particulars, however, the condition of the molmen class in the later East Anglian extents seems to be of special significance. There is, for example, a transaction in the Binham extents which is somewhat curious. There the heading to the molmen category runs as follows: 'Incipit tenura tenentium mollond facta per quandam indenturam inter priorem et tenentes infrascriptos anno regis Edwardi filii regis ...'[4] The remainder of the sentence is unfortunately left blank, but the rubric certainly describes a specific arrangement embodied in a legal act at a definite date. This is of

---

[1] This type of commutation was common at Littleport in the early fourteenth century, but it has left no trace in the extents. Cf. Maitland, *E. H. R.*, vol. ix, pp. 317 seq.

[2] Many instances might be found of this; e. g. at Feltwell the owners of 'half lands' are described thus: 'et arabit quolibet mense a festo omnium sanctorum quousque blada domini fuerint perseminata unam acram et dimidiam rodam. Et si dominus non indiget de illa aratura tunc dabit pro ea tres denarios et unam quadrantem et dimidiam' (Cott. Claud. C. xi, fol. 249). Or again at Walpole of a customary tenant it is remarked: 'Et si placeat domino vel si non indiget de aratura unus quisque eorum dabit pro caruca integra qualibet warneta tres denarios et non habebit cibum' (ibid., fol. 189 b).

[3] This occurs in the obligations of the 'censuales' class throughout the Ely manors. Cf. *supra*.

[4] Cott. Claud. D. xiii, fol. 10 b.

itself remarkable. Binham is not ancient demesne, and it was in practice highly exceptional and in common law impossible [1] for a lord to enter into such relations with his unfree tenants. A villein could not in common law be a party to a contract with his lord. Yet judged by any of the normal legal standards then in use there is no doubt of the unfree status of these men. They all pay merchet, and several of them are described as ' nativus domini '.[2] It would thus seem difficult to provide an adequate explanation of this remarkable rubric, which reflects directly upon the status of these molmen tenants. In some ways the most tempting solution to the problem is afforded by the suggestion that we are here dealing with an irregular contract concerning newly acquired assart land. But the whole question is made at once more interesting and more complex by a comparison of this extent with the very curious earlier record embodied within it. There we find a molman class already in existence long before the creation of the ' indentura '. Moreover, the conditions of their tenure are curious. Though the text is very corrupt the most probable reading would seem to suggest that the commutation was at that date no stereotyped arrangement, but varied from time to time, and that the widest possible meaning which could possibly be given to ' mollond ', as applying to the holdings of all these tenants as a whole, was to signify land that on occasion paid money in place of week work.[3] It would thus be very difficult to make any generalization from this remarkable text. What, however, would appear from a comparison of it and the later ' indentura ' is that this identical category of tenants takes in both extents the same place in manorial economy, and that the later holdings are unlikely to have been mainly the result of later acquisitions from the waste. If, on the other hand, as is more probable, the ' indentura ' was made to reorganize the commutation itself, it is clear that such commutation existed in much earlier days on this same manor, and the most which could have been

---

[1] Vinogradoff, *Villainage in England*, pp. 43 seq.
[2] Cott. Claud. D. xiii, fols. 10 b seq.
[3] This seems the most probable explanation of the first three sentences of the early molmen tenure at Binham. Cf. Appendix II, No. 3. It depends on the opposition of ' sin autem non ' to ' si ad opus '.

accomplished by the transaction was a rearrangement of conditions which were in their essence of much higher antiquity.

The difficult evidence of the Binham surveys thus seems to point to the early existence of a molmen class on that manor, and the position of that class is throughout peculiar. The total absence of free tenants throughout both records, coupled with the very large numbers of 'tenentes mollond', suggest the presence of free elements in the latter class, and in later days the men of the same class are entering into a contract as in common law only freemen could. On the other hand these men pay merchet, and in the earlier extent there is evidence that some at least of them have performed, and still occasionally do perform, week work, though there is the opposition common alike in the Burton cartulary [1] and the Bolden book [2] of 'ad opus' to 'ad censum' or 'ad malam'. Altogether, on the one hand, it seems highly probable that these molmen in this manor represent a composite class; and on the other, that the Binham evidence in general serves as a warning against any attempt to limit the action of even a widespread process of commutation to the thirteenth and fourteenth centuries.

The testimony from Binham thus tempts speculation concerning the origin of the molmen class. Not only is it fairly clear that at Binham the class is derived from many diverse elements, but the early fourteenth-century surveyors thought of it as being as old as the Priory itself, and postulated its active existence within twenty years of Domesday. Whatever the actual date of this document it certainly represents what to these men of the fourteenth century were considered to be archaic conditions, and it is surely not too rash to lay considerable stress upon the comparison of the early Binham extent with Domesday Book. In the account in the great survey of Peter's manor we have to deal with a community divided fairly equally into socmen and bordars.[3] Then

---

[1] Ed. Wriothesley (William Salt Society). Cf. Round, *E. H. R.*, vo xx, pp. 275 seq.　　　　　　　　　　[2] Ed. Camden Society.

[3] Here again there is a corrupt text, but the population seems to have consisted in Domesday of 16 socmen, 3 villeins, 13 bordars, and 2 serfs (*D. B.* ii, fol. 257 b). Cf. *V. C. H. Norfolk*, vol. ii, p. 180.

comes the extent dividing the manor again almost equally between a population of 'tenentes mollond' holding irregular tenements and a collection of servile groups with regular holdings.[1] There thus seems to be every reason for supposing that the 'tenentes mollond' of the extent represented in part at any rate the socmen of the Domesday record. And the evidence from the Ely registers tends on the whole indirectly to confirm this. If the 'censuales' were on those manors the outcome of a recent commutation, it is difficult to understand why already by 1222 their holdings showed infinite variety in size as opposed to the regular 'plenae terrae' and 'dimidiae terrae' of the 'operarii' class.[2] The distinguishing marks of the molmen of the extents are in many ways remarkably like the little we know of the eleventh-century socmen, and from many points of view the East Anglian evidence concerning this intermediate class of money-paying tenants suggests its very early existence and perhaps opens the way for a consideration of the social position of one of the most baffling of the peasant classes of the Domesday Survey.

The conditions of the tenure of the socmen in the latter years of the eleventh century are very obscure. To what is already known of this matter the East Anglian evidence only in one instance adds directly. In the St. Benet of Hulme survey there is given one very early statement of services which seems to be connected with a soke. In the third quarter of the twelfth century Abbot Thomas gave to one, Reginald the clerk, the land which had been held by 'Estanus Fitele de socagio in Northwalsham'.[3] Fortunately in a marginal note[4] there is added a list of the 'consuetudines quas fecit Reginaldus clericus pro terra sua in tempore abbatis Thome et antea'. The main part of Reginald's obligations consists of money payments of various kinds. He performs extensive carrying services. He gives a goose, a hen, and eggs at stated periods. He mows one day in winter and

---

[1] The number of tenants has in each case, however, greatly increased. See Appendix II, No. 3.
[2] Vide *supra*. Conditions such as those at Northwold are rare. Normally no regular principle can be discovered.
[3] Cott. Galba E. ii, fol. 66.   [4] Ibid., and see Appendix II, No. 6.

one day he reaps. Eight times in the year he 'works', providing his own food, and one day 'ex prece cum cibo'. For two days also he 'digs'. Now these services are interesting by comparison with what we know of the early socman's tenure. In the 'precariae' which figure so largely and in the very noticeable absence of week work which is the most striking feature of the tenure, they are very like both the duties of the socmen of the Peterborough lands and those which are described in the Ely 'placita'. But the most interesting fact in this description is the remark ' Hoc totum fecit Ethelstan cuius fuit eadem terra ante eum'. Reginald the clerk held the land before the time of Abbot Thomas, that is to say before 1167. So even without risking a possible identification between the Estan Fitele of the charter with the Ethelstan of the statement of services, it is clear that the latter probably dates at least from the earlier half of the twelfth century. This description is the earliest known statement of East Anglian services, and it does not seem too much to suppose that the services which Reginald performed in the soke of Northwalsham were in essence the same as those performed by certain of the socmen of Domesday.

The description of the services of Reginald the clerk thus indicates that the tenurial position of the East Anglian socman in the period immediately subsequent to Domesday was very similar to what we know of it elsewhere. It also, by comparison with the Binham evidence, brings into prominence the fact that many of the characteristics of the early ' molmen ' class in this district conform somewhat remarkably to the conditions which appear to have attached to the socman's tenure. The terms on which Reginald held his lands were very like those undertaken by the molmen of the Binham ' foundation ' extent. And in general the analogies presented by the tenurial arrangements of the two classes are very striking. Like the Blythe socmen of Nottinghamshire, the molmen pay merchet.[1] Like the Ely,[2] the Revesby,[3] and the Peterborough [4] socmen

[1] Stenton, *Northern Danelaw*, pp. 22–4 (O. S. L. S. ii).
[2] Maitland, *D. B. B.*, p. 77.
[3] Stenton, *Northern Danelaw*, pp. 24–7 (O. S. L. S. ii).
[4] *Registrum Nigrum Petroburgense*, ed. Camden Society.

they are normally exempt from week work. Like the East Anglian socmen of Domesday they hold irregular tenements.[1] The name by which the molmen are designated in itself supplies analogies to that of the socman, for as 'mal' in its jurisdictional sense gave place in English terminology to 'mal' in its normal fiscal sense,[2] so also did soke in its jurisdictional sense pass very early into the fiscal ' socage '.[3] It would seem very probable that in considering the original composition of this molmen class in later East Anglia, we must allow some part to have been constituted by the members of the numerous sokemen class of Domesday, and it is even possible that some line might be drawn on the basis of recent commutation between the 'liberi homines' and the 'socmanni' of the Survey.[4] But in any case it seems highly probable, in view of the Binham evidence, that some of the socman class of the Survey, already too heavily burdened for the later jurors to speak of them as ' libere tenentes', must have passed directly into the intermediate category of non-free rent-paying tenants.

It is impossible, therefore, not to attach considerable importance to the possibility of the existence in Domesday of a class of men paying a money rent which itself was the result of a recent commutation from labour services. Anything like a complete proof of this would be impossible in view of the inadequacy of the evidence, for the distinctions of work and service were alien to the purpose of the survey and were for the most part unrecorded therein. But in Domesday and in the documents nearly contemporary therewith it is possible to watch in many parts of East Anglia the gradual transformation from an economy of natural husbandry to one of money payments. As will be seen, it is hardly possible to over-emphasize the importance of the cash nexus even in twelfth-century East Anglia,[5] but there are not a few instances of social arrangements of a different nature which even then

---

[1] Vide *supra*.   [2] Stevenson, *E. H. R.*, vol. ii, p. 332.
[3] Cf. Cott. Charters, ii. 1.
[4] This might fit in well with the distinction on ability to alienate land at will. Cf. Johnson, *op. cit.*, p. 28. This of course, like every other criterion in this matter, cannot be rigidly applied. Vide *infra*.
[5] Vide *infra*, pp. 113 seq.

present the appearance of antiquity. Food rents are intimately connected with labour services of some kind or another, and such rents are not uncommon in the earlier East Anglian documents. The farm of so many nights is no very rare feature of the East Anglian Domesday,[1] and the organization of twelfth-century Wells on the border of Norfolk and Cambridgeshire shows a manor which was of profit to the Abbey of Ramsey solely on account of its render of eels.[2] There are traces of food rents in twelfth-century Brancaster.[3] An original twelfth-century charter which has been preserved in the Bodleian Library is concerned with the tenure of Robert Picot in the village of Grenevill ' pro sexaginta sellis frumenti ',[4] and the St. Benet of Hulme cartulary also contains a charter of a still earlier date concerning the same land, which was before 1127 still held at the same rent by William Curcun, the predecessor of the Robert Picot of the Bodleian charter.[5] There are also records of similar East Anglian rents before the Conquest. The Wells render of eels goes back to the foundation of Ramsey by King Edgar,[6] and there is an early grant of extensive food rents to that abbey from Hickling.[7] But what may here be specially stressed is the specific commutation which can be early seen in nearly all these particular cases. With regard to the Domesday farm, the conditions in the soke of Necton may be regarded as a good example of this commutation acting, so to speak, between the T.R.E. and the T.R.W. entries. This large soke, we are told, paid Harold a six-nights' farm, but now it pays 60 pounds by weight.[8] Again, before 1130 we have a definite instance of the commutation of the Wells rents into money payments.[9]

---

[1] *D. B.*, vol. ii, *passim.*

[2] Cf. the two extents, one taken in the twelfth century (*R. C.*, vol. iii, p. 296), and the other in 1206 (vol. ii, p. 318).

[3] *R. C.*, vol. iii, p. 265.

[4] *Norfolk Charters*, 607. See Appendix I, No. 26. This document also makes its appearance in the St. Benet of Hulme Cartulary, Cott. Galba E. ii, fol. 59 b.

[5] Cott. Galba E. ii, fol. 55. Cf. Appendix I, No. 41.

[6] *R. C.*, vol. ii, p. 55.

[7] Thorpe, *Diplomatarium*, p. 532.

[8] *D. B.*, vol. ii, p. 235. For the evidence concerning this soke, vide *infra*, pp. 179-89.　　　　[9] *R. C.*, vol. i, p. 134.

Still more significant, perhaps, is the transitional stage which is shown by another charter [1] concerning the Grenevill tenure, by which before 1140 William de Curcun is instructed to bring his render at certain definite times of the year probably in order that it might then be sold by the abbey. Already the food payment is valued by the landlord primarily for its pecuniary equivalent, which may be regarded as a first step towards its complete commutation.

Such changes can hardly have been without effect on the tenure of the freemen and socmen whose payments they involved, and such earlier evidence as we possess seems thus to fit in with the testimony of the extents of the twelfth and thirteenth centuries. And it therefore seems clear that the molmen and 'censuales' class, whilst it is constantly being increased by later commutation, nevertheless contains elements of high antiquity. It was probably recruited in many cases from the socmen of Domesday, who sometimes pass into it neither through a depression from the position of manorial free tenants nor from an elevation from the position of full manorial villeins. Further, there is a distinct probability that in some cases also the money rent from these men represented a commutation from the food rents, which in the eleventh or twelfth century can sometimes be seen changing into money payments. It would be impossible to say how many of these men ever represented an original tenure by money which was never the outcome of a rent in kind, but in East Anglia, where money was early so plentiful,[2] it is probable that this was very often the case. It is, however, certain that a distinction between work and service reacting directly upon peasant status is of early origin in this district; the transformation from the one to the other type of tenure and the particular class of the peasantry which it produces are probably as old as Domesday; and it is consequently necessary to allow for the operation of commutation in the formation of a tenure by money rent in East Anglia as early as the eleventh century.

The history of early commutation in this district thus

---

[1] Cott. Galba E. ii, fol. 56, and see Appendix I, No. 43.
[2] Vide *infra*, pp. 97 seq.

brings out very clearly the importance of the contrast between work and money rent on the later manors. The alteration from the one tenure to the other in particular classes of men at once reacted upon their status, and was chiefly responsible for producing as early, at any rate, as the twelfth century an intermediate class of men personally unfree like the villeins, but economically akin to the free tenants in their tenure by a money rent. In the main, that is to say, on the ecclesiastical lands the personal standing of the peasant depended very largely upon his relation to the manorial husbandry, and a tenure by money rent, even where it was of servile origin, at once created analogies in the minds of the jurors between the non-free rent-paying tenants and the freeholder. In this the condition of the manorialized estates was in no way peculiar as far as the thirteenth century is concerned. But the real difficulty of such contrasts, of the problem of money rent and of the free tenure of which the money rent was in a sense the distinguishing mark, lies in their origin, and it is here that the loose arrangements of twelfth- and thirteenth-century Norfolk and Suffolk may be of peculiar importance as illustrating the development of such distinctions in the thirteenth-century records. The reasons for the intimate connexion of personal freedom with the payment of a money rent are still somewhat obscure, and the variations of these rents paid in the twelfth and thirteenth centuries and their relation to the size of the tenements from which they were due present problems which have a wide bearing on early social history. Further, it is in the early organization of a district such as East Anglia that there might be discovered concerning the later free-rents in money the proportion among them of those which are derived from an original contract, those which have survived from old rents paid by tenants in pre-Conquest days, and those which have been evolved through the intermediate stage of later labour service. For therein it might be possible to determine how far any primitive money rent peculiar to freemen and to free tenure could ever be postulated. On the manorialized estates such as those of St. Edmunds and Ely, that is to say, a special opportunity seems to be offered of determining the causes of the pecuniary side of free tenure and the earlier development of the manorial rents. Definition is difficult in such matters, but in the main the broad distinction between the customary and the contractual [1] serves as the best classification of the nature of these later payments. And whilst no very exact standards can be devised, in that a rent contractual in one period could very often become customary in another, nevertheless there is one fairly satisfactory criterion which, in view of the date of the Ely Registers, may be devised. A reference to the relation of money rent to acreage in the case of the free tenants, and a comparison of this with that supplied by the rents of the other classes of the manor, should perhaps afford a general solution of the nature of these payments. For a money rent reckoned throughout according to a given ratio to the number of acres held, and varying from manor to manor, would indicate the survival of older customary payments, whilst a rent which bore no fixed relation to the size of the holding, but which depended to all seeming on the nature and quality of the tenement itself and the mutual advantages accruing to the lord and to the tenant therefrom, might well be at once supposed to be the result of contract.

The employment of such a test on the East Anglian manors of the Bishop of Ely leads to somewhat interesting results. If, for example, at Pulham in 1222 the holdings of the molmen class are examined, it is at once revealed that there is a customary regulation of rents in the manor on the basis of a fourpenny acre.[2] These holdings conform to that standard with the utmost regularity, and there are very few exceptions to the rule.[3] Moreover, these conditions can be compared to those prevailing in the 'libere tenentes' class. In the 1222 extent of Pulham there are thirteen free holdings described where the acreage was given and where no services are due to distort the comparison, and where the holding is not

---

[1] Neilson, *Customary Rents*, pp. 5–14 (O. S. L. S., vol. ii).
[2] Cott. Tib. B. ii, fol. 186.
[3] If the first paragraph, for instance, of these holdings be examined it will be found that out of thirty-five tenements only seven fall outside the reckoning.

the result of recent purpresture. Out of these thirteen holdings five are assessed according to the customary standard[1] and in such a way as to involve an elaborate reckoning.[2] With regard to the ' new land ' the valuation has risen and again is reckoned according to a uniform standard, this time of six-pence.[3] Similar conditions prevailed at the same date at Bridgham, which in this respect is interesting by comparison with Pulham, in that at the former manor we have at once the same uniformity and yet a wholly different monetary standard ; for the customary ration of acreage to rent on this manor is based upon a penny acre.[4] Here also the customary holdings show a remarkable uniformity, and here also the standard makes its appearance with reduced force in the case of the free holdings.[5] In both manors, that is to say, the customary regulation of rent according to a fixed standard[6] has affected the free as well as the unfree tenants, though in both cases the greater divergence from the norm on the part of the free holdings testifies to the greater influence of non-customary forces in the regulation of the rents of the free tenants.

Pulham and Bridgham, however, represent the maximum introduction on the Ely lands of a customary standard into

[1] Cott. Tib. B. ii, fol. 184 b.

[2] 35 acres will, for instance, pay 11 shillings and 8 pence, 10 acres and 1 rood will pay 3 shillings and 5 pence.

[3] Cott. Tib. B. ii, *loc. cit.*

[4] Cott. Tib. B. ii, fols. 181 b seq.

[5] In the case of the Bridgham free rents the exact reckoning on a one penny standard is 7 out of 16.

[6] The rigid and customary nature of this standard is brought out very clearly from a comparison between the two extents of 1222 and 1277. As an example the tenement of Adam Buxton at Pulham may be instanced.

1222	1277
Adam Buxton tenet tres acras pro duodecim denariis equaliter. Idem tenet unam acram pro sexdecim denariis. . . . Idem tenet de novo duas acras pro duodecim denariis. (Cott. Tib. B. ii, fol. 185 b.)	Adam Buxton tenet unam acram pro sexdecim denariis. . . . Idem tenet duas acras pro duodecim de-nariis. (Cott. Claud. C. xi, fol. 203 b.) Johannes Buxton tenet tres acras pro duodecim denariis. (Ibid., fol. 204.)

Here we have a tenement with the three types of payment all of which remain permanent though the tenement splits up. Many other examples of a similar nature could be found from a comparison, for instance, of Cott. Tib. B. ii, fols. 185–186 b with Cott. Claud. C. xi. 203–206.

the regulation of the free rents.   In other manors, it is true, similar conditions may be observed.   There are, for instance, traces of a fourpenny acre at Dereham,[1] and at Glemsford there is a very marked tendency towards a rigid reckoning at threepence.[2]   But such conditions are exceptional.   The normal conditions on the East Anglian Ely manors is for the rents outside the 'operarius' class to bear no fixed proportion to the acreages of the holdings from which they are due.[3]   In the majority of the manors of the See of Ely, that is to say, in the thirteenth century the relation of the money rents paid by the free tenants to the acreage of their tenements suggests a contractual origin of these payments, though the conditions on exceptional manors suggests the occasional persistence of other and customary arrangements.

Such conditions may be of very diverse origin.[4]   Nevertheless, the occasional intrusion on the Ely lands of customary reckonings into the arrangements governing the payments of all rent-paying tenants within their manors suggests a line of previous development which the terminology of the extents indicates and the exceptional earlier history of the district makes clear.   It is a striking feature of the Ely records that they frequently describe the holdings of the peasantry in terms of 'ware' acres.[5]   This phraseology is exceptional in the thirteenth century, and it is of interest to note that it also appears on the East Anglian lands of the Abbey of St. Edmunds.[6]   The same curious terminology also makes its appearance in two original charters which concern land in Raydon, Suffolk, and date from the close of the twelfth century.[7]   The 'ware' acre, we have been taught, was a unit

---

[1] Cott. Claud. C. xi, fol. 219.   [2] Ibid., fol. 256.

[3] An analysis of the rent conditions in the East Anglian manors has shown that no fixed ratio of acreage to rent outside the 'operarius' class is to be found at Terrington, Walpole, Walton, Tilney, Wiggenhall, Walsoken, Emneth, Shipdham, Hartest, Rattlesden, Hitcham, Barking, Wetheringsett, Brandon, or Bramford.

[4] Cf. Miss Neilson's monograph, O. S. L. S., vol. ii, *passim.*

[5] Of the East Anglian manors, Hitcham and Barking are good examples of this (Cott. Claud. C. xi, fols. 286, 295 b).

[6] e. g. Harl. MSS. 2977, fol. 82.

[7] Harl. Charter 53, A. 31, and Harl. Charter 53, C. 51. See Appendix I, Nos. 11 and 12.

of tributary assessment and represented a geld unit [1] originally
derived from an actual agrarian holding, but like the hides of
an earlier time frequently deflected from its field prototype.
In its character of a geld symbol it is probably implied in
the numerous cases where the term does not occur, but the
acreages, whether real or fiscal, rigidly conform to a fixed
standard throughout the manor. The term 'wara', however, is
clearly archaic in the thirteenth century, and any explanation
of its significance must be sought for in the past, where it
might be supposed that the exceptional conditions of earlier
East Anglian history would make its earlier history clear.
'Wara' in its various compounds in Domesday is common,
and closely associated both in the Survey [2] and earlier [3] with
the king's geld. It might, therefore, be supposed that, starting
from the terminology of these East Anglian extents, an
examination of the conditions of Domesday and the twelfth
century might reveal the extent to which such ancient public
burdens formed in this district the basis of the manorial money
rents of the thirteenth century.

In Domesday Book itself there is clear evidence of the
existence of a free peasant class which discharged all or most
of its obligations by means of money payments. Ralf Bainard
had, for instance, seized a freeman at Southwold. Now Rabell
the carpenter holds him. But in the time of King Edward
this freeman paid rent (censum) to the king's manor.[4] At
Kildingham, again, there were four freemen of whom Stigand
had held the soke, but they 'have been added to the rent
roll of the hundred of Earsham'.[5] Variations of such pay-

---

[1] On the 'wara' acre cf. Vinogradoff, *Villainage in England*, p. 242.
[2] Cf. Maitland, *D. B. B.*, p. 123.
[3] Vinogradoff, *Growth of the Manor*, pp. 225-7. Cf. Stenton,
O. S. L. S., vol. ii, pp. 10-11.
[4] 'Fuit in censu manerii regis,' *D. B.*, vol. ii, fol. 279 b.
[5] 'In Kildincham xii liberi homines iii carucatis terrae et ix bordariis.
Tunc viii carucae modo v. xii acrae prati. Silva viii porcis i aecclesia
xxx acris libere terrae. Ex his fuere ix antecessores Radulfi de bella fago
commendatione T. R. E. et unus Alwi Deted et unus et dimidius abbatis
de Sancto Eadmundo et dimidius Stigandi. In eadem iiii liberi homines
xv acris et dimidia caruca. Stigandus habuit socam T. R. E. et sunt
additi in censu de Ersham. Et totum hoc est in censu.' *D. B.*, vol. ii,
fol. 141 b.

ments[1] could be found in plenty scattered throughout the Survey, and they are reproduced in the earlier twelfth-century charters. In these the free peasant normally appears in a money-paying capacity,[2] and in many very early twelfth-century documents the term socage already bears its later fiscal connotation.[3] Sometimes a comparison between the two sets of records brings this out very clearly. William the first earl of Warenne gave to Lewes Priory ' mansionem in Norfolk Hecham nomine totum quod ibi habui cum terra Pagani prepositi et cum omnibus liberis hominibus quorum censum idem Paganus recipiebat '.[4] In the Survey Heacham appears as a normal Warenne manor with a dependent population of thirty-five socmen, out of whom the rent-paying freemen of the charter must surely have come.[5] Such evidence as this is quite in conformity with the general testimony of the East Anglian Domesday, where similar conditions appear under many different forms. All the freemen, for example, on the king's land in the hundreds of Walsham and Blofield pay the sum of twelve pounds ' in consuetudinibus ' and one pound ' de gersuma '.[6] Fersfield, again, is worth twelve pounds and six shillings and eight pence, and of this the freemen of the

---

[1] At ' Torp ' (*D. B.*, vol. ii, fol. 138) Robert Blund, who was probably a steward of the king, has added a freeman to his rental (*censum*), and he has also done the same to some freemen at Plumstead (*D. B.*, vol. ii, fol. 199).

[2] The socmen, for instance, are normally separated from the main gift of land and estimated in terms of money; cf. Appendix I, Nos. 60, 62. A Warenne charter to Lewes grants in ' Catestona ' in Norfolk ' dimidiam marcatam terre et de socamennis x solidos ' (Cott. Vesp. F. xv, fol. 19). Another Warenne charter, this time to Castleacre, grants to the Priory ' apud Stanhoe terram socemannorum que reddebat per annum iii solidos ' (Harl. 2110, fol. 3 b), and Hugo de Wanci gave to the same church ' ecclesiam de Barseham cum terra ad eam pertinente et decimam manerii et tres sochemans eiusdem manerii ' (ibid., fol. 1 b).

[3] Vide *infra*, Appendix I.

[4] Cott. Vesp. F. xv, fol. 10 b.

[5] *D. B.*, vol. ii, fol. 163: ' hic iacent xxxv socmanni i carucata et dimidia terrae. Semper vi carucae iiii acrae prati.'

[6] *D. B.*, vol. ii, fol. 129 b: ' Et isti omnes cum aliis qui sunt in alio hundredo reddunt viii libras blancas et c solidos de consuetudinibus ad numerum et xx solidos de gersuma. Super omnes istos qui faldam comitis requirebant habebat comes socam et sacam. Super alios omnes rex et comes.' The other hundred is probably Blofield, though there are traces of a common evaluation between Walsham and West Flegg.

manor pay 106 shillings and 7 pence,[1] whilst a similar arrangement is noted at Bedingham.[2] It would be easy to multiply
such examples,[3] and there seems no doubt of the widespread
existence of a money-paying peasantry in East Anglia at the
time of Domesday.

The interest of such entries as these lies, however, in the
peculiar arrangements which they postulate. Much is vague
about these payments, and the names under which they are
described admit of no precise definition. It is impossible
to distinguish between ' consuetudo ', ' censum ', ' geltum ', and
' gersuma '.[4] Many of these payments are to royal manors,
and in general they may be said to bear both a public and a
private character. Further, most significantly they illustrate
with especial clearness that there was a general tendency in
all cases for the freemen and socmen to make their payments
independently of the manors to which they were attached.
This appears very clearly in the examples which have been
given, and in one case we actually hear of an unsuccessful
attempt being made to bring the freemen into the common
payments. At Caston on Terra Regis we learn that Godric,
who held the manor for the king, used to pay thirteen pounds
thirteen shillings and four pence and a fine of twenty shillings,
but that now, ' since he lost the soke ', he pays seven pounds,
and ' super socmannos quos amisit ' are seven pounds.[5] It is
clear that in these payments to the royal manors the free

---

[1] *D. B.*, vol. ii, fol. 130 b: 'Fersfeuella cum beruiuita et Borstuna tunc
valuit lx solidi postea vii librae et vi solidi et viii denarii inter censum et
consuetudines. Modo valet xii librae et vi solidi et viii (denarii) blanci
et de his xii libris dant liberi homines centum solidos et vi et vii
denarios.'

[2] *D. B.*, vol. ii, fol. 131: 'Bedingaham—Tunc totum valet iiii librae
postea et modo viii blancae et xx solidi de gersuma. De his viii libris dant
hi vi liberi homines xxvii solidi et iiii denarios.'

[3] They occur most frequently round royal manors, and the royal
manor of Snaring forms a good example of the concentration of these
payments. At Barney the seventeen freemen who hold there of Peter of
Valognis 'reddunt in Snaringa xvii solidos et iiii denarios' (*D. B.*, vol. ii,
fol. 258), whilst at the berewick of Thursford there were three groups of free
peasants. The whole was worth T. R. E. 8 pounds, but now it pays ' de
gersuma' 11 pounds 10 shillings and 8 pence (*D. B.*, vol. ii, fol. 122 b).
These payments are described quite separately from the geld contributions, and Snaring was not the manor to which the hundred court was
attached, for this belonged to Wighton (*D. B.*, vol. ii, fol. 112 b).

[4] Cf. Maitland, *D. B. B.*, pp. 78–9.   [5] *D. B.*, vol. ii, fol. 126.

peasantry, while they normally contributed a money sum, yet did so separately from the manors in which they lay.

This becomes of great importance in dealing with the geld and its assessments, where the same principle seems to have been applied. The ' valet ' entries of the Survey clearly have some bearing on the geld payments, and it is normal through-out the East Anglian Domesday for the freemen and socmen to be valued apart from their manors, and usually when a single assessment is given a special note is made to the effect that the freemen and socmen have in this case been included in the valuation.[1] This is highly significant and coincides with the information given in the descriptions of the other pay-ments not specifically described as geld. Consequently it is of some importance to note how on one occasion we have a definite application of the same principle to the hundred's geld itself according to the peculiar East Anglian method of assess-ment. The soke over the whole hundred of Midford is the Abbot of Ely's and was attached to the manor of Dereham.[2] In the assessment of Dereham and ' Torp ' in the Survey we are, however, told that each of these manors paid fifteen pence to the pound paid by the hundred, and that upon all the socmen of these two manors was charged another fifteen pence of geld.[3] In the hundred of Midford it seems that we have recorded the separate geld assessment of the free peasantry of the hundred apart from the manors to which they were individually attached, and this fully bears out the implications involved in the separate ' valet ' entries.

The import of this distinction between the two geld pay-

---

[1] Cf. Maitland, *D. B. B.*, p. 126. Examples of this might be found on nearly every page of the East Anglian Domesday.

[2] *D. B.*, vol. ii, fol. 214 : Later at Shipdham. Vide *infra*, and Appen-dix II, No. 4.

[3] *D. B.*, vol. ii, fol. 214 : ' Mitteford Hundred et dimidium. Derham tenuit semper Sancta Ætheldreda. . . . Tunc ualuit x librae modo xiii. Habet i leugam in longitudine et dimidiam in latitudine et xv denarios de gelto. Tota soca istius hundredi et dimidii iacebat ad sanctam Aethel-dredam T. R. E. et ualet lx solidi.'

' Torp tenuit semper Sancta Ætheldreda. . . . Tunc ualuit lx solidi modo xi librae et habet i leuga in longitudine et i leuga in latitudine. Et xv denarii de gelto. Et super omnes socmannos de istis ii maneriis xv denarii.'

ments which runs through the Survey is extensive and bears directly upon the problem of the development of the later manorial rents. Primarily it raises two questions of considerable magnitude. In the first place we would fain know to what extent the lord was responsible for the geld of his villeins and possibly exacted from them labour services in return for his own payment. Of this, however, we have no direct information. The comprehensive statement of the value of the geld liabilities of the manors and of the villeins within them conceals all the subsequent arrangements which may have been made. It is, however, in the separate payments of the free peasantry that an opportunity is presented of examining somewhat more closely the operation and the subsequent significance of the geld payments.

It is firstly important to notice the close connexion between the public and private aspects of these payments. Certainly the relation between the socman's geld and that of the manor to which he was attached was a loose one, but it is at least probable that in case of default it would be on the shoulders of the socman's lord that the burden would eventually fall, and if that were so the modern distinction between 'rent' and 'tax' would be completely inappropriate to apply to a payment which was like a contribution to the royal geld and yet also at the same time relieved the lord from paying the same sum to the king. Moreover, there is certain positive evidence in favour of such a suggestion, which at least was true on the lands of the king which were held of him by a steward. On the estates of the king which Godric held at Mileham there was a poor widow who held 12 acres once the property of Aluid the freeman, and there were also three socmen with 15 acres and half a plough. In the time of King Edward it was worth twenty shillings. But now all is changed, 'Modo nichil reddit quia nichil habet'. The widow has become poor indeed. But the king goes not without his money : 'Godric pro ea censum reddit'.[1] Here is a case of the payment ultimately falling on the shoulders of the lord, and we may well suppose that similar conditions

[1] *D.B.*, vol. ii, fol. 121.

prevailed elsewhere. They would be in strict accord with
the arrangements described in the twelfth-century documents.
In general, it seems probable that the socmen's payments
might equally be considered as a tax to the king or as a rent
to their lord for their land. And even if this could not be
rigidly applied, it is clear that the smallest depression on
the part of the peasantry or the least grant of immunity to
the church by a king or a lord would have effected the
change. On the whole the descriptions of the peasant geld
payments in the East Anglian Domesday have a peculiar
interest with regard to the development of the later rents.
Firstly, throughout the Survey there is a tendency to reckon
the free elements of the population separately to the geld, and
secondly, such payments take on both a public and a private
character. Further, it seems reasonable to suppose a direct
connexion between these two aspects of the geld in the
probable ultimate seignorial responsibility in regard to the
free payments.

The consideration of such peasant payments in Domesday suggests directly the origin of the ' wara ' elements
in the later manorial extents. The development can, moreover, be fairly clearly seen from a comparison of both sets of
records with the twelfth-century charter evidence which
chronologically lies in between them. The essence of both
systems lies in the repartition of the liability to contribution
among the peasant holders according to the number of acres
held. This on the transference of the geld into private hands
would result in a customary rent depending absolutely on the
acreage of the tenement. And that such repartition actually
took place there can be little doubt. A collective responsibility of groups of freemen and socmen to the geld must have
been subdivided according to the size of the tenements which
the individual peasants held. All that we know of the allocation of the Domesday geld points to this conclusion. As
the shire arranged its geld at so much per hundred and the
hundred at so much per leet and so much per vill on the
basis of geld carucates, so also is it probable that a similar
process took place in the case of the liabilities of these groups

of free peasants.[1] In other directions in the East Anglian Survey we can see the same notion. Whilst no uniformity is to be expected, nevertheless outside the geld proper, there are frequent indications in the case of small isolated tenements of a fixed ratio between acreage and value. Throughout the Suffolk Domesday there is a marked tendency towards a reckoning based upon a twopenny acre,[2] which is of too frequent occurrence to be merely the result of coincidence. In Norfolk the land of the churches seems very frequently to have been assessed on a penny basis, and this sometimes leads

---

[1] Already it is apparent that in the time of Domesday the essentially tenurial aspect of the payment is stressed. It is the tenement which pays very frequently, with the express statement ' whoever holds there'. The number of tenants thus seems often of very little importance. Such the estate, such the rent, and it is sometimes added ' others hold there'.

[2] Examples of this could be found scattered through all parts of the Suffolk survey. An instance might perhaps be selected in eight consecutive entries on the Ely land, only two of which fall outside the fixed scale, and those not to any great extent.

' In Deploham dimidius liber homo soca et commendatione iiii acras et ualet viii denarii. . . .

In Assefelda i liber homo soca et commendatione iii acras et ualet viii denarii.

In Henlea i liber homo commendatione et soca dimidiam acram et ualet i denarius.

In Torp Alsi liber homo soca et commendatione x acras et ualet xx denarii.

In Scaruetuna i liber homo soca et commendatione ii acras et ualet iv denarii. Galt' tenuit.

Pereham dimidium hundredum.

In Balcheshalla v liberi homines in soca et commendatione abbatis xxvi acras. Semper dimidia caruca et ualet iiii solidi.

In Wantesduna xii acrae de dominio de Sutbourne et ualent xxiv denarii.

In eadem tenet Moruinus liber homo ii acras et ualet iiii denarii.'— D. B., vol. ii, fol. 384.

It is noticeable also how often in the passages in which the constant ratio is sustained that it will remain unaffected by varieties of internal organization. One man will be under soke, another under soke and commendation, another will have a plough or a serf, but the relation of acreage to value will, in spite of these changes, often remain the same. Again, a good example may be found on the Ely lands.

' In Hamingstuna i liber homo Iricus commendatus abbati et in soca eius xv acrae et ii bordarii et ualet ii solidi et vi denarii.

In Uledana i liber homo Aluricus commendatione tenet i acram et dimidiam et ualet iii denarii. Rex et comes socam. Hoc est in dominio.

In Codenham xvi acrae dominice terre et fuit in pretio de Bercham.

In Hassa i libera femina Listeua commendata abbati i acram et ualet ii denarii. Rex et comes socam. In eadem i liber homo commendatione tenet dimidiam acram et ualet ii denarii. Rex et comes socam.'— D. B., vol. ii, fol. 383.

to elaborate equations.[1] On the whole there can be little doubt of the similar repartition of the geld contributions of the free peasant groups. Just as the team-land came elsewhere to represent subpartitional shares of the geld, so [2] also these acres of freemen and socmen in East Anglia must often have served as the basis of their individual geld liabilities.

The terminology of the twelfth-century charters shows that this was indeed the case. In them there frequently occur statements which show that the villar liability was subdivided according to the acres within the vills. Whoever may have been ultimately responsible for the geld of the unfree in the constituent manors of the vill, it is clear that the separate payments of the free peasantry must have been rigidly assessed according to acreage and something very like the peasant 'warloths' of Lincolnshire [3] and Yorkshire [4] set up. One of such charters, for instance, describes how the granted land is to defend itself against the king, 'secundum communitatem quam uilla Mendleshe de xxx acris prosequitur'.[5] And of another tenant it is mentioned, 'de tenemento suo xl acras inter uillatum defendit'.[6] And elsewhere there are clear indications of the same system. The ware acres themselves appear in twelfth-century documents. But what is much more important is that these deeds bring out very clearly the arrangements which the Domesday conditions postulate. The free geld payments of the survey were assessed according to acreage, and with the confusion of public obligations and private rights conditions were established very like those to be seen later in the customary rents of the extents. In certain of the Ely manors it has been shown how traces of a constant relation between acreage and rent could be found, though the ratio varied from manor to manor. The

---

[1] The ratio varies very often in these cases, but cf. the two churches at Shouldham in Norfolk with 73 acres, being worth 6 shillings and 1 penny (*D. B.*, vol. ii, fol. 250). This and the following folio give very good examples of this artificial reckoning of the church lands.

[2] Cf. Maitland, *D. B. B.*, p. 472.

[3] *Lincolnshire Gilbertine Charters*, Ormesby Series, No. 1 (Lincoln Record Society).

[4] *Y. C.*, vol. ii, p. vii.

[5] Harley Charter 49, C. 1, and see Appendix I, No. 5.

[6] Harley Charter 46, E. 31, and see Appendix I, No. 3.

only explanation which can be given of these conditions seems to be that we have here to deal with the results of an arbitrary allocation of geld units to each tenement in proportion to the amount originally owed to the public geld and now transformed into a private rent.

From the peculiar character of the East Anglian evidence, we thus seem able to trace fairly clearly the process by which on the ecclesiastical lands certain of the later manorial rents were evolved from public payments. In many ways the essence of this development lies in the extensive grants of geld immunity to the great religious houses, which in East Anglia as elsewhere were very numerous. The vast lands of Ely, Ramsey, and St. Edmunds[1] paid no geld. The geld payments of St. Benet of Hulme were limited to a very small portion of the estates of the abbey.[2] Under these circumstances, it is clear that the public payments of the free peasantry were hardly to be distinguished from customary rents. An interesting writ of the Confessor to St. Edmunds shows the abbot stepping into the place of the king with regard to public payments.[3] And it seems clear that every extensive grant of lands in frankalmoign must have affected in a similar way the smaller tenants which it involved. The frequent exclusion of forinsec service and all that it implied from the frankalmoign immunity in the twelfth-century charters shows the importance of the numerous grants where the exclusion was absent.[4] Altogether, we can see in such

---

[1] See the early grants to these houses scattered through Kemple, *C. D.*, and later in the cartularies.

[2] 'Et non geldet terra sua iniuste nec sicut geldare solebat tempore regis Henrici aui mei et anno quo fuit uiuus et mortuus nominatim illa hundreda de Happingehundrededi et de Waxstonesham cum omnibus aliis.' Charter of Henry II to St. Benet of Hulme (Cott. Galba E. ii, fol. 31 b).

[3] Thorpe, *Diplomatarium*, p. 417 : 'And ic wille him þat se fredom stonde on his welde þat so fele siðe so men gildeð here gilde to heregild oþer to schipgild gilde se tunschipe so oþere men don to þe abbates nede 7 þere muneke þe þer binnen sculen for hus seruen.'

[4] An agreement as to the incidence of the forinsec service due from the granted tenement is a normal feature of a twelfth-century charter, as appears alike from the charters in such a text as the Castleacre Cartulary, and also from the Yorkshire and Danelagh documents. Forinsec service certainly included the geld liability as well as military services and scutage payments, and the immunities from this in the twelfth-century

previous development the probable origin of the later customary rents rigidly based upon acreage, and of the ' wara ' acres to which they are so closely akin. On the lands of St. Edmunds we are fortunate in being able to watch this development at an early date. The extensive immunities of the abbey, including the possession of eight and a half hundreds in Suffolk, make this house a very good example. Consequently it is of great interest to watch the tenemental conditions described in the document known as Abbot Baldwin's feudal book,[1] where we have an extensive list of the holdings of some of the minor tenants of the abbey which dates from the period immediately subsequent to Domesday.[2] Here it is very noticeable how the correspondence of acreage to rent on the basis of a penny acre is maintained very generally throughout the Survey. Late in the twelfth century we have also the record which Jocelyn of Brakelonda describes as the Kalendar of Abbot Samson. And here, again, there is the same close correspondence, and still upon the reckoning of a penny acre.[3] The St. Edmunds evidence from the eleventh and twelfth centuries is in fact in strict accord with the terminology of the Ely extents alike in the ware acres and in the rigid assessment of rent according to acreage, and in both it seems that we may see an illustration of the manner in which, on the ecclesiastical lands, the free geld payments which are so prominent a feature of the East Anglian Domesday form the basis of many of the later manorial rents.

There are, furthermore, two aspects of the transformation of public payments into private rents in East Anglia which may perhaps be specially noticed. The general character of the evidence which has been considered indicates once again

---

charters vary from a complete discharge of the whole service by the grantor to the exclusion not only of the royal service but also of that owed to the mediate lords of the land.

[1] Registrum Nigrum Sancti Edmundi (Cambridge University Library), fols. 124–43 b.

[2] Vide *supra*, p. 7.

[3] A section of this is printed in Gage, Introduction to *History of Suffolk*.

that no theory which views the manor as the ultimate gelding unit can possibly be applied to this district. As far as the freemen and socmen are concerned, it is the vill and not the manors which lie within it that constitutes the basis of the assessment. As has been seen in the charters, the fiscal acreage of the peasants gelds ' inter uillatum ' or ' secundum communitatem quam uilla . . . de xxx acris prosequitur '.[1] The East Anglian evidence thus tends strongly to reinforce the attacks[2] which have been made on Maitland's theory of the Domesday manor[3] as being a technical term representing the house against which geld is charged. The arrangements of the district show that whatever may have been the measures adopted with regard to the unfree, the free peasants were viewed in respect of the geld as holding fiscal shares of the village, which was the geld unit. In this matter, as in so many others, the lack of coincidence between the East Anglian manor and vill cannot be too strongly emphasized. And taking into account this fact and the arrangements of the free peasantry, it must be concluded that the most definite part which these manors could have played in the geld administration was as possibly representing collective fiscal divisions of the vill, including villeins and serfs, but excluding freemen and socmen.

From another point of view, it is just possible that we may see in the separation of the geld payments of the free peasants from those of the manorial villeins traces of that distinction between inland and sokeland which was of such importance in the Northern Danelagh.[4] The contrast between inland and sokeland in the Danelagh is in many respects akin to that between inland and warland in the south and west, and it has been noted that the warland bears the ' double implication of land in the occupation of the dependent peasantry and land rated to the king's geld '.[5] The Danelagh inland appears also in its latinized form as ' dominium ', but in that region it signifies ' the whole of that portion of an estate over which the lord has

[1] Vide *supra*.
[2] e. g. Tait, *E. H. R.*, vol. xiv, p. 768, and Round, *E. H. R.*, vol. xv, p. 293. [3] Maitland, *D. B. B.*, pp. 107–28.
[4] Stenton, O. S. L. S., vol. ii. [5] Ibid., p. 10.

most immediate and direct control, the land of the villeins and
bordars as opposed to the socmen ',[1] and the extended form of
the term is probably ' dominium aule '.[2] This formula occurs
in the early Hulme charters, and in these documents generally
the term ' aula ' often appears to take the place of the ' manerium '
of the Survey.[3] A kindred idea is expressed in certain passages
of the Domesday of Norfolk itself. The payments of certain
freemen and socmen of the hundreds of freemen of Walsham
and Blofield to the royal manor of Walsham have already
been noted.[4] They are of considerable importance in the
Norfolk Domesday, and they were clearly of permanent value
to the king, for they were the subject of a charter of Henry II
to the Bishop of Norwich.[5] But in two cases this part of the
revenue of the Domesday manor is described as its ' outsoke ',[6]
an expression which in its context thus seems to indicate an
organization very much like that with which we have been
made familiar in the Danelagh. The types of the soke
structure of the two districts, as will be seen,[7] present far more
striking similarities than has usually been supposed, and it is
in that connexion that such contrasts are of most interest.
But without pressing such distinctions too far, it may perhaps
in this place be suggested that in the separation of the free
peasants' contributions to the villar geld from those of the
villeins and bordars comprised in the manorial assessments, we
have in many respects between the two districts a link which
would be more complete could we assume that the contributions of the villeins were discharged by the lord on whom they
were directly dependent.

---

[1] Ibid., p. 11.   [2] Ibid., p. 12.

[3] Cf. especially the twelfth-century abbots' charters in the St. Benet
Cartulary (Cott. Galba E. ii). For an early instance of this term cf.
Appendix I, No. 42 (Cott. Galba E ii, fol. 55).

[4] Vide *supra*, p. 98.

[5] Cott. Charter ii. 4. See Appendix I, No. 21.

[6] The first of these clearly establishes the connexion between the two
terms. The description on *D. B.*, fol. 123 b, of certain freemen in the
hundred of Blofield, closes with the remark, ' Et hi omnes liberi homines
sunt appreciati in xiii libris de lut soca de Walessham '. The outsoke
seems to have stretched into the hundred of West Flegg, where ' Radulfus
Stalra xl acras. Semper i caruca et dimidia salina et iiii acrae prati. Et
ualet ix solidi in ut soca de Walsam. Rex et comes soca ' (*D. B.*, vol. ii,
fol. 135).   [7] Vide *infra*, pp. 180 seq.

In the lack of definite evidence it would be highly unwise to overstress such similarities, but in general it is clear that we may trace in East Anglia the formation of many of the later manorial rents to a public origin, and by that means explain both the later 'ware' acres and the frequent close correspondence of acreage and rent upon a customary basis on the thirteenth-century ecclesiastical lands. The broad separation of peasant classes in the church manors upon a basis of service and money rent seems reflected in the earlier distinction which the East Anglian Domesday makes so especially prominent between the free peasant liable to public tribute and the unfree man whose tribute is paid by the lord, and over whom that lord has in return rights of labour service. The inclusion at a later date within the manors of the free elements of society would produce just the conditions which are later to be found on the ecclesiastical lands. And the evidence for such a development in East Anglia is not wanting. For whilst in a sense the same criteria of status can be applied both in Domesday and in the thirteenth-century extents, nevertheless no study of peasant conditions during the intervening period can afford to neglect the great contrasts which are presented by the two sets of documents. The society portrayed in the Ely extents is in many ways radically different from that of the normal Domesday vill, and it is thus that any detailed comparison of the ranks and classes described in the two documents breaks down. For in the later record, as has been shown, it is the relation of the peasant to the manorial husbandry which is the determinant of status, but in the earlier record it is primarily personal considerations which are important. The ranks and classes of Domesday have been the subject of much profound speculation,[1] and East Anglia is in this respect not remarkable save in the large proportion of free peasants to be found there. Here, as elsewhere, the distinction between the freeman and socman has baffled all inquirers,[2] and the most that can be said is that the line drawn

---

[1] Vinogradoff, *English Society* ; Maitland, *D. B. B.*
[2] Cf. Maitland and Vinogradoff, *op. cit.*, and note the remarks of Johnson, *V. C. H. Norfolk*, vol. ii, p. 28.

between the two classes was fluctuating and irregular. Not only is it probable that the terminology differed from place to place,[1] but also it may be suspected that sometimes the socmen of Domesday appear in the early charters as ' liberi homines '.[2] Still, a theoretic distinction there undoubtedly was, and an explanation of it based upon a wergild difference seems to meet with fewer obstacles than most.[3] It is possible also that the operation of a recent process of commutation, as in later times, was already creating a rent-paying class similar to the ' liberi homines ', but without the claim to complete freedom possessed by the descendants of the original Danish settlers.[4] But in the main the somewhat vague distinction seems to have been enforced rather in connexion with the ability to alienate land, which frequently appears as the distinguishing mark between the two classes.[5] Whilst, however, much remains vague about the Domesday peasant classes, the contrast between the society presented in the great survey and that described in the later ecclesiastical extents is so great that the only possible explanation of the change is a widespread depression of the peasantry to which reference has so frequently been made.

There is fortunately no need to labour this point, which has often been stressed.[6] A comparison between the T. R. E. and the T. R. W. entries of Domesday itself shows everywhere the encroachment of the lords upon the liberties of the peasant

---

[1] Johnson, *op. cit.*

[2] The socmen, for instance, who form the gift in the very curious charter (Harl. 76, F. 35; Appendix I, No. 14) are almost certainly represented by the ' liberi homines ' discussed on fol. 395 b of the Survey.

[3] Cf. Stenton, O. S. L. S., vol. ii, pp. 18–19, for a discussion of the twelfth-century wers and their relation to Domesday. The differentiation of the socman's wer from that of the villein is, however, unlikely. A distinction, however, between a ' twelfhund ' ' liberi homines ' category, corresponding to the thegns of Wessex (' Leges Henrici Primi ') and a twyhund sokemen class in East Anglia does not seem impossible. This might well be the outcome of the wergild rearrangements of the Danish invasions. But anything like proof is impossible.

[4] Vide *supra*, pp. 85 seq. This would fit in well with the suggested wergild distinction.

[5] Vide Johnson, *V. C. H. Norfolk*, vol. ii, pp. 1 seq., though of course the distinction cannot be pressed. Cf. Vinogradoff, *English Society*, pp. 431 seq.

[6] e. g. Maitland, *D. B. B.* ; Vinogradoff, *English Society*.

class.[1]   The possession of the vague superiorities involved in
commendation is, for instance, very frequently made the starting-point for an assertion of the full rights involved in complete lordship.[2]   Men are everywhere making manors by the
simple process of creating a few acres of demesne land and
arranging round it the obligations of the free peasantry.[3]
A striking instance of this has been, for example, noted at
Martham, where the Bishop of Norwich can be seen transforming the Domesday colony of 'liberi homines' into manorial
villeins at the beginning of the twelfth century.[4]   The constant
gifts of freemen and socmen from one lord to another must
also have contributed to this depression.   In one case we have
from Suffolk a highly significant record of such a transaction.
In the earlier half of the twelfth century Gilbert, Earl of Clare,
confirmed by a charter, of which we possess the original,
a gift of socmen in Stansfield.[5]   These men can be identified
with reasonable certainty as being the descendants of the
Domesday 'liberi homines' recorded as the Earl of Clare's men
in these vills.[6]   But over them the earl had only commenda-

---

[1] e. g. the large notices of 'Invasiones' in both the Norfolk and
Suffolk Domesdays.

[2] It would be easy to multiply examples of this.   Lords are very
frequently described as possessed of full customary right over men over
whom their 'antecessores' had 'nothing but the commendation'.   'Perhaps
the most striking change to which Domesday bears witness is the conver-
sion of these "commendati" into "consuetudinarii" or customary tenants.'
Johnson, *V. C. H. Norfolk*, vol. ii, p. 30.

[3] Frequently we have the phrase 'Of this X. made a manor'.
Equally significant are the numerous cases where the same process can
be seen under the normal D. B. terminology.   A good example of this is
to be found, for instance, in the village of Caister.   'Castre tenuerunt
lxxx liberi homines T. R. E. et modo similiter iiii carucatae terrae.   Tunc
xxii carucae et ex hoc toto Radulphus comes manerium.   Modo i caruca in
dominio et xxi hominum' (*D. B.*, vol. ii, fol. 134).   Manor-making has in
this case been a simple process, and superficially the social structure of
Caister is very little affected.   It is easy, however, to see how vitally the
status of these freemen has been compromised in relation to the new
feudal tests of tenant right.

[4] *Trans. R. H. S.*, vol. iv, Series iv, pp. 1 seq.   It is interesting to note
in this connexion the stress which Mr. Hudson lays upon the part played
by the village geld in promoting the peasant depression in this case.

[5] Harl. Charter 76, F. 35.   See Appendix I, No. 14.

[6] 'Isti sunt liberi homines qui T. R. E. potuerunt terras suas uendere et
donare.   Wisgar antecessor Ricardi habuit commendationem et socam et
sacam preter vi forisfacturas Sancti Eadmundi.' *D. B.*, vol. ii, fol. 395 b.

tion and very limited soke rights, and the grant of these men within half a century of Domesday show alike how widely such rights could be used and also how, with the constant liability to change of ownership, they were prone to be extended with the increasing seignorial pressure. The frequent litigation [1] at the time of the Survey between the Church and the lay lords represents but another aspect of the general seignorial encroachment, and the charters bear witness also to frequent peasant distress at the time of the anarchy.[2] A very striking feature of the St. Benet of Hulme cartulary is the constant increase of rents on change of ownership,[3] and when this affected men of some importance it certainly reacted upon the peasants who held of them. Nor was this depression confined to the twelfth century. It is, for instance, important to note how, between the dates of the two Ely registers, there is sometimes an increase in the amount of week work exacted from the villein tenements in the manors.[4] The growth of the manorial organization must in this district have operated with peculiar force, as has been seen, in transforming the geld payments of the free peasantry into rents to private lords, and this would be most prominent on lands comprised in royal grants or in gifts to the Church by the lay lords, both of which are very common in the twelfth century. The loss

[1] Besides the famous Ely trials, for which see Bigelow, *Placita Anglo-Normannica* and the *Inquisitio Eliensis* (ed. Hamilton), it is clear that the encroachments of the Domesday period frequently lead to subsequent litigation. The twelfth-century charters often refer to such trials. For instance, Cott. Aug. ii, No. 25, mentions a trial at Kenetford; whilst a very remarkable document in the Binham cartulary (Cott. Claud. D. xiii, fol. 20; see Appendix I, No. 35) shows the end of the disputes between the Bishop of Norwich and Peter of Valognis, in Binham, and links up with the description in Domesday (vol. ii, fol. 194).

[2] Appendix I, No. 38.

[3] The case of Godric dapifer and Ralph his son is a very good case of what was very common; Appendix I, Nos. 39, 40, 41, 45.

[4] This occurred at Littleport; cf. Maitland, *E.H.R.*, vol. ix, pp. 417 seq. On the East Anglian manors of the bishopric it took place at Dereham. In 1222 the full villein there performed from Michaelmas to All Saints' day two days each week; from All Saints' day 'usque ad tempus quo ordeum perseminatum fuerit' one day; from then to August 1st two days, and from August 1st to Michaelmas five days (Cott. Tib. B. ii, fol. 205). In 1277 he performs a uniform two days each week from Michaelmas to August 1st, and then five days from August 1st to Michaelmas (Cott. Claud. C. xi, fol. 229).

of the position of 'gafolgelder' by the free peasant was always of great importance in lowering his status, and the process is by no means confined to pre-Conquest times.[1]

On the ecclesiastical lands it is thus possible to trace in detail, in the exceptional East Anglian evidence, a fairly clear development from the early geld payments to the later manorial rents, and to estimate with some degree of accuracy the extent to which, on the ecclesiastical lands, such rents had a public origin. The transition can best be watched in the transformation of the separate geld payments of the Domesday free peasantry to manorial rents rigidly based upon acreage, and this process was marked chiefly by the numerous grants in frankalmoign, the royal gifts to the churches, and the general extension of manorial control by the ecclesiastical and lay lords. It is through the growth of lordship and its responsibilities, and through the lavish grants of ecclesiastical immunities, that 'wara' in this district comes to signify more a private than a public obligation. From another point of view, also, the inclusion within the manor of the free class originally liable to a separate geld payment was responsible for much of the later employment of the distinction between rent and service as the dominant criterion of peasant status. In any consideration of the origin of thirteenth-century rents and services on the ecclesiastical lands, due weight must thus be given to the public geld payments made by the free peasants of an earlier age.

The social organization of twelfth-century East Anglia shows thus clearly the previous development of many of the customary rents on the later manors. But that organization itself postulates a society in the main radically different from the manorial communities upon the lands described in the extents which have been the subject of our investigation. Even on these estates it has been seen that free rents were in the main the outcome of other forces, and elsewhere, where the seignorial organization was much weaker, it might be expected that such a divergence would be more pronounced. In the sphere of

---

[1] On the pre-Conquest development in this direction see Vinogradoff, *Growth of the Manor*; cf. Maitland, *D. B. B.*, Essay II.

contract, that is to say, it is probable that the East Anglian conditions might also show with peculiar clarity yet another aspect of the earlier history of free tenure which bears directly upon the problem of its origin.   But the main value of the earlier evidence of such conditions lies rather in the fact that it concerns a society held together by no manorial control and villages whose operative agricultural unity was not enforced by any unified seignorial pressure.

Even on the ecclesiastical lands this is very noticeable.   The widespread disintegration of peasant tenements which is so striking a feature of the tenemental structure of the district [1] inevitably introduced at an early date into the relations of man and lord a contractual element which, when reflected in the payment of money, led to a formation of a rent which was peculiarly 'free'.   The outward sign of a contractual tenure is the charter, and though this cannot be straitly pressed, there are some signs in certain of the manorial extents that the free tenant was there considered as being possessed of a charter by the very nature of his tenure.   At Salhouse, for example, the free holdings of the Priory of Binham were described as ' tenementa libera que tenentur per cartam et debent redditum et sectam curie '.[2]   On the Ely lands the tenure by charter is recorded only exceptionally in the extents, but examples of it are by no means infrequent.[3]   On the general evidence of the later extents it would be altogether impossible to grant the possession of a charter to all or even to most of the free tenants,[4]

---

[1] Vide *supra*.   [2] Cott. Claud. D. xiii, fol. 111.

[3] e. g. Tilney: 'Thomas Dix tenet sexdecim acras terreque fuerunt Wydonis filii Elwan pro octo solidis equaliter per cartam domini Johannis episcopi.'   Cott. Claud. C. xi, fol. 195 b.

Dereham : ' Johannes filius Roberti le frere tenet quadraginta acras terre ex dono episcopi Galfridi per carta pro una marca per annum equaliter.' Ibid., fol. 223.

Terrington : ' Johannes de Sibilla filius Wace tenet unum mesuagium et duodecim acras terre que fuerunt patris sui et triginta tres acras quas perquisivit de husbundis episcopi . . . pro quattuor denariis per annum equaliter per cartam.' Ibid., fol. 174 b.

Hitcham : ' Galfridus filius Alani de Thorneye tenet viginti acras de ware cum pertinenciis que fuerunt quondam Arnulfi de Hegge pro duodecim solidis per annum equaliter sicut carta prioris et conventus de Ely testatur.' Ibid., fol. 276 b.

[4] It would be impossible thus to discover in the Ely extents any practical illustration of the theory that the distinguishing mark of free

but that such possession was a common attribute to the tenure there can be no doubt.

But it is outside the manorialized lands and in the earlier charters themselves that the full importance of this element in early East Anglian social organization is made fully clear. From documents of the twelfth century it is shown plainly that not only were tenurial relationships normally in this district expressed in money payments, but that also the constant fluctuation of peasant ownership had already resulted in the formation of a contractual complex which has no parallel in the south and west. A gift of land in these charters usually seems to have implied an annual money payment accruing from that land ; the frequent occurrence of land assessed in librates, solidates, and even denariates [1] implies in this district the widespread peasant payment of a money rent.[2] On the other hand, the very existence of such a text as the Castleacre Cartulary itself is sufficient evidence of the prevalence in the century following the great Survey of a multitude of contractual tenures, which introduced into the whole scheme of social organization an inextricable confusion, and which precluded in twelfth-century East Anglia the operation of any rigid well-organized manorial system. In this cartulary and others of a similar nature,[3] the very large number of peasant contracts which are themselves attested by men who are themselves of the peasant class and bear names

tenure as opposed to socage was the possession by the free tenant of a charter. (Cf. Vinogradoff, *Villainage*, pp. 199 seq.) It would, of course, be highly rash to deny the possession of a charter to all those whose tenure is not thus specifically described, and in this connexion it is interesting to note that the Thomas Dix who holds by charter in the 1277 Survey appears as holding 16 acres again in the 1222 Survey, but without any reference to the charter which antedates the Survey. On the other hand, it would be impossible to assume a tenure by charter in the extents in the vast majority of cases where it is not mentioned. The holding at Terrington already referred to seems to make a contrast between the land which the free tenant holds by right of succession to his father and the other land which he holds by charter.

[1] This is especially prominent in the Castleacre Cartulary, Harl. 2110.

[2] Cf. the Danelagh conditions described by Professor Stenton, *D. C.*, Introduction, p. lxxxvii.

[3] There are a fairly large number of grants by peasants both in the St. Benet of Hulme register (Cott. Galba E. ii) and in the Binham cartulary (Cott. Claud. D. xiii).

of English or Scandinavian origin,[1] implies an extreme freedom of land alienation on the part of such men and a highly contractual organization of society. Such charters are by no means always granted to the Church, and they very frequently record an agreement as to tenure between one small holder and another.[2] There can be no doubt that there was much circulation of money in twelfth-century East Anglia,[3] and prosperous peasants were constantly buying and selling land and entering into new contractual relations with each other. From the general testimony of these documents it is in fact unmistakably clear that any estimate of East Anglian social conditions must recognize as early as the twelfth century the existence of a cash nexus which involved a very large section of the peasant class, and implied the widespread payment by freemen of contractual money rents.

Individual examples of the operation of this tenurial development could easily be found, both in the cartularies and in such original charters which have survived. As an illustration of the manner in which an individual tenant could enter into such relationships might be cited the five remarkable charters which have been preserved concerning the tenure of Peter of Edgefield in the twelfth century. The first of these describes the elaborate conditions under which he inherited his father's land in Edgefield.[4] Two more record separate leases of small parcels of land.[5] The fourth is concerned with the sale to Peter of a small tenement,[6] and by the last the Prior of Binham confirms to Peter the lands which he had formerly held in the village under Alexander the clerk.[7] The form and content of these charters are of interest in other connexions. What, however, may here be stressed, is that despite the great destruction of such deeds there here remains the record of a man of no particular pre-eminence entering into five contractual

---

[1] Stenton, *op. cit.*, p. cii *n.*
[2] Especially common in the Castleacre Cartulary (Harl. 2110).
[3] This is even more pronounced than in the corresponding Danelagh documents. Cf. Stenton, *op. cit.*, p. 1.
[4] Harl. Charter 49, G. 22. See Appendix I, No. 6.
[5] Harl. Charters 50, B. 37 ; 52, E. 22. See Appendix I, Nos. 7 and 10.
[6] Harl. Charter 45, F. 15. See Appendix I, No. 2.
[7] Harl. Charter 44, A. 18. See Appendix I, No. 1.

relationships, acquiring from three separate small owners small and scattered parcels of land, and holding from several lords by a variety of tenures whose only common feature is their contractual and fluctuating character.

Perhaps, however, the best example of the prevalence of such conditions in the period immediately subsequent to Domesday is to be found in the series of early charters contained in the cartulary of St. Benet of Hulme. These documents deal for the most part with the affairs of people of somewhat more importance than the grantors and witnesses in the Castleacre register, but they serve to bring out afresh the fact that in all ranks of society tenemental arrangements were constantly changing as the result of frequent sales and contracts. In one charter, for instance,[1] in the first half of the twelfth century, the abbot is recognizing the gift of land by one of his tenants to another as a marriage portion for his daughter, and this at once forms the basis of a new contractual rent to be paid by the grantee to the abbey. Another grant of about ten years later by another abbot narrates in full the various recent purchases and acquisitions of which it is made up.[2] Here, as in the Castleacre lands, we are faced with a rapidly fluctuating tenemental organization and the ever increasing implications of the contractual nexus.

These documents, remarkable as they are, merely confirm the evidence obtained elsewhere. The peculiar value of the St. Benet of Hulme text in this respect is that the long series of documents concerning the business transactions of the twelfth-century abbots shows with the utmost clearness the fact that continuously, from a generation after the Survey, the obligations of the tenantry to the abbey were normally expressed in the payments of contractual money rents. The variations of this are numerous and elaborate. Before 1170 we have examples of hereditary grants[3] by the abbey, of life leases,[4] and of other more elaborate contracts.[5] And there are

[1] Cott. Galba E. ii, fol. 59. See Appendix I, No. 47.
[2] Ibid., fol. 61. See Appendix I, No. 49.
[3] e. g. Cott. Galba E. ii, fols. 54 and 60.
[4] e. g. ibid., fol. 58.
[5] Vide *infra.*

clear indications of a general policy on the part of the abbots of letting their estates to tenants in return for an annual money payment.[1] Further, in the opposite direction the same result is being achieved. Men were giving land to the abbey and arranging to hold it themselves for one or two lives by rent.[2] Something very like the later ' use ' was no uncommon thing on the St. Benet of Hulme lands of the twelfth century.

The widespread operation of the contractual movement affected all ranks of society. Amongst the earliest documents in the Hulme register are four charters which concern the family of one of the most obscure of the minor East Anglian Domesday tenants-in-chief. In both Norfolk and Suffolk large estates were held in Domesday by Godric the ' dapifer '.[3] In both surveys this man appears both as a tenant-in-chief and also as holding certain of the king's lands in farm. The St. Benet charters show his family already in his lifetime appearing as contractual subtenants of the abbey of St. Benet of Hulme. In the first of these documents,[4] some time before 1125, Godric himself gave to the abbey his land in Little Melton[5] on the understanding that Ralph his son should hold it at a yearly rent of ten shillings. But at the same time Letselina, the wife of Ralph, gave a curtain to the abbey in return for the right to hold the land at the same rent if she survived her husband. Furthermore, if Ralph had a son he was to succeed to the land, but at a rent of forty shillings. But if Ralph died without heir the land was to go unconditionally into the hands of the abbot. Such a deed is quite typical of the highly complex contracts which were common in twelfth-century East Anglia. But the second of these charters[6] shows that Ralph had already entered into another similar contract with the abbey for lands which by this deed he renounced in return for a substantial money payment. The third docu-

---

[1] Lands which revert to the abbey are promptly relet to tenants at a money rent. Good examples of this are to be found in Appendix I, Nos. 38–55.

[2] Cf. Appendix I, No. 49.

[3] *D. B.*, vol. ii, fols. 202 seq., 355 b seq., and 191, 284 b seq.

[4] Cott. Galba E. ii, fol. 54. See Appendix I, No. 39.

[5] *D. B.*, vol. ii, fol. 204 b.

[6] Cott. Galba E. ii, fol. 54. See Appendix I, No. 40.

ment[1] concerning Ralph is some twenty years later in date, and confirms to him his rights in Little Melton. But the fourth charter,[2] which is very little subsequent to this, shows a wholly new contract concerning the same family and the same land, which is now granted to Basilia the wife—presumably the second wife—of Ralph, who is to hold the land at a life lease, but this time for the rent of one silver mark yearly. These four charters cover the tenemental history of a small part of the estates of the family for about twenty-five years. They show very clearly how the contractual and fluctuating conditions of East Anglian tenures were affecting from the time of the Survey itself the tenurial arrangements of such men as the lesser Domesday tenants-in-chief.

Such contractual relationships, which thus involved many varieties of money rents and leases, affected the whole tenurial structure of East Anglia in the two generations immediately subsequent to the Survey. And there can be little doubt that they also in great measure helped to determine the slowly consolidating seignorial rights of the great lords in this district in the century after the Conquest. It is in this connexion that the history of the Ely manor of Wiggenhall in the twelfth century is probably of importance in supplying a parallel to the formation of similar social conditions a century earlier. In the Ely registers the manor is in a sense highly peculiar. It is recorded in the later Survey as containing a population consisting entirely of free tenants.[3] In 1222 it is surveyed in connexion with the manor of Tilney. This record is also peculiar. There are no rubrics to indicate categories of tenants, but they seem to fall into two groups, the one paying merchet and the other being exempt.[4] There is no week work mentioned and no demesne. Nor do any of the later services associated with the villein or 'operarius' class exist in the manor. It is, moreover, in the past history of Wiggenhall that the interest and the explanation of these

---

[1] Cott. Galba E. ii, fol. 56. See Appendix I, No. 44.
[2] Cott. Galba E. ii, fol. 56. See Appendix I, No. 45.
[3] Cott. Claud. C. xi, fol. 196.
[4] Cott. Tib. B. ii, fol. 172 b, and see Appendix II, No. 2.

curious conditions lie. Wiggenhall was a marshland manor,
and its formation by reason of adverse natural surroundings
was very late. At the time of Domesday there was but one
peasant there.[1] By the end of the thirteenth century it is
a small but prosperous community consisting, so far as the
Bishop of Ely was concerned, exclusively of free tenants.
What had happened there may be stated in the words of
Blomefield,[2] who bases his account on the Castleacre Cartulary.[3]

'It appears from an ancient pleading that before the year
1181 there was neither any habitation or ground yielding
profit within that part of Wiggenhall St. Mary Magdelene
from a place called Bustard's Dole to the south side of the said
town except the monastery of Crabhouse with certain lands
belonging thereto—all of which then being waste and in the
nature of a desolate fen. But afterwards diverse inhabitants
came and by draining and banking gained as much by their
industry as they could and that they might the more securely
enjoy the same were content to be tenants forunto and to such
great men and upon this agreement was made the old
podike . . .'

The formation of the manor brought into being by a late
colonization of marshland thus seems to have brought into
being a contractual group of peasants. And this characteristic
of the settlement persisted. By 1187 we have a fine concerning
the transfer of land in Wiggenhall.[4] And from that time
forth the amount of sales and exchanges there is very
remarkable. The Castleacre Cartulary shows twenty-six
charters of this nature.[5] There are some in the cartulary of
the Priory of Crabhouse,[6] whilst the West Dereham Register,
with the exception of a few pages towards its close, is
exclusively devoted to the transfer of land in Wiggenhall.[7]
But the chief consideration which arises from the peculiar
history of Wiggenhall is the fact that, judging by the events
of the twelfth century, these free tenants in the Ely extents
represent primarily men who, whatever their condition else-

[1] D. B., vol. ii, fol. 274.
[2] Blomefield, *Norfolk*, ed. 1808, vol. ix, p. 176.
[3] Harl. 2110, fol. 144. Cf. also the allusions in the *Liber Niger Scaccarii*, ed. Hearne, p. 364.
[4] P. R. O. Fines.
[5] Harl. MSS. 2110, fol. 82 seq.
[6] Add. MSS. 731, *passim.*
[7] Stowe MSS. 929.

where,[1] have got possessed (probably by purchase) of land newly acquired from the marsh. They are men who stand in a loose economic relation to their lords; they are outside any strictly manorial organization; for such organization did not exist at the time when the 'podike' was made at Wiggenhall. Indeed, even in the thirteenth century the word 'manor' seems a misnomer when applied to Wiggenhall. For a 'manor' in which we are expressly told that there was no demesne,[2] and whose whole population then consisted solely of free tenants, bears much more resemblance to one of those freeman or socman groups which are so common in the Little Domesday than to any of the later forms of normal manorial structure.

The twelfth-century evidence displays in East Anglia a society organized very largely upon a contractual plan in the period subsequent to the Survey. And it thus seems probable that in a similar manner must be explained at once the miscellaneous character of the peasant tenements in Domesday itself and the variety of obligations to which their holders are subject. The number and irregularity of the tenements in the Survey offers a complete analogy to the conditions of later times. Most of them are far too small to have supported even one peasant, quite apart from his family.[3] If the figures

---

[1] The very presence of merchet-paying free tenants suggests that these men might possibly have been villeins from elsewhere. A similar case, of the confusion of liabilities which might easily result in a similar confusion of status, may be cited from Wells, a Ramsey manor very similar to Wiggenhall on the Ely estates, where we learn that 'Ailbrith filius Walteri est nativus domini abbatis sed dicit se esse hominem domini Episcopi'. *R. C.*, vol. iii, p. 299. Cf. a similar case in the adjoining manor of Walsoken, belonging to the Abbey of Ramsey, of a twelfth-century tenant: 'Godwinus (non est homo noster) duodecim acras.' *R. C.*, vol. 291.

[2] 'In dominio nichil' (Cott. Claud. C. xi, fol. 196).

[3] The exact amount of arable necessary to support a household in the eleventh century must remain a matter for conjecture. It was clearly more than 5 acres. Cf. Vinogradoff, *Growth of the Manor*, pp. 352-3. A partial explanation of these small holdings must be that their possessors supplemented their produce by hiring themselves out as casual labourers, and conditions in East Anglia were peculiarly favourable to this; but this would only account for about a third of the population, especially for a section which in Domesday often seems to be bound to no particular service or manor.

recorded have anything but a fiscal meaning,[1] the only possible
explanation of the majority of these Domesday entries is that
they are the outcome of a twofold contractual process.   The
absence of the cohesive influence of the lord's will has opened
the way to the formation of numberless contractual relations
among the peasants themselves, and on the other hand, in this
miscellaneous society the beginnings of manorial organization
have also assumed a contractual form.   A small but prosperous
peasant who had bought land in the semi-manorialized estate
of some great East Anglian landholder would be bound to
his lord only by the slightest economic tie, and would, with
regard to each of such holdings, be remarkably ' free '.   He
would further, as far as that particular tenement was concerned,
have been recorded by the Domesday jurors as a freeman
holding so many acres of land, whatever might have been
his status elsewhere.   It is therefore reasonable to expect
much reduplication in these descriptions in the Little Domesday
of tiny holdings of land.   In the West of England it has been
shown that there was, after the Survey, a small increase in the
number of free tenants.[2]   This phenomenon, occurring on the
lands such as those of the abbey of Worcester, can only be
explained by the lords making a new and advantageous
agreement with new tenants on the basis of contract as a money
organization of society spread itself over the land.   The
process had become general by the thirteenth century.[3]   In
East Anglia, however, it is clear that it very largely moulded
twelfth-century social arrangements, and must be carried back
to the Survey itself.   This is probably the explanation of that
curious complex which in Domesday everywhere shows small
tenements of a few acres apiece held by freemen and socmen,
and of the strange tangle by which freemen appear as

---

[1] Cf. Vinogradoff, *Villainage in England,* for the importance of ware
acres, and vide *supra.*   It is, however, in the highest degree improbable
that the Domesday figures bore no relation to the actual holdings.

[2] Hale-Hale, *Worcester Register,* Introduction (Camden Society),
especially p. 39.

[3] ' Item quia multi magnates Anglie qui feoffaverunt milites et libere
tenentes suos de parvis tenementis in magnis maneriis suis.'   Statute of
Merton, cl. ix.

economically dependent upon freemen, and occasionally even upon socmen.[1]

The nature of the Survey tends to conceal all but the results of this process. One aspect of the development may, however, perhaps be specially mentioned. The twelfth-century extents of the Ramsey East Anglian manors show[2] that there has been much sub-letting of the demesne, and it is interesting to note that individual references to similar proceedings can be found in Domesday.[3] Definite examples could also be found in the Great Survey, both of the creation of individual holdings in return for the payment of an annual money rent and[4] also of the institution of life leases.[5] But

[1] Vinogradoff, *English Society*, pp. 431 seq. The whole Norfolk Domesday is a commentary on the confusion caused by the constant creation of new relationships. The following examples may perhaps be given :

Freemen under freemen : *D. B.* ii, fol. 273 (Moulton).

Socmen under socmen. Perhaps amongst many examples the curious complex at Hemelington deserves notice : In Hemelington : 'vi socmanni de xxx acris terre. ii acrae prati. Semper ii carucae. In eadem ii socmanni et i homo in soca hundredi. Dimidia carucata terrae et i bordarius. vi acrae prati. Et habet sub eis vii socmannos de xx acris terre.' *D. B.* ii, fol. 129.

Of socmen under freemen : *D. B.* ii, fol. 247 b. Wickhampton may be taken as typical.

Freemen under socmen. This is, of course, the most abnormal arrangement. Vide the examples given in Vinogradoff, *English Society*, p. 431, and also *D. B.*, vol. ii, fol. 182 : 'In Hadescou unus socmannus Edrici de Laxsefelda xxx acras et iii bordariis et una caruca et dimidia. vi acras prati et iiii liberi homines sub illo xxx acris terrae.'

[2] Cf. *R. C.*, vol. iii (Brancaster), and *R. C.*, vol. iii, p. 291 (Walsoken). For an Ely early example of this may be taken an entry from Hartest (Suffolk) : ' Thomas de Burgo tenet decem acras terre a tempore Willelmi episcopi scilicet de dominio ' (Cott. Tib. B. ii, fol. 223). This was William Longchamp, who died in 1189.

[3] ' In Dice i liber homo tenet v acras de dominio manerii quem tenet Willelmus Malet ' (*D. B.*, vol. ii, fol. 276 b). Parenthetically this has some bearing on what is now a somewhat outworn controversy, for Seebohm observed that it was impossible to look for concealed freemen on the manorial demesne in Domesday. The development, however, which has been observed in East Anglia suggests that this is one of the places where freemen might most likely have been concealed. Cf. *E. H. R.*, vol. vii, p. 445.

[4] ' Hanc (terram) emit ipse Beorn liber homo ab abbate eo conuentione quod post mortem suam rediret ad aeclesiam Sanctae Aeldredas testante hundredo.' *D. B.*, vol. ii, fol. 372 b.

[5] ' Istud supradictum manerium Nachetuna tenuit Gutmundus die quod rex Edwardus obiit de Sancta Edeldryda ita quod non potuit vendere nec dare de ecclesia pro ista conuentione quod post mortem suam debebat redire in ecclesia in dominio et hoc testatur hundret.' *D. B.*, vol. ii, fol. 406 b.

quite apart from the occasional appearance of such transactions even in a survey which was not concerned to record them, the important point to notice is that the society described in the Little Domesday of itself implies their prevalence. In the light of the twelfth-century documents, it seems quite clear that much of the peculiar social conditions of the East Anglian Domesday can only be explained with reference to a contractual movement. Throughout the earlier Middle Ages the free peasants in this district were entering constantly into new tenurial relationships both with each other and with the great landowners. The social organization of the late eleventh century has to a large extent an economic interpretation. And the numberless freemen and socmen of the Little Domesday are in fact not to be considered only as the product of Danish influence. They appear in the bewildering form of the East Anglian Survey also as the result of the establishment of a cash nexus. The complicated network of liabilities there presented is largely the result of sales and contracts which have created a large number of new ' free ' relationships that entitle the jurors in respect of these holdings to term their tenants ' freemen '. Wherever we find a freeman in Norfolk or Suffolk holding a tiny tenement we have not necessarily to deal with the descendant of a free Danish warrior. Very often we have merely the record of the purchase of land by a prosperous peasant. The manor in East Anglia is still a very artificial institution. The freemen and socmen are still to a very large extent outside it, and throughout we may ascribe their position in society not only to historical tradition or to legal survivals, but to an economic and contractual movement already potent in the time of Domesday.

It is also only in connexion with this widespread contractual movement that can be understood the importance and the significance of East Anglian commendation. Commendation was a contract, and it took many different forms.[1] It is in the Survey the loosest of the bonds between lord and man, and

---

[1] Cf. Maitland, *D.B.B.*, pp. 66 seq.

is sometimes involved in and sometimes contrasted with both economic dependence [1] and jurisdictional right.[2] Sometimes it affected the land of the commended man and prohibited its sale, but this was exceptional, and normally in commendation we have to deal with a contractual arrangement which instituted a slight and a personal dependence.[3] Here, as in the other forms of contract, it is highly significant that the Domesday evidence is of the same character as that from the period immediately subsequent to the Survey. The importance of the appearance of the 'manreda' in certain of the St. Benet of Hulme charters has been pointed out.[4] The various aspects of commendation indeed appear in other charters of the twelfth century. Maitland [5] showed how the process of commendation in Domesday was in large measure conditioned by the importance attached in judicial matters to the oath of the magnate. Consequently, when we find a grant made [6] about 1125 by the Abbot of St. Benet of Hulme to an important tenant on the condition that he shall render 'fidelitatem sancto Benedicto et abbati et fratribus et fortitudinem et auxilium in omnibus que posset ad placita et ad hundreda et ubicunque necessarium videtur', it seems that we are dealing with strictly similar ideas. Commendation easily shaded off into the later homage,[7] which is perhaps the best translation of

---

[1] Cf. Maitland, *D. B. B.*, on the contrasts of soke with all custom which runs through the Norfolk Domesday. Many other examples might be given, in particular the numerous passages on the same lines, as : ' In Brambetuna xii liberi homines ix Ulketelli commendatione i sancti Edmundi alteri ii de feudo Stigandi. Inter x tenent xl acras terrae. Inter ii de feudo Stigandi. T.R.E.' 'xxxiii acras terrae modo xv acras. Inter xi caruca et dimidia semper. Inter ii tunc dimidia caruca.' *D. B.*, vol. ii, fol. 175 b. Such contrasts could be found on nearly every page of the Domesday Survey. The very frequent use of the phrase 'mere commendation' testifies to their weight.

[2] Cf. Maitland, *op. cit.* As an example might be given the socmen freemen in Fordham, who held by commendation of Hermo de Ferrers. Of these St. Benet of Ramsey had the soke over three, and St. Edmunds the soke over one. *D. B.*, vol. ii, fol. 275.

[3] Cf. Maitland, *loc. cit.* This is borne out by the character of the St. Benet of Hulme manreds (*E. H. R.*, vol. xxvi, p. 225), where the burden seems primarily personal.

[4] Stenton, *E. H. R.*, vol. xxxvii, pp. 225 seq.

[5] Maitland, *D. B. B.*, p. 71.

[6] Cott. Galba E. ii, fol. 55, and see Appendix.

[7] Stenton, *E. H. R.*, vol. xxxvii, pp. 225 seq.

the Saxon 'manred',[1] and the twelfth-century charters on occasion show very clearly the connexion between the two terms. For instance, as we have seen, a remarkable deed of the former half of the twelfth century confirms a gift of soc-men on the Clare lands 'cum eorum humagio'.[2] But the ancestors of these men are almost certainly to be found in Domesday in a group of men over whom Richard Fitz Gilbert of Clare had acquired only commendation and partial soke.[3] The 'humagium' of the charter is certainly the commenda-tion of the Survey. Within a few years of the Survey, William, the second Earl of Warenne, is giving to the monastery of Acre four men 'et tenuram eorum cum humagiis et consuetudinibus et seruitiis cunctis',[4] which can be almost exactly paralleled in the frequent Domesday references to 'commendation and all custom'. The third Earl of Warenne gave to the same house his demesne at Snettisham 'cum humagiis et aliis pertinenciis',[5] which is in form strikingly like the Hulme manred grants. And at Snettisham, also, Prior Henry, about 1160, gave away 'terram Richardi filii Iurewi et terram Offing et terram Edild cum pertinenciis et humagiis suis'.[6] Commendation is not only part of a large contractual complex, but its Domesday prevalence reappears in the charters immediately subsequent to the Survey, which show how gradual was the process by which it was absorbed into more regular and more strictly tenurial types of subjec-tion. The Domesday references to the commended man putting himself between the hands of his lord [7] are frequently paralleled in the early charters.[8] Outside the normal 'pro homagio et servitio suo' there are many variations of formulae, some of which present the appearance of antiquity and implied quite clearly physical acts of a ritual significance.[9] Commendation, too, like the other contracts of which mention

---

[1] Stenton, *E. H. R.*, vol. xxxvii, pp. 225 seq.
[2] Harl. Charter 76, F. 35, and see Appendix I, No. 14.
[3] *D. B.*, vol. ii, fol. 395 b, and vide *supra*.
[4] Harl. 2110, fol. 2 b, and see Appendix I, No. 27.
[5] Harl. 2110, fol. 4 b, and see Appendix I, No. 28.
[6] Add. Charter 15508. See Appendix I, No. 15.
[7] Cf. Maitland, *D. B. B.*
[8] Vide *supra*.   [9] Vide *supra*, pp. 13–15.

has been made, was primarily an affair of money, and it is thus that must be explained its frequent division in this district from an early time. The well-known East Anglian eleventh-century document [1] in which Alfric Modercope bows to the abbots of St. Edmunds and Ely is paralleled both in the divided commendations of the Survey and in the divided manreds of the Hulme register in the early twelfth century. And throughout the earlier Middle Ages commendation may be regarded as but one aspect of the contractual and fiscal complex which went far to involve all East Anglian social organization in the period immediately subsequent to Domesday.

The importance of the East Anglian evidence of this wide-spread contractual movement operating throughout society lies in its unity. The early twelfth-century charters presuppose the same conditions as the Domesday Survey and clearly illustrate the great influence of contract in forming the tenurial relationships in such a loosely organized society, where the action of any form of seignorial pressure was extremely weak. It is to the same cause that must be attributed the origin of many of the later free rents, and the contractual nexus clearly modified the conditions of tenure even on the ecclesiastical lands where its operation was most restricted. Moreover, the ability to enter into new contractual relationships based upon money payments is a fair test of peasant freedom and the prevalence in Domesday of men who could go with their land, where they would be strictly analogous to the large number of peasant charters in the twelfth century, and shows the continuance of similar conditions. While, therefore, the evidence of peasant depression in this district and in this period is very strong, it would be easy to exaggerate its import. It must be remembered that for the most part it comes from the lands of the church and from the sections of the district which underwent the most rapid process of post-Domesday manorialization. The charters thus serve as a warning not to generalize too freely from the ecclesiastical

---

[1] Thorpe, *Diplomatarium*, p. 416, and cf. Stenton, *E. H. R.*, vol. xxvi, p. 231.

estates. Outside these lands, not only is the evidence of the charters and the Survey strictly similar in character, but it is no uncommon thing to find a peasant grantor in the twelfth century tracing back his tenure to the period of the Survey itself,[1] and certain rare documents have been preserved where the descent is traced without interruption back into pre-Conquest times.[2] The preservation of such deeds as these has naturally been uncommon, but the stability of individual peasant tenures in the twelfth century could often be shown, and the widespread ability of the peasantry to alienate their land in the twelfth century is itself a proof of the continued existence of the free peasant class which is so prominent in Domesday. It has been shown that there is a presumption in favour of the freedom of any man who attests a charter, and [3] the peasant witness, frequently bearing a name of English or Scandinavian derivation, is 'ubiquitous in East Anglia '[4] in the twelfth century. The very existence of such documents as those contained in the Castleacre Cartulary dealing with peasant grants and attested by witnesses of native ancestry [5] itself postulates the survival into the twelfth century of the free peasantry of Domesday, and the chaotic and heterogeneous obligations of such men as they are recorded in the St. Benet of Hulme register is also in strict accord with the evidence of the Survey. The failure of a manorial organization to fit itself on to the villar arrangements in East Anglia by the beginning of the fourteenth century also points in the same direction. And whilst it is necessary to see throughout the period a general development in the direction of depressing the status of the peasantry, whilst the causes of this can be isolated and its effects watched, nevertheless, outside the ecclesiastical lands

---

[1] Cf. the evidence discussed in *E. H. R.*, vol. xxxvii, pp. 225 seq. The character of the Castleacre Cartulary is strictly similar.

[2] Cf. *E. H. R.*, vol. xxxvii, p. 229, and the conditions in Necton soke vide Appendix I, Nos. 56, 57, 58, 59.

[3] Stenton, *Danelaw Charters*, pp. cii seq.

[4] Ibid., p. cii.

[5] Peasant witnesses with Anglo-Scandinavian names are common in the Hulme register. In the Castleacre Cartulary they occur in almost every charter, and it is probable that the application of philological tests to this register as a whole would reveal a percentage of such witnesses exceeding that of 50 per cent.

no conception of the social conditions of medieval East Anglia can afford to neglect the survival in the twelfth century of a free peasant class composed of men who were the descendants of the freemen and the socmen of Domesday Book.

This, indeed, must be considered as the distinguishing mark of East Anglian peasant history in the Middle Ages, and the cause of the peculiarities of the social organization of the district. With the modifications which such a condition inevitably produced, the broad classification of the peasantry according to rents and service seems to hold in East Anglia as elsewhere. It cannot, however, be accepted in all its details without qualification, and it resolves itself in the thirteenth century in East Anglia, as in other parts of England, into a test based upon the relation of the peasant to the manorial husbandry, so that whilst the normal criteria of peasant condition can be applied, the test of week work is here also of primary importance. This, too, supplies the interest of the movement towards commutation. That movement in this district can be watched at a remarkably early date, and in the twelfth century has already been largely responsible for the creation of a class of non-free rent-paying peasants which, however, seems also to contain elements of higher antiquity. The distinction between money rent and service is again illustrated in the development by which the geld payments of the free peasants, so minutely recorded in the Survey, became transformed on the manorialized lands into private money rents, producing at times the recorded 'ware' acre and also the close correspondence between acreage and rent so prominent in the later ecclesiastical estates. This transformation was largely the result of grants of immunity and also of a general depression of the peasantry, though in this latter respect it is necessary to distinguish clearly between the highly organized lands of the churches and the looser arrangements which prevailed on lay estates until the thirteenth century. For the main value of the East Anglian evidence of peasant status lies in the picture it gives us of a society arranged primarily upon contract. The absence in the greater part of the district of any strong seignorial control led to the formation of a contractual complex at an early date. This, it is clear, was very largely responsible for the classification of East Anglian peasants in Domesday. It is reflected in the multitude of peasant charters of the twelfth century, and even on the extented lands it was certainly in the thirteenth century the origin of the bulk of the free rents. In this respect there is a striking agreement between the testimony of the Survey and that of the twelfth century, and in general there is no reason to suppose any immediate or widespread diminution of the free peasantry of Domesday, who held their land by means of heterogeneous obligations largely contractual in their nature. No strictly manorial explanation of peasant status is adequate to explain the East Anglian conditions, which were largely dictated by the rival rights over the peasant of king and the great ecclesiastical and lay lords. But in the main, extra-manorial forms of lordship, though they frequently involved economic superiorities, were most strongly reflected in juris-dictional right, and must be considered in that connexion.

CHAPTER IV

JUDICIAL ORGANIZATION

In the formation alike of the social and political structure in the Middle Ages, a predominant part was played by judicial considerations. Legislation and the administration of justice are for the most part still indistinguishable, and not only was status determined by tenure and reflected in the payment of rents and services, but in judicial rights and obligations was also to be found one of the formative influences at work in society. This intimate connexion of jurisdiction at once with political administration and personal status, suggests that any treatment of its organization must be twofold. In the first place it is important to ascertain in what relation the institutions through which justice was dispensed stood towards the agricultural and political groups which otherwise regulated the life of the community. The position, therefore, of manor and hundred in the general jurisdictional scheme is of great importance; and of equal moment is the relation of these institutions to the owners of large 'soke' rights. Thus arise those questions which centre round the rights of the lord, his franchises and their origin, and the conflict of the royal and baronial claims. But at the other end also of the social scale the problem of the organization of 'soke' has a wide significance. The connexion of jurisdiction with status has frequently been noticed, and the fundamental importance of the legal position of the various classes of the peasantry has been duly emphasized. Perhaps, however, insufficent attention has been paid to the procedure adopted by the men of the Middle Ages in the imposition of jurisdictional obligations upon their fellows. In point of fact it may be asked what, if any, was the underlying principle actually applied in regard to liability to 'soke', and how far can the variations in such obligations be used as criteria of peasant status?

K 2

These are wide questions, and some of them may have
already been answered as well as the evidence concerning
them permits.   But it may perhaps be hoped that a review
of certain aspects of them, in the light of new evidence,
may not be without profit.   In this respect also the early
history of East Anglia has a general importance.   The main
characteristics of the society revealed in the Domesday Book
of Norfolk and Suffolk suggest the existence of jurisdictional
conditions of especial interest.   The stress laid throughout the
Survey on 'soke' and its implications, coupled with the presence of large numbers of freemen and socmen, show the
importance which such factors exercised in the growth of
East Anglian society,[1] and raise the expectation that in the
history of the district might perhaps be found an exceptionally
clear illustration of processes more obscurely at work elsewhere.
In such a loosely organized community, where for instance in
the eleventh century the obligations of the peasantry were by
no means blended in an all-embracing manorial scheme,[2] it
might be hoped that the causes of such general processes
would at times be at least partially exposed.   And whilst this
is true of the seignorial aspect of 'soke', it is even more
apparent in the relation of the jurisdictional obligations to
peasant status and the importance of these in determining the
vexed questions of freedom and servitude.

It has long since been shown [3] how the freeholder was distinguished from his fellows by the protection offered to him in
the king's courts; and we may suspect that, even in the confusion
caused by the growth of private jurisdiction, the distinction
between classes outside the manor was greater than that which
existed within it.   Of course, it is important to note that this
was the result rather than the cause of freedom of tenure, and
that during the thirteenth century there were indications that
the legal distinction might break down, either as the result
of an innovation or from the persistence of more ancient

[1] Cf. Seebohm, *English Village Community*, pp. 34, 87, 102; Vinogradoff, *English Society*, pp. 403 seq.
[2] Cf. Maitland, *D. B. B.*, pp. 66 seq.
[3] Pollock and Maitland, *History of English Law*, vol. i, pp. 357-60.

customs.[1] Yet in the actual allocation of judicial liabilities it may be suggested that no such definite distinctions were drawn, and we must not lay down precise rules for men who knew them not. But quite apart from legal theory, with which this essay is not concerned, there is always the question how far, in the actual organization of medieval English society, it was found possible in practice to follow any definite principle in the assignment of judicial obligations.

In such an inquiry the Ely extents are excellent evidence. Not only do they occasionally contain fairly full statements of the duties of individual tenants in regard to 'soke', but, what is more important, by means of a comparison they afford an opportunity of discovering traces of the modification or development of such duties during half the thirteenth century, exactly, that is to say, at a time when the judicial organization of the country was taking its permanent shape.

It must, however, be remembered that extents are usually silent as regards the detailed arrangements of the more normal jurisdictions; and in particular is this so concerning the simplest of all the judicial relationships of the peasantry—that of the individual tenants to the court of the manor to which they belong. There are, however, certain broad characteristics concerning manorial suit which the Ely Registers serve to illustrate. In 1222 all mention of obligations to suit at the manor court are omitted, with the exception of two entries.[2] And one of these is itself somewhat curious by contrast with the common 'debet sectam curie' of the later extents. At Hartest, Suffolk, in 1222, 'Johannes filius Willelmi le Rede tenet triginta acras terre pro quattuor solidis equaliter et debet sectam ad Hallemot'.[3] This furnishes an apt illustration of the statement of Maitland, that in early days the court of the manor was simply the moot of the hall, that as yet there was no distinction between court, baron court, leet, and court customary, no separation between villein and

---

[1] Pollock and Maitland, p. 359, note. Cf. Vinogradoff, *Villainage in England*, pp. 78–81.
[2] At Wiggenhall (Cott. Tib. B. ii, fol. 177 b), where manorial suit seems to be included in a complicated list of obligations, and at Hartest, vide *infra*.   [3] Cott. Tib. B. ii, fol. 194.

free courts.[1]   But, as a whole, it is the silence of the 1222 extents on the question of manorial ' soke ' obligations which is in this respect their most important characteristic.

The 1277 register presents a contrast to the earlier extents. Suit to the manor court is frequently mentioned as part of a tenant's liability.   In these later Surveys it is the allocation of the burden which is curious.   Suit to the manor court is never specifically noted as one of the obligations of the unfree ; rarely in the case of the customary tenants ; and sporadically, though frequently, in the case of the freeholders.   For instance, at Pulham in 1277, suit to the manor court is never mentioned,[2] whilst at Bridgham it is stipulated for in the case of nearly every free tenant.[3]   What is the meaning of this discrepancy ?   It cannot be said that Pulham existed without a court.   In fact, beyond the ordinary manorial jurisdiction, the Hundred Rolls show that there the Bishop possessed the assize of bread and beer, that he had both a gallows and a pillory.[4] Again, when we approach a manor such as Feltwell[5] and find there suit to the manor court sometimes specified and sometimes not, we dare not say that some of the free tenants are here specially exempted from attendance.   Beyond the free tenants there are also the unfree, who, from the mere wording of the Surveys, might have been totally free from all judicial burdens whatsoever.

A comparison of the two registers serves to explain these apparent contradictions.   In 1277 it has been noted that if suit of court seems to be allotted as a burden upon freeholders quite without method, in the case of the definitely unfree it is never mentioned.   In the 1222 Survey an almost complete silence reigns concerning the whole question. If we cannot, as has been seen, exempt those from suit of court in 1277 whose obligations are not stated, it is equally impossible to grant our exemption to those in a similar position in 1222.

[1] Maitland, Selden Soc., vol. ii, p. xviii.
[2] Cott. Tib. B. ii, fol. 184 b ; Cott. Claud. C. xi, fol. 202.
[3] Cott. Claud. C. xi, fol. 241 seq.
[4] H. R., vol. i, p. 472.
[5] Cott. Claud. C. xi, fol. 246 seq.

Turning to the seemingly haphazard notifications of the later Survey, is it not possible to see in them a transitional phase in the development of the freeholders' liability to the manor court? The middle of the thirteenth century was precisely the time when the lawyers were attempting to enforce the practice of stipulation for suit of court. The Provisions of Westminster decreed in 1259 that unless there was a special stipulation, no freeman enfeoffed by charter should in any wise be compelled to render suit.[1] At the same time it was ordained that free tenants whose enfeoffment was not by charter could not be compelled to render suit unless it could be proved to have been paid before 1232.[2] Between the dates of the two extents the conditions of the liabilities of manorial soke were for the free tenant becoming stereotyped. The legislation on the matter coincides with the period of the success of the baronial movement under Henry III, and the framers of the regulating clauses were not likely to allow them to operate against themselves. Much more likely were they, by increased stipulation and greater insistence on prescriptive right, to safeguard their own interests. This is the explanation of the curious condition of East Anglian peasant liability in the matter as revealed in the later Ely extent. All is still in confusion in 1277. At Pulham, for instance, it has not been thought necessary to stipulate for the suit. It has been felt that prescription will there suffice. ' De sectis autem quae ante tempus supradictae transfretationis subtractae fuerunt currat lex communis sicut prius currere consuevit.' [3] Very different, however, has been the case in a manor such as Bridgham. In the 1222 Survey [4] suit of court is never mentioned. It is considered unnecessary so to do. But between this and the 1277 extent have come the Provisions of Westminster and other kindred enactments. Suit of court is a valuable service, and in Bridgham the lord, even at the risk of weakening his theoretical position, has thought it profitable to stipulate for suit in each case from his free tenants. But this does not mean in any

---

[1] Provisions of Westminster, clause 1.
[2] Ibid.   [3] Ibid.
[4] Cott. Tib. B. ii, fol. 181 b.

sense that such suit was not obligatory before, in that it was not mentioned. Even in 1277 it is not mentioned in the case of the unfree tenants, who could certainly be compelled to come to court. Nor, in surveying the East Anglian manors of Ely as a whole, is this tendency towards increased stipulation confined to one manor. At Walton, ' et debet sectam curie ' is added to all the entries concerning freeholders in 1277, to none in 1222.[1] It is the same at Rattlesden,[2] at Hitcham,[3] and at Wetheringsett.[4] We have, in fact, certainly to deal with a general development, and this in the direction not of stricter but of laxer jurisdictional ties over the free tenant. The unfree shall come to court as a matter of course. In 1222 it was the same with the freeholder. But by 1277 new circumstances have operated in his favour. Already in the extents and elsewhere we have references to the dependence of the suit on the charter.[5] Soon the freeholder will be able successfully to maintain that if suit of court is neither stipulated in his enfeoffment charter nor embodied in a very limited prescription, he shall by no means be compelled to perform it. But that in practice seems still in 1277 to be a question of the future. Still, a marked development in that direction has already taken place. In 1222 the old idea of suit of court as a normal part of the rent of every free tenement seems to be assumed. In 1277 there can be seen in operation another system, which will in time mark off more definitely the free tenant from his unfree neighbour in the manor. In the Ely extents, in fact, can be seen the connexion of statute legislation with the gradual modification of peasant duties.

[1] Cott. Tib. B. ii, fol. 170 b ; Cott. Claud. C. xi, fol. 192.
[2] Cott. Tib. B. ii, fol. 177 ; Cott. Claud. C. xi, fol. 269.
[3] Cott. Tib. B. ii, fol. 173 b ; Cott. Claud. C. xi, fol. 276.
[4] Cott. Tib. B. ii, fol. 225 b ; Cott. Claud. C. xi, fol. 292.
[5] At Shipdham, for instance, a free tenant owes suit of court ' per cartam episcopi Galfridi'. Cott. Claud. C. xi, fol. 228. At Dereham a charter of Bishop Hugh is cited in the same manner. This is probably why in the manumission charters of the period the continued suit of the freed man is almost always mentioned. Cf. the interesting series of such charters in a St. Edmunds Register, Add. MSS. 14849. For example, ' Nicholaus', the son of ' Adam of Botoluesdale ', is to hold 'faciendo sectam ad curiam nostram de Redgrave sicut alii libere tenentes faciunt in eadem villa ', fol. 65 b, and the manumitted Robert Pikeham has to attend ' ad curias nostras de Ringeton generales ', fol. 64 b.

Apart from this general trend of development, the extents give little information as to the details of liability to suit at the manor court. The phrase 'debet sectam curie' conceals all else. Still, it may be suggested that here, too, some distinction between the freeholders' duty and that of the unfree can occasionally be made.

We have already noticed that at Herthyrst in 1222, one John le Rede was noted as being peculiar in the soke duties which he performed. Fifty years later the holding which was once his is still a very curious one. Another John now holds the tenement, which is described as containing 30 acres in 'Rede'. Its judicial obligations are summed up in the sentence: 'Et debet sectam curie bis in anno. Et eciam quociens opus fuit per annum pro afforciamento curie vel pro brevi domini regis.'[1] Such an elaboration finds its parallels throughout the extents of Ely and Ramsey and illustrates certain variations in manorial soke obligations.

He owes suit twice a year. The explanation seems simple, and points to a special liability to attend the exercise of the most common and the most important of all the manorial franchises, the view of frank-pledge.[2] But the details of the franchises possessed by the Bishop of Ely in Hartest show the entry to be of special difficulty and interest. For Hartest appears as exceptional as being one of the very few manors in which the bishop was not entitled to hold the view. The later register remarks of Hartest, 'Istud manerium est in comitatu Suffolch et in hundredo de Badbergh quod est in libertate Sancti Edmundi'.[3] Not a word of the extensive liberties which are quoted elsewhere. In the Hundred Rolls Hartest is repeatedly mentioned.[4] The bishop has there 'placita de vetita namii': he has there a gallows and the assize of bread and beer;[5] he has there free warren.[6] But he has *not* view of frank-pledge as he has in his other Suffolk manors

---

[1] Cott. Claud. C. xi, fol. 263.
[2] Cf. Maitland, Selden Society, vol. ii.
[3] Cott. Claud. C. xi, fol. 262 b.
[4] *Hundred Rolls*, vol. ii, pp. 142, 143, 152, 153.
[5] *H. R.*, vol. ii, p. 143.
[6] Ibid., p. 152.

—at Hitcham, at Rattlesden, at Glemsford, and at Wetheringsett.[1] Yet it may not be necessary to give up this explanation
of the six-monthly suit.   Rather it may be suggested that we
have here an explanation of the wholly unusual entry in the
1222 Survey.   The man's tenement was in ' Rede ', though
by his rent he was economically bound to Hartest.   Yet the
bishop's rights as to view of frank-pledge have been made from
some other manor to cover this man, and he is therefore noted
as owing suit for view of frank-pledge to a privileged manor
court and not to the hundred.   In 1222 he owes ' sectam ad
hallemot ' ; in 1277 ' sectam bis in anno '.   It is all one, and
shows at once the still undivided nature of the manor court
and also the curious tangle that a franchise like that of view
of frank-pledge could cause in a country as loosely organized
as East Anglia.

This is largely supposition, but we would fain see in certain
other entries the limitation of the free suit, if not to the view
of frank-pledge, at least to certain special sessions of the
manorial court.   A knight at Lyndon, for instance, owes suit
' ad curiam de Lyndon in adventu senescallus '.[2]   It is the
same with an important freeholder at Duddington.[3]   Here
again it may be suggested that we have to deal with a peculiar
obligation.   In the Ramsey manors the tenure of the view
seems to be the chief duty of the abbot's ' senescallus ', who is
hardly ever mentioned save in this connexion.[4]   Furthermore,
attendance thereat is on occasion emphasized as specially
incumbent upon certain of the free tenants.   Alexander the
monk and all his tenants attend the manor court of Upwood
for that purpose.[5]   It is the same with the monk Berengarius
at Holywell.[6]   It is possible that the record of these obligations
is in these manors the result of previous disputes on the
matter.[7]   But the inference from such meagre evidence as is
forthcoming seems again to point to the conclusion that a

---

[1] *Placita Quo Warranto*, p. 726.
[2] Cott. Claud. C. xi, fol. 46.   [3] Ibid., fol. 55.
[4] e. g. *R. C.*, vol. i, pp. 285, 286, 295, 343; vol. ii, p. 282 ; vol. iii, p. 57.
[5] *R.C.*, vol. i, p. 343.   [6] *R. C.*, vol. i, p. 295.
[7] Cf. the case of the Prior of St. Ives, *R. C.*, vol. i, p. 296, and vol. ii,
p. 282.

free tenant might well owe suit only to certain important sessions of the manor court, and that these tended to be connected with the view of frank-pledge and the appurtenant 'leet' jurisdiction which was rapidly growing up around it.[1]

The distinction drawn between the different sessions of a court and between the obligations thereto was no uncommon one in medieval practice. Besides the special meeting of the hundred court at the tourn and the view, there are abundant examples of similar conditions elsewhere. To take but one example. In the Abbot of Ramsey's honour court at Broughton there is a very clear distinction made between the six-monthly and the ordinary sessions of the court. These special meetings of what was a feudal court composed exclusively of freemen[2] were not connected with view of frank-pledge.[3] But they illustrate a similar distinction between different types of function and the different types of judicial liability. In the manor court also in the thirteenth century contrasts such as these were being made, and among them that occasioned by the holding of the view of frank-pledge was already beginning to be prominent. As the view was in theory a regality in private hands,[4] attendance could be forced to it in a more

---

[1] Cf. Hearnshaw, *Leet Jurisdiction*, p. 55. In the *Mirror of Justices* the view is still separated from the tourn, and we can suppose a similar confusion in the manor court. The transformation of the view into a system of presentment of offences was after all of slow growth.

[2] Selden Society, vol. ii, p. 53. This can be seen in the frequent references to a six-monthly suit owed to the honour court at Broughton. e.g. *R. C.*, vol. i, pp. 274, 280 ; vol. ii, pp. 36, 47, 357 ; vol. iii, p. 323.

[3] A court composed of freemen only could not exercise the view, and the Broughton court confined its activities to supervising the tenure of the view in the various manors of Ramsey. e.g. Selden Society, vol. ii, pp. 53, 64, 74. But at the same time it cannot be too strongly insisted that at the time of the extents the view with its appendant jurisdiction was not a court but a jurisdiction which could be exercised by its holder either in his private hundred court or in his manor courts, though the latter was of course the more common. The apocryphal statute 'de visu frankipleg' makes this perfectly clear. In Fleta the normal place for a private view seems to have been supposed to be a private hundred court. But even as late as the sixteenth century a writer such as Kitchin will assert that the 'Leet shall be held in any place within the precinct of the lordship where it pleaseth the lord' (*Jurisdictions*, p. 90). On these points cf. Hearnshaw, *Leet Jurisdiction*, pp. 25, 50, 72, 80.

[4] This is the view of the Edwardian lawyers, though it was resisted ; cf. Hearnshaw, *op. cit.*, pp. 19 and 50. Fleta's designation of the leet as 'Curia Regis' illustrates this view. In more modern times this is

thorough manner than for the other business of the court; and as liability to such attendance depended upon a personal obligation [1] and not upon tenure, any increasing exemptions from suit to the manor court on the part of the free tenants would not operate in this direction. Further, there are certain indications in later times that the great lords on occasion followed the procedure of the sheriff in his tourn. At the manor of Littleport, within fifty years of the last Ely extent, we find *two* juries presenting at what is now very like a fully formed court leet. On the one hand there are the 'capitales plegii'; on the other a revising second jury of twelve free-holders.[2] But such conditions must always have been rare, and we need not even at Littleport put them back into the mid-thirteenth century. At the time of the extents men did not think so clearly about the view or the leet; [3] nor were these institutions as yet perfectly blended together. Still there was but one court—the halimote. But in the apparent limitation of the 'sectae' of certain privileged free tenants to certain specified sessions of the court we can see the beginnings of the break-up of the manor court. The duties of this court were becoming sharply distinguished, and though they as yet performed by what is technically the same body, the separation of duty is already becoming reflected in the ' soke' obligations of the peasantry. Thus can be seen a stage in the separation of the later court leet. In the history of English judicial institutions it is no uncommon thing for a differentiation of function to precede the formation of a new court, and in these limitations and elaborations of peasant liabilities to suit it is probable that we can see such a process at work in the small courts of these East Anglian manors.

Sometimes also the free tenant's liability to attendance at court is more distinctly limited. John le Rede comes to court

expressed more clearly, 'suit to the leet court is suit royal and the court is proclaimed with a triple Oyez'. Maitland, Selden Society, vol. ii, p. xviii.

[1] Cf. Vinogradoff, *Villainage in England*, p. 363.

[2] Selden Society, vol. iv (The court Baron), p. 139—the court roll of Littleport for December 29, 1324. Cf. Maitland, Selden Society, vol. ii, pp. xvi seq., and iv, p. 110.

[3] Fleta, as we have seen, still separated the view and the tourn.

when necessary for its 'afforcement'. Here again he is subject to a special obligation common to many free tenants on these manors. The same condition is applied to the manorial 'suit' owed by a knight at Rattlesden on the Ely lands. The probability that 'certain of the larger franchises— e. g. that of sending thieves to the gallows—could not be exercised without free suitors ',[1] may in part serve to explain these entries. At Shipdham a tenant is forced to attend the Bishop of Ely's private hundred when thieves were to be tried.[2] In 1244 one Vitalis Engayne agrees to attend the honour court of the Abbot of Ramsey for the same purpose.[3] And the Ramsey Cartulary also shows the same principle applied to suit at a manor court. At Shitlington a knight owes suit to the court of that manor for the trial of thieves,[4] and it is the same with the lords of two sub-manors attached to Shitlington.[5]

But from another point of view this new characteristic of free suit is interesting. The free tenant occasionally is obliged to afforce the manor court whenever that court is occupied at all with pleas concerning freemen—'cum placita inter liberos fuerit motum '.[6] The notion that the hearing of cases concerning freemen necessitated in the manor court the presence of freemen thus seems to be behind many of these otherwise vague 'afforcement' notices. And in these statements of the judicial liabilities of the free tenant in the Ramsey and the Ely extents there may be seen a practical illustration of the theory that a certain number of tenants were necessary to the existence of the manor court, a doctrine that afterwards found its place in the 'arbitrary and sterile terminology' of Coke.[7] Professor Vinogradoff has shown the probable connexion of this with 'an earlier conception of the court as a court of free and lawful suitors taking in villeins and excluding slaves ',[8]

---

[1] Selden Society, vol. ii, p. lxxi. [2] Cott. Claud. C. xi, fol. 233 b.
[3] *R. C.*, vol. ii, p. 356. [4] *R. C.*, vol. i, p. 458.
[5] *R. C.*, vol. i, p. 460. [6] *R. C.*, vol. i, pp. 458, 468.
[7] Maitland, Selden Society, vol. ii, p. lxiii.
[8] Vinogradoff, *Villainage in England*, p. 396. For another discussion of the significance of the doctrine cf. Holdsworth, *History of English Law*, vol. i, pp. 69–71.

and the bearing that this has on earlier social conditions.   The
necessity of freemen in the manor court would thus need to be
considered quite apart from the conditions under which the
larger franchises were exercised, and quite apart from any
theories of ' iudicium parium ', though doubtless, as has been
seen, these also exercised an influence in the same direction.
Here, however, it may primarily be noticed how, with the
substitution of the free tenant for the mootworthy ceorl as the
essential suitor to the manor court, a new line is in practice
being drawn, marking off the suit of the free tenant from that
of the unfree inhabitants in the manor.   As yet these entries
seem to show the process was not yet complete: the future
was to show its importance.

In yet another way also was the free tenant's suit occasionally
distinguished from that of his fellows.   Again John le Rede is
a good example.   He must attend court when necessary ' pro
brevi regis '.   John is not alone in this.   On the Ely lands
at Rattlesden a knight has the same qualification made as to
his duties.[1]   On the Ramsey manors Vitalis again adds this
to the agreement which he made with the abbot.[2]   In the
higher courts, also, both of the bishop and the abbot, the same
distinction is made.   ' Pro brevi regis ' is, however, an elastic
phrase, and we may suspect that its application was varied.
It might be applied to the higher franchises.   The Bishop of
Ely repeatedly claims to exercise all the pleas which the
sheriff holds both by writ and without writ.[3]   To such pleas,
as in the case of the trial of thieves, the freemens' attendance
would be required.   But usually the writ in question must
have been the writ of right which was sent direct to the
mesne lord,[4] though again, since this writ was solely concerned
with free tenure, the obligation of the free tenants to attend
court on these occasions was in reality the same as that
involved ' cum placitum liberorum motum fuerit '.

It is this double tautology which suggests the possibility
that in this qualifying clause there is perhaps an illustration
of a more obscure process.   We have already noted the

---

[1] Cott. Claud. C. xi, fol. 271.   [2] *R. C.*, ii, p. 356.
[3] Vide *infra*.   [4] Pollock and Maitland, vol. i, p. 386.

connexion of the Provisions of Westminster with the growth of custom on these East Anglian manors. And here, too, there would seem to be another example of the occasional crystallization in statute law of a procedure but gradually evolved in scattered manors. May not these sporadic references to the king's writ indicate the special relation in which the free tenant stood not only to the curia as a whole, but also to the jury of trial as opposed to the jury of present-ment? With the advent of the inquest system into manorial court practice a peculiar situation was created in the manor court. In Maitland's words ' the lords in imitation of their royal master took to selling the right to have questions tried by inquest. But here a distinction disclosed itself between the two classes of tenants. The lord could force his villeins to swear; he could not force his free tenants to swear; they resisted and made good their point '.[1] Now this appears in the Provisions of Westminster in the following terms, which have their parallel in the Statute of Marlborough.[2] The lord, we read, ' nec iurare faciat liberos tenentes suos contra volun-tatem suam desicut nullus hoc facere potest sine precepto regis '. It is therefore suggested that in these frequent references to the king's writ in the description of the judicial liability of the free tenants we have the embodiment of the necessary royal precept which alone could secure a competent jury of trial. It is possible, that is to say, that in these some-what elaborate and confused entries of the freeholders' obliga-tions on these manors we have also the record of a successful resistance to innovations introduced by the extension of the inquest system to manorial court procedure. And the final triumph of the freeholders on this point was already by 1277, in practice as well as in theory, sufficiently assured to separate them in yet another way from the other classes of the manor in their relation to suit of court.

Whilst, therefore, the evidence of the extents is very meagre as to the details of the peasant liabilities to manorial suit,

---

[1] Maitland, Selden Society, vol. ii, p. lxvi.
[2] *Statutes of the Realm*, Statute of Marlborough, clause 22 ; Provisions of Westminster, clause 18; Stubbs, *Charters*.

which for the most part in the earlier register is unmentioned and in the later survey concealed under the vague word 'secta', nevertheless, it has been possible to see in the phraseology of the registers traces of development in the practical working of the courts on these manors. In particular it may be noted that the obligations of the free tenants are becoming limited and specialized. In some cases he will owe suit only to special sessions of the court, or only to view of frank-pledge. In others his attendance will be required specially for the exercise of the greater franchises or for the trial of his fellow free tenants, and a practical illustration is thus offered of the growth of an important judicial theory. Lastly, in the registers may perhaps also be seen the special position in which the free tenant found himself after the introduction of the inquest into the manor court. Thus in many ways through the thirteenth century a broad line of distinction is in practice being gradually drawn between the judicial obligations of the two main classes of the peasantry. The manor court is still one, and there is as yet no definite suggestion of a division of the curia itself. The same court is still the embodiment of such franchisal jurisdiction as the lord possesses; it is still but one of the many feudal courts to which the lord may require the suit of his tenant, though this obligation is in practice breaking down; and it is also still the institution by which the lord manages his estate. The court as yet embraces all these jurisdictions. But this diversity of function has already begun to reflect itself in the peasant obligations to suit. To the franchisal court as to a royal jurisdiction all men must come; at the feudal court all the tenants must be present where statute does not exempt them; from the third aspect of the court, however, the free tenants are beginning to shake themselves loose by means of a limitation in the burden of their attendance. Already the future division of the still homogeneous halimote is foreshadowed in the differentiation of the suit owed by the various classes of the peasantry. Already by 1277 in these manors the court is beginning to demand a different personnel for the discharge of its different functions.

With regard also to the suit owed to shire and hundred the Ely extents are of peculiar value, as has been shown by the late Professor Vinogradoff,[1] who has pointed out the importance of the presence of a special class of 'hundredors' in certain of the Cambridgeshire manors of the bishop. These tenants occupied a unique position in the manors to which they belonged, and though their tenure varied from place to place, Professor Vinogradoff was able to make certain generalizations concerning them. These men have tenements specially burdened with the obligation to suit at the courts of shire and hundred. And though this duty is constantly reckoned as a free serjeanty, it is not in itself bound up with free tenure, for whilst the hundredor by reason of his soke service is usually freed from all other service, only a few holdings are selected for the performance of these special duties. The interest of the class has thus been found to lie in its dual nature. It combines within itself the elements of freedom and villeinage. Its tenure is at once allied to and distinct from freeholding. As such Professor Vinogradoff saw in it an indication that 'the administrative constitution of hundred and county is derived from a social system which did not recognize the feudal opposition between freeholder and villein' and that —since this feudal opposition is a superimposition upon society—'we must look upon feudal villainage as representing to a large extent a population originally free'.[2]

In view of the importance which has been attached to the hundredor system on the Cambridgeshire lands of the Bishop of Ely, it may be useful to examine the arrangements of 'soke' obligations to shire and hundred as they appear on the Norfolk and Suffolk manors of the same fee. The name 'hundredor' does not occur, but the system remains the same, and certain tenements in the manor are specially burdened with the obligation of attendance at the courts of the hundred and county. In one case in particular we are fortunate in possessing a somewhat detailed account of the system in

[1] Vinogradoff, *Villainage in England*, pp. 441 seq.; and cf. also pp. 188 seq.
[2] Vinogradoff, *op. cit.*, p. 196.

working. Shipdham was the capital manor of the Bishop of Ely's 'hundred and a half' of Midford. And attached to the extent of the manor is a detailed account of the method by which the burden of suit to the hundred court is apportioned in the various dependent manors.[1] For instance, the suit from North Woodham to Shipdham is described in the following terms :

'Ricardus filius Willelmi unam sectam. Rogerus de Seynder unam sectam. Thomas Thurford dimidiam sectam. Ricardus de Bauaunt unam sectam. Iohannes clericus et participes sui unam sectam. Homagium constabularii unam sectam. Willelmus de Aqua et participes sui unam sectam. Homagium de Belhus in Northwodeham unam sectam.'[2]

What is at once clear from such descriptions is the fundamentally tenurial aspect of the obligation. Just as the suit was attached in the Cambridgeshire manors to the holdings of certain ' hundredors ', so here, too, it is the tenement and not the tenant from which the suit is primarily due. This merely confirms the widespread testimony of the Ramsey Cartulary and other well-known sources. At Cranfield, for instance, on the Ramsey lands, Avicia, daughter of Robert, owes suit to the hundred for one virgate of his half-hide tenement.[3] Two hides at Barton are said to be free of all service except that due to the king, save that they also render suit to shire and hundred.[4] And the same obligation is affixed to one of the two virgates which a tenant holds at Elsworth.[5] But also the Shipdham description presents an admirable illustration of Maitland's theory[6] that as these tenements split up or descended

---

[1] Cott. Claud. C. xi, fol. 226: ' Istud manerium est in comitatu Norfolch et in hundredo et dimidio de Midford quod spectant ad libertatem Elyensem et pertinent ad istum manerium domini Elyensi.' And see Appendix II. 4.

[2] Cott. Claud. C. xi, fol. 225 b.

[3] *R. C.*, vol. ii, p. 4: 'Avicia filia Roberti tenet dimidiam hydam. Pro una virgata illius dimidiae hydae sequitur comitatum et hundredum.'

[4] *R. C.*, vol. iii, p. 274: ' Duae hidae predictae liberae nihil nisi servitium Regis faciunt et sequuntur comitatum et hundredum.'

[5] *R. C.*, vol. iii, p. 300: ' Robertus filius Thurkilli tenet duas virgatas. Pro una sequitur comitatum et hundredum. Pro altera dat quinque solidos.'

[6] *E. H. R.*, vol. iii, pp. 417 seq.

to a number of heirs the obligation of attendance was not thereby increased. The actual performance of the duty was left to be agreed upon among the co-tenants themselves. From other manors of the bishop we get a very clear view of the same process. At Brandon in Suffolk, for instance, Stephen the clerk in 1277 'debet sectam hundredi secundum turnum septem percennariorum suorum . . .',[1] and in the same manor the heirs of Matilda and the daughters of Edith, Adelicia, Agnes, and Isabell 'debent sectam hundredi secundum portionem tenementi sui'.[2] Everywhere the disintegration of tenements has confused but has not increased the primitive obligations of suit to these extra-manorial courts. In what other way can the suit owed by 'Willelmus de Aqua et participes sui' or the 'homagium de Belhus in Northwodeham' be explained?

The other outstanding characteristic of these 'soke' obligations to the hundred of Shipdham lies in their 'representative' character. It is in a sense the suit of the whole manor that these specially burdened tenements are performing. Nor is this in the Ely extents confined to the Shipdham hundred court. The 'representative' character of the suit obligation is sometimes expressed in so many words. In 1222 at Walpole, Richard, the son of Hildebrond, has 40 acres for which 'debet sectam comitatus et hundredi pro manerio'.[3] In 1277 his heir performs the same suit with the same qualification.[4] This aspect of the obligation is, of course, not confined to East Anglia, but it can hardly be too strongly emphasized. In a Croyland Register taken in the early thirteenth century the manors are arranged in hundreds. Each owes so many

---

[1] Cott. Claud. C. xi, fol. 300 b.
[2] Ibid. The same process receives an admirable illustration in the Ramsey Survey of the manor of Ripton, in the following entry: 'Radulfus de Broughtone, Aspelon Pincerna, Iohannes Gernone, Nicholaus Stalkere, Philippus de Clervaus, Gilbertus Faber, Thomas filius Willelmi Textoris, et elemosinarius Ramesiensis, tenent tres virgatas et dimidiam terre quas Nicholaus Freman tenuit de Abbate pro quibus fecit homagium Abbati sectam curie de Broughton et ad comitatum et hundredum et aliqui istorum respondeant in modico servitio pro dicto tenemento per annum et alii non.' R. C., vol. i, p. 333.
[3] Cott. Tib. B. ii, fol. 167 b.
[4] Cott. Claud. C. xi, fol. 185.

'sectas' to the hundred, in some cases with curious variations in the repartition of the suit within the manors.[1] In the Ramsey Cartulary the same idea is frequently expressed. At Cranfield, for instance, Robert, the son of Christiana, holds half a hide 'et defendit villam in comitatu et hundredo'.[2] The specially burdened tenants were in a very special sense representative at the hundred of the manors in which they dwelt.

But in yet another way also does the Shipdham evidence afford the opportunity for the examination of the details of the system. In the case of the suit owed to the hundred, from the manor of Dereham and from the capital manor of Shipdham itself it is possible to compare the statement of the suit given in the account of the hundred with the statement of the incidence of the suit in the extents of the individual manors. Not only, that is to say, is it occasionally possible to note from the Survey of the hundred the tenants from whom suit is due, but it is occasionally possible to compare this with the position ascribed to these tenants by another set of jurors in the manorial extents. The importance which has been attached to the hundredors would seem to render such a comparison desirable.

In the description of the hundred court we read that the suit is owed from the capital manor by 'Iohannes ate Kote et participes sui', 'Robertus ate Buk et participes sui', 'Rogerus de Verly', 'Symo Prudbern et participes sui', 'Homagium Friuill', 'Alexander de la Rode', and the 'Homagium de Caston'.[3] Now in the extent of the manor itself there is no mention of any of these names among the free tenants. On the other hand, among the 'consuetudinarii' there is an entry as to the holding of 'Robertus filius Hugonis de Buk et Adam et Radulfus filius Petri'.[4] It is hard not to identify this with the Robertus atte Buk of the hundred court description. And it is peculiar that in the one case where at Shipdham an identification can be made between the accounts of hundred and manor, the 'hundredor' should prove to be

---

[1] Add. MSS. 5845 (Cole Transcripts), fols. 89, 90.
[2] *R. C.*, vol. ii, p. 4.
[3] Cott. Claud. C. xi, fol. 225 b.			[4] Ibid., fol. 232.

a customary tenant. The case of the suitors from Derham is also interesting in the same connexion. In the hundred court description we are told that a certain ' Ricardus Wlfketel et participes sui ' owe suit.[1] Turning to the Dereham extent we find again that no such name occurs among the free tenants. It is in the category of customary tenants that there is described the holding of ' Ricardus filius Ulfketel '.[2] Nor is this customary holding of recent creation. Fifty years earlier the same tenement was held by another Richard Ulfketel, and it was even then not a free but a customary holding.[3] But the Dereham evidence also goes to show the existence of other conditions. In the hundred court description there is mentioned one ' Hugo de Camera ',[4] and it is possible to identify this with a free tenant in the Dereham extent.[5] In another entry, also, it is possible to see an instance of a hundredor as a free tenant. Among the suitors to the hundred from Thurston is one Robert the son of Richard of Worthstead.[6] Thurston is, however, included in the Survey of Dereham, and among the free tenants therein there is described a tenement which once was the property of Robert of Worthstead and now belongs to the heirs of Richard of Worthstead.[7] Whether we identify the Shipdham suitor with the ' heres ' or Robert in the Derham Survey, it is clear that there is here another instance of a hundredor who is also a free tenant.

The evidence from the Shipdham hundred court is thus somewhat perplexing. The soke burden in these manors seems to be scattered about in a most haphazard way. A

---

[1] Ibid., fol. 225 b.   [2] Ibid., fol. 219.
[3] Cott. Tib. B. ii, fol. 204.
[4] Cott. Claud. C. xi, fol. 225 b.
[5] Ibid., fol. 215.   [6] Ibid., fol. 226.
[7] Cott. Claud. C. xi, fol. 215. The probable explanation of the reference is, of course, that the Robert of the extent is the grandfather of the Robert of the hundred court description, which is supported by the presence of a Robert of Worthstead in the earlier extent—Cott. Tib. B. ii, fol. 201. This identifies the ' hundredor ' with the ' heres ' of the extent. If it could be shown that this was not so—that hundredor Robert was not the heir of Richard but a younger brother—there would be provided an interesting case of a peculiar arrangement of the soke burden. It would imply that in this case the heir succeeded to the family tenement which, however, supported also his brothers, whilst the duty of attendance at the hundred was discharged by one of the younger brothers. But of this there is unfortunately no proof.

' tenurial ' theory will explain much, but it will not explain everything. There certainly seems no indication that the specially burdened suitors to the hundred court should be freeholders. The most that can be said of these Ely manors of Norfolk and Suffolk is that, as far as the evidence goes at Shipdham and elsewhere, the hundredor or his unnamed equivalent never seems to have been selected from the ' operarius ' or villein class. If he is not a freeholder the infer- ence is that he must be a non-free rent-paying tenant. This, again, is in the main in conformity with the general evidence of the Ramsey Cartulary. It is true that the villeins at Chatteris all in their turn perform suit to the hundred at Wichford :[1] and this represents a condition unknown on the Ely lands. But with this exception the suit to the hundred court is almost invariably[2] performed by tenants who are undoubtedly free. This is so predominantly true that it needs no exemplification. Sometimes the freedom of the burdened tenement is insisted upon in such a way as to suggest that its very freedom was bound up with the suit. John, the son of Adam, at Cranfield holds half a hide for which in the time of Henry I his father ' sequebatur comitatum et hundredum et fuit liber a servitio '.[3] The suit at Elton[4] and Upwood[5] is confined to the free class in a most striking manner. Richard at Barton holds half a hide ' quae sequitur hundredum et comitatum et fuit libera '.[6] For one part of the half-virgate which a villein holds at Warboys the tenant ' sequitur comi- tatum et hundredum et curiam de Broughtone ', but only ' si liber esset et terra libera '.[7] In general, the overwhelming majority[8] of the cases in the Ramsey Cartulary, where the suit is performed by a free tenant or, more strictly, by free land, is sufficient to suggest that the notion of the courts of shire and hundred as consisting of free suitors was still opera-

---

[1] *R. C.*, vol. i, p. 432.
[2] The doubtful cases are those at Elsworth, *R. C.*, vol. iii, p. 300, and at Ringstead, *R. C.*, vol. iii, p. 269.
[3] *R C.*, vol. iii, p. 301.   [4] Ibid., pp. 257 seq.   [5] Ibid., p. 270.
[6] Ibid., p. 225.   [7] *R. C.*, vol. i, p. 314.
[8] Besides the examples quoted cf. e.g. *R. C.*, vol. i, pp. 296, 491; vol. iii, pp. 242, 248, 261, 267, 273, 275.

tive in the thirteenth century, and in general to confirm the Ely evidence that the performance of such suit by a villein tenement was, to say the least, unusual.

On the whole, therefore, the East Anglian evidence which has been discussed, supported by certain testimony from elsewhere, has revealed three prominent characteristics of the allocation of the burden of attendance to the hundred which throughout is attached to land rather than to persons. The holders of these tenements are viewed as 'representatives' of the manors in which they live. But, on the other hand, they tend with very few exceptions to be free or rent-paying tenants. And though the fluctuation of the burden on the Ely lands between the free tenants and a class which owed its origin largely to a process of commutation dating from the twelfth century raises certain important questions as to the origin of the system, nevertheless the general exclusion of the villein class from the duty points to the permanence of the notion of the shire and hundred court as consisting of free suitors.

It is the implied opposition between the 'representative' and the free aspects of this suit which constitutes the primary difficulty of the peasant obligation to suit at these extra manorial courts in the thirteenth century. And it is suggested that this contrast is on occasion brought out with exceptional clearness in the Ely extents in the description given of the liabilities of certain tenants in relation to the shire court. There is throughout both Surveys a tendency to give a most minute definition as to the liabilities to discharge the cost of the suit. For instance, at Barking in 1277 there is a curious entry concerning the freeholders which runs as follows :

' Hubertus de Hawet et Iohannes Edus tenet quattuor acras que fuerunt Willelmi Gernegon pro duodecim denariis equaliter in termino Sancti Michaelis. Et erunt coram iusticiariis ad custum suum proprium et ceteris diebus ad custum villatae. Et debent ire cum summonitore pro districtionibus faciendis sine cibo . . .'[1]

We can fortunately find the ' antecessor ' of these two men

[1] Cott. Claud. C. xi, fol. 285.

in the 1222 Survey.[1] William Jernegon has there very distinct
judicial obligations.   Again, too, there is the distinction as to
cost.   One day he goes to court 'super custum suum'; on
other days 'reliquis diebus', 'super villatam'.   In the
extent of Pulham there is a somewhat similar entry which
describes the tenure of Richard Lord and Richard Ketelshaw
in 1222 : [2]

'Hi duo debent sectam comitatus et hundredi et debent esse[1]
coram iusticiariis super custum suum.'

In these entries we have a distinction drawn between the
two obligations of the suitor to the ordinary and to the special
sessions of the county court.   For John Edus and Hubert
Hawet can hardly have gone to meet the justices elsewhere.
But far more important is this distinction as to cost in another
connexion.   It seems possible that we have here an illustration of the limitation of liability to the suit which was imposed
upon all by the Assize legislation of Henry II.   This may be
used by analogy to throw some light upon the earlier process
by which the obligation to suit at the ordinary county court
became fixed upon a few tenements.   May it not be suggested
that all these entries refer to one and the same thing, though
it is expressed in different ways.   Let us note what these
jurors had to record as regards this aspect of judicial obligations.   In the Assize of Clarendon we find a definite new
burden laid upon the shoulders of the freemen.[3]   The older
obligation to attend the county court is becoming limited
already.   But these special sessions before the king's justices
all freemen are to attend.   'Vult etiam dominus rex quod
omnes veniant ad comitatus ad hoc sacramentum faciendum
ita quod nullus remaneat pro libertate aliqua quam habeat vel
curia vel soca quin veniant ad hoc sacramentum faciendum.'
Now in Magna Carta 1215 these special sessions were limited
to four in the year,[4] and in the reissue of 1217 to one yearly
meeting.[5]   Then in 1222 we find William Jernegon having to

[1] Cott. Tib. B. ii, fol. 230.   [2] Ibid., fol. 184 b.
[3] Assize of Clarendon, clause 8.
[4] Magna Carta, clause 18.
[5] Magna Carta (1217 reissue), clause 13.

perform one suit in the year at his own cost and the rest at the cost of the vill. Richard Lord has to go before the justices at his own cost, and the usage has survived until 1277, when John Edus goes to court 'coram iusticiariis ad custum suum proprium et ceteris diebus ad custum villatae'.

The significance of these entries thus seems clear. They all apparently refer to the relics of the essential difference drawn between the freeman's older obligation to attend the shire court and the newer liability imposed by the judicial reforms of Henry II. And if this is true, the traces of the limitation of the burden may serve by analogy to illustrate the limitation of the more ancient liability. The duty of attendance at the shire court has, as has been shown, become attached to certain definite tenements. That, however, has been a matter of time. The same course has also been followed in the case of the other obligations, laid down in the Assize of Clarendon, of all men to meet the justices. But the one has necessarily lagged behind the other. It began later so to speak. So that now, when the two duties have become concentrated on the same special tenement, there remains this difference to show their different origins. In the one case John Edus is performing a duty once obligatory on all free men, though now in practice confined to certain tenants. He therefore goes to court at his own cost. In the other case the limitation of the suit to certain holdings is of older standing. He is already going in an almost 'representative' capacity. He is therefore paid by the vill. Certainly the free tenant is in 1277 placed in a very peculiar relation to the courts of shire and hundred. As he is evading the obligations to serve as the result of his tenement in the court of the manor, so also in the other courts, where once he appeared in his position of free tenant, he is transferring his obligations to a few burdened members of his class. Already in 1277 the transfer is complete in the case of the ordinary shire court; in the case of the special shire court held before the justices it is all but complete also.

It would thus seem that in these curious entries of the liabilities of certain men to suit at the shire court there is a clear indication of the twofold nature of the status of these specially burdened tenants. Part of the suit of these tenants seems to be considered as being theoretically incumbent upon all freemen. But part also is viewed as a representative duty discharged by certain men on behalf of their fellows. There is in practice much confusion in the allocation of 'soke' burdens in these East Anglian manors. And in the thirteenth century itself it has been possible to see certain forces tending towards its increase. The growth of the notion that the burden is strictly a tenurial one and affixed to land has prevented the increase of the ' sectae ' and attached them to certain tenements. But at the same time the free tenant has been eager, and able, to limit his attendance at court. He has imposed conditions. He has introduced into the obligation a contractual element. He has also succeeded in shifting the burden on to the shoulders of a few of his number.

But the confusion does not end here. In one or two entries we can see yet another phase of this dual problem concerning suit at the hundred and shire courts. At Brandon the Bishop of Ely had a manor. In 1277 Master William, the parson, held therein one full land upon the following conditions:

' Et inveniet unum hominem ad quemlibet turnum precarium ad cibum domini ut supra. Et unum hominem in quolibet adventu iusticiarum et inquisitorum domini regis in eodem comitatu ad custum suum proprium ad perficiendum quattuor homines et prepositum.' [1]

This at once suggests an analogy to the usage described in the Leges Henrici Primi, whereby the reeve priest and four best men have to ' represent ' the vill in the courts of hundred and shire.[2] Nor, with this curious entry in mind, is it perhaps too fanciful to see some significance in the fact that the suit from Shipdham from the subject vills was frequently discharged by six men, of whom the parson was sometimes one.[3] In one of these cases the parson is one of the suitors.[4] And in another of the subject vills he owes suit, though the number

---

[1] Cott. Claud. C. xi, fol. 300 b.
[2] L. H. P., vii. 8, and cf. also viii. 1.
[3] Cott. MSS. Claud. C. xi, fol. 231 b ; cf. Appendix II, No. 4.
[4] Ibid.

six is not there made up.[1]   Such conditions are by no means
peculiar to the Ely lands.[2]   Yet it is worthy of remark that,
with all the other schemes of suit allocation, there exists on
these manors the notion that the priest and the reeve should
play some special part in the discharge of the suit of the vills.
More than this can, however, hardly be said, for the system on
these manors in the thirteenth century has been distorted
and nowhere bears the uniformity laid down in Leges.   It is
noteworthy that here we have recorded yet another system at
once 'personal' and 'representative' under which the judicial
obligations of these thirteenth-century peasants might be
arranged, a system which has the appearance in the extents
of being archaic, which presents analogies to certain twelfth-
century customs, and which even at the end of the subsequent
century, when new conditions had produced new arrangements, had not been entirely effaced.   The suit of these
manors is based upon a system of specially burdened tenements, but also there can be seen traces of two other types of
arrangement, the one founded on the notion of the liability of
all freemen to attend the courts, the other upon a representa-
tional scheme in which the priest and reeve of each vill have
a special function to perform.

The detailed illustration of this confusion upon a particular
group of manors tempts speculation as to the origin and interrelation of these various schemes.   In particular, it might be
asked how far the prevailing tenurial system was the outcome
of one or the other of the differing arrangements of the suit.
Was it created by a distortion of the suit of the reeve priest
and four best men, or was it the result of a limitation of suit

---

[1] Ibid.
[2] Cf. e. g. the well-known instances in the Ramsey Cartulary.   In
Burwell in the thirteenth century, 'Ivo clericus tenet tres virgatas terre
et sequitur hundredum et comitatum pro villa et facit inde forinsecum
servitium' (ii, p. 25).   The position of Ivo the clerk in the manor is, however, of course uncertain.   At Cranfield in the twelfth century, however,
we learn, 'Ecclesia ipsius villae possidet dimidiam hidam liberam.   Et
presbiter debet esse quartus eorum qui sequuntur comitatum et hundredum cum custamento suo' (iii. 301).   At Shillington, in the twelfth
century also, 'Ad ecclesiam pertinent quinque virgatae terrae.   Pro
quibus persona debet esse quartus homo coram iusticiis cum custamento
suo' (iii. 307).   Cf. Vinogradoff, *Villainage in England*, p. 191.

once universally incumbent upon all freemen ?   Without tres-
passing into the domain of wide general questions, it may be
suggested that here, perhaps, we have an illustration of what
may have been a general development.   What may be called
the ' hundredor ' system was the normal one on these manors,
and it may be traced back into the twelfth century, both on
the Ramsey lands [1] and in these manors themselves in certain
enfeoffment charters [2] in which the suit, according to previous
custom, is the reserved service in the granted tenement.   The
suit owed by the reeve, priest, and four best men may be seen
as early as the 'Leges Henrici Primi',though it would be easy to
read into these clauses more than they actually mean, for they
are very vague as to the application of the system which they
describe.   Beyond the Leges there is utter darkness—the
nearest approach to a kindred idea being contained in the
method by which the data for the Great Survey were col-
lected,[3] in which the reeve, priest, and six townsmen from each
vill were employed.   Before the Conquest there is not a single
unequivocal reference to the institution.[4]   The notion, on the
other hand, of the hundred and shire courts as being primarily
assemblies of free suitors can be seen in certain pre-Conquest
documents.   The common freeman in Anglo-Saxon days, in
a famous charter, was considered mootworthy as well as fyrd-
worthy and foldworthy,[5] and the moot certainly comprised the
meetings of hundred, shire, and wapentake.[6]   In the East
Anglian Domesday also the idea is prominent, and amid much

---

[1] Cf. *R. C.*, vol. iii, pp. 273, 274, 275, 277, 301, 307.   The frequent
reference to the service in the days of Henry I is itself interesting.
[2] Cf. a charter in the Ely Cartulary (Liber M, Muniment Room), by
which land is given in the time of Bishop Nigel in Straham as being
entirely free, ' salvo servicio quod ad hundredum pertinet', fol. 158.   Or,
again, Bishop Longchamp gave to the monks of Ely ' totam terram quae
fuit Radulfi clerici de Wycham quam tenuit de nostro socagio in eadem
villa'—to be held—'pro eodem seruicio pro quo idem Radulfus inde facere
solebat hundredis', fol. 168.
[3] Stubbs, *Select Charters*, p. 101.
[4] Cf. Maitland, *D. B. B.*, pp. 1, 47.   The nearest approach to anything
similar to the institution is in Edgar's Ordinances for the witnessing of
sales, but the whole is too vague to supply anything like proof.   Cf.
Vinogradoff, *Growth of Manor*, p. 191.
[5] Kemble, *C. D.*, DCCCLIII.   Cf. Vinogradoff, *Growth of Manor*, p. 273.
[6] Aethelred, iii. 3, and cf. Vinogradoff, *op. cit., supra.*

inextricable confusion it seems clear that the ' liber homo ' and the socman were regarded as being the normal suitors to the courts of hundred and shire.[1]   In Norfolk, for instance, the whole description of a hundred such as Wayland shows the tendency of the freemen and socmen to be attached to the royal manor in which the jurisdiction of the hundred lay.[2] The same is true of the hundred of Guiltcross, where the jurisdiction seems to have been attached to the manor of Kenninghall.[3]   The king, it is said, had the soke of all the freemen in the half-hundred of Diss,[4] and elsewhere there are clear indications of the old connexion of mootworthiness and fold-worthiness as characteristics of freedom.[5]   Any wide generalizations are impossible, in that the whole soke complex in East Anglia is inextricably confused by the growth and variety of private jurisdiction: but even in spite of this, the idea that hundred court is in essence the assembly of the freemen of the hundred, that the normal freeman owed suit there as a mootworthy ceorl, seems to be latent in the East Anglian Domesday.

The East Anglian evidence tends strongly to suggest that the notion of the reeve, priest, and four men of the township as the suitors *par excellence* of that township, in so far as it was ever widely prevalent, was equally with that of the

---

[1] Vinogradoff, *English Society*, pp. 91 seq.

[2] Throughout there is a strong tendency for the free elements in the population of this hundred to render their soke in the royal manor of Saham.   Sometimes this occurred in spite of attempts on the part of lords to keep the soke, and we read how Godric in Caston lost the soke of his freemen, who thereafter went to the hundred court at Saham, *D. B.*, vol. ii, fol. 126.   To Ellingham also in the same hundred used to belong the soke of six sokemen before Ralph made forfeiture.   Now we read their soke also is in Saham and the whole hundred witnesses it, fol. 126 b. Cf. also fols. 110, 227, 232 b, 252.

[3] This in spite of the presence in the hundred of a large private soke, cf. fol. 178, and in spite also of an occasional limitation of the jurisdiction to the six forfeitures, fol. 223.   The general tendency is quite clear, cf. fols. 202, 209 b, 262 b, 270 b, 277 b.

[4] *D. B.*, vol. ii, fol. 114, and cf. *V. C. H. Norfolk*, vol. ii, p. 33.   This hundred also contains the well-known distinction between the soke of those who holds 30 acres and those who hold less, the jurisdiction of the former lying in the hundred and of the latter in private hands.   *D. B.*, vol. ii, fol. 130, and cf. Vinogradoff, *English Society*, p. 104.

[5] e. g. Walsham hundred, *D. B.*, vol. ii, 129 b, and cf. *V. C. H. Norfolk*, vol. ii, p. 34.

' hundredors ' the outcome of an older notion of a general free suit to the hundred court. The scheme vaguely seen in the Leges and still dimly visible in the extents would appear to be the result of two processes. On the one hand, the general insistence upon tenure which came in with the Conqueror tended to affix the liability to the suit to certain definite parcels of land ; but at the same time, as is seen in the method by which the Great Survey was drawn up, the application of the royal inquest system to the smallest local unit of society tended to limit the suit to a few ' representative suitors '. Whether or no these representatives ever acquired a constitutional importance, whether they were ever more than the embodiment of a special royal device fashioned to meet exceptional needs, may perhaps be doubted. There is no indication that the regulations of the Leges were ever rigidly applied or that the number of the suitors from the vill ever remained constant.   And in any case, whatever may have been the extent of the application of these regulations, it may well be supposed that such arrangement shaded off very easily into the vaguer hundredor system into which they had been almost completely absorbed by the time of the Ely Register. This coalescence would be the more easy in a district such as East Anglia, where the manor and the vill seldom coincided.

In the thirteenth-century confusion in these Ely manors it appears that we can see the results of a somewhat complicated process. This development seems in the main to have been characterized by certain fairly definite phases. It starts with the conception of the courts of hundred and shire as consisting of the freemen dwelling therein. With the advent of the feudal lawyers at the Conquest the mootworthy freeman tends to surrender his position as a suitor to the free tenant ; and at the same time the burden of attendance becomes attached to various tenements irrespective of their owners. To the period immediately after the Conquest, too, it seems clear that the vill, through the action of the central government, particularly in respect of the inquest system, began to assume a less vague and more definitely ' corporate ' responsibility in the matter of the soke obligation.   Both processes thus contributed to establish in the several manors a system by which certain scattered holdings owed suit to hundred and shire, and the free tenants by their successful attempts to limit their liabilities in the thirteenth century helped to make this system permanent. Consequently, in the thirteenth century the hundredor or his equivalent is at once a representative of the vill and also he is in a sense the institutional descendant of the mootworthy ceorl. Thus, too, it is said that at one and the same time three different notions of suit to the courts of hundred and county can be seen prevailing in these East Anglian manors.

As regards manor, shire, and hundred it has thus been possible to note a certain development in the judicial organization of these manors during the thirteenth century, and in the arrangements of that century to see traces of earlier systems. Throughout we must beware of applying any too definite statement of legal obligation to a society which was governed primarily by custom, albeit a custom constantly subject to modification. What above all must be stressed is the complexity of the whole soke nexus. The peasant, and especially the free peasant, is compassed about by a great confusion of judicial obligations, and this confusion is by no means absent from the regulation of his suit to the more normal jurisdictions. But such suits represent in East Anglia but one part of the problem of judicial organization. The free tenants, and occasionally the other peasants, owe suit to other courts besides those of manor, shire, and hundred. Their soke may be rendered elsewhere. So we are told, even at the end of the thirteenth century, when the shapeless matter of actual fact is being beaten into shape by the hammers of controversy. And since in the struggle between rival theories of justice contradictory ideas were urged by the immunists on the one hand and the king on the other, it may be profitable to look at the matter from the point of view of the facts recorded in these East Anglian documents. But as it is now necessary to deal with the jurisdictional rights of the lord as well as with the obligations of the tenant, a different method should be pursued. For we must perforce inquire not only what were the obligations of the peasantry to the royal courts, but how far these

courts were indeed royal and how far the peasantry were subject
to other jurisdictions.   And in the light of recorded fact rather
than of legal theory it might be possible to trace the growth of
some of these seignorial jurisdictions which can be sometimes
observed in the controversial publicity of the thirteenth century.

Across the threshold of the question of seignorial jurisdiction lies the problem of the nature and origin of manorial
jurisdiction itself.[1]   There may be no ' direct answer ' to the
question whether this jurisdiction was the outcome of the
relation of lord to man, or the result of the inevitable
arrangements involved in the management of the open fields.
Yet the social condition of East Anglia at least allows the
examination of the contrast involved in these two views in its
most acute form.   The entire lack of coincidence between
manor and vill throughout the district must have provided a
unique opportunity for the observation of any agrarian
jurisdiction that existed, apart from the jurisdiction implied
in feudal practice.   The two aspects of manorial jurisdiction,
indissolubly blended together elsewhere, would tend in East
Anglia to separate, for the administration of agrarian custom
in the courts of several manors, each possessing perhaps a
small share in the common fields of one village, would present
almost insuperable difficulties.   If there was a jurisdiction
springing out of the soil and its management, it was the village
and not the manor in East Anglia which would exercise it.
From the general circumstances of the social organization of
the district, it might be supposed that it was no very uncommon thing for the villagers of a township such as Fincham,[2]
divided among several lords, to meet together to discuss
infringements of common custom and to adjust the agricultural
arrangements involved in common ploughing.   The absence
of any records of such proceedings save those which, like the
account of custom at Aston,[3] come from a very much later

---

[1] A well-worn subject : cf. Maitland, Selden Society, vol. ii, pp. xxxviii-
liii, and Vinogradoff, *Growth of the Manor*, pp. 193 seq.

[2] Vide *supra*, p. 3.

[3] Cf. *Villainage in England*, pp. 392 seq., and also Maitland's articles
on the survival of Archaic Communities, *Law Quarterly Review*, vol. ix,
pp. 36, 211.

date, makes any theory of such jurisdiction at the time of Domesday rest largely upon probability.

There are, however, certain definite indications that the several manor courts of an East Anglian village had at times great difficulty in coping with the jurisdiction which in its essence involved the village as a whole; and in some cases we know that it was found unprofitable to administer a village which was divided into many lordships by means of their separate courts. There is, for instance, an agreement[1] made between the lords who shared in the possession of the vill of West Rudham as to the common administration of their jurisdictional rights. In this they were going back to the only unity which had remained in the village since the time of Domesday,[2] when it had been split up among various lords, in which divided condition it remained until the fourteenth century.[3]

More definite illustrations are, however, to be found of the way in which in East Anglia a village could succeed in judicial matters in imposing its agricultural unity upon the manors within it. In the Binham cartulary there is a charter[4] by which Adam de Valognis, a grandson of Peter the Domesday tenant, gave to the church of Binham a croft, three acres of arable and one acre of meadow. This charter is first witnessed in the normal way. But afterwards we hear of another and more curious attestation, for the charter is again witnessed, this time 'in villa de Ingaldesthorp coram omni villa presente domina Beccha uxore mea et Rogero fratre meo et presbitero ipsius ecclesie de Ingaldesthorp'. A reference to Domesday supplies additional interest to this; for at the time of the Survey the village was by no means unified under one lordship. It was held in the first place by Roger son of Renaud, whose 'antecessor' there was one Turchetel, a freeman who had held 1½ ploughlands with two ploughs on the demesne and half a plough belonging to the men. And the soke had been Stigand's.[5] In Ingoldisthorpe however,

---

[1] Harl. MSS. 2110, fol. 40, and see Appendix I, No. 31.

[2] D.B., vol. ii, fols. 146, 165, 165 b *bis*, 257 b. An excellent example of a split-up East Anglian Domesday vill.

[3] *Feudal Aids*, vol. iii, p. 461.

[4] Cott. Claud. D. xiii, fol. 173, and see Appendix I, No. 37.

[5] D.B., vol. ii, fol. 266 b.

M

Peter de Valognis also held land which afterwards became the Binham manor.[1] His predecessor was one Torvert. Further, in the same village there were also T.R.W. three freemen with 38 acres of land. The foldsoke and the commendation over these had belonged to the antecessor of Peter, but Stigand had held all the other soke.[2] In Ingoldisthorpe, then, at the time of the Survey, there was concentrated a fairly complex collection of varying superiorities involving different lords. But within two generations of the Survey 'all the village of Ingoldesthorp' meets to witness a charter independently of such disintegrating rights of lordship, which could hardly within so short a time have been unified into a single seignorial control.

It is, however, with two original charters concerning the village of Nettlestead in Suffolk that we come nearer to a complete illustration of a village imposing in a semi-legal matter its unity upon the different manors within it. Late in the twelfth century, Peter Boterel gave to the church Godwin the reeve of Nettlestead.[3] The conditions of this gift are in many ways peculiar, but the most interesting point about it is that the charter is witnessed by 'tota villata de Nettlestede'. Nor is this all. We would gladly know what exactly is meant by this villar attestation; and this information seems to be supplied by a still earlier charter of an ancestor of this Peter in the same village. This is a notification [4] by an earlier Boterellus to Baldwin his reeve in Nettlestead, that this reeve and his successors in that office should pay every year to the monks of Hatfield Broad Oak priory one mark. This charter was witnessed, we are told, in 1134 by two of the 'barons' of Count Alan. But the reeve is further given instructions 'ut cartula hec in ecclesia coram tota parrochia legatur ut parrochiani omnes huius doni mei testes sint'. This supplies an instance of a rare type of attestation, 'for a village community does not often witness charters in its ecclesiastical capacity',[5] and we are forcibly reminded

---

[1] Ibid., fol. 256 b.   [2] Ibid., fol. 256 b.

[3] Add. Charters 28331, and see Appendix I, No. 16.

[4] Add. Charters 28322, and see Appendix I, No. 17.

[5] Stenton, *D. C.*, Introd., p. lxxii, and see *D. C.*, p. 270, for a comparative instance. For the early interrelation of village and parish cf. Stubbs, *Constitutional History*, vol. i, pp. 224 seq.

of the clear and intimate connexion in the Danelagh district of the church with the village as distinct from the manors it contained.[1] There can, that is to say, be little doubt that here we have a more detailed account of the witness of the vill described in the later charter—an attestation which clearly implied in fact as well as theory the presence of the villagers. But again it is by a comparison with Domesday that the full importance of these charters is brought out. Nettlestead at the time of the Great Survey was situated on the lands of Count Alan, and T.R.E. one Gouti, a freeman, held 5 carucates of land within it ' pro manerio ', which after the Conquest were held by Halanalt of the Count.[2] In the same village another freeman held 60 acres also ' pro manerio ', which Halanalt ' now holds of the Count '.[3] In ' Scarestuna '[4] also there were in 1086 three freemen who were for some reason ' included in the valuation of Nettlestead '.[5] Lastly, we are told that Ulmar the king's reeve had also encroached upon the land of one freeman in Somersham whose commendation was in Nettlestead.[6] In the time of Domesday, that is to say, Nettlestead, though more compact than many East Anglian villages, was a highly complex entity. There were at least two ' manors ' within it, and to it were attached commendation rights. Nevertheless, within fifty years of Domesday the villagers of Nettlestead are meeting together in the church of the vill to witness a charter, and in another fifty years there is record of the ' villata '—not the ' manerium '—of Nettlestead attesting to a deed concerning land within it. We have in these charters clearly to deal with the jurisdictional action of an agricultural entity quite distinct from the seignorial units it contained.

But the most striking instance of a village acting independently of the confused rights of lordship which existed therein is to be found again in the Binham Cartulary, and this time in a document which is yet nearer to Domesday in date.

---

[1] Cf. Stenton, *D. C.*, Introd., pp. lxx–lxxviii.
[2] *D. B.*, vol. ii, fol. 294 b.
[3] *D. B.*, vol. ii, fol. 294 b : ' Netlestedam tenuit Gouti liber homo T.R.E. v carucatis terrae pro uno manerio. Modo tenet Halanalt de comite. . . . In eadem i liber homo lx acras pro manerio.'
[4] Probably Sharpstone, cf. *V. C. H., Suffolk*, vol. ii, p. 436.
[5] *D. B.*, vol. ii, fol. 295.   [6] Ibid., fol. 448 b.

It occurs in a charter [1] by which Ralph the son of Thorold of Dalling gave to the monastery of Binham 10 acres of land and the service of Peter his nephew. He then explains :

'Hanc donationem feci pro anima Petri de Valognis qui eandem terram de conquestu Anglie patri meo in hereditatem dedit.'

This gives a very early date to the deed. It is thus of considerable interest to find that this charter is witnessed by 'all the village of Dalling'. Turn now to Domesday. On the lands of Peter de Valognis we read that in Dalling one ' liber homo,' Fisc, held one ploughland there, and there were also five sokemen, and the soke of the whole was in the king's manor of Foulsham.[2] Under Walter Gifford there were in Dalling also three ' liberi homines ' with 70 acres of land. Of these also the king had the soke.[3] And under William of Warenne there were five ' liberi homines '.[4] At the time of the Survey, that is to say, Dalling was occupied by fourteen freemen, the rights over whom were shared by the king, William of Warrenne, Walter Gifford, and Peter de Valognis—magnates who lived far away and had no personal interest in the vill. Yet within a generation of the Survey the whole vill of Dalling is witnessing a charter. The village is acting as a unity quite independently of the individual seignorial rights within it. Have we not here something very near to a sense of unity sufficiently strong to enable the village not only as a village to witness a charter—a definite juristic act—but also to regulate its own economic business ? Save the vill there was no other unit of husbandry in Dalling; none in Domesday; none even in 1316 when the village is shown to be even then divided into four lordships.[5] The only unity is to be found in the village itself, and within a generation of Domesday the village can and does act in a semi-judicial capacity.

In East Anglia there are then not wanting instances of villages imposing their agricultural unity upon the manorial

---

[1] Cott. Claud. D. xii, fol. 12.   See Appendix I, No. 36.
[2] *D.B.*, vol. ii, fol. 258 b.   [3] Ibid., fol. 241.
[4] Ibid., fol. 157 b.
[5] *Feudal Aids*, vol. iii, p. 465.

and seignorial judicial arrangements, and the distinction in manorial jurisdiction between those rights accruing from husbandry organization and those implied in the feudal contract is made especially clear. Nor need we hesitate to see in the former type of jurisdiction something clearly in East Anglia pertaining to the village rather than to the manors which it contained. And it only became part of the manorial procedure as the villages were very slowly and artificially subjected to a single manorial control. It is hard to see how the management of the open fields could continue without some sort of regulation, and this in East Anglia could not have been performed through the small manors. On the other hand, we have had proof that early in the twelfth century the village had even then acquired sufficient 'self-consciousness' to witness a charter; and it seems likely, therefore, that such jurisdiction as was later implied in the mere possession of a manor, in so far as this was dictated by husbandry conditions and concerned with their management, came into the hands of the lords not through the exigencies of manorial organization, which even until the fourteenth century never fitted completely on to the agricultural units, but from the village, which alone was the unit of corporate husbandry and alone possessed the common fields in their entirety.

The testimony of twelfth-century vills which in Domesday were divided up among many lords is an important factor in the explanation of many of the problems connected with medieval East Anglia. It also raises several important questions of general interest. The old problem of the existence of the village court appears in a new light by a comparison of these charters with the survey of a district in which the manor and village were very far from coincident. It has been held that the township was 'too automatic to be autonomous and too homogeneous to be highly organized',[1] and the rarity of the word in the Anglo-Saxon laws[2] has been con-

---

[1] Maitland, *Township and Borough*, p. 36. Cf. also p. 35: 'If our villages had remained lordless they might have exhibited in time the decisive symptoms of corporate unity.'

[2] Maitland, *D. B. B.*, pp. 349-51, and cf. p. 21. Cf. *Law Quarterly Review*, January, 1893.

sidered to be of great weight in the case against the existence of a moot or a court pertaining to the vill. On the other hand, again, it has been urged that the arrangements involved in the fields of the village presupposed some regulation of the customs of husbandry which could only be supplied by the existence of some sort of court, however crude.[1] The reference to the 'tunscipemot' in Richard I's charter,[2] though significant, is by itself insufficient to prove anything. But the conditions of East Anglian eleventh-century society, where the village, as distinct from the manor, was the unit of agriculture, suggest that here, if anywhere, traces of such village arrangements might be observed. It seems certain that the attestation described in these early charters actually took place in the very presence of the villagers; and the step from a meeting of the villagers in order to perform a juristic act to the existence of a village court is not a difficult one in times when mens' notions of 'personality' were of the vaguest. And if such a meeting or such a court of the village, irrespective of the disintegrating influences of many concurrent seignorial superiorities, could assemble to witness a charter, it is hard not to conclude that it could and did also so do in order to manage those common economic arrangements which were the sole basis of its unified existence. Without arguing too closely from the more to the less definite, or endowing 'archaic communities'[3] with more modern attributes, it may certainly at least be said that this East Anglian evidence gives considerable additional support to the case for the existence of a pre-Conquest village court in England.

And upon another general problem of early manorial juris-diction these charters seem to bear somewhat directly. The origin of the presenting jury in the court baron for the purpose of the detection and punishment of offences against agrarian custom has been held to lie in the imitation by the manorial lords of the royal procedure instituted by the Assize of Clarendon.[4] Whilst Maitland's conclusions as to the origin

[1] Vinogradoff, *Growth of the Manor*, pp. 194-6.
[2] Cf. Stubbs, *Constitutional History*, vol. i, p. 90 *n*.
[3] Maitland, *Law Quarterly Review*, January, 1893.
[4] Maitland, Seldon Society, vol. ii, pp. xxvii seq.

of presentment at the tourn seem to be final, it nevertheless
seems by no means a necessary consequence of this that the
similar employment of the frank-pledge system for the same
purposes by the manorial lords was also necessarily the result
of this.[1] The blend of the agricultural and jurisdictional
aspects of the sokes of the Northern Danelagh has already
been used as evidence in favour of this suggestion, and the
same is true in the case of the sokes of East Anglia. The
appearance in these early charters of witnessing villages and
of the unity imposed by common husbandry conditions and
juristic activity also point to the same conclusion. What is
more likely, then, that on coming into possession of a village
accustomed to manage its own agricultural affairs, and finding
there not only this economic autonomy, which is reflected in
these charters, but also the frank-pledge system, the lord
blended the two institutions for the regulation of manorial
custom in the same way as the king later co-ordinated them
for the purposes of criminal justice. The origin of the presenting jury of the later court baron is very far from being
proved to lie in the Assize of Clarendon.

There is little doubt that the jurisdictional rights of the
manorial lord in East Anglia as the predominant member of
an agricultural community had their origin in the village
rather than the manor, and the important part played by the
village in the early development of judicial organization is
well illustrated in the documents of this district. Beyond the
possession of such ' agrarian ' jurisdiction the lord might of
course possess certain special rights and regalities. On these
the extents tend to dilate and to supply a mass of detail, most
of which is inconclusive. The rights, for instance, of the
Bishop of Ely may be regarded as typical of those of a large
franchise in East Anglia. As a rule his manors are exempt
from the jurisdiction of the hundred when that hundred is in
their hands. Bridgham, for example, was in Shropham
hundred, which was held by Robert of Chateshall. But in
that manor the bishop had ' libertatem suam et de furcis tum-
berellis visum franciplegii bussellorum lagenarum et huiusmodi

[1] Cf. Stenton, *English Social and Legal Studies*, vol. ii, p. 27.

aliarum mensurarum et de omnibus placitis que vicecomes potest placitare tam per brevem domini regis quam sine brevi '.[1] This may be regarded as the normal statement of the bishop's manorial franchises, and the same statement with very small modification is repeated in the case of Northwold,[2] Wetheringsett,[3] Hicham,[4] Barking,[5] Brandon,[6] and Feltwell,[7] and in the last two instances the additional note is added, 'sicut ad alia maneria similia'. Such were quite typical rights of a great lord in his manors when these were situated in the hundred of some other lord. Strictly similar rights had the Abbot of Ramsey in his East Anglian manors.[8] Sometimes, as in Hartest[9] and Glemsford[10] in Suffolk, the bishop had a more limited jurisdiction, but on the whole it might be said that the manor of Bridgham represents his normal franchisal rights in his manors. Such judicial rights in East Anglia seem to present no peculiar characteristics and to be in conformity with conditions throughout England.

More interesting is the question of the higher feudal courts which such franchises tended to produce on the lands of the great immunists. The Abbot of Ramsey's court at Broughton has been made the classical example of such a court.[11] But it seems probable that the Bishop of Ely held a similar court at Ely, which he called his council, and to which cases could be reserved from his manor courts.[12] The existence of this court is also reflected in the suit owed by certain tenants in the extents. In this sense will a tenant at Straham in 1256 owe 'sectam hundredi per totam annum ad quodlibet hundredum et

---

[1] Cott. Claud. C. xi, fol. 240.　　　　　[2] Ibid., fol. 250.
[3] Ibid., fol. 291 b. For Wetheringset see also *P. Q. W.*
[4] Cott. Claud. C. xi, fol. 275 b.
[5] Ibid., fol. 284.　　　[6] Ibid., fol. 249 b.　　　[7] Ibid., fol. 246.
[8] Cf. *R. C.*, vol. i, pp. 113, 114.
[9] Cott. Claud. C. xi, fol. 262 b.
[10] Ibid., fol. 255.
[11] For the whole matter of the court at Broughton, see Maitland, Selden Society, vol. ii, Introduction.
[12] Selden Society, vol. iv. In the court roll of the manor of Littleport a dispute is referred to a given day 'apud Ely ad curiam ibidem ad audiendum iudicium suum'. And again in another dispute a day is given to the disputants 'apud Ely coram domino Roberto de Maddingele et Iohanne de Canto et aliis de consilio domini ostensuris si quid pro se habeant vel dicere sciant'.

sectam ad curiam de Ely et de Stratham '.[1] In 1277 a knight
at Duddington owes ' duas sectas per annum ad curiam de
Ely '.[2] Such glimpses as we can obtain of the honour court
of Ely suggest that its character and organization were similar
to that of the Abbot of Ramsey at Broughton, and the arrangements as to honorial jurisdiction on these manors seem to have
been in no way peculiar.

But while these aspects of honorial and franchisal jurisdiction present in East Anglia the same appearance as elsewhere,
there is one phase of seignorial judicial organization which in
this district is exceptionally prominent. The Danelaw provinces provide in Domesday the best evidence for the discussion of all ' soke ' organization in so far as that organization was
distinct from the more normal manorial machinery. And in
relation to the Danish provinces East Anglia occupies a peculiar position. The scattered and varying obligations of small
groups of freemen and socmen, who would often pay their
judicial liabilities to different lords and could frequently ' go
with their soke where they would ', have no parallel among
the counties of the Northern Danelaw.[3] The confusion thus
caused in the whole social nexus can hardly be exaggerated,
and it has been well emphasized in a famous book.[4] The
liability to render soke was frequently involved in, and often
contrasted with, the other relations of man and lord, both
in connexion with commendation [5] and with economic subjection; [6] and the criteria which governed such liability
were fluctuating and irregular. The sporadic appearance
of vendible soke [7] suggests that here, too, on occasion we have
to deal with arrangements which were often in their essence
contractual. The full explanation of these confusing ' soke '
liabilities has probably yet to be found. What may, however,
here be stressed is that this peculiar description of East Anglian

[1] Coucher Book (Ely Muniment Room), fol. 15.
[2] Cott. Claud. C. xi, fol. 55.
[3] For a general comparison of East Anglian and Danelagh conditions
see Stenton, *Oxford Social and Legal Studies*, vol. ii, p. 39.
[4] Maitland, *D. B. B.*, pp. 66 seq.
[5] Cf. *D. B.*, vol. ii, fol. 207, and cf. *V. C. H.*, *Norfolk*, vol. ii, p. 29.
[6] Vide *infra*.
[7] Maitland, *D. B. B.*, p. 100.

society was not due to any mere terminological eccentricity of
the Little Domesday. A sharp line within that book can be
drawn between the Survey of Suffolk and that of the adjoining county of Essex.[1] And what is more important, the
East Anglian soke confusion is reproduced in the documents
of the century immediately after the Conquest. From the
early charters of St. Benet of Hulme it is clear that the acquisition of personal soke rights was still in process, and these
documents show also ' that seignorial justice was a privilege to
the tenant as well as a source of profit and influence to the
lord '.[2] Moreover, an original charter [3] of the last quarter of
the twelfth century shows how such arrangements still persisted at that date. By this deed Maino, the prior of Castleacre Priory, grants to a tenant the land that had once been
held by one ' Wreghe Scule '. Among the conditions of the
grant it was stipulated ' Et si placitum aut uerbum aliquod inter
predictum Alanum et homines suos surrexit quod ipse Alanus
per se terminare non poterit et ante nos pervenerit medietas
placiti nostra erit et alia medietas sua '. It is clear that the
division of the profits of soke over individual peasants, which
is so characteristic of the East Anglian Domesday, persisted
on occasion well on into the twelfth century. And it is certain
that the Domesday descriptions of these confused peasant
liabilities represented actual conditions which were of a permanent nature, and mark off the district in a jurisdictional as
well as an economic sense from the Northern Danelagh.

The exceptional conditions in these counties render it
important to discover whether this soke nexus was ever
arranged in East Anglia upon anything like the definite plan
which was adopted in the Danelagh proper, and to what extent
it is possible to find in East Anglia, besides a confusion of
heterogeneous obligation, the permanent existence of units of
private jurisdiction analogous to the great sokes of Lincolnshire. The territorial aspect of soke is connected with, though
distinct from, the personal,[4] and whilst it is the latter which is

---

[1] Vinogradoff, *English Society*, p. 94.
[2] Stenton, *E. H. R.*, vol. xxxvi, p. 225.
[3] Topham, *Charters*, p. 15, and see Appendix I, No. 20.
[4] Vinogradoff, *English Society*, pp. 120 seq.

stressed in the East Anglian Domesday, it is necessary to ascertain to what degree the former also contributed to the social organization and development of the district.

In this connexion the very exceptional judicial complex which centres round Bramford in Suffolk at the end of the thirteenth century is of peculiar interest. The 1277 extent of this opens with the following note:

'Istud manerium est de perquisitione Domini Hugonis episcopi et in comitatu Suffolch et in hundredo de Bosemere. Sed quidam de forinsecis socmannis manent in hundredo de Claydone. Et habet in re libertatem scilicet tol et team et infongenthef visum francii plegii et furkas tumberellum et visum et iudicium lagenarum et aliarum mensurarum, taurum liberum et verrum liberum. Ita quod nullus alius in manerio et in sokna potest hec habere nisi solus episcopus. Et similiter breve recti magnum et parvum et liberam warennam suam in toto manerio et bestias estratas que vocantur waif.'[1]

Later in the extent we learn that soke was owed to this manor from no less than fourteen vills,[2] the incidence of the suit being assigned separately to the various individual vills in question.[3] Then follows a list of the 'forinseci socmanni' themselves.[4] These are described for the most part as possessed of quite small holdings. In two cases[5] they can be identified with tenants holding land in the Berking extent, and this comparison tends to suggest that they varied greatly in their wealth and position. The descriptions both of the dependent vills and of the 'forinseci socmanni' are added to what otherwise would have been the extent of a normal manor.

Now it is clear that we are here brought face to face with

---

[1] Cott. Claud. C. xi, fol. 305.
[2] Westerfield, Whitton, Thurlston, 'Charesfeld', Claydon, Summersham, Hemingstone, Esk, Tudenham, Stonham, Olden, Blakenham, Battisford, Barking.
[3] Cott. Claud. C. xi, fols. 311–12, and see Appendix II, No. 4.
[4] Cott. Claud. C. xi, fol. 312.
[5] In those of Hubert of Berking and John Edus (fols. 284 b–285). The case of John Edus is a very good instance of the accumulation of soke obligations on the lands, and the very small lands, of a single peasant. This small peasant owes suit to the court at Bramford and to the manor court at Berking. He owes suit probably to Bosemere hundred and certainly to the Suffolk county court.

an organization highly exceptional in the thirteenth century. At the first glance, in view of the magnitude of the jurisdiction, we are tempted to suppose that here we have another example of a hundredal jurisdiction in private hands. A closer examination proves this to have been quite impossible. Not only is the judicial unit described in the extents quite different from that noted at Shipdham, but the very fact of much of the suit being owed from Claydon hundred invalidates the suggestion that at Bramford we have to deal with a private hundred court. In a royal inquisition taken in 1316 the Bishop of Ely is recorded as possessing Bramford, but the hundred is said to be in the king's hands and to be administered by his sheriff.[1] Bosemere was never one of the five hundreds which belonged in Suffolk to the Bishop of Ely,[2] and the description of this hundred in Domesday also shows that its court was not connected with the manor of Bramford.[3] We therefore seem faced in this late thirteenth-century extent with an active soke court on the ancient model.

It is in the past history of Bramford that the chief interest of this curious thirteenth-century organization lies. And it is therefore fortunate that it is possible from other documents to reconstruct this history in considerable detail. In the Ely Cartulary there is an interesting series of charters relating to Bramford. In the first of these[4] Henry I gives to the Bishop of Evreux ' manerium de Brantfort et xl solidatos in sochemannis in Claiendone hundredo et in Bosemere hundredo '. The presence of the sokemen in these two hundreds at once shows the connexion of this grant with thirteenth-century organization. The further history of the jurisdiction can also be seen in the Cartulary. Henry I's charter is confirmed by Stephen,[5] Henry II,[6] and Richard I.[7]

---

[1] *Feudal Aids*, vol. v, p. 35.
[2] *D. B.*, vol. ii, fol. 385 b ; *R. H.*, vol. ii, p. 197.
[3] Vide *infra*.
[4] Ely Cartulary (Muniment Room, Liber M), fol. 80. See Appendix I, No. 60.
[5] Ibid., fol. 83.   [6] Ibid., fol. 88.
[7] Ibid., fol. 90.

Then there is a new charter of Henry III,[1] by which that king confirms to the Bishop of Ely the manor of Bramford, which the Bishop of Ely has bought from the Bishop of Evreux. This charter also mentions the earlier grant of Henry I, and further it shows clearly that the Bishop of Ely has bought not only the manor but also the jurisdiction, for in this grant, too, the sokemen are mentioned, and with them the elaborate if vague judicial privileges involved in the possession of Bramford. This charter is dated at 1247. Nine years later, in the Coucher Book of Ely,[2] the jurisdiction is described in almost the same terms as we have found it in the later extent of 1277.

We can thus see this soke organization at work continuously through the twelfth century as far back as the time of Henry I. What of Domesday Book? In the Survey the manor of Bramford is on 'terra regis',[3] as might be expected from the mention of the 'little writ' in the thirteenth-century extent. Before the Conquest it was held by Stigand,[4] and it passed thence into the king's hand. In the light of the Ely evidence we can see beneath the terminology of the Survey that Bramford was in 1086 the centre of a large organization, and that this was substantially the same as that described in the thirteenth-century Register. Following the Bramford entry and in the same paragraph there are described the king's lands in four vills. These are all from their position dependent upon Bramford, and the tenants of one of them are noted as being in 'soca regis'.[5] All these estates are held by freemen. The next entry is concerning the hundred of Claydon, and therein is a freeman holding 30 acres whom Ulmar the reeve has added to 'the king's farm at Bramford'.[6] Most important of all is the fact that all these five vills, the tenants in whom are described in these entries as being dependent upon Bramford,

---

[1] Ibid., fol. 113. See Appendix I, No. 62.
[2] Coucher Book (Ely Muniment Room).
[3] *D. B.*, vol. ii, fol. 281 b.   [4] Ibid., fol. 289.
[5] In Blakenham, 'ix socmanni de dimidio carucatae terre in soca regis', fol. 281 b.
[6] Claindune Hundredum, 'In Haminghelanda i liber Aluuinus commendatione Guit xxx acris ... Ulmar prepositus adjunxit hunc liberum hominem ad firmam regis de Bruntford,' fol. 282.

are among the dependent vills in the thirteenth-century extent.[1] It may be further noted, also, how throughout the description of the hundred of Bosemere a distinction is drawn between land held 'in soca regis' and the soke which belongs to the king and the earl. This latter is the hundred jurisdiction which was probably exercised through the manor of Mendlesham.[2] The king's soke with one small exception is always mentioned in this hundred in connexion with an estate held in one of the vills dependent in the later extents upon the manor of Bramford. Nor is this all. A curious section of the Suffolk Domesday is concerned with the 'terra Vavassorum'.[3] This is entirely composed of entries concerning places in the hundreds of Bosemere and Claydone. There are sixteen such entries. With the exception of two, every one of these concerns an estate in one of the dependent vills of the later extent.[4] All describe the holdings of freemen and socmen, save that in one a burgess of Ipswich is mentioned.[5] The intimate connexion of these men with the king and also with Bramford is also made clear. Four freemen are said to have been added to the farm in King William's time.[6] One is more specifically described as having been added 'to the king's farm at Bramford'.[7] In the Bosemere entries two separate estates are said to lie 'in soca regis',[8] whilst in the Claydon description three are given as being held 'in manu regis'.[9] We are also told that in the hundred of Claydon there are thirty freemen, twenty-nine of whom are mentioned by name.[10] These men the sheriff holds 'in manu regis', and the same is true of two other freemen in another of the dependent vills.

---

[1] Blakenham, Summersham, Olden, Stonham, Hemingstone.
[2] Cf. *D. B.*, vol. ii, fol. 285, in the description of Stonham—though the passage seems to me obscure. But cf. *V. C. H.*, *Suffolk*, vol. i, p. 424.
[3] *D. B.*, vol. ii, fol. 446.
[4] Hemingstone (3), Olden, Thurlston (3), Battisford, Claydon, Whitton, Westerfield (2), Coddenham (a part of Olden). The unidentified places are 'Facheduna' and 'Cratigas'.
[5] At Thurlstone, fol. 446 b.   [6] At Olden, fol. 446.
[7] At Hemingstone : 'Ulmar prepositus adjunxit hunc liberum hominem de Brumford.' Cf. the entry already quoted on fol. 281 b.
[8] At Hemingstone and 'Facheduna', fol. 446.
[9] 'Isti supra in manu regis,' fol. 446 b.
[10] Fol. 446 b.

Altogether it has been possible to find all of the subordinate vills of the Ely Register in Domesday, and all except three have proved in the Survey certainly to contain estates in a close and peculiar relation to Bramford.[1] In short, Bramford at the time of Domesday seems to have been a large administrative unit held together partly by money payments and partly by judicial ties.[2] It consisted of a central manor in which were contained villeins, bordars, and a serf,[3] and also of widely scattered dependent estates held by freemen and sokemen who were attached to the central manor by rents and jurisdictional obligations. It was administered partly by the direct action of the king's officials and partly through the medium of the king's vavassors, who probably were smaller tenants-in-chief.[4] And what is the most significant fact of all, this ' soke ', itself a complex institution, continued in spite of two changes of ownership as a working unit without essential modification until the last quarter of the thirteenth century.

The exceptionally full character of the Bramford evidence suggests that the territorial soke was in East Anglia anything but a moribund institution at the time of Domesday. The widespread prevalence and the permanent nature of such a type of social organization would, if proved, be of considerable importance in determining the forces at work in the twelfth century in the formation of a more rigid seignorial control over the scattered ' free ' elements of East Anglian society. Fortunately, too, there is a certain amount of evidence to show the strength of such institutions in the centuries subsequent to Domesday. The essence of a soke was after all its court, and

---

[1] Thus of the names in the Ely Register. Westerfield appears in this way on *D. B.*, vol. ii, fol. 446 b; Whitton on *D. B.*, fol. 446 b; Thurlston, fol. 446 b; Claydon, fol. 446 b; Summersham, fol. 281 b; Hemingstone, fols. 281, 446; Coddenham (? Tudenham), fol. 446 b; Stonham, fol. 281; Olden, fols. 281, 446; Blakenham, fol. 281; Battisford, fol. 446. The unidentified places are ' Esk ' and ' Charesfeld '. The history of Berking is fairly obvious. In *D. B.* it is one of the considerable manors of the Bishop of Ely in Bosemere hundred, and was probably added to the soke of Bramford after Henry III's grant.

[2] The variations of the terms ' firma ' and ' soca ' suggest this.

[3] *D. B.*, vol. ii, fol. 281 b.

[4] On vavassors see Vinogradoff, *English Society*, pp. 62, 73, and *V. C. H.*, *Suffolk*, vol. i, p. 401.

the ability of a soke to witness charters may be taken as an indication of its active existence. There are scattered through the cartularies a not inconsiderable number of charters and agreements witnessed by the sokes which they concern, and sometimes specifically ratified in the presence of the soke court. These are sufficiently important to deserve a detailed examination.

Among the Lewes charters in the Public Record Office [1] there is one which dates from the twelfth century and describes a grant made to that priory by Walter the son of Sernebrune. It concludes with the remark 'Hanc venditionem feci coram socna de Hecham . . . Teste socna et multis aliis'. This charter presupposes a very definite 'soke' organization at Heacham. In the thirteenth century, also, this organization can be seen in working in two charters in the Lewes Cartulary. In the former [2] an agreement between Alan of Ingoldisthorpe and the monks of Lewes is witnessed by the 'soca de Hecham'. In the latter [3] a convention between Osbert the Dean of Lewes and Ranulf de Kalli is witnessed in the normal manner and then ratified 'coram socha de Hecham'. In Domesday Heacham is described as being on the lands of William of Warenne, and to the manor belong thirty-five sokemen. [4] There is thus clear evidence that this soke at Heacham continued in working from the time of Domesday to the thirteenth century.

To Massingham, also, in the thirteenth century there was a soke attached, for a gift to the Priory of Castleacre was then witnessed by 'tota soca de Massingham'. [5] This case is also curious by comparison with Domesday. For Massingham is divided into two portions which are somewhat difficult to distinguish in the Survey. Both appear as centres of wide jurisdictional rights. The former, in which subsequently lay the manor of St. Benet, [6] was in Domesday Book a royal

---

[1] P. R. O. Misc. Books, A. 75/4. See Appendix I, No. 24, and cf. Cott. MS. Vesp. F. xv, fol. 251.
[2] Cott. Vesp. F. xv, fol. 251, and see Appendix I, No. 54.
[3] Cott. Vesp. F. xv, fol. 284 b, and see Appendix I, No. 52.
[4] *D. B.*, vol. ii, fol. 163.
[5] Harl. MS. 2110, fol. 21 b, and see Appendix I, No. 30.
[6] Cf. Blomefield, *Norfolk*, vol. ix, pp. 1, 13.

manor [1] to which belonged twenty-five socmen, and ' from this manor were wanting twenty-five socmen who T.R.E. belonged there " cum omni consuetudine " ', and also fourteen freemen and twelve villeins whom Ralph Baignard had taken away. There are various tenements in Great Massingham mentioned sporadically throughout the Survey, and the soke of two [2] of these is in the king's manor. Little Massingham was also the centre of a soke. This was held in Domesday by Count Eustace, and to it in Harold's time were attached twenty socmen who were handed over with the manor.[3] A royal inquisition of 1316 [4] shows both the Massinghams reckoned as one village in the hands of three lords, and we may fairly see here, too, the continuation of a pre-Conquestual soke through the twelfth century.

Wendling also appears as a soke in the thirteenth century, and as a soke it witnesses a quit-claim in the Castleacre Cartulary.[5] The interest of this example is that there is in the Domesday Survey nothing to suggest a soke connected with that vill, which appears as a manor of St. Edmunds to which but one sokeman is attached.[6]

Two other charters in the Castleacre Cartulary offer a further illustration of the post-Domesday East Anglian soke. One of these [7] is witnessed by the soke of Rudham. In another a quit-claim is witnessed after fourteen other names by ' pluribus aliis de soca de Baggethorpe '.[8] In Domesday Bagthorpe is part of a large organization which is attached to West Rudham, and it is described as a berewick of that manor.[9] In all, there are six outlying estates of West Rudham, comprising a population of some forty-six sokemen. Both West Rudham and Bagthorpe passed together into the possession of Castleacre,[10] so there is no doubt that both these

---

[1] *D. B.*, vol. ii, fol. 109 b.   [2] Ibid., fol. 173 and fol. 222.
[3] Ibid., fol. 151.
[4] *Feudal Aids*, vol. iii, p. 449.
[5] Harl. MSS. 2110, fol. 103, and see Appendix I, No. 34.
[6] *D. B.*, vol. ii, fol. 209 b.
[7] Harl. MSS. 2110, fol. 39 b, and see Appendix I, No. 32.
[8] Harl. MSS. 2110, fol. 55, and see Appendix I, No. 33.
[9] *D. B.*, vol. ii, fol. 169 b.
[10] Blomefield, *Norfolk*, vol. vii, pp. 40, 152.

charters are referring to the same organization which persisted from the time of Domesday to the thirteenth century.

Evidence similar to that for Rudham and Bagthorpe is supplied by an original charter[1] concerning a gift of land in 'Stanlond' in the early years of the thirteenth century. At the end of the list of witnesses to this we are told that the ratification took place 'coram soca elmhamie'. Referring back to Domesday[2] we learn that Elmham was held by William the Bishop of Thetford in 1086, and was then a large organization held for a manor and 8 carucates. To it were attached twenty-four sokemen whose soke Stigand had once possessed, though now they render it in Mileham. There is also a dependent berewick at Beetely which consists of 1 carucate. The whole was worth the·large sum of thirty-six pounds. The reappearance of this organization in the early thirteenth century is thus of considerable importance in illustrating the permanence of the territorial soke in this district.

A more remarkable illustration of a large and complex soke hidden under the confused terminology of the Little Domesday is, however, afforded by a comparison of the Survey with an early charter in the St. Benet of Hulme Cartulary.[3] By this charter Thomas, who was abbot of that house from 1175 to 1186, notified a gift of $10\frac{1}{2}$ acres of land, and the charter is witnessed by 'tota soka de Houetone'. The relation of the Domesday descriptions to this document is very striking. Hoveton St. John, to which the charter refers, is mentioned no less than six times in the Survey. It appears prominently in the description of the lands of St. Benet of Hulme,[4] and in the account of the manor we are presented with a normal manorial estate to which are attached one sokeman with 28 acres and seven sokemen with 110 acres. Elsewhere we read that at Belaugh[5] there are two sokemen, one of whose soke belongs to St. Benet, and ' $10\frac{1}{2}$ ' more who have passed to the abbey

[1] Campbell Charters, i. 12, and see Appendix I, No. 18.
[2] D.B., vol. ii, fol. 191 b.
[3] Cott. Galba E. ii, fol. 65 b, and see Appendix I, No. 50.
[4] D.B., vol. ii, fol. 218 b.
[5] Ibid., fol. 218 b.

from Ralph Stalra who held them T.R.E. The whole of
Belaugh is in the valuation of Hoveton. At Wroxham, also,[1]
there are four sokemen who belong to Hoveton. These
also Ralph gave to St. Benet in King William's time. The
whole of ' Estuna '[2] is also included in the Hoveton valuation,
and was probably a berewick of that manor. On the lands
of William of Warenne at Hautbois[3] there is one sokeman
also belonging to Hoveton through the gift of Ralf, and two
more sokemen who belong to St. Benet, though their connexion with Hoveton is not specifically noted. Again, on the
land of Ralf de Bellofago there is another sokeman, this time
again in Belaugh.[4] He also belongs to Hoveton. But his
fortunes have been more chequered. For though Ralph
Stalra again gave, Eudo took away, and now Ralph de
Bellofago has got possession of him. Lastly, it is perhaps
worthy of note that in the vills on the land of the same Ralph
and in the same hundred there are numerous sokemen of
St. Benet, though their connexion with Hoveton is not stated.[5]
Altogether in the light of the later charter we can thus see a
soke centreing round Hoveton in the scattered Domesday
references to that vill, and this organization persisted till it
makes its appearance again as an active organization about a
hundred years after the Conquest.

But probably the most interesting evidence of East Anglian
soke organization in the period immediately subsequent to the
Survey is to be found in four very remarkable charters in
the cartulary of the house of Warwick. Two of these charters[6]
were granted by Ralph de Toeni, a Norfolk Domesday tenant-
in-chief, and two by his son and heir Roger de Toeni.[7] Roger
de Toeni was alive after 1130,[8] so that these charters cover the
dark period which lies between the Survey and the middle of
the twelfth century. They concern the great Toeni estate in
Norfolk which centred round Necton. The charters of Ralph

---

[1] Ibid., fol. 217 b.　　　　　　[2] Ibid., fol. 218.
[3] Ibid., fol. 159.　　　　　　　[4] Ibid., fol. 229 b.
[5] Cf. entries concerning Scottow, Skeyton, Hautbois, on the same folio.
[6] Add. MSS. 28024, fols. 183, 183 b, and see Appendix I, Nos. 56, 57.
[7] Add. MSS. 28024, fol. 183 b, and see Appendix I, Nos. 58, 59.
[8] Cf. Round, *Feudal England*, p. 177.

are addressed to ' omnibus de soca Neketoine tam Francis quam Anglis' and to ' omnibus hominibus suis de soca de Neketoine presentibus et futuris'. Those of Roger to 'omnibus suis hominibus tam Francis quam Anglis' and to 'toti socce de Neketon'. In two of the documents the soke appears as a witness in the midst of a list of testators. And the charters throughout give the impression that the whole organization is extremely active. In Domesday itself the great extent of this soke is made plain.[1] After the notice of Necton in the Survey there follow the notices of no less than twenty estates belonging to Ralph. These lie in nine different hundreds. The lands in the hundred of Greenhoe, where lay the capital manor, we are told were bound to Necton by payment of commuted food rents. All the estates in the other hundreds are specifically noted as being ' included in the valuation of Necton'. In the case of this soke we are thus dealing with an extremely large and complex institution, which nevertheless persisted as an active unit into the twelfth century.

The combined testimony of these documents is sufficient proof of the continued existence of the territorial soke in the period subsequent to Domesday ; and it seems quite clear that this type of social organization cannot in any way be considered as a sporadic survival at the time of the Survey, but that in East Anglia the soke remained in the twelfth and thirteenth centuries an important factor in the social structure of the district. A comparison of these documents with the record of Domesday also serves to throw some light on the general characteristics of the territorial soke in the period after the Conquest.

The absence of the word soke in its territorial significance in the East Anglian Domesday in many cases where we have later record of its existence[2] suggests that sometimes we have to deal with a development which must be relegated to post-Conquest times. Frequently we have in the Survey

---

[1] *D. B.*, vol. ii, fols. 235–236 b.
[2] Cf. throughout the reluctance with which the Little Domesday uses the word in its territorial sense, and note also especially the case of Wendling.

merely a description of the socman holding frequently of many different lords. And whilst the close connexion of the personal and territorial aspects of soke must always be borne in mind, nevertheless it is important to note in East Anglia the absence of anything like the rigid classification of estates into the categories of soke, manor, and berewick which runs through the Survey of the Northern Danelagh.[1] But on the other hand, though the presence in East Anglia of the socman who could go where he would with his soke remains the mark which distinguishes the two types of social organization, yet on occasion the Domesday notices of social complexes, which afterwards appear as sokes, sometimes suggest that the difference was on occasion largely of method in description. However, conditions in East Anglia were in the main undoubtedly more loosely organized, and it is quite possible sometimes to see in the twelfth-century soke the result of a consolidation of earlier and more chaotic arrangements. The territorial conception of 'soke' is the product of a more rigidly organized society than the personal, and the tendency in East Anglian post-Conquest history was in the direction of the general consolidation of scattered rights into definite institutions. The socman who could go where he would soon drops out of East Anglian society. But the socman forming part of a large territorial unit remains, and it is natural to see in him the institutional descendant of the men who in the Little Domesday are described as being personally subject to soke. In one case we can see the transition between the two ideas, which were never very dissimilar. At Brockley three freemen are described as being unable to sell their soke, but two others there were who could sell their soke only within the soke of St. Edmunds.[2] From another point of view also the same development may be seen. Gifts of sokes we know were no uncommon thing in twelfth-century Yorkshire,[3] and in Suffolk the twelfth-century gift of Bramford shows

[1] Cf. Stenton, *O. S. L. S.*, vol. ii.
[2] *D. B.*, vol. ii, fol. 349, and cf. Vinogradoff, *English Society*, p. 131.
[3] Cf. the remarkable charter of Henry I which enjoins that certain churches are not to lose their parishes 'propter socas quas inde dedi quibusdam baronibus meis', *Y. C.*, No. 428.

how a private soke could be formed by the gift of men in two hundreds who previously owed their soke to a royal manor. On the whole, it may be said that there was a tendency in East Anglia after the Conquest to create out of the scattered obligations of freemen and socmen not only compact manorial estates but also the territorial soke. In this district, just as it is quite incorrect to think of the soke as being a decaying institution in the time of Domesday, so also is it impossible to limit the origin of sokes to pre-Conquest times.

But undoubtedly in the soke we are dealing with what frequently, and perhaps usually, is a pre-Conquest institution, and it is the peculiar value of certain of these documents that through them we can trace the development of these often large and complex organizations through the period of the Conquest. In Domesday alone the comparison of the T.R.E. and the T.R.W. entries shows how frequently a soke was taken over by the conquerors as an existing unit.[1] It is reasonable to suppose that the soke of Elmham was not unconnected with the ancient bishopric; and at Hoveton the soke of St. Benet of Hulme was clearly a pre-Conquest institution possessed by Ralph Stalra and given to the Church about the time of the advent of the Normans. But at Necton we can see this continuity much more clearly marked. In the two generations subsequent to the Survey we have noticed this organization in full activity. Turning to Domesday, we have also seen there the extent of this great soke. But Domesday also shows how this institution existed in the time of Harold, whose property it was, and that it had been taken over by Ralph de Toeni with little or no modification. The basis of at least part of the soke lay in the payment of food rents to the capital manor by the subordinate estates, and this also suggests an institution of some antiquity.[2]

---

[1] To take but two examples, Wymondham, fol. 137 b, and Costessy, fol. 144 b.

[2] *D.B.*, vol. ii, fol. 235 b, 'Hoc totum simul reddebat H(aroldo) vi noctes de firma. Modo reddit lx libras ad pensum', and cf. also the note in the description of Fransham, 'Modo eam habet Radulfus de Toeni ineketuna ubi iacuit T.R.E.' Throughout the whole complex appears from the Survey to have been taken over from Harold.

It is clear that the Conquest made little or no difference to the internal organization of this soke; and what is far more striking is the fact that the charters show how little the individual tenants in the soke were affected by the great political change. In one of these documents [1] Ralph de Toeni, the Domesday tenant, describes how one Richard alienated his land 'que fuit Bunde aui sui et Ade patris sui ', and the grantee, it is added, is to hold that land ' ut aliquis predecessorum suorum illa melius vel liberius tenuit '. A clearer example of the continuity of pre-Conquest tenurial conditions into Norman times could scarcely be afforded, and it agrees with the similar evidence which has been brought forward to show how conditions on the lands of St. Benet of Hulme remained for the tenant substantially the same from the period immediately preceding the Conquest.[2] There was much ' invasion ' taking place, yet apart from this within the great ecclesiastical lands the conditions of the peasantry remained substantially unchanged between ' the day when King Edward was alive and dead ' and the beginnings of the twelfth century. And it is interesting to find that at Necton we have an instance of a soke also being strong enough to preserve its form and its conditions of tenure throughout that troubled period. The soke in East Anglia seems frequently to have been a pre-Conquest institution which preserved its characteristics despite the changes of the Conquest, and in the documents concerning Necton we have an admirable illustration of how complete such a preservation could be.

That the soke in East Anglia, as elsewhere, was primarily a jurisdictional institution is brought out very clearly in these documents. The witnessing of a charter by a soke would seem to imply the meeting either of the men or the court of the soke, and it is no uncommon thing for this attestation to be specifically described as taking place ' coram socna '.[3] When Ralph de Toeni proclaimed to the soke of Necton that a transfer of land had been made ' coram me ',[4] he could hardly

---

[1] Appendix I, No. 56.
[2] Cf. Stenton, *E. H. R.*, vol. xxxvii, pp. 225 seq.
[3] Appendix I, Nos. 24 and 18.   [4] Appendix I, No. 56.

refer to any other occasion than a meeting of the court of that soke. There are several instances of courts appearing as witnesses in twelfth-century Danelagh charters.[1] And the address of the Necton charters to the whole soke presupposes its active and common interest in the jurisdictional affairs which these charters discuss. Bramford in the thirteenth century was an operative judicial entity. It does not, therefore, seem too much to suggest that this series of witnessing sokes which stretches from the morrow of the Survey to the thirteenth century conclusively proves the continuous existence of active judicial units taking a prominent place in the jurisdictional organization of the country.

But these sokes appear also very strikingly in another light. Not only were they in East Anglia units of jurisdiction, but from these documents they seem also to have been units of agriculture and economic units also. The importance of the money payment in the organization of the soke is shown by the prominence which it assumes in almost all the documents relating to sokes. There seems to be no break in the development which ended in the later use of the word 'socage' as implying a money rent.[2] Already in the twelfth century the word is being used in a sense very nearly akin to this. And although due weight must always be given to the conception of justice as being primarily fiscal, nevertheless it seems impossible to account solely by this for the predominantly financial privileges which always appear to be involved in the possession of a soke. It is thus that with Bramford are bestowed 'lx solidatas socmannorum',[3] or that the third Earl of Warenne will give to Lewes '1 solidos de sochagio'.[4] Of the origin of these money rents much has already been said, and the soke organization probably represented but one aspect of development which had also been taking place elsewhere. Nevertheless, in these sokes certain peculiar arrangements may be observed. The bond which attached a man to

---

[1] Cf. *D. C.*, pp. 459, 460.
[2] Vinogradoff, *English Society*, p. 125, note I.
[3] Vide *supra*, and Appendix, Nos. 60, 62.
[4] Cott. Vesp. F. xv, fol. 19.

a soke was usually of a highly contractual nature and usually also implied a money rent. Ralph de Toeni, within his own soke of Necton, will pay one of his tenants money in return for hunting rights, whilst the tenant himself is paying a money rent.[1] In many cases we may suspect that the characteristic payments within the soke are the result of public royal duties in money or in kind which have been transferred to private hands with the soke itself. The farm of Bramford was of very considerable importance in Domesday, and probably originally formed the basis of the rents of the 'forinseci soc-manni' after the soke had passed into private hands. At Necton, too, we have an example of the same process. All the Greenhoe manors of the soke rendered Harold six nights' farm. Now they pay 60 pounds by weight. The repartition of such a commuted burden among the various tenants would, after the soke had passed into private hands, result as we have seen [2] in something very like a money rent rigidly based upon the amount of acreage held.

But in a more fundamental manner is the soke in East Anglia economically consolidated as an agrarian unit. The whole description of Rudham and its dependencies shows a manor with scattered berewicks as well as sokemen attached thereto, and the Elmham Domesday description is very similar. It was indeed the agrarian aspect which later came to be pre-dominant in the surviving sokes in this district, just as elsewhere the soke of Rotheley [3] was primarily an agricultural organiza-tion, and the Bishop of Ely's sokes at Duddington [4] and Summersham [5] were agricultural as well as judicial units. The latter was a coparcener as a soke in the intercommoning rights of a wood.[6] In East Anglia, as elsewhere, the details of such

---

[1] See Appendix I, No. 57.   [2] Vide *supra*.

[3] *Archaeologia*, vol. xlvii, pp. 99 seq.

[4] Cott. Claud. C. xi, fol. 64: 'Item sciendum quod unusquisque anilepiman et anilepiwoman de tota sokna de Duddington debet venire ad magnam precariam autumpni ad cibum domini.'

[5] Cott. Claud. C. xi, fol. 96 b.

[6] Cf. *Hundred Rolls*, vol. ii, p. 605: 'Summersham cum sokna . . . et in dicto manerio i magnum boscum in quo quidem bosco homines propin-quarum villatarum ut Wardeboys Wodehirst Woldhirst Sancti Ivonis Nidigworth et Haliwell communiant omnes suas bestias cum sokna de Summersham tenet.'

organization varied greatly. For instance, in the soke of Costessy [1] there was a blend of the ordinary manor consisting of a home farm and tenant land, with an administrative dependency stretching over a wide area. At Heacham [2] and Wymondham [3] the manorial centre seems to have played a more important part in the agriculture of the soke, and in both, as at Elmham, the presence of large numbers of bordars attached to the home farm and probably holding small portions of demesne land testifies to the importance of the centre of an administrative area enriched by the tribute of the scattered estates. At Necton, again, whilst the manorial centre is of considerable importance, the main value of that large complex must have lain in the food rents and tribute accruing from the satellite berewicks. In short, in spite of the different terminology of the East Anglian Domesday, there seems no reason to doubt the existence of the various types of Danelagh soke in this district also.

In another way also do the soke arrangements of East Anglia and the Danelagh invite comparison. Professor Stenton has shown how, in the Survey of the Northern Danelagh, a contrast is made between ' inland ' and ' sokeland '.[4] This is analogous to the distinction drawn in the south and west between ' inland ' and ' warland ',[5] which, as has been seen, is reflected in East Anglia in the fiscal contrast between the geld payments made by the manor proper and those of the freemen and socmen.[6] The distinction of the Danelagh Domesday also appears in the Liber Niger of Peterborough as between ' dominium ' and ' soca ', and it appears from a comparison of the two records that the term ' inland ' is frequently reproduced

---

[1] Cf. Vinogradoff, *English Society*, p. 316.

[2] *D. B.*, vol. ii, fol. 163 b. : 'Hecham tenuit Toche liber homo T.R.E. Semper vii carucae in dominio et lxx bordarii et xii acrae prati et vii caruca hominum. . . . Hic iacent xxxv socmanni (cum) i carucata et dimidia terrae. Semper vi carucae iii acrae prati.'

[3] *D. B.*, vol. ii, fol. 137 b : 'Wimundham tenuit Stigand T.R.E. iv carucatis terrae. Semper lx villani et l bordarii et viii survi Semper iiii carucae in dominio Tunc lx carucae hominum modo xxiiii. Huic manerio iacebant T.R.E. lxxxvii socmanni modo tantum xviii.'

[4] *O. S. L. S.*, vol. ii, pp. i seq., from which the following description of Danelagh conditions is entirely taken.

[5] *Op. cit.*, pp. 6 seq.

[6] Vide *supra*.

by the vaguer and equivocal 'dominium'.[1]　The Peterborough antithesis is rare in the Survey, but it does occur, and once takes the form of a contrast between ' in soca ' and ' in dominio aule ', which appears to be the correct extension of the phrase.[2] Elsewhere, too, the word 'aula' appears as taking the place both of 'inland' and 'dominium'. Whatever may have been the rights implied in the possession of a ' dominium' in Domesday, it is clear from the evidence from the Northern Danelagh that there is a distinction drawn between these rights and the vaguer privileges involved in the possession of soke, and, secondly, that the word ' dominium' is occasionally being used to cover not only the manorial demesne in the narrower sense but also the lands of the tenants in contrast to the estates over which the lord has only judicial and seignorial rights.　It appears, therefore, that this notion of ' dominium ', which ' was fully established by the time of Bracton ', ' is carefully defined' in the Dialogus de Scaccario, and ' underlies the arrangement of the Liber Niger of Peterborough ', was employed also in the Domesday of the Northern Danelagh.[3]　As the consequences of this doctrine were somewhat important as regards peasant status, it is of some interest to discover how far the distinctions observed by Professor Stenton in the Danelagh are to be found also in the East Anglian district at an early date.

In East Anglia it is impossible outside the geld arrange- ments to find any such categorical contrasts, but in this district also there seem to be traces of similar ideas governing the administrative arrangements of the sokes.　Leaving aside altogether the many references to the demesne of the Church which stand by themselves, there are not a few cases where the word ' dominium' appears in early documents with the same sense as the Danelagh 'inland'.　In an early charter of St. Benet of Hulme six acres of land are described as being held ' de dominio aule ',[4] which at once suggests comparison

---

[1] *D. B.*, vol. i, fol. 283.　See Stenton, *op. cit.*, p. 12.
[2] Stenton, *loc. cit.*　　　　　　　　　[3] Ibid.
[4] Cott. Galba E. ii, fol. 55, and see Appendix I.　Cf. also Cott. Galba E. ii, fol. 64.　Note also the curious use of the word in the account of the same survey of Roger Bigod's invasions on the lands of the same house. *E. H. R.*, vol. xxxvi, pp. 227 seq.

with the Nottinghamshire Domesday entry. A phrase in a twelfth-century charter of the same house also makes a contrast between the rights which a lord enjoyed over his socmen and those which he exercised over his manorial tenants.[1] But perhaps the most interesting individual example of the early use of 'dominium' in this sense in an East Anglian document is to be found in a very curious charter of Henry I [2] to one of the Domesday subtenants of St. Edmunds.[3] In this deed the term 'dominium' occurs four times, never in the normal restricted sense and once in direct contrast with the lands of the knights and socmen, with the meaning normally given to it in the Peterborough Black Book. It is not without importance to note how a charter concerning the lands of a Domesday tenant in East Anglia can already make the emphatic distinction between the possession of 'dominium' and that of knights and socmen, and use the word throughout, not in its common restricted Domesday sense but with the wider meaning attached to it in later days. But it is in a series of Suffolk entries in the Survey itself that we come nearest to the Danelagh use of the term. A number of these, indeed, make such a pointed contrast between the possession of 'soke' and the possession of 'dominium' that it is hard to believe that the distinction was not intentional.[4] From many

---

[1] 'Terras landsettorum et terras leuicias et socmannos,' Cott. Galba E. ii, fol. 33.

[2] Cambridge University Library, Liber Niger Sancti Edmundi, fol. 96, and see Appendix I, No. 63.

[3] *D. B.*, vol. ii, fols. 358 (Rede), 359 (Cockfield), 368 (Layham), 369 (Whatfield).

[4] This distinction is made frequently throughout the Suffolk *D. B.*, vol. ii, fols. 296, 296 b, and 297 are good examples. Here are to be found, e. g., the following entries. 'In Brantham Goduinus liber homo xxxv acras pro uno manerio tempore regis Euuardi et tenuit Goduinus de comite.... Modo tenet comes in dominio. Soca in Bercolt.'
'Pereham dimidium hundredum. In soca abbatis de Eli. In Wanttesdena xvi liberi homines dimidii subcommendati antecessori Malet et dimidii commendati abbati de Eli et in soca eius omnes.... Modo comes in dominio. In eadem Eduin liber homo xiii acras ... Comes in dominio.'
'In Blachessala tenet Brotho liber homo xii acris et valet ii sol'. Comes in dominio. Soca abbatis.'
'In Wantesdena tenet Oslac liber homo iii acras et valet vi den'. In eadem Edilt liber homo viii acras et valet xvi den'. Modo comes in dominio. In Blachessala Uluricus liber homo iiii acras et valet viii den'.

points of view, indeed, it seems probable that the direct relation in which the free peasantry stood to the royal geld was
strictly paralleled in the position occupied by these men in the
internal administrative arrangements of the sokes themselves.
And whilst in East Anglia the contrast is never rigidly applied
in the definite Danelagh sense, yet it is clear at least that the
word ' dominium' was already in Domesday and in documents nearly contemporary therewith in this district used with
its later extended meaning, and that the proprietary rights
involved in its possession were in the Survey sharply contrasted
with the less rigid superiorities enjoyed by a lord over the
tenants subjected to his soke. And without applying later distinctions too emphatically to the Domesday conditions, the
apparent presence as early as the time of Domesday of a doctrine
which denied to the lord in respect of the men of his soke the
rights which he exercised over the men of his ' dominium'
may contribute materially to the explanation of the chaotic
and ' free' position which the freemen and socmen occupied
in these counties.

Throughout, therefore, it seems that in the East Anglian
soke we are dealing with an institution which is not in any
sense to be regarded as a mere survival in the time of Domesday, but one which played during the subsequent centuries an
important part in the social life of the district. The soke
frequently had an economic or agrarian basis, but it was held
together primarily by the judicial ties which bound its
members to its lord, and there seem to be traces of a sharp
distinction being made between these and the more extensive
rights involved in the possession of ' dominium'. In its origin
it can sometimes be traced to post-Conquest times, but more
usually it seems that we must regard the soke as a pre-
Conquest institution. The relation of the soke to the hundred,
therefore, is of some importance. One aspect of this relation
has already been noticed in the definite connexion which the

In dominio. Soca abbatis. . . . Gliemham tenet in dominio supradictus
Edricus et pertinet in Chetelberia et valet xl denarii. Soca abbatis . . . In
Sternxsfelda Osbern' liber homo T.R.E. xxiiii acras . . . Modo Comes
in dominio. In eadem ii liberi homines additi viii acris et dimidia et
valent xviii den' in dominio Soca abbatis.'

free elements of society succeeded in maintaining with the
hundred court. From another point of view, however, it may
be noticed that the East Anglian sokes present a contrast to
those of the northern Danelagh. There, we have been taught,
'it was unusual for an important soke to extend beyond the
borders of a single wapentake or group of adjacent wapen-
takes', and 'highly exceptional for any wapentake to include
more than a single soke of wide extent '.[1] Such was not the case
in East Anglia. Thus, for instance, in Forehoe hundred there
are the two sokes of Gurth and Stigand at Costessy and
Wymondham,[2] and Necton soke lay in no less than nine
different hundreds. In spite of this it would be rash to
conclude that the gift of hundredal jurisdiction had nothing
to do with the formation of the East Anglian soke. Such
gifts were by no means infrequent in the early history of
the district. St. Edmunds, for instance, in Suffolk held soke
over eight and a half hundreds, and the same county contained
the famous five hundreds of St. Etheldreda.[3] Occasionally
we may suspect another development in the formation of the
private soke which is connected with the hundred. In East
Anglia there is a constant tendency for the soke of all
unattached freemen to be regarded as the king's;[4] and the
grant of such jurisdiction to private individuals within one or
two hundreds may have sometimes been the origin of the
soke. The soke of Bramford probably took its origin in such
a grant of men in the hundreds of Bosemere and Cleydon.
But on the whole it would seem that the interrelation between
the soke and the private hundred was in East Anglia far less
strong than in the Danelagh proper. Perhaps this may be
accounted for by the artificial character of the East Anglian
hundreds,[5] and it is somewhat significant in this respect that
one famous gift of a soke in East Anglia did not coincide

---

[1] Stenton, *O. S. L. S.*, vol. ii, p. 44.
[2] *D. B.*, vol. ii, fols. 137 b and 144 b ; cf. *V. C. H.*, *Norfolk*, vol. ii, p. 33,
and vide *supra*.   [3] *V. C. H.*, *Suffolk*, vol. i, p. 387.
[4] *D. B.*, vol. ii, fol. 185 ; cf. *V. C. H.*, *Norfolk*, vol. ii, p. 33, and Stenton,
O. S. L. S., vol. ii, p. 45.
[5] The whole arrangement of the geld suggests this, and there are also
other indications of the same thing. Cf. *V. C. H.*, *Norfolk*, vol. ii, p. 5,
and *Suffolk*, vol. i, pp. 358, 359.

with the hundred it purported to grant.[1]   Still, the hundred in East Anglia was in the time of Domesday a very real unity. It could witness the transfer of land [2] and give judgement on private rights.[3]   It could have a common pasture.[4]   And while it seems necessary usually to give the soke an origin in this district independent of the grant of hundredal jurisdiction, it would be highly unwise to push this too far as an indication of the recent formation of the East Anglian hundred.   Nevertheless, the presence of the *leet* and the important part it played in East Anglian geld calculations in Domesday very strongly suggests that the hundreds of the district were of peculiar composition, and it is at least a plausible hypothesis that the leets represented early hundreds.[5]   On the other hand, it seems probable that these leets, like the similar 12-carucated hundreds of Lincolnshire, may have been connected with certain peculiar agrarian arrangements [6] which

[1] The wording of the later confirmations of the jurisdictional right of the abbey of Ramsey on Clackclose hundred with the original grant by Edward the Confessor is interesting.   In the later documents the jurisdiction is always referred to as consisting of the hundred to which sixty-four socmen ' within Bichamdich' are attached.   Cf. e. g. *R. C.*, vol. i, p. 241 ; vol. ii, p. 95.   This compares very curiously with the phrases used in the Confessor's charter, where that king gives the jurisdiction in the following words : 'Volo etiam ut soca quae est infra Bichamdiche in omnibus ad sanctum Benedictum pertineat . . . Volo preterea ut sancta Maria et Sanctus Benedictus et abbas et fratres Ramesiae habeat socam in omnibus super omnes homines qui sunt motwrthi ferdwrthi et foldwrthi in illo hundredo et dimidio cuiuscunque homines sint', *R. C.*, vol. ii, pp. 73-6.   From a comparison of these two terminologies it seems clear either that the original grant was of a soke which was not coterminous with the hundred or that the hundred itself was modified in form after the charter.   Of these the latter seems the more reasonable conclusion.

[2] This is common throughout the Little Domesday.   Note also the importance in this connexion of the witness of a twelfth-century 12-carucated hundred in Lincolnshire, *D. C.*, pp. 93, 94.

[3] The best example of this again is the well-known Brungar case, Maitland, *D. B. B.*, p. 104.

[4] Cf. the case of the hundred of Colneis in Suffolk, *D. B.*, vol. ii, fol. 339 b ; cf. *V. C. H., Suffolk*, vol. i, p. 359.   It is interesting to note in this connexion how in the Ramsey hundred of Clackclose in the thirteenth century a villein's threshing is confined within the hundred in which he lived.   *R. C.*, vol. i, p. 365.

[5] Corbett Tribal Hidage, *E. H. R.*, Trans., vol. xiv, p. 213.

[6] Vinogradoff, *English Society*, p. 103.   The importance of this theory is increased by the unity of the 12-carucated hundred as shown in the witnessing hundred of the twelfth century.

have been discovered as being common to the two districts.[1]

But apart from such theories of origin, it is in this connexion that the early social history of East Anglia throws light not only on the various types of private jurisdiction but also upon a general problem concerning the judicial history of medieval England. It is well known that the word 'leet', which was 'somewhat suddenly adopted by the lawyers for the purpose of expressing . . . the distinction between the delegated royal jurisdiction and the properly feudal jurisdiction',[2] 'seems to spread outwards from East Anglia'.[3] This may be said to be a late thirteenth-century development.

It has also been shown how the Domesday geld payments in that district were apportioned in a peculiar manner. For each pound owed by the hundred the villa within the hundred paid so many pence. But for this repartition an intermediate unit was used; and the hundreds were subdivided for the geld payments into approximately equal parts which usually each contributed either one Danish 'ora' or two shillings to the hundred's pound.[4] Two headings in the Norfolk survey show that these units were termed 'leets'.[5] Between this geld-paying entity of the eleventh century and the wholly different judicial unit which came into prominence towards the end of the thirteenth, the sole connecting link has been the extent which, according to Jocelyn of Brakelonda, Abbot Samson drew up and called his 'Kalendar'.[6] The portion of this 'Kalendar' which has survived relates to the hundred of Thingoe in Suffolk,[7] and, as Dr. Round has pointed out, it

---

[1] Vide *supra*.

[2] Maitland, Seldon Society, vol. ii, p. lxxiv. This note still remains the best source of information.   [3] Ibid.

[4] *V. C. H.*, *Suffolk*, vol. i, pp. 360 seq., and *Norfolk*, vol. ii, pp. 5 seq. Cf. analysis of the geld payments at the end of the Domesday translations in the *V. C. H. of Norfolk and Suffolk*.

[5] *D. B.*, vol. ii, fol. 119 b, 'Hundredum de Grenehoe de xiv letis', and fol. 212 b, 'Hundredum de Clakeclosa de x letis'. Cf. Round, *Feudal England*, p. 101.

[6] Vide *supra*, and cf. *Memorials of St. Edmunds Abbey*, vol. i, p. 234 (Rolls Series).

[7] This is printed in Gage, *History of Suffolk*, pp. xii seq. Miss Lees also incidentally mentions a reference to a leet in a twelfth-century cartulary of St. Edmunds. (*E. H. R.*, Jan. 1926.)

'gives us the names of the twelve leets into which that hundred was divided'.[1] What is also interesting is the fact that these leets of Abbot Samson's book are not merely geld-paying units, but also units of jurisdiction which owe suit to the hundred and have a separate suit of their own.[2] By the end of the twelfth century, in Suffolk the leet is no mere arbitrary arrangement of vills for geld-paying purposes, but a judicial unit also. Thus in this curious term we have to deal with a fiscal division of Domesday, with the judicial and fiscal unit of Abbot Samson's register, and with the judicial 'leet' which emerges into the full glare of fourteenth-century publicity. Between each of these there is an interval of about a century, and each form appears to present individual and distinct characteristics.

The widespread prevalence of the leet in later times renders it in the highest degree desirable to ascertain the connexion between these three isolated and different applications of the term in East Anglia. From two points of view the problem of the leet has already been touched upon. On the Ely manors it has been shown how the alteration of the suit obligation of the tenantry prepared the way for the break-up of the manor court into its later component parts, of which the leet was the chief. But more important than this is the fact that an analysis of the geld statistics of the East Anglian Domesday and their relation to the tenemental organization of Norfolk and Suffolk has indicated that the leet already occupied an important place in the social structure of the district, and that it was an institution probably strictly similar to the 12-carucated hundreds of Lincolnshire. The curious phenomena associated with the early leet merit close investigation; and in particular, in the sphere of jurisdiction, it is very desirable not only to ascertain the judicial significance of the leet before the fourteenth century, but also to discover how the gulf between the fiscal unit of Domesday and the ubiquitous court leet of the fourteenth

---

[1] Round, *Feudal England*, p. 99.
[2] This is quite clear from the wording of the document, cf. Gage, *History of Suffolk*, pp. xii seq.

century is bridged over by the institutional growth of the
intervening period.

It is the former of these two lines of inquiry which supplies
the interest of the very remarkable foundation charter of
Wymondham Abbey.[1]   For when William of Albini founded
that house he conferred the jurisdictional privileges of the
abbey in Wymondham in the following words: ' Volo et
concedo quod predicti prior et conventus habeant curiam
propriam in eadem villa et omnia amerciamenta hominum
suorum tam liberorum quam lancetorum in leta mea in foro
in curia et in quocunque loco amerciati fuerint.'   William
was the chief butler of Henry I, and this charter is witnessed
by Roger Bigod who died in 1107.[2]   Here, then, we have the
earliest post-Domesday mention of the leet which has yet been
recovered, the charter antedating the Kalendar by about half
a century.   What, however, is more important is the fact that
here, too, the leet is regarded as a definitely judicial unit.   It is
closely connected with the ' curia ' and with the amerciaments
which accrued to that court.   Thus within some thirty years
of Domesday the same jurisdictional characteristics which
appear in the late twelfth-century Thingoe leets appear also
in this leet which was given to Wymondham Abbey ; and it is
hard in view of this not to conceive of the Domesday leet also
as being a judicial unit as well as a geld-paying subdivision of
the hundred.   This suggestion receives strong support from
the curious relation in which the charter stands to the
Domesday entry concerning Wymondham.   For the vill of
Wymondham in Domesday pays six shillings and eight pence
to the geld.[3]   It contains, that is to say, in the assessment
reckoning exactly four of the one shilling and eightpenny—
or ora—leets into which parts the hundred of Forehoe appear
to have been divided.[4]   It does not seem too bold to think of

---

[1] Dugdale, *Monasticon*, vol. iii, p. 330.

[2] *V. C. H., Norfolk*, vol. ii, p. 336.

[3] *D. B.*, vol. ii, fol. 137 b : ' Hoc manerium cum tota soca T.R.E. valebat
cum soca xx librae.   Modo lx et habet ii leugae in longitudine et i in
latitudine et vi solidos et vii denarios de gelto.'

[4] Cf. *V. C. H., Norfolk*, vol. ii, p. 210.   The ora leet is the predominant
form in Forehoe hundred, though a 2s. unit also makes its appearance.

William's leet as one of these. But in any case the connexion between the two documents is too striking to admit of any other conclusion than that the 'leet' which was a centre of jurisdictional rights in 1109 was no mere artificial geld entity in the time of Domesday.[1] It seems, therefore, that the leet of Domesday, which has hitherto been held to have performed merely a fiscal function, was itself a judicial unit also. And this being so, its development into the leet of later days becomes far less obscure.

But it is in the history of certain manors of the Bishop of Ely in the north-west corner of Norfolk that the best illustration can be found of this development, and the records of these manors tend to throw light on a new aspect of the early leet and its origin. When describing the judicial rights of the Bishop of Ely in his manors of Walton, Walpole, Terrington, and Walsoken, the jurors in 1256 and 1277 use a curious phrase. These manors are said to be 'infra letam integram libertatis domini Eliensis in marisco'.[2] Tilney and Wiggenhall are described as 'extra letam domini Eliensis '.[3] We seem in fact here to be dealing with a curious unity. And this unity we can trace also in other nearly contemporary documents. In the 'Placitorum Abbrevatio', for instance, it is told how the men of Marshland made complaint in 1325, and in the course of the plea we learn that the 'villate de Marshelande' comprise Walsoken, West Walton, Tilney, Wiggenhall, and South Lynn, and we are further informed that the men of these vills had to combine together to keep the sea from their lands.[4] In the Hundred Rolls [5] also we find references to the same unity. There the jurors complain that the bishop will in no wise allow the bailiffs of the lord king to enter ' infra libertatem suam in Marshalane tam in feodis alienis quam in propriis scilicet infra iiii villis, Walton, Walsoken, Walpol, Tyrrington '. Under another heading [6] the four vills are

---

[1] The presence of large numbers of socmen at Wymondham strongly supports this view.

[2] Cott. Claud. C. xi, fols. 173, 184 b, 191, 196 b, 198 ; and Coucher Book, fols. 96, 100, 103, 114.

[3] Cott. Claud. C. xi, fols. 195, 196 b; and Coucher Book, fols. 112, 112 b.

[4] *Placitorum Abbrevatio*, p. 362.   [5] *H. R.*, vol. i, p. 461.

[6] *H. R.*, vol. i, p. 461 : ' Dictus episcopus excedit fines warennie sue eo

mentioned in close connexion with each other, and in yet a third [1] the bishop is said to have certain rights ' de hominibus suis de Marshlande '. At the end of the thirteenth century the vills of Walton, Walpole, Tirrington, and Walsoken seem to constitute a unity among themselves; and this unity is closely related both to the constant references to Marshland in the thirteenth century and to the ' leta integra de marisco ' of the Ely extents.[2]

That the connexion of these vills had an economic foundation is clearly brought out in the Ely extents. These minutely describe the extensive intercommoning rights which these villages enjoyed in the West Fen. In 1277 the jurors of Walsoken for instance remark : ' Tota ista villata debet communare in marisco qui vocatur Westfen cum villatis de Tyrington, Walepole, Walton, et Tylneia tam fodiendo quam pascendo horn under horn eo excepto quod nullus debet nec potest turbam dare vendere vel carriare extra predictas villas sine licentia domini episcopi et assensu et consensu aliorum percennarum predictarum villatarum.' [3] The same statement occurs in respect of all the other vills mentioned in 1277,

---

quod inwarennat tam in terris alienis et communis (*sic*) quam in terris suis propriis in villis de Tirrington, Walsok, Walton, Walpol.'

[1] *H. R.*, vol. i, p. 461.

[2] It is interesting to see how in certain Ministers' Accounts of the See of Ely dating from the beginning of the fourteenth century, preserved in the P. R. O. (1124/8), the term is used in a different sense. The possessions of the see are there divided into ' Bailiwicks '—that of Norfolk, of Suffolk, and of Cambridgeshire. Then we find the heading ' Balliva Merrsheland ', which, however, includes only the manors on the Cambridgeshire side of the boundary which runs beside the four Norfolk villages. There are indeed signs that the county boundary in these districts was itself a matter of considerable doubt. In the twelfth century there was, for instance, drawn up a record which makes its appearance in the Spalding Register, by which eight knights from Lincoln, eight from Northampton, and one from Norfolk met to decide on the boundary of the three counties in that district (Harl. MSS. 742, fol. 2). In the time of Edward I the ' hundred ' court of Wisbeach was certainly dealing with the affairs of villages on the Norfolk side of the border (Wisbeach Court Rolls, Ely Muniment Room), and in the extents a tenant of Wiggenhall owes suit to the courts of both Wisbeach and Walton (Cott. MSS. Claud. C. xi, fol. 195). It was also a common thing for tenants in Walsoken to perform carrying services to both Walton and Wisbeach (Coucher Book, fol. 113).

[3] Cott. Claud. C. xi, fol. 196 b. The statement is repeated in respect of the other vills on fols. 173, 184 b, 191.

and in the 1256 Coucher Book.[1] These fen-sharing rights
were supplemented by a common burden in keeping up
the dykes necessary to preserve the common pasturage.
This was not only minutely apportioned among the various
vills but even among the scattered acres within them, and
neglect of the duty was punished by special fines.[2] But the
strength of the economic unity of these marshland vills can
best be measured by the fact that it was strong enough to
impose itself upon the great ecclesiastical lordships which
converged upon it. Two charters in the Ramsey Cartulary
illustrate this well. In 1250[3] a grant of rights in 'Westfen
infra fossatum de Pokediche versus Mereslande' at once
involved 'Episcopus Eliensis Abbas de Rameseia Prior de
Lewes Thomas de Ingoldesthorpe et omnes alii parcennarii
marisci et fossati'. Between 1133 and 1160[4] the Abbot of
Ramsey is stipulating that the land which he holds between
Wells and Emneth is 'nona pars contra Episcopum Eliensem
et Priorem Sancti Pancratii participes nostros illius terrae'—
a stipulation which can only refer to common payments made
by the district as a whole. But the clearest example of the
early economic interrelation of these vills, both with regard
to the marsh and with regard to the duties and payments
necessary for its preservation, is an agreement concerning the
marsh which was drawn up in the early thirteenth century
between Bishop Eustace of Ely, the Prior of Lewes, and
Abbot Samson of Bury St. Edmunds, and no less than
forty-seven other coparceners.[5] The contracting parties in this
agreement are divided into two large groups. The one is led
by Abbot Samson and is comprised by 'hominibus participantibus de Tilneya et Ilsington'. The other, whose most
prominent members are the Bishop of Ely and the Prior of

---

[1] Coucher Book, fol. 113; cf. fols. 96, 103, 108, 114.
[2] *British Academy Records of Social and Economic History*, vol. iv,
p. xlvi. For the general significance of these intercommoning rights
cf. the whole of Miss Neilson's Introduction to the Terrier of Fleet in
this volume.
[3] *R. C.*, vol. ii, pp. 320, 321.
[4] *R. C.*, vol. ii, p. 268; cf. *Cartularium Abbatie Ramesiensis* (Rolls
Series), p. 273.
[5] Cott. Vesp. F. xv, fol. 284 b. See Appendix I, No. 53.

Lewes, is described as '*participes qui sunt de leta integra de Merslond*'. In this twelfth-century document we are thus confronted again with the strong unity of Marshland ; again we have reference to the economic basis of that unity ; and again most significantly this unity is connected with the leet of the marsh alluded to by the thirteenth-century jurors.

In short, it is possible throughout the twelfth and thirteenth centuries to trace clearly the presence of an economic connexion between the vills which comprise the leet of the marsh. The foundation of this seems to lie in the possession of a common marsh, and it is made the more secure by common payments and works to keep out the sea. It is quite clear that from the early twelfth century the vills of Marshland are bound very closely together, and the constant references to the 'leet' involved show the connexion of this unity with the Domesday terminology. The 'leet of the marsh' mentioned in the late thirteenth century by the Ely jurors was no new thing. It can be traced back through the twelfth century, and it appears to have been based upon an economic foundation.

Turn now to the jurisdictional sphere. When the jurors described this leet, they added that the bishop had therein very extensive judicial rights ;[1] and the Hundred Rolls also give in detail the bishop's franchises within that area. The connexion of this marshland entity with jurisdiction can be seen in the previous history of the district. In the Public Record Office[2] there is a court roll of Walsoken which dates from the year 1295, and which offers, in Maitland's words, a curious instance of 'a leet with three lords'.[3] An examination of this roll shows the very strange nature of the jurisdiction described therein. In the first place the court is described as the ' Leta Episcopi Eliensis, Abbatis de Rameseia, et Prioris Lewensis tenta in communia '. And in the second place we may note from a curious arrangement concerning the tithings that this was not the manor court of Walsoken at all, but

---

[1] Vide *supra*, notes.
[2] Court Rolls, Walsoken, 23 Edward I, P. R. O.
[3] Maitland, Selden Society, vol. ii, p. lxii.

something quite distinct. The roll states: 'Quia testatur in plena leta quod multi aetatis duodecim annorum et amplius sunt extra decennas . . . predictis iuratoribus qui sunt de homagiis prioris et episcopi quod respondeant de nominibus eorum qui sunt extra decennas et eorum receptatura ad letam de Walton. Et predictis iuratoribus de homagio Abbatis quod de nominibus eorum qui sunt extra decennas et eorum receptatura ad proximam curiam separalem dicti abbatis . . .' The separate court of the Abbot of Ramsey must be the manor court of Walsoken—the only manor which he held in these parts. And that the leet which was held before the three stewards was something very different from a manor jurisdiction is made clear from a comparison of the court roll with the very curious twelfth-century extent of Walsoken given in the Ramsey Cartulary. There we read that: 'Episcopus Eliensis habet aulam in Waltona. Et Prior Sancti Pancraci similiter habet aulam in eadem villa. In Walsoken autem abbas Ramesiae solus habet aulam et saccam et soccam et tol et team et infangethef et alias libertates regales sicut habet in caeteris terris suis.'[1] The jurisdictional union of the three lords of the leet only came about in 1294, for we have record of the fact,[2] and it is couched in somewhat significant terms. In that year, we are told, the bishop and the abbot in view of the contentions which had arisen between them in the past agreed 'quod leta de Walsoken coniungatur et de tenentibus dictorum Episcopi Abbatis et Prioris de Lewis et per eorum senescallos coniunctim et in communi teneatur'. The comparison of the court roll and the extent of Walsoken has shown that the bishop and the abbot were creating no new jurisdiction, and that in uniting the judicial rights of the three lords in the leet they were building upon a foundation which was already old. There is also a curious charter of Richard I[3] which appears to refer to this leet, and in any case illustrates very well the vitality of the twelfth-century leets in this district. The king

---

[1] *R. C.*, vol. iii, p. 289.
[2] This is given twice in the Ramsey Cartulary, vol. i, p. 215, and vol. iii, p. 57.
[3] Ely Cartulary (Liber 'M' Ely Muniment Room). See Appendix I, No. 61.

enjoins his officials 'quod firmiter et inviolabiliter faciatis obseruari racionabile divisam inter Tilneam et Tyrrinton inter letam qui est Episcopi Elyensis cancellarii nostri et Prioris de Lewes et Abbatis de Rameseya et Willelmi de Warenna et dimidiam letam que est Comitis de Clara et Abbatis Sancti Ædmundi et Godefridi de Lisewi' et Roberti de Cherville et participancium eorum'. In this connexion it is also well to recall that Abbot Samson's Thingoe leets were jurisdictional units, and it is hardly likely that the same abbot would use the same word in a wholly different sense in his agreement with Bishop Eustace,[1] which has already been noticed as referring to the Marshland leet in a phrase almost identical with that employed by the thirteenth-century jurors in describing the bishop's jurisdictional rights in that district. Further, we have already noted evidence of a leet jurisdiction existing in another part of Norfolk as early as 1109.[2] All things considered, it seems certain that we can trace back the marshland leet in its judicial as well as in its economic aspects well into the twelfth century, and even in the earliest references in that century in both connexions it bears the appearance of antiquity.

Turning to the Domesday Survey it is therefore somewhat disappointing to find that too few of these vills are recorded as paying geld to admit of a complete identification between this twelfth-century leet and a leet of Domesday-Book. But it is significant that Walton in its geld payments is reckoned as a leet in itself, and that the other three adjacent vills are not described as paying any geld at all and therefore do not fall into any other leet division.[3] It thus seems probable that we have in the Walton leet the later Marshland leet of Ely. But be this as it may, taking into consideration both the twelfth-century history of these four villages and the analogous and earlier Wymondham evidence, it seems clear that in the Marshland district there is a direct connexion

[1] Vide *supra*, p. 197.
[2] Vide *supra*, p. 194.
[3] *V. C. H., Norfolk*, vol. ii, p. 204. Since none of the other vills are mentioned, it seems probable that they were included in the leet assessment of West Walton, which was a leet in itself.

between the leets which can be seen as judicial and economic units from the early twelfth century to the late thirteenth, and the fiscal units of the Domesday Survey.

It is thus possible to trace the development of the application of the word leet from the time when it appears in Domesday in connexion with the Danegeld to its emergence in the late thirteenth century as a technical jurisdictional term ultimately applied over the whole of England. The history of the leet during that period can now be clearly seen. The Domesday leet must not be regarded as merely an artificial geld subdivision of the hundred. Judging from a comparison of the Domesday entry with the record of a charter which is to be dated not later than 1107, the leet was already in the Survey a jurisdictional unit. The judicial character of the leet can also be seen very clearly in a group of vills in the north-west corner of Norfolk, whose leet jurisdiction can be actually observed at work in the thirteenth century and discovered in the records of the twelfth in such a way as to leave little doubt that it was based upon the Domesday organization. Lastly, the same group of vills show also how between 1133 and 1160 the leet could appear as an economic as well as a jurisdictional or fiscal entity. We therefore conclude that the word which the lawyers of the fourteenth century accepted and rendered popular as a symbol of a peculiar sort of jurisdiction had already a long and a continuous history in East Anglia, as representing a district and a jurisdiction smaller than that of the hundred and larger than that of the normal manor or vill. The final transition in the meaning of the term is to be explained by one of those confusions so common in medieval terminology between the district, the court of the district, and the jurisdiction embodied in the court.[1] With the slow evolution of a distinct franchisal court out of the once undivided hallemot,[2] the lawyers had to seek a term to express this new judicial entity which comprised as it were a fragment of the hundredral jurisdiction.[3] Their choice of the term leet

---

[1] The analogy of the term hundred is sufficient evidence of this.

[2] Vide *supra*.

[3] Vinogradoff, *English Society*, p. 214.

was thus apt. But what must, however, most emphatically be stressed in connexion with the origin of the leet in its wider significance is the fact that there was in East Anglia no break in development from the time of Domesday to the fourteenth century. The institutional growth is constant and can be traced throughout the period. From the eleventh century onwards in East Anglia the leet can continuously be seen as an operative institution. Probably analogous to the 12-carucated hundreds of Lincolnshire,[1] it formed a unit quite distinct from manor and village and knit together both by jurisdictional and by economic ties. Certain it is that in Norfolk and Suffolk there existed the leet court long before men formed the more modern and universal notion of the court-leet.

From many points of view a survey of the judicial organization of medieval East Anglia thus throws some light upon questions of general interest, whether that organization is considered with regard to the liabilities of the peasantry or the rights of the lords. In the Ely manors, for instance, throughout the thirteenth century there is a tendency to define more strictly the details of the suit owed to the manor court. And the result of such specification is beginning to confine the suit of the free tenants to certain special occasions. Thus, as the old distinction between free suit and villein suit becomes more marked, so does the curia itself tend to be different in composition according to the different functions which it performs ; and it seems that in this fluctuation of the soke obligations of the peasantry (partly as a result of statute legislation) must be sought in practice the beginnings of the disintegration of the halimote into the three well-known divisions of later days. Again, in the details of suit owed to the courts of hundred and shire also a general development may be observed. In the later thirteenth century the burden of attendance is regarded as being ‘ tenurial ’. It is affixed to certain holdings which perform the suit for the manors in which they lie ; and a detailed example of this system in working can be found in the case of Shipdham hundred. But

----

[1] Vide *supra*, pp. 55-6.

whilst this is so, there are to be found in the extents traces of other systems. The notion that the village should be represented by its priest, its reeve, and its four best men can be seen, and also the conception that the normal suitors to the hundred and shire courts are the free men. By a comparison of this confusion with the Domesday Survey, the main features of the early history of such obligations appear to be the substitution of the free tenant for the mootworthy ceorl and the limitation of the former's suit to certain representative tenements. But it is outside the more normal jurisdictions that the main interest of early East Anglian judicial arrangements lie. The jurisdictional rights of the lord, in so far as they have an agricultural basis, demonstrably in East Anglia have their origin in the village rather than the manor; and the twelfth-century testimony of the communal action of vills in this district which are subdivided into many lordships in the time of Domesday, illustrates very forcibly the importance of the economic unity of the village in the development of English judicial organization. Jurisdictional arrangements in East Anglia frequently took the form of large administrative sokes. These were at once judicial and economic units; their active existence can sometimes be traced through the period of the Conquest, and they were clearly responsible for absorbing much of the chaotic personal ' freedom' described in the Survey. In spite of the descriptive method of the Little Domesday, a comparison of the charter evidence with that of the Survey itself shows many points of similarity in this respect between the arrangements of East Anglia and those of the Danelagh proper; and in Norfolk and Suffolk it is abundantly clear that the territorial soke can in no wise be regarded as a mere survival in the time of Domesday. Its active existence and the important part which it played in the social and judicial organization of the district can be closely watched from the Conquest to the thirteenth century. These sokes in their origin were sometimes not unconnected with the hundreds of the district, which in turn present peculiar features. In spite of the important function which these performed, in respect both of jurisdiction and the

Danegeld, the late origin of the East Anglian hundreds is suggested, and their formation was probably posterior to that of the leets into which they were later divided. These leets, indeed, are the most curious and in many ways the most important of East Anglian judicial institutions. Here again an economic backing is to be found to their jurisdictional unity, and, what is most significant, a continuous development can be watched from the fiscal entity of the Little Domesday to the fourteenth-century court-leet, which became one of the most prominent instruments for the administration of English law. In the sphere of jurisdiction that is to say, as elsewhere, an examination of East Anglian social history in the Middle Ages contributes materially to the solution of many of the problems connected with the judicial development of medieval England.

CHAPTER V

CONCLUSIONS. GENERAL SIGNIFICANCE OF THE EAST ANGLIAN ARRANGEMENTS IN THE SOCIAL HISTORY OF ENGLAND

THE social structure of medieval East Anglia may be examined from many points of view, but in every case it possesses a dual significance. The social organization which can be seen in these highly remarkable shires is itself so distinctive as to merit attention. But on the other hand these arrangements bear a peculiar relation to the Scandinavian north and to the Saxon south and west, and may thus be said to have played a unique part in the general social history of England.

Nowhere is the isolation of East Anglia more marked than in the tenemental organization of the district. Here, as elsewhere in the east of England, in the nucleated village and a strip method of cultivation the countryside presents the normal agricultural features indicative of a division of share land worked upon a basis of co-operative husbandry, in spite of certain modifications introduced by pastoral practices. But outside such general similarities the arrangements in Norfolk and Suffolk seem to have been highly irregular. In the sixteenth century a comprehensive survey had shown, for instance, that the peasant holdings were not divided into even approximately equal proportions amongst the fields of the township ; nor was any scheme of crop rotation worked upon the basis of the village fields. The virgate was thus all but unknown, and the vaguer ' tenementum ', usually called after the name of some previous holder, serves to designate the holdings of the peasantry. Alike, that is to say, in the presence of this unit coexisting with a strip system of agriculture and in the absence of anything like the normal virgate or of a scheme of field rotation, the tenemental organization of sixteenth-century East Anglia marks it off sharply from the surrounding counties.

The widely scattered evidence of the medieval extents shows unmistakably that these conditions were also to be found in the district in the Middle Ages. In the thirteenth and fourteenth centuries the holdings of the peasantry were arranged independently of the village fields and allocated in named furlongs or precincts. The 'tenementum', strictly similar to that of the sixteenth century, is still to be seen, though it appears under names which sometimes suggest a primitive origin. The rarity of the virgate and bovate both in name and in fact is as remarkable as in the later documents, and where the former is to be found in certain of the extents its introduction should probably be attributed to a late seignorial reorganization of older and smaller holdings which corresponded to the 'tenementa' of the later centuries. The virgate is in fact clearly exotic in East Anglia from the time of Domesday; and throughout the medieval period the tenurial arrangements of Norfolk and Suffolk are as distinct in character as those prevailing in the district under the rule of the Tudors. The village fields in the Middle Ages also played no part in the scheme of crop rotation, and whilst a strip system points to an original division of the arable according to fixed shares, the tendency of the strips of each particular tenant to be concentrated in one section of the village land suggests peculiar methods of farming and an exceptional tenurial development. The tenemental history of this district shows clearly through some six centuries the continued existence of exceptional conditions which constitute an important variation of the practices dictated by the exigencies of early husbandry.

Such arrangements also suggest a connexion between the 'tenementum' of later days, and an original scheme of land-sharing, and point to primitive farming practices which early stabilized the peculiar conditions of this province. But if such a continuity of development could be discovered, it is clear that it has been subject to much modification. In no district

in England in the medieval period was there such widespread
disintegration and reintegration of the peasant tenements.
This was clearly responsible for the unique terminology of
the East Anglian Domesday. It was reflected in a multitude
of twelfth-century peasant charters, and it can be watched
even in the thirteenth-century extents on the estates where its
action was the most restricted. This, in fact, is the most
conspicuous mark of East Anglian tenemental arrangements
at the earliest time at which they can, in detail, be examined.
Of itself it makes any investigation into the regular arrangements which preceded these conditions very difficult, and suggests that the subsequent social development of this district
must have been peculiar.

Not only with regard to the peasant holdings themselves
but also in respect of the manner in which these tenements
were held does the East Anglian evidence present features of
interest. An initial contrast is indicated between those lands
which were under the control of ecclesiastical landlords, where
a highly organized manorial régime was in force and from
which come our later extents, and those other parts of the
country where no such rigid organization had ever taken
place—villages under divided and miscellaneous lordship,
sparsely represented in our documents by means of isolated
charters. On the later ecclesiastical manors the main divisions
of peasant tenure and status followed the same lines as in
other parts of England, and seem to have been dictated by
the relation in which the individual tenant stood to the
manorial husbandry. Thus with certain exceptions a broad
distinction between the 'free' payment of a money rent and
'unfree' service can here also be applied. It is thus that the
question of the performance of week work is here as elsewhere
of cardinal importance, and its commutation affected directly
the arrangement of the peasant classes. Such commutation
can be watched in East Anglia at an exceptionally early date,
and it is even possible that it may have affected the Domesday
arrangement of classes. Apart from this, however, on the
later manors the variations of peasant tenure were also reflected in judicial obligations, and already in the thirteenth

century the segregation of these into different categories was beginning to split up the still homogeneous manor court into its later component parts. The freeholder is gradually winning for himself a special place in the jurisdictional organization of the manor, and the same is true with regard to the courts of shire and hundred. The variations of the peasant obligation to attend these latter courts are to be seen with especial clearness in the Ely records, where can be watched a development which begins with the liability of all moot-worthy men to attend these courts and ends with the burden becoming fixed tenurially upon the shoulders of certain specified tenants.

The broad separation of money rent and services as determinants of peasant status has other implications also. It seems to be possible roughly to distinguish on these later manors between customary and contractual rents, and the earlier history of these is of considerable importance in an interpretation of the social history of twelfth-century East Anglia. A comparison of the Domesday evidence with that of the later extents suggests very strongly that the origin of many of the later customary rents, frequently expressed in terms of ' wara ' acres, is to be found in the contributions to the geld made by the eleventh-century free peasantry independently of the manors to which they were otherwise attached. The slow consolidation of the estates of the great religious houses in a district as loosely organized as East Anglia renders such a transition unusually clear, and it is probable that in this district considerable importance must be attached to the public origin of many of the later manorial rents.

But it is in the sphere of contract that the peasant tenures of East Anglia are most remarkable. Outside the ecclesiastical lands and to a certain extent even upon them the right of the free peasant to alienate his land seems to have existed from an early date and to have been exercised with unusual frequency. The ability to sell or give his land is the distinguishing mark of the freeman of the East Anglian Domesday. The twelfth-century charters show the constant formation of peasant contracts and demonstrate unmistakably that there was much circulation of money in this district even in the former half of that century. This is, indeed, but another aspect of the rapid movement towards the disintegration of the peasant tenements. It affected the tenure of all ranks of society. The abundant evidence of the twelfth century shows everywhere the formation of a contractual complex which has no parallel elsewhere at the period in England. This profoundly modified the whole social structure of the district from the eleventh century onwards. As in the case of the tenemental organization, that is to say, and outside the more regularly arranged ecclesiastical lands, we have to deal with constantly fluctuating tenurial conditions. And whilst underneath this constant change it is possible at times to see more regular arrangements and the customary regulations which the royal administration or the claims of lordship imposed, nevertheless from the time of Domesday the predominant feature of East Anglian peasant tenure is to be found in the operation of a contractual movement, which was largely responsible for breaking up any regular scheme of holdings which might ever have existed and for creating a variety of money rents often temporary in their nature and normally contractual in their scope.

The distinction between the manorialized and the non-manorialized sections of this district postulates the antithesis between village and manor in its most extreme form, and there is considerable evidence to show their complete dis-severance in East Anglia. The general evidence of Domesday shows the total inability of the manor in this district either to coincide with the village as the unit of agriculture or to comprise the heterogeneous obligations of the free peasantry. The typical East Anglian eleventh-century village was divided up into many 'manors', which in turn varied both in their size and in the rights which their 'lords' enjoyed. The evidence from the other end of the medieval period shows that this lack of coincidence between the two institutions had persisted. The returns embodied in the 'Feudal Aids' inquisitions for Norfolk and Suffolk show clearly that the coalescence between manor and village was still incomplete. Throughout the medieval period the distinction in practice between manor and village which can so seldom be made in the south and west is a normal feature of East Anglian society. The village, for instance, and not the manor was clearly in the East Anglian Domesday the unit of geld assessment, contributing so many pence to each pound paid by the hundred, and the later charters show that this remained so into the twelfth century when the village liability to royal imposts was maintained and was subdivided according to the number of geld acres held in the village. Yet more significant than these cases, however, are those in which the village attests charters. A few of these rare documents relative to East Anglia have come to light, and in all cases they deal with villages broken up among several lordships in Domesday and still minutely divided in the fourteenth century. They thus afford a very clear illustration of the village performing semi-legal acts in virtue of its economic unity, and this in spite of the disintegrating factors involved in its feudal composition. The independent and distinct action of the village in the eleventh and twelfth centuries is probably nowhere illustrated with such fullness as in the East Anglian material.

Distinct alike from manor and from village is the soke, and in spite of the terminology of the East Anglian Domesday it is clear from a comparison of that record with the later charters that the territorial soke was one of the component parts of the social structure of the district. The personal aspect of soke is stressed in the Survey, but the attestation of sokes in later charters and the occasional ratification of these deeds before soke courts makes it possible to piece together the widely scattered soke entries of Domesday and in them to discover the existence of similar units in the eleventh century. In most of these cases it is clear that we are dealing with entities which are pre-Conquestual in their origin, and in some instances there was certainly very little institutional change involved in the transition of ownership. On the other hand, it is possible that occasionally the soke, like the manor, formed part of the Norman machinery of consolidation, and that some at any rate of these sokes seem of post-Conquest formation. This was exceptional, but it would be in the highest degree incorrect to think of the soke as a moribund institution in East Anglia at the time of Domesday. In one case the continued existence of such a soke can be seen from the time of the Survey through a series of twelfth-century charters in which it twice changes ownership until it finally appears in a thirteenth-century extent. The frequent and active existence of the territorial soke is a marked feature of the East Anglian evidence in spite of the confusing method of Domesday, and no criticism of the social structure of Norfolk and Suffolk in the Middle Ages can afford to neglect its importance.

The soke stands in a special relation not only to the manor but also to the hundred, and its close connexion with the latter institution is sometimes suggested in the East Anglia evidence. The hundreds of Norfolk and Suffolk have indeed much in common with those of the south and west, though they are perhaps of later formation. They are of fairly regular size and have the appearance of being ideally composed of a given number of carucates. The eleventh-century East Anglian hundred court was probably in theory attended by the freemen of the hundred, and this court in this and the subsequent century was competent to witness the transfer of land and to undertake the ratification of charters. The modification of the liability to suit at the hundred court can be watched in East Anglia, and the tendency towards basing this upon tenure becomes more and more prominent throughout the medieval period. But the peculiar interest of the East Anglian hundred lies in the exceptional relation in which it stood to the geld arrangements of the district. Not only was it a territorial unit but it was also the pound-paying unit in the geld assessment, and the division of this geld into fairly regular shares among leets constitutes the real peculiarity of the hundred in Norfolk and Suffolk.

The leet is, in fact, in many ways the most interesting of the social institutions of East Anglia and one whose earlier history bears directly upon a problem of general import to the development of jurisdiction in England. The transition from what appears in Domesday as a geld division of the hundred to the court leet of later days is no easy one, but it is exemplified fairly clearly in the documents of this district. A very early twelfth-century charter already uses the term in a jurisdictional sense, and there seems no reason to deny this quality also to the unit in Domesday a few years before. Further, in the twelfth-century records of a small group of vills in north-west Norfolk, we have a series of documents terming this group a leet and treating it at once as a jurisdictional and an economic unit, the one aspect being emphasized by the possession of a common and a non-manorial court and the other by extensive intercommoning rights appertaining to all these villages. Finally, these same vills in the late thirteenth century all form part of a leet jurisdiction of the later model. It is thus impossible to regard the leet merely as the jurisdictional unit of the fourteenth century or merely as the fiscal unit of Domesday. Both records refer to one and the same institution which was frequently held together also by an economic tie. The scattered evidence concerning the leet at the time of Domesday and in the subsequent centuries makes it possible in short to reconstruct its earlier history, and it is clear that there was no break in the development. The word that was afterwards used to represent what was in essence a fraction of the hundredal jurisdiction in private hands was taken from an actual jurisdictional and economic unit representing a district and its court. The fiscal unit of Domesday was thus something more than a geld division. It represented a subdivision of the community, and an analysis of the Domesday geld statistics shows it to have been of fairly regular size. In these East Anglian documents it is thus possible to bridge over the gulf between the leet of the Norfolk Domesday and the well-known institution of later legal parlance and to watch at various points the process by which an East Anglian territorial unit came to give its name to a particular judicial court throughout England.

No attempt at an interpretation of the highly remarkable arrangements prevailing in medieval Norfolk and Suffolk can fail to impinge upon certain of the general questions affecting English social development as a whole. In particular is East Anglia important in its relation to the social cleavage between the Danish districts and those of the south and west. Norfolk and Suffolk cannot be included in either of these categories, and the individual character of their social structure gives them a place apart among the English provinces. Still, it is important to estimate the extent to which Scandinavian influence contributed towards the development of these curious conditions. No exact test can of course be applied in such a matter, but in the evidence which has been examined it may be suggested that in certain directions a close connexion between the organization of East Anglia and that of the Danelagh can be seen.

The explanation of the tenemental arrangements of the district offers one line of approach to the problem, and from many points of view it seems strongly suggested that the early allocation of share land, which in spite of much disintegration seems postulated by the later conditions, probably took place under a Scandinavian scheme. The names under which the ' tenementum ' appears in the later documents suggest Danish systems of land-sharing, and an analysis of the average size of these holdings points to a normal acreage of roughly $12\frac{1}{2}$ acres or 50 roods, the eighth part of the Danish carucate of 100 acres. This it is suggested was the ideal bovate which in turn represented the manloth or manshare, the fundamental holding in the Danish scheme corresponding to the toftlands of the solskift or heimskift systems. It was the typical peasant holding at the time of the Scandinavian settlements and the carucate itself was derivative therefrom. The strength of this theory is furthermore very much increased when we apply it to the peculiar geld statistics of the East Anglia Domesday, whereby a correspondence is obtained between the purely fiscal and the quasi-agrarian figures. The hundred thus appears not only as ideally containing 120 carucates of 8 bovates each, but also as the pound-paying unit it contains 960 farthing units, which thus exactly correspond to the manlots of the agrarian reckoning. These fundamental bovates or manloth holdings thus possibly not only formed the foundation of the original land division, but translated into fiscal terms they also were the basis of the peculiar geld arrangements of eleventh-century Norfolk and Suffolk.

If such a theory is in any way correct it affords an example of a very remarkable exhibition of Danish influence upon the tenemental arrangements of the district, and one which goes far to suggest a considerable modification of the social structure of the district at the hands of the invaders. But the East Anglian geld figures imply also a more complete analogy between the East Anglian and the typical Danelagh institutions. For working from the pound-paying hundred of 120 carucates the most common two-shilling leet would give a unit of 12 carucates, the exact equivalent of the hundreds of Lincolnshire. This is important in that it removes the leet from its position of isolation and brings it into harmony with the arrangements in force the other side of the Wash. It adds also considerable strength to the supposition that the leet was itself an early hundred and goes far to explain the divergence between the statistics of Domesday and those of the 'Tribal Hidage' for this district.

No feature of the social order of the Danish provinces in the time of Domesday is more distinctive than the widespread existence therein of the territorial soke. The frequent occurrence therefore of such sokes in East Anglia forms a new link between the two districts. From the twelfth-century charter material it is clear in fact that the peculiar method of the Little Domesday often conceals an institutional organization strictly similar to that presented in the Survey of those parts of the country where the Scandinavian influence was admittedly the greatest. The regular categorical division of estates into sokes, manors, and berewicks could indeed not be applied to East Anglia, but in many respects the arrangements in both provinces are strictly analogous. In East

Anglia as in the Danelagh the soke is, for instance, an economic as well as a jurisdictional unit. The distinction between inland and sokeland, though again by no means so regular in its incidence as in the Danelagh, makes its appearance both in relation to the king's geld and also to the services due to the lord. There can indeed be little doubt that the numerous and active sokes of eleventh- and twelfth-century East Anglia were constructed upon a very similar plan to that employed in the Danelagh proper.

Such considerations warrant the suggestion that far-reaching Scandinavian influence modified in many respects the social structure of medieval Norfolk and Suffolk. These shires were parts of Guthrum's kingdom, and remained for some time under Danish influence, though for a shorter period than the Danelagh itself. The port of Lynn became associated with the Danish trade at an early date, and peaceful infiltration probably took place from thence after the Conquest. A survey of the peasant names of the peasantry as they appear in the attestations to twelfth-century charters and of the field and village nomenclature would probably display a high degree of Norse influence. Consequently it is not surprising to find a similar correspondence in many respects in the institutional development of East Anglia and the Danelagh. The territorial soke and the 12-carucated hundred are not found outside the Danish districts, and the possible basis of the peculiar tenemental organization of Norfolk and Suffolk in manloth or bovate can most easily be compared to Danish arrangements within and without England. A delimitation of the Scandinavian influence on English society must certainly include East Anglia within its scope.

The differences between the two districts must, however, not be minimized. The social organization of East Anglia was much looser than that of the Danelagh and for many purposes much further removed from the normal manorial scheme of the south and west. The permanent and regular organization of the Danelagh soke, comprising economic as well as jurisdictional rights over its dependents, has much more in common with the manor proper than the fluctuating and heterogeneous rights over scattered groups of free peasants which in the main constituted East Anglian lordship. For the territorial soke is but one aspect of East Anglian social structure, and in the main in Norfolk and Suffolk the possession of commendation, custom, or personal soke over men who could often take even these where they would was the most frequent attribute of seignorial superiority. There is nothing in the Danelagh to correspond with this loose organization. The all but universally contractual character of the peasant tenure on the morrow of the Conquest is only to be found in Norfolk and Suffolk, and the widespread disintegration of peasant tenements which is so marked a feature of East Anglian eleventh- and twelfth-century society has no parallel in the Danish districts. Alike in the absence of any organized territorial lordship throughout the district and in the presence of large numbers of free peasants only loosely and often temporally subjected to seignorial control, the social conditions of medieval Norfolk and Suffolk were unique in England.

These characteristics, indeed, constitute the general importance of the East Anglian arrangements. The social organization of medieval England resulted from two sets of forces which often operated in close conjunction but can at times be separated. On the one hand, the agricultural groups moulded their institutions on the lines dictated to them by the practices of their common farming. On the other hand, the rights involved in lordship ultimately connected as they were with tenure created a parallel set of institutions which were of their essence seignorial. By the one process, for instance, was formed the share holding in the fields; by the other the compact peasant tenement constituting the unit of service. The result of the one arrangement was the village as the unit of agriculture; of the other, the manor, a unit wherein agriculture, jurisdiction, and lordship were inextricably blended together. This duality runs throughout early English social history, and the peculiar importance of the East Anglian social institutions is that they show in their most extreme form in England what may be called the non-feudal elements in English medieval society.

This is to be seen when any aspect of East Anglian social history of the eleventh or twelfth century is examined, and too much stress can hardly be laid on the harmony in this respect of the very different documents which come from the two periods. The only explanation, for instance, of the tenemental disintegration to be found in both is that in this district there has been no seignorial pressure sufficiently organized to check it. The same consideration also applies to the early widespread formation of contractual peasant tenures. Nowhere is this, however, of more significance than with regard to the existence of a large free peasant population in this district. This can be seen on every page of the East Anglian Survey, and it is the importance of the East Anglian evidence considered as a whole that it shows that the special terminology of the Little Domesday is accurately adapted to the facts. The numerous charters of the twelfth century presuppose the conditions described in the Survey. The ability of a peasant to alienate his land is itself indicative of personal freedom, and the very existence of large numbers of peasant charters is thus of itself a remarkable corollary to the Survey. The constant attestation of these deeds by peasant witnesses bearing English or Scandinavian names shows the continuous existence of the large class which appears so prominently on the pages of the East Anglian Domesday. In short, in view of the East Anglian evidence, no general theory of English social development can afford to neglect the continuous recorded existence of a large free peasant population in Norfolk and Suffolk between 1050 and 1150.

The relation borne by the village to the manor in this district has the same general importance, which is again enhanced by the remarkable way in which the Domesday testimony is corroborated by that of the earlier charters. The manor was clearly a very artificial institution in eleventh-century East Anglia. It did not coincide with the village as the unit of agriculture. It did not comprise the free elements of the population. The village and not the manor was the geld unit, and the strength of the village as opposed to the manors within it is witnessed by its recorded legal acts. Here, again, any general seignorial explanation of English medieval society breaks down in face of the East Anglian evidence. The ' free ' village, the ' lordless ' village, is not an exception in East Anglia. It is the basis of the social structure of the district. Its active existence is not a matter of hypothesis but of recorded fact.

Nevertheless, any purely static conception of East Anglian society during the earlier medieval period would be wholly false. The contrast between the conditions of Domesday and those of the later extents is so great that even if we regard the latter as exceptional some attempt must be made to explain it. The peculiar circumstances of Norfolk and Suffolk make it especially easy to watch the gradual depression of the peasantry which we know to have taken place elsewhere in England. In this district can often be seen the stages by which the village organization could on occasion be merged into that of the manor, and members of the free peasant class of Domesday become transformed into manorial tenants sometimes passing directly into the category of non-free rent-paying tenants distinct alike from the freeholder and the working villein. The East Anglian evidence alone is sufficient to indicate that there were forces at work in medieval England capable of transforming in time a free peasant population into one of manorial tenants to whom a new legal theory would soon deny the liberty that they had once possessed.

In many ways, therefore, the social history of medieval East Anglia would seem to have a general importance. The peculiar characteristics of the Domesday record are in part to be attributed to Scandinavian influence, but in the main they show the social organization resulting from the lack of any uniformly organized seignorial control over a society consisting for the most part of free peasants holding their lands by virtue of contracts and farming them according to the system prescribed by their co-operative methods of agriculture. The post-Domesday material demonstrates the continuance of these conditions until the middle of the twelfth century, and it is clear that even in the thirteenth century the social structure of Norfolk and Suffolk had not conformed to the normal manorial pattern, though a widespread depression of the peasantry had taken place. Such conditions are of themselves remarkable. They must be taken into consideration in any general estimate of the social development of medieval England.

APPENDIX I

CHARTERS

Nos. 1–26. Original Deeds from various quarters.
Nos. 27–34. From Castleacre Cartulary (Harl. MS. 2110).
Nos. 35–37. From the Binham Register (Cott. Claud. D. XIII).
Nos. 38–51. From the St. Benet of Hulme Register (Cott. Galba E. II).
Nos. 52–55. From the Lewes Cartulary (Cott. Vesp. F. XV).
Nos. 56–59. From the Warwick Cartulary (Add. MS. 28024).
Nos. 60–62. From the Ely Cartulary (Liber 'M' Ely Muniment Room).
No. 63. From the 'Black Book' of St. Edmunds (Cambridge Univ. Library).
Nos. 64–66. From the York Register (Rylands Library).

1

Harley Charters 44, A. 18.

Sciant presentes et futuri quod ego Petrus prior de Binham et totus eiusdem loci conuentus unanimi assensu et consilio dedimus et concessimus et hac presenti carta nostra confirmauimus Petro de Egeffeld et heredibus suis totam terram quam predictus Petrus de Egeffeld tenuit de Alexandro clerico in uilla de Egeffeld et quam terram idem Alexander tenuit de nobis hereditario iure et quam reddidit quietam de se et heredibus suis in manus nostras et que terra appellatur Adhelingesdele et a Croftegate usque ad ductum de Hemsted' pro homagio suo et seruicio tenendam de nobis libere et honorifice et hereditarie et quiete pro sex solidis et quinque denariis nobis inde annuatim reddendis ad quattuor terminos uidelicet ad Natale Domini xx denarios et ad Pascha xix denarios et ad festum sancti Johannis Baptiste xix denarios et ad festum Sancti Michaelis xix denarios. Et idem Alexander et heredes sui adquietabunt predictam terram quam nobis reddidit et quam predicto Petro dedimus et confirmauimus de omnibus consuetudinibus et exactionibus preter predictos sex solidos et quinque denarios et preter duodecim denarios de releuio pertinente ad successores predicti Petri. His testibus. Willelmo de Egeffeld. Ada de Pereres. Willelmo de Stodere. Hamone de Hemsted. Ricardo de Egeffeld. Ricardo filio Simonis. Alexandro clerico. Hugone peregrino. Ricardo anglo. Waltero de Walecote. et multis aliis.

Slit for seal tag.
Date: 1189–1198.

2

Harley Charters 45, F. 15.

Sciant tam presentes quam futuri quod ego Rogerius filius Alani de Hatfeld uendidi Petro de Edisfeld pro xxxta solidis totam terram quam Alix soror Bartholomei ad Hunew' in eadem uilla habuit et ego Rogerius tenui de predicto Bartholomeo et quidquid iuris in illa terra habui. Que terra hoc modo distinguitur, scilicet v acras in ascheteles-hirne usque ad terram que fuit Ulfi Fretehois et unam acram et dimidiam que fuit bruntclimhehod que iacet iuxta semitam que uadit de birsti usque ad molendinum Bartholomei et unam acram que iacet iuxta acram Reddburg et duas acras quas Aschetel tenuit iuxta bruarium de Stody et terram Ricardi clerici. Et hanc uendicionem et hanc terram debeo ego Rogerius warantizare Petro et heredibus suis quam assignatis. His testibus. Petro Scano. Willelmo filio Petri de Edisfeld. Simone Butery. Thoma presbitero de [   ].[1] Stoma de Waberg'. Petro de Bodham. Randulfo de Hayl'. Roberto de Rellmekes. Ricardo de Marbos. Rogero de Saxeheham. et aliis multis.

Slit for seal tag.
Date : Late twelfth century.

3

Harley Charters 46, E. 31.

Willelmus Blundus omnibus hominibus suis francis et anglis tam futuris quam presentibus salutem. Sciatis me concessisse et dedisse et hac presenti carta confirmasse Anselmo filio Brihtwini de Ixewrthe et heredibus suis ad tenendum de me et heredibus meis totum tene-mentum patris sui libere et quiete sicuti pater suus illud unquam melius et liberius tenuit scilicet in bosco in plano in pratis in pascuis in exitibus in turbariis in uiis in semitis scilicet singulis annis reddendo nouem solidos ad tres terminos tres solidos ad festum sancti Michaelis tres ad Natalem et tres ad Pascha et preterea concessi et dedi ei et heredibus suis de me et heredibus meis ad tenendam terram suam luitiam in feudum et hereditatem pro quattuor solidis et duobus denariis pro omni seruitio et illos reddet ad festum sancti Johannis. Et de tenemento suo xl acras inter uillatum defendet. Et preterea dedi ei toftam quam Egelaf tenuit in eschambiam tofte que fuit patris sui Brihtwini quam Aldwinus tenet. Et preterea fermam quam ego quesiui

---

[1] Illegible.

ab eo singulis annis per consuetudinem ei et heredibus suis quietam clamo nisi honorem mihi per amorem facere uelit. Et pro hac donatione et confirmatione et quietantia dedit mihi Anselmus predictus unam marcam argenti. Huius rei sunt testes. Alanus capellanus. Albericus de Dammartin. Adelitia soror eius. Walterus filius Gileberti. Robertus de Rikinhehale. Alexander de Wridwel'. Robertus de Ixew'. Normannus filius eius. Gilebertus clericus de Hunterest'. Eudo berton. Odo de Walesham. Radulphus clericus de Ixeworth. Huo prepositus. Warinus. Odo. Willelmus Grim. Herbertus filius Hugonis.

Tag for seal.
Date : Late twelfth century.

4
Harley Charters 47, H. 45.

Willelmo dei gratia Norwicensi episcopo et domino suo Willelmo comiti de Warenna et omnibus sancte ecclesie filiis tam presentibus quam futuris Johannes de Querceto salutem. Sciatis me concessisse deo et Sancte Marie et canonicis de Rudeham duas ecclesias ipsius uille cum omnibus pertinentiis suis et totam preterea terram laicam quam Bruno et Willelmus presbiteri tenuerunt scilicet quam auus meus Radulphus de Querceto et Willelmus filius eius patruus meus et ego liberam ab omnibus consuetudinibus et exactionibus et ecclesiasticam possessionem fecimus. Sciatis etiam me dedisse eis hortos Frehe Godwini Lamberti Wlnoti et Warini et Almari et molendinum de Cokesforde et uiuarium et Caldewellewang et totam terram qui est inter Caldewellewang et aquam de Tatersate et Ketelesmerewang et totam Noremerewang et Radulphum filium Wlmari et totam terram suam et Burstanum et terram suam et hoc in escambio propter terram Almari de Gaituna quam Moyses tenet et seruitium Sumerledi sacerdotis et terram suam quam patruus meus Willelmus de Querceto dedit ei et Godwinum scriptorem et totam terram suam et Tocheswda et totam terram de Marham quae de feudo meo esse dinoscitur, et molendinum de Torp de uiuario et ipsum uiuarium et opera quae homines ipsius uille facere solebant ad stagnum predicti uiuarii reficiendum et duos homines iuxta predictum molendinum manentes scilicet Godwinum et Uluingum fratrem suum et terram illorum et dimidium nemus de Besefen quod est extra parcum. Et ut ipsi canonici pro anima aui mei Radulfi de Querceto et uxoris eius et anima patris mei et matris mee et Willelmi de Querceto patrui mei et Rogeri et sororum eorum et Walerani de Rocesforde et omnium parentum meorum et pro mea et uxoris mee et fratrum meorum et sororum mearum. Omnia supradicta inconcusse et honorifice et quiete iure perpetuo teneant. Ea et presentis scripti attestatione et sigilli mei appositione corroboro et confirmo, saluo seruitio comitis. Huius autem donationis sunt testes. Reinaldus de Warenna. Radulfus de Wiburuilla. Radulphus filius Osmundi. et Sibilla uxor domini Johannis. Petrus de Caineto. et Mattheus frater eius. Nicholaus clericus. et Godwinus frater eius Scule. et Willelmus frater eius. Radulphus sacerdos de Saxtorpe. et magister Willelmus Maurinus. Willelmus sacerdos. Nicholaus de Stanhoe. Wache diaconus. Gaufridus de Westrudeham. Radulfus auis. et Nicholaus clericus de Barsham. et Walterus clericus. et Albertus. et Rigolf. et Warinus. et Robertus de Croft. Ista [1] conuencio renouata fuit coram domino Willelmo Norwicensi episcopo apud Toenedis in uigilia Ascensionis domini die Sancti Dunstani presente ipso Johanne de Caineto. Huius autem donationis et renouationis teste [*sic*] sunt. Willelmus Norwiciensis archidiaconus. Turoldus capellanus. Radulphus de Snaringes. Ernaldus capellanus. Adam de Calna. Radulphus clericus de Saxlingham. Johannes dapifer. Petrus constabularius. Willelmus de Backetuna. Arthur. Adam filius Johannis dapiferi. Willelmus filius Ranulfi.[1]

Seal Tags.
Date: 1146–1148.
Occurs also Dugdale, Mon. Ang., vol. vi, p. 369.

5

Harley Charters 49, C. 1.

Manas de Dammartin omnibus hominibus et amicis suis tam clericis quam laicis tam francis quam anglicis Suffolchie salutem. Sciatis me dedisse et concessisse Reginaldo de Cottona et heredibus ipsius totam terram suam et humagia sua omnia que tenuit in die quo dominus noster Henricus Rex Anglie transfretauit in Hiberniam in bosco et in plano tam in pratis quam in pascuis et in omnibus tenementis tenendum de me et heredibus meis per seruicium xvi solidorum et ii denariorum soluendum pro omnibus consuetudinibus et uersus regem defendendum pro xxx acris secundum communitatem uille Mendleshe' de xxx acris prosequitur. Quare uolo et firmiter precipio quod idem Reginaldus et heredes sui de me et heredibus meis bene et in pace et libere et quiete istum concessum in feodo et hereditate teneant per seruicium prelibatum. Hiis testibus Huberto capellano qui hanc cartam composuit. Reginaldo clerico de Cottona. Benedicto clerico. Hugone

---

[1] In different ink.

clerico. Willelmo de Brisew'. Manaso iuuene. Hugone camerario. Huberto de Brisew'. Karlone. Nicolao clerico. Wichmaro fratre suo. Teobaldo de Brisew'. Rodberto de Boseuill'. Ricardo filio Lefwi.

Seal : equestrian figure in red wax.
Date: 1171–1172.

6

Harley Charters 49, G. 22.

Willelmus de Edesfeld' omnibus hominibus suis vicinis et amicis et omnibus qui hoc scriptum videbunt et audient tam presentibus quam futuris salutem. Sciatis me dedisse et concessisse et hac presenti carta confirmasse Petro filio meo et proximo heredi meo et heredibus suis hereditarie totam terram meam de Edesfeld' et totam terram meam de Wallekote cum omnibus pertinentiis que ad predictas terras appendent. Scilicet in dominiis et redditibus et in homagiis et in patronatu ecclesiarum cum omnibus aliis pertinentiis que ad prenominatas terras appendent. Et ego Willelmus de Edesfeld' me ipsum dimisi de omnibus predictis terris et ipsum predictum Petrum filium meum intus saisiaui. Et ego Willelmus concessi predicto Petro dotare uxorem suam Hawisiam de tercia parte omnium predictarum terrarum faciendo seruitium quod debui dominatibus meis de quibus istas terras tenui. Scilicet trium militum feodum. Et sciant omnes quod ego Willelmus non possum manum mittere in predictis terris nec in redditibus nec in pertinentiis nisi per commissionem predicti Petri. Et ego Willelmus warantizabo predictas terras cum omnibus prenominatis pertinentiis predicto Petro filio meo et heredibus suis contra omnes homines. Pro hac autem donatione et concessione predictus Petrus dedit mihi quindecim marcas argenti. His testibus Symone fillio [*sic*] Simonis. Galfrido filio Petri de Maunt'. Gileberto de Norfoldche. Eborado filio Radulfi. Roberto de Baunei. Thoma de Waburne. Hamone de Henstede. Willelmo de Miliers. Ricardo de Migun. Eustachio de Bernigham. Richero de Withewelle. Radulfo de Curcun. Willelmo de Edesfeld' filio Willelmi. Ricardo de Edesfeld' filio Willelmi. Thoma de Walekote et multis aliis.

Tag for seal.
Date: late twelfth century.

7

Harley Charters 50, B. 37.

Simon filius Simonis omnibus hominibus et amicis suis francis et anglis salutem. Noueritis me concessisse et dedisse et hac mea presenti carta confirmasse Petro filio Willelmi de Edesfeld totam terram meam quam habui in Lotfal et totam partem meam communis Bruere quam habui infra Lotfal et extra communem Hamonis de Henstede et totam partem meam terre et communis Bruere que iacet inter magnum chiminum que tendit de Holt usque ad molendinum Willelmi de Edesfeld et inter eundem chiminum que tendit de eadem Holt usque ad Hunewurthe. Tenendum illi et heredibus suis de me et heredibus meis in feodo et hereditate libere et quiete et honorifice pro una libra piperis annuatim reddendo scilicet ad festum Sancti Michaelis pro omnibus seruiciis et consuetudinibus. Pro hac predicta concessione est prefatus Petrus meus affidatus et dedit mihi unum talentum gersumie. Has prefatas terras et brueras et concessionem ego et heredes mei warantizabimus illi et heredibus suis. Hiis testibus. Ada de Pereres. Hamone de Henste. Ricardo de Marebof. Willelmo Blundo. Willelmo filio Radulfi. Gileberto de Klopwud. Hagone le pelerin. Rogero de Mundam. Rogero de Metingham. Roberto filio Saffrei. Iohanne filio Sibaldi. et pluribus aliis.

> Slit for seal tag.
> *Date* : late twelfth century.

8

Harley Charters 50, C. 14.

Rogerus filius Warengeri omnibus hominibus suis et amicis presentibus et futuris salutem. Sciatis me concessisse et dedisse et hac carta mea confirmasse Stephano de Brokedis et heredibus suis terram de feudo meo que iacet inter terram Willelmi filii Erlwin' et Walteri filii Turchil in Hintrecroft et terram de feudo meo in eadem cultura iuxta pascuam Huberti clerici de Simpling et terram de feudo meo que iacet inter terram Wydonis de Simplinge et Walteri filii Turchil que adcheuiat Roreker. Tenendum de me et heredibus meis sibi et heredibus suis pro vi denariis annuatim reddendis hiis terminis scilicet tribus ad pascha et tribus ad festum sancti Michaelis pro omni seruicio saluo seruicio domini regis scilicet i obulum ad xx solidos ad hospitatum regis et sicut ascendit et descendit. Et pro hac donacione predictus Stephanus dedit mihi unum bisancium de gersuma. Hiis testibus Bartolomeo de [   ].[1] Iohanne Britone. Rogero [   ].[1] Hugone de [   ].[1] Helya de Simplinge. Iordano de Burstone. Petro filio Willelmi capellani. Ricardo filio Willelmi.

> Tear in charter where there has been seal tag.
> *Date* : T. R. H. ii.

[1] Illegible

9

Iohannes de Godritorp omnibus amicis et uicinis et hominibus suis francis et anglicis tam presentibus quam futuris salutem. Sciatis me concessisse et dedisse et hac carta mea confirmasse Willelmo de Coleuilla pro homagio et seruitio suo tres partes de Aspaleshage iacentes uersus orientem et terram quam Robertus pater meus totam tenuit in crofta Pilehund et totam terram quam Robertus pater meus tenuit in crisehage preter unam acram quam Simon de Aspal' de me tenuit scilicet ipsi et heredibus suis ad tenendam de me et heredibus meis libere et quiete reddendo inde annuatim xii denarios scilicet ad Pascha vi denarios et ad festum sancti Michaelis vi denarios pro omnibus seruitiis et omnibus consuetudinibus. Has terras debeo ego et heredes mei warantizare ipsi Willelmo et heredibus suis contra omnes homines et contra omnes feminas propter hanc concessionem et donationem et huius carte mee confirmatione predictus Willelmus dedit mihi de gersuma i marcam argenti. Hiis testibus Seher' de Bischel'. Nigello de Ulueston'. Martio de Belfo. Waltero de Waltham. Willelmo filio Roberti. Gerardo filio Hernaldi. Walchel fratre eius. Huberto filio Saxe. Simone de Aspal'. Roberto Uisdelii. Roberto Barate. Roberto Hahi. Huctred de Brocford'. Daniel de Aspal'. Helias Puher. Roberto de Boseuilla.

Seal tag.
Date: late twelfth century.

10

Sciant presentes et futuri quod ego Ricardus filius Elfuini Kingesman de Nortune dedi et concessi et hac carta mea confirmaui Petro de Edisfeld' totam terram meam de Hokedam usque de Kaketorpgate versus occidentem del chemin usque ad Iungiere et totam terram meam versus orientem illius chemin a porta Edduardi hominis Oliueri Dages usque ad Kaketorpgate et dimidiam acram terre que iacet iuxta molendinum predicti petri ante portam que fuit Willelmi Dipre tenendam de me et de heredibus meis ipsi et heredibus suis libere quiete plenarie et hereditarie reddendo mihi annuatim unum denarium ad Pasca pro omnibus seruiciis et exaccionibus et consuetudinibus. Pro hac autem donacione et concessione et carta mee confirmacione devenit predictus Pletrus [*sic*] homo meus et dedit mihi unam marcam argenti de gersumia. Quare uolo et firmiter concedo quod predictus Petrus et heredes sui habeant et teneant integre totum prefatum tenementum de me et de heredibus meis per prefatum seruicium. His testibus Galtero de Raueniggeham. Henrico de Brom. Elia. Beniamin. Petro de Mundham. Rogero de Mundham. Moricio de Silande. Heruico filio suo. Willelmo Wacelin. Ada de Hubber. Steffano Kingeman. Gocelino Gingesman. Roberto Geldenefot. Galfrido Prudfot.

Tag for seal.
Date: late twelfth century.

I I
Harley Charters 53, A. 31.

Sciant presentes et futuri quod ego Robertus de Lindholt dono et concedo et hac mea carta confirmo Rogero filio Elwi terram Born cum omnibus ad ipsam pertinencibus et duas acras terre et dimidiam de warre de Elfricesland pro humagio et seruicio suo de me et heredibus meis sibi et heredibus eius in feudo et hereditate libere et quiete habendam et tenendam et defendendam per seruicium triginta denariorum oboli annuatim reddendorum scilicet ad festum sancti Æadmundi quindecim denarios argenti et ad pascha quindecim denarios et obolum et ad scutagium regis uiginti solidorum tres denarios ad plus plus et ad minus minus. Pro hac donatione et concessione dedit mihi Rogerus prefatus sex solidos argenti de gersuma et iiii denarios Roberto filio meo. Hii sunt testes. Iohannes de Peitune. Iohanes filius Ricardi. Sired filius Nigelli. Petrus filius Iohannis de Peitone. Petrus. Iohannes filius Ricardi. Ricardus filius Oldam. Galfridus filius Elwi. Iohannes filius Ernoldi. Willelmus de Lindholt. Gilbertus filius Hugonis prepositi. Hugo capellanus qui cartam composuit.

Seal in green wax: equestrian figure.
Date: circa 1200.

I 2
Harley Charters 53, C. 51.

Radulfus de Mandauilla omnibus hominibus suis et amicis suis presentibus et futuris salutem. Sciatis omnes me dedisse et carta confirmasse Acelino filio Giliberti de Reind' totam terram Giliberti patris sui scilicet quindecim acras terre de ware cum omnibus pertinenciis suis et totam terram que fuit terra Alfrici de Reind' scilicet quindecim acras terre de ware cum omnibus pertinenciis suis in uilla de Reind' scilicet Brunescroft et Crouenhel et Pilecothetland cum omnibus pertinenciis suis in bosco in plano in pratis in pasturis in alnetis in uiis in semitis in aquis in mariscis in redditibus in omnibus rebus, illi et heredibus suis tenendum de me et de heredibus meis libere et quiete et hereditarie reddendo mihi et heredibus meis octo solidos per annum et uxori mee iiii denarios scilicet ad festum Sancti Andree xxxii denarios, ad Pascha xxxii denarios; ad festum Sancti Iohannis xxxii denarios et uxori mee ad festum Sancti Michaelis iiii denarios pro omnibus seruiciis et omnibus consuetudinibus qui ad me pertinent et ad heredes meos saluo seruicio domini Regis scilicet ad xx solidos iii solidos et ad plus plus et ad minus minus. Et pro hac donatione et carte predicte confirmatione dedit mihi predictus Acelinus xx solidos de gersumia et seruicium suum quindecim annorum et uxori mee unum besancium et deuenit homo meus. Isti sunt testes. Galfridus de Mandauilla frater meus. Robertus filius Warini Willelmus de Cheueruilla. Hugo frater eius. Radulfus filius Etard. Gilibertus filius Norman. Warinus filius Walehir'. Wade de Reind'. Ricardus filius eius.

Seal tag.
Date: circa 1200.

13

Harley Charters 54, H. 5.

Sciant tam presentes quam futuri quod ego Iohannes de Peitune concedo et hac mea carta confirmo Willelmo fratri meo pro seruicio et humagio suo unam dalam terre al crupht et alteram dalam terre in minori redeles et terciam dalam al perier de fuerstrete et quartam dalam al perier ailred de me et heredibus meis sibi et heredibus eius in feudo et hereditate libere et quiete et honorifice habendas et tenendas et defendendas pro omni seruicio propter xiiii denarios per annum reddendos. Et preter hoc quod totam terram quam habuit pater meus Nigellus in segagio defendere debet ab omni seruicio. Has partes terre predictas debeo ego Iohannes et heredes mei warantizare Willelmo et heredibus eius adversus omnes homines et feminas. Quas si warantizare non poterimus, dabimus eis escambiam de terra que vocatur Walhaghe. Pro hoc concessu et donacione et pro carte mee confirmacione dedit mihi predictus Willelmus xii solidos argenti de gersuma. Termini predicti census reddendi tales sunt. Ad festum sancti Ædmundi vii denarios et ad pascha floridum vii denarios. Hii sunt testes Robertus de Lindholt. Martinus de Nuost'. Galfridus frater eius. Willelmus filius Rogeri de Polst'. Iohannes filius Ricardi. Gilbertus filius Hugonis. Iohannes filius Eruold. Brihtmer faber cum filiis suis.

Fragment of seal.
No early endorsement.
Date: T. R. H. ii.

14

Harley Charters 76, F. 35.

Gilbertus comes Clare omnibus suis hominibus et amicis francis et anglicis salutem. Notum sit vobis omnibus me concessisse donationem quam Adam filius Warini fecit Hugoni filio suo et Prince uxori sue scilicet terram Martini capellani de Poseligwrdia que fuit Burnardi et quicquid ad eam pertinet. Et apud Claram pratam que Martinus tenebat et mansuram in qua monachorum grancee fuerunt cum gardino et sochomannos de Strateseleia et de Ferneleia quoque in Stanesfeldia xx solidos et vi denarios cum eorum humagio. Hanc autem donationem concedo Hugoni et Prince matri sue in feudo et hereditate eis et heredibus suis de me et heredibus meis. Et ad tenendum de Adam eo uiuente et si de Hugone male contigerit Herveio fratri suo et si de Herveio male contigerit ceteris pueris huius mulieris scilicet Prince siue sit masculus siue femina. Et post obitum Ade teneant de me et de meis heredibus per seruitium quinte partis militis et ista quinta pars militis est infra seruitium unius militis de Pebenersia. Et dum Princia sine marito suo fuerit post decessum Ade omnem predictam tenuram ei concedo et do ad educandos pueros suos. Si autem virum ceperit tantum ei do et concedo predictos sochomannos xx solidos et vi denarios reddentes et tres mansuras de burgagio in Sudberia ex parte Esexie et x marcas quas ei Adam dabit in dotem. Testes sunt. Rogerus frater meus. Rodbertus de Creuechor. Simon de Thoni. Rogerus de Hastinges. Walterus filius Humfridi. Radulfus Walensis. Alanus de Dampmartin. Stefanus frater eius. Hugo de capello. Toma de capello. Gillbertus filius Humfridi. Willelmus de Mundauilla. Warinus filius Ade. Gerardus nepos Ade. Galfridus nepos eius. Fulco frater eius. Willelmus filius Ansgodi. Mattheus de Lundoniis. Rogerus de Dalham. Willelmus clericus. Baldewinus clericus. Elinal et Alured fratres eius.

Tag for seal.
Date: 1139-1151.

15

Additional Charters 15508.

Sciant presentes et futuri quod ego Henricus prior de Acra consilio et assensu totius conventus nostri dono et concedo et hac carta confirmo Alano filio Rodberti de Snetessam et heredibus suis iure hereditario terram Ricardi filii Turewi et terram Offing et terram Edild cum participibus suis et aliis pertinenciis suis et humagiis suis ad tenendam de nobis pro quattuor solidis reddendis singulis annis pro omni seruitio excepto auxilio quod de eo capiemus sicuti de aliis nostris liberis hominibus. His terminis ad purificationem xvi denarios. Ad pentecosten totidem ad festum sancti Michaelis totidem. His testibus. Osberto decano. Rogerio capellano. Gaufrido capellano. Willelmo de Lechesam. Herberto de Hillegetuna. Hamone serviente. Ricardo de Rudam. Radulpho de Brecham. Radulpho filio Adewaldi. Willelmo de Resam. Willelmo de Ribur. Lamberto clerico de Chemeston.

Slit for seal.
Date: T. R H. ii.

16

Additional Charters 28322.

Gaufridus cognomento Boterel Baldwino prefecto suo de Nettestede salutem. Ego Gaufridus tibi precipio precipit quoque uxor mea precipiunt et filii ut monachis beati Melanii qui in Hetfeldo uilla regis manent marcam argenti anima pro mea meorumque uxoris scilicet mee filiorumque et antecessorum successorumque meorum monasterio eorum dedi singulis annis quamdiu rerum mearum procurator eris absque omni contradictione reddas. Volumus autem et precipimus tam ego quam uxor mea Vigolent' filiique mei Willelmus et Petrus ut omnes qui in officio quod modo agis tibi successuri sunt marcam de qua loquor predictis monachis omni anno in festiuitate sancti Michaelis recte dant. Volumus etiam et precipimus ut cartula hec in ecclesia coram tota parrochia legatur ut parrochiani omnes huius doni mei testes sint et monachi illud de cetero libere et absque labore habeant. Hoc [1] a nobis precipi audierunt ex baronibus comitis Alani Alanus Aimeric Gaufridus Aldroini anno ab incarnatione domini MCXXXVIIII.[1]

Tag for seal.
Date: 1139.

[1] In different ink.

17

Additional Charters 28331.

Willelmo dei gratia Norwiciensis episcopo. Walchelino archi-diacono. Conano comiti domino suo. omnibusque sancte ecclesie filiis Petrus Boterellus salutem. Sciatis me dedisse et concessisse pro salute anime patris mei et matris mee et predecessorum meorum et mea ecclesie sancti Melanii Redonis Godwinum prepositum de Netle-stede et eius heredes cum omni tenura sua quam de me tenuit in perpetuam elemosinam solutum et liberum et quietum ab omni seruicio et exactione et consuetudine et ab omnibus que ad me pertinent et exutum ab omni mea potestate saluo regis seruicio et comitis. Concedo etiam quod idem Godwinus et heredes sui habeant in uilla mea de Nettlestede eandem communionem in bosco in plano in pascuis in aquis in uiis in semitis et in omnibus locis quam ante habebat. Preterea do et concedo prefate ecclesie duodecim acras de dominio meo in sorlund quietas solutas et liberas ab omni seruicio tam regis et comitis quam meo. Quod si Godwinus vel aliquis heredum suorum de aliqua forifactura ad me pertinente ponatur in placitum in curia monachorum prefate ecclesie super eundem feodum [1] iusticiabitur a monachis. Idem vero Godwinus et heredes sui non cogentur per me aut ministros meos ire ad underz et syras sed dato scoto suo solito domi in pace remaneant. Volo autem ut prefata ecclesia hoc donum meum de me et de heredibus meis libere solute et in pace imperpetuum teneat. Testes huius rei sunt. uxor mea Matildis que huic donationi interfuit et eam concessit. Adam presbiter eiusdem ville. Arnaldus medicus. Richardus presbiter. Willelmus presbiter de Pileberge. Ranulfus parmentarius. Godricus filius eius. Godricus de fonte Willelmus filius Lifrum. Rogerus prepositus. Petrus de Chalgrafe. Andrea filius Arnaldi. Galfridus presbiter de Blacheham. Robertus de Wilasham. et tota villata de Netlestede.

Date: 1153-1160.
Tag for seal.

18

Campbell Charters i. 12.

Sciant omnes tam futuri quam presentes quod ego Robertus Huse-bonde dedi et concessi Roberto filio Bartolomei de Sancroft totam meam terram in Staniland cum uia scilicet tres acras et dimidiam in

---

[1] Interlined.

terra arabili tenendam in feodo et hereditate illi et heredibus suis de me et heredibus meis libere et quiete reddendo annuatim pro omni seruicio quod ad terram pertinet vi denarios ad iiiior terminos scensus episcopi scilicet ad quemlibet terminum iii obolos. Pro hac donatione et concessione prefatus Robertus de Sancroft dedit predicto Roberto Husebonde vii solidos in gersumiam et ut hec donatio et concessio firma habeatur hac carta mea illi legitime confirmaui. Hiis testibus Roberto de bosco. Radulfo filio Safridi. Waltero filio Eustacii. Alano filio Rogeri. Iuone. Simone de Stort. Herberto dispensatore. Ricardo filio Walteri. et Rogero eius filio. Radulfo filio Willelmi filii Godwini. Hugone Babbard. Rogero Leueg'. Willelmo filio Ricardi. et pluribus aliis coram soca Elmhamie.

Seal : flower device.
Date : early thirteenth century.

19

Campbell Charters xii. 3.

Omnibus sancte matris ecclesie filiis Willelmus dei gratia Norwicensis episcopus salutem. Sciant uniuersi fideles dei tam presentes quam posteri quod Ernaldus Lupellus spontanea ductus uoluntate in manum meam mihi reddidit sochagium quod ei dederam tota uita sua tenendum scilicet terram Turchilli filii Ketelli in Humeresfeld et omni modo quietum clamauit et penitus abdicauit. Ego uero eandem terram ita in manu mea liberam et absolutam concessi et dedi Bartolomeo homini meo de Humeresfeld. dandam uni ex fratribus suis uel uni ex heredibus suis cui uoluerit. tenendam libere et hereditarie de me et de meis in posterum successoribus episcopis in capite reddendo inde annuatim dimidiam marcam argenti et faciendo inde debitas consuetudines. Hanc quoque donationem meam presenti scripto confirmo et sigillo meo corroboro. Testibus Gaufrido dapifero. Petro constabulario. Magistro Nicholao. Magistro Stangr'. Radulfo capellano. Rogero presbitero de Humresfeld. Rogero clerico episcopi. Herberto dispensatore. Radulfo filio Saffridi. Warino ostiario. et Rogero filio eius. Randulfo coquo. et Gilleberto filio eius. Waltero filio Wlmari. Waltero filio Odonis. Rogero filio Anchetil. Eberardo Halthein. Richero filio Philippi de Martham.

Seal in brown wax : episcopal figure.
Date : 1146-1175.

20
Topham Charter 15.

Sciant presentes et futuri quod ego Maino prior de acra consilio et assensu fratrum nostrorum do et concedo et hac carta confirmo Alano filio Rodberti totam terram que fuit Wreghe Scule cum omnibus perti nentiis suis in omnibus rebus in feudo et hereditate illi et heredibus suis tenendam de nobis annuatim reddendis xvcim solidos pro omnibus seruiciis scilicet ad pentecosten v solidos ad festum sancti Michaelis v solidos ad purificationem sancte Marie v solidos saluo in omnibus auxilio nostro. Et si placitum aut uerbum aliquod inter predictum Alanum et homines surrexerit quod ipse Alanus per se terminare non poterit et ante nos pervenerit medietas placiti nostra erit et alia medietas sua. Hiis testibus. Steing' archidiacono. Gaufrido decano. Willelmo presbitero de Sculetorp. Symone de Cailli. Rogero de Paueli. Petro de Peleuile. Willelmo fratre suo. Rogero de Cailli. Willelmo de Cailli. Radulpho de Sancto Germano. Bernardo Grim. Lamberto clerico. Eustachio dapifero. Willelmo clerico de Dunham. Willelmo clerico de Fuheldun.

Date: 1174–1180.
Seal : Episcopal figure.

21
Cott. Charters ii. 4.

Henricus rex Anglorum Ricardo Basset et Alberico de Ver et vice-comitibus et baronibus et omnibus fidelibus suis francis et anglis de Nortfolc salutem. Sciatis me dedisse et concessisse Ebrardo episcopo de Nortwic c solidatas de redditu hundretorum meorum de Walesham et Blafelda de x libris quas reddere solebant per annum pro escambio ecclesie sue de Stiuentona. Et ita quod ipsa hundreda teneat in tota vita sua et reddat mihi inde per annum reliquas c solidatas qui remanent de istis x libras. Testibus cancellario et Roberto de Sigillo et Ricardo Basset et Alberico de Ver apud Westmonasterio.

Date: 1129–1135.
Remnants of Seal Tag.

22
Cott. MS. Nero, C. iii, fol. 190, fig. 1.

Noverint omnes qui cyrographum istud viderint legerint vel de hac conventione aliquid audierint quod ego Ricardus filius Gileberti de Rising concedo dominis meis monachis de Lewes dimidium sochagium

quod habeo in Lettuna cum redditibus et omnibus rebus quas ego
haberem si in manu mea illud tenerem. Ad tenendum quindecim
annis a festo Sancti Michaelis post adventum domini regis in Angliam
quando misit abbates et comites per totam Angliam scrutari actus
vicecomitum et prepositorum id est post incarnationem domini anno
millesimo centesimo sexagesimo primo. Postquam terminum supradictum dimidium sochagium in manu mea revertetur. Nam aliam
medietatem eiusdem sochagii videlicet tenementum Wlui presbiteri et
Iohannis fratris eius et advocationem ecclesie de Lettuna supradictis
dominis meis monachis concessi et donaui liberam et quietam in
perpetuum. Hanc conventionem sine fraude et ingenio tenendam
affidauimus ego Richardus et Willelmus frater meus et Robertus
Iordanus et Osbertus clericus de Sipedham in manu Willelmi dapiferi
in preseneia [*sic*] domini Henrici prioris de Acra et Roscelini
Camerarii et Ade monachi. Domini vero mei monachi dederunt mihi
per Osbertum decanum pro hac convencione v marcas. Huius con-
vencionis testes sunt. Wlui presbiter. Iohannes filius eius. Gaufridus
presbiter. Lambertus diaconus. Willelmus dapifer. Reinerus frater eius.
Hamo serviens. Radulphus Tusard. Radulphus Calet. Henricus de
Warnestona. Robertus Testard. Thomas de Trunfled. Ricardus de
Arundel. et quia hec conventio in presentia prioris de Acra est facta
sigillo eius petitione utriusque partis est munita.

Date : 1161.
Cyrographum (down left side and cut through).

23

Cott. MS. Nero, C. iii, fol. 191, fig. iv.

Iohanni Norwicensis ecclesie episcopo omnibusque sancte matris
ecclesie filiis presentibus et futuris Matillis de Muntchenesi salutem.
Sciatis me concessisse et dedisse deo et ecclesie sancte Trinitatis de
Gypeswico et canonicis ibidem deo seruientibus ecclesiam sancte Marie
de Hegham in perpetuam elemosinam cum pertinentiis prefate ecclesie
pro salute anime mee et patris et matris mee et Rogeri domini mei de
Munchenesi et filiorum et omnium predecessorum meorum. His
testibus. Walkelino archidiacono. Hugone decano. Willelmo decano.
Nigello decano. Alano de Bellofago. Hugone filio Garini. Osberto de
Gladfen. Galfrido de Reind'. Willelmo de Possewic. Roberto Bagard.
Iohanne Sund. Alano clerico. Garino sacerdote. Hoc factum est
coram capitulo de hundredo de Sanford.

Date : late twelfth century.

24

D. of L. Misc. Books A. 75/4 (Public Record Office).

Sciant presentes et futuri quod ego Walterus filius Wlmari de Sernebrune vendidi et forisiuravi domino priori de Lewes et conventui pro quinque. solidis. redditum trium denariorum per annum quem Galfridus mihi reddidit pro illis terris scilicet pro duabus rodis et dimidia. inter viam de fferinges et pro duabus rodis et dimidia ad Brechamgate. et pro tribus rodis et dimidia adfole. et pro una roda in Sudbriche. Hanc autem venditionem feci coram socna de Hecham. Teste socna et multis aliis.

> Slit only for seal tag.
> Occurs in Lewes Cartulary Cott. Vesp. F. xv, fol. 251.
> *Date* : late twelfth century.

25

Bodleian Library, Norfolk Charters 602.

Notum sit tam presentibus quam futuris dei fidelibus quod ego Adam prior et totus conventus ecclesie sancti Benedicti de Hulmo concessimus et dedimus et presenti cyrographo nostro confirmauimus Willelmo Saluagio terram nostram de Gernemutha in longitudine et in latitudine illi et heredibus suis habendam et tenendam iure hereditario in perpetuum terram scilicet illam quam Wido nepos Aky prioris tempore regis Henrici primi tenuit in eadem uilla cum omnibus libertatibus et liberis consuetudinibus que ad eandem terram pertinent sicut predictus Wido eam umquam melius et liberius tenuit in vita sua pro quinque solidis de redditu per annum ad festum sancti Martini pro omnibus seruiciis. Willelmus uero prenominatus in eadem terra inueniet fratribus ibidem redeuntibus idoneum hospicium sed ad sumptum eorum proprium. Huius donationis et concessionis sunt testes. Magister Adam de Gernemutha. Willelmus Latimarus. Richerus Mazelin. Rogerus filius Ædwardi. Robertus clericus. Iustinus. David Ruffus. Alexander de Berewic. Theodericus. Humfridus. Osbertus. Wlward. Willelmus scip'. Arnaldus frater eius. Iohannes filius Richeri. Willelmus filius Humfridi. Willelmus clericus filius Ædrici. Willelmus filius Suiert. et Walterus frater eius. Wlfricus

filius Sprottolf. Karolus clericus. et multi alii seniores et iuniores de
uilla.

CYROGRAPHUM

Date: 1168–1173.
(The cyrographum is cut through in a straight line.)
Occurs also in Cott. Galba E ii. fol. 59.

26
Bodleian Library, Norfolk Charters 607.

Notum sit omnibus matris ecclesie filiis tam presentibus quam
futuris quod ego Daniel dei gratia abbas ecclesie Sancti Benedicti de
Holm communi consensu et concordi uoluntate totius capituli prefate
ecclesie concessi et dedi Rotberto Picot in feudo et hereditate totam
terram quam predicta ecclesia habet in Grenesuilla pro sexaginta sellis
frumenti de redditu unoquoque anno ad mensuram prefate ecclesie.
Ipse vero Rotbertus concessu et voluntate mea totiusque conventus
dedit eandem terram Beatrici uxori sue in dote sibi et suis heredibus
habendam et tenendam de eadem ecclesia pro predicto seruicio
scilicet lx sellis his terminis. Ad festiuitatem Sancti Andree per-
reddet xx primos sellos. Ad Pentecosten secundos xx sellos. Ad
festiuitatem Sancti Michaelis ultimos xx sellos. Hanc vero concessionem et donationem quam isdem Rotbertus fecit prefate uxori sue
Beatrici in dote in presentia nostri et totius capituli et nos ei concedimus et donamus in feudo et hereditate et hac carta nostra
confirmamus et his subscriptis testibus premunimus. Turbertus
decanus. Stephanus capellanus. Bartholomeus de Glanuilla. Willelmus
filius Herem. et Petrus filius eius. Odo arbalistarius. et Richardus et
Ebrardus filii eius. Richardus filius Stanhardi. et Willelmus filius eius.
Rogerius de Glanuilla. et Rotbertus filius eius. Osbertus de Glanuilla.
Richardus filius Bond. Outi. Alexander. Herebertus nepos episcopi
Iohannes. Garinus. Hamundus cocus et multi alii.

CYROGRAPHUM

Date: 1140–1145.
Occurs also in Cott. Galba E ii. fol. 59.

27
Harl. MS. 2110, fol. 2 b.

Notum sit presentibus quam futuris quod ego Willelmus comes de
Warenna confirmo et concedo donationem xl solidatarum terre quam
Rainaldus frater meus in liberam et quietam elemosinam dedit deo et
sancte Marie de Acra pro salute anime sue et omnium parentum suorum.

Nomina autem illorum qui in terra illa manent hec sunt. Godwinus filius Hagne de Wichingham et Azur et Henricus frater eius et Gilbertus de Branteston. Hos homines et tenuram eorum cum humagiis et consuetudinibus et seruitiis cunctis uolo et precipio ut monachi de Achra bene et libere et quiete et in pace teneant et possideant iure perpetuo duas quoque partes decime de Wistona quas Rainaldus supradictus ecclesie donauit et duas partes decime Radulfi de Baliol in Dockinges et duas partes decime Gaufridi de Quiluer-duilla uidelicet in Dockinges. Has donationes concedo et confirmo nominatim pro anima patris mei et pro redemptione anime mee et pro animabus illorum qui hec beneficia ecclesie Sancte Marie de Achra contulerunt.

Date: 1089–1135.

28

Harl. MS. 2110, fol. 4 b.

Willelmus comes de Warenna Willelmo dapifero et omnibus homini-bus francis et anglicis salutem. Sciatis me donauisse et concessisse deo et sancte Marie de Acra et monachis ibidem deo seruientibus pro anima patris mei et pro animabus omnium parentum meorum et pro me ipso in liberam elemosinam et quietam ab omni consuetudine et seruitio terram meam de Wittona et quicquid in ea habebam cum ecclesia et omnibus aliis pertinenciis. Do etiam predictis monachis in liberam elemosinam terram meam de Senetesham quam habebam in dominio meo cum homagiis et aliis pertinenciis. Hiis testibus Reginaldo de Warenna. Ela comitissa. Rogero capellano. Willelmo dapifero. Radulfo de Warrenna. Roberto Freiuilla. Osmundo dispensa-tore. Galfrido de Quiluerduilla. Osmundo de Stuteuill.

Date: 1138–1148.

29

Harl. MS. 2110, fol. 31 b.

Sciant presentes et futuri quod ego Aileue filius Turchilli de Rucham dedi concessi et hac presenti mea carta confirmaui deo et sancte Marie de Acra et monachis ibidem deo seruientibus in liberam et puram et perpetuam elemosinam totam terram quam Galfridus frater meus tenuit de predictis monachis die qua obiit tenendam libere et quiete in per-petuum. Hanc autem donationem consilio et assensu Thome Albi nepotis et heredis mei feci. Hec sunt partes terre prenominate. Tuftum inter tuftum Thome Albi et tuftum Vincentii. Et terra ad

Witewelle inter terram Rogeri Kolling et terram Thome Albi. Et
terram ad Cathorgate inter culturam Willelmi pincerne et terram
Thome Albi. Et ex meridionali parte terra inter terram Alexandri
et terram Thome prefati. Et terram in Nethercroft iuxta terram
Ricardi filii Ranulfi. Et terram ad Grumbaldeshacre inter terram
Hugonis de Sokentun et terram Thome prefati. Et terram ad
Grenegate inter terram Alexandri et terram prenominati Thome.
Et terram ad Meredele inter terram Rogeri Dusing et Thome
prenominati. Et item ad Merdele terram inter terram Beatricis et
terram Thome prefati. Et ad Merdelepit terram inter terram Thurkil
Dusing et terram Thome predicti. Et ad Merdeleslede terram inter
terram Willelmi filii Rogeri et terram Thome prefati. Et terram ad
Stanardesgate inter terram Willelmi filii Bike et terram Thome
prenominati. Et terra ad Wudegate. Ego uero et heredes mei
warrantizabimus prefatam terram predicte domui contra omnes.
Hiis testibus. Richardo de Resham. Seniore comite Warrennie. Waltero
filio Hamonis. Hugone fratre eius. Godrico dapifero. Willelmo filio
Reinaldi. Eustacio Seniore. Alexandro dapifero. Ricardo port'.
Iohanne de Swafham. Galfrido de Swafham. Simone abbate. Magistro
Simone de Acra. et multis aliis.

Date : thirteenth century.

30

Harl. MS. 2110, fol. 21 b.

Sciant presentes et futuri quod ego Robertus filius Radulphi
consilio voluntate et assensu Claricie uxoris mee et liberorum meorum
dedi et concessi deo et Sancte Marie et monachis de Acra iii acras
terre mee ad Teofordegate in liberam et perpetuam et quietam
elemosinam pro anima patris mei et antecessorum meorum. Et pro
hac donatione monachi clamauerunt mihi quietam calumpniam quam
habebant in terra de bromwong. Teste Yuone presbitero. Teoberto
clerico. Rogero de Anemere. Eustacio Willelmi nepote monachi. et
tota soca de Massingham.

Date : thirteenth century.

31

Harl. MS. 2110, fol. 40.

Sciant presentes et futuri quod ista conventio inter Robertum
priorem et conventum monachorum de Acra et Willelmum priorem et
conventum de Cokesford quod predicti Robertus prior et monachi
quietum clamauerunt et remiserunt clamium quod habuerit in mora

de Estrudham et pastura eiusdem more. Et quod predicti Robertus
prior et monachi et eorum successores numquam movebunt queri-
moniam erga predictos Willelmum priorem et canonicos et eorum
successores super eadem mora et eiusdem imperpetuum pastura. Cum
uero opus fuerit ut puraleamentum fiat in uilla de Westrudham de uiis
et semitis et fossatis iniuste levatis homines canonicorum de Cokesford
cum hominibus monachorum de Acra et hominibus aliorum
partionarum in uilla de Westrudham ibunt ad hoc emendandum.
Sed ad merciamentum hominium prioris et monachorum de Acra
remanebit dicto Priori monachorum et monachis et eorum successoribus.
Et minute decime curie dictorum monachorum in Westrudham
remanebunt dictis monachis. Sed decime garbarum et agnorum
et uellerum et caseorum manerii eorum integre soluentur dicto
Willelmo priori et conuentui de Cokesford et eorum successoribus imperpetuum pro firma solita. Aueria uero estraeta et homines
aduentii in feudo dictorum monachorum in Westrudham advenientia et
iuuenta more solito dicto Willelmo priori et canonicis remanebunt
similiter cum mensuris et galonibus saluo dictis priori et monachis ad-
merciamento de hominibus suis. Et in huius rei testimonium dicti
priores et conuentus alterna scripta idem represententia sigillorum
capitulorum suorum appositione corroborauerunt. Hiis testibus
Ricardo de Seinges. Herueo de Stanho. Galfrido le Sirede
Massingham. Henrico de Ferrariis de Rudham. Iohanne de Keyney'.
Dauid de Hout'. Willelmo cambellano. Rinaldo de Dunt'. Waltero
filio Hamonis. Hamone filio suo. Willelmo filio Godefrido.

> *Date*: 1239-1250.

32

Harl. MS. 2110, fol. 39 b.

Iohannes de Querceto ministris et omnibus hominibus suis
de Rudeham salutem. Sciatis quod calumpniam humagii Gaufridi
fratris Matthei prioris de Rudeham quietam clamaui deo et Sancte
Marie et monachis de Acra et meam firmam pacem illi dono et
communem pasturam meam illi concedo, ita ut faciat mihi tales consuetudines quales ceteri homines de Rudeham mihi faciunt qui nullam
terram de me tenent in eadem uilla. Hiis testibus. Henrico decano.
Pagano de Taterford. Roberto fratre meo. Rogero Sparco. Willelmo
filio Alfled. Walchel filio Brithl. et pluribus hominibus de socha. Hanc
supradictam pasturam illi concedo quamdiu manserit in feudo meo in
eadem uilla. Hiis testibus quod supra.

> *Date*: 1140-1170.

33
Harl. MS. 2110, fol. 55 b.

Sciant presentes et futuri quod ego Milo filius Willelmi de Baggethorp reddidi et quietum clamaui Roberto priori et monachis de Acra et
eiusdem loci conuentui totum tenementum quod tenui de feodo predictorum monachorum in Baggethorp' de me et heredibus meis imperpetuum scilicet xxiv acras terre in campis de Baggethorp' cum mesuagio
quod fuit Willelmi patris mei in eadem uilla pro x marcis argenti quas
prefati prior et monachi michi dederunt. Et ut hec quieta clamantia
stabilis et firma permaneat imperpetuum sigilli mei impositione et tactis
sacrosanctis abiuratione pro me et heredibus meis confirmata. Hiis
testibus. Willelmo de Burham. Waltero de Cheureuilla. Reinaldo de
Dunt'. Willelmo de Bellem'. Willelmo de Garnei. Waltero filio Hamonis.
Alexandro dapifero. Alin' de Acra. Galfrido camerario. Hamone filio
Godefridi. Willelmo filio Willelmi. Ada portario. Iohanne aurifabro.
Willelmo de Heringham. et pluribus aliis et soca de Baggethorp'.

Date: circa 1250.

34
Harl. MS. 2110, fol. 103.

Noverint hoc scriptum visuri vel audituri quod ego Willelmus filius
et heres Galfridi Geynecolt de Wenling, reddidi resignaui et quietum
clamaui dominis meis priori de Castelacra et eiusdem loci conventui
totum tenementum et totam terram quam habui et tenui uel habere potui
de eis simul et totum ius et clamium quod habui et habere potui in
dicta terra in Wenlinge cum omnibus ad dictam terram pertinentibus.
Hanc resignationem et quietam clamationem feci ego dictus Willelmus
prefatis dominis meis pro me et pro omnibus meis imperpetuum. Et
in huius rei testimonio presens scriptum sigillo meo roboraui. Hiis
testibus. Alexandro dapifero monachorum. Galfrido ianitore. Ebor'
Grang'. Willelmo Brett'. Roberto de Creic clerico. Nicholao camerario
prioris. Ada de Wigenhall. Gilberto de Franchevilla. Iohanne de
Norwic'. Willelmo de Wenling clerico. et tota soka de Wenling'.

Date: thirteenth century.

35
Cott. Claud. D. xiii, fol. 20.

Anno ab Incarnatione domini mcviii facta est hac concordia inter
Herbertum episcopum et Petrum de Valoniis de quibusdam con-

trouersiis quas habebant inter se propter quasdem terras quas
Herbertus clamabat in manerio de Binham et Petrus similiter in
manerio de Langham. Herbertus dimisit calumpniam quam faciebat
et clamauit illam terram quietam quam clamabat infra terminos de
Binham uidelicet duos hospites cum duabus carucatis terre et prata et
aliis particulis terre quas ibi clamabat. Similiter Petrus clamauit
illam terram quietam quam habebat infra terminos de Langham et
quam se clamabat ibi habiturum. De pasturis uero huiusmodi
conueniencia facta est ut pasturae communes essent sicut fuerunt
temporibus predecessorum uidelicet Edwardi regis et Willelmi
senioris et terre que illis temporibus colebant essent arabiles et que
eisdem temporibus inculte erant iacerent deserte servata utrius manerii
auctoritate. Ex parte Herberti fuerunt Radulfus de Bellofago. Radulfus
Passelewe. Radulfus dapifer Godrici. Wydo dapifer. Alanus conestabol'.
Willelmus Longaspata. Alanus de Secefford. Ranulfus de Stratune. Et
de monachis. Goffridus. Ingulfus. Macharius. Stemardus. Ex parte Petri
fuerunt. Ricardus Alb'. Andoen' capellanus. Willelmus de Hoctune.
Gaufridus de Fanarchis. Willelmus Veltr'. Albertus francigena. Odo de
Nueres. Walterus de Valoniis. Turoldus de Dallinges. Ricardus de
Spineto. Iwynus de Stiuekeye. Edwinus de Warham. Turkellus Rufus.
Toche de Withuna. Odulfus. Chetellus.

Date: 1108.

36
Cott. Claud. D. xiii, fol. 121.

Sciant tam presentes quam futuri quod ego Radulphus filius
Thoroldi de Dalling' concessi deo et sancte Marie de Binham et
monachis ibidem deo servientibus iii acras in Britriztoft et seruicium
Petri nepotis mei de quadraginta acris quas tenet de me in parva
Riburg ii solidos reddendos annuatim ecclesie sacre Marie de Binham
in perpetuam elemosinam hiis terminis xii denarios ad Pascha et xii
denarios ad festum sancti Michaelis. Idem persolvent heredes sui
post eum et si aliquid suo iusto herede remanserit illa terra liberam et
quietam in manus monachorum remanebit. Hanc donationem feci pro
anima Petri de Valoniis qui eandem terram de conquestu anglie patri
meo in hereditatem dedit et pro anima patris et matris mee et pro salute
corporis et anime mee et omnium amicorum meorum. Hiis testibus
Ricardo de Nugun. Willelmo filio Radulfi. Rogero de Saxlingham.
Waltero de Hosedon'. Nicholao de Titebi. Willelmo de Causton'. Et
omnia [*sic*] villata de Dalling' teste.

Date: circa 1125.

37

Cott. Claud. D. xiii, fol. 173.

Notum sit omnibus tam presentibus quam futuris quod ego Adam filius Alueredi pro amore dei et Sancte Marie matris domini et pro salute mea et uxoris mee et pro animabus Petri de Valoniis avi mei et Rogeri de Valoniis filii eius awunculi mei et Petri iunioris cognati mei et pro animabus patris mei et matris mee omniumque parentum meorum do libere et quiete ab omni seculari seruicio assensu uxoris mee ecclesie Sancti [*sic*] Marie de Binham in perpetuam elemosinam possidendam in villa de Ingaldesthorp unam mansionem id est croftam ad in hospitand' et iii acras in agro et i acram de prato quinque videlicet acras et pasturam et turbariam in commune. Croftam vero dedi in loco qui nominatur Southcroft. Predicta autem ecclesia nihil mihi vel successoribus meis pro hac donacione unquam aliquid recompensabit preter oracionum suffragia. Hanc itaque donationem prius feci super altare sancte Marie de Binham coram priore Milone astante conuentu et subscriptis testibus. Ricardo clerico videlicet de Ingaldesthorp. Ade de Franche terre. Rogero de Appulia. Willelmo de la Haia. Nicholao. Wlmero. Cane. Halwardo. et Wymondo. Magistro de Wict'. Ade de Berneya. Michaele portario. Roberto Tresgot. Willelmo Grangiario. Gosso. Stirgaro coco. Rogero. et Reinaldo carpentario. Ricardo filio Turkil. Thoma coco. Deinde in villa de Ingaldesthorp coram omni villa presente Domina Beccha uxore mea et Rogero fratre meo et Ricardo presbitero et Ricardo presbitero ipsius ecclesie de Ingaldesthorp Hugone de Insula. Hanc itaque elemosinam feci pro salute mea tam corporis et anime et pro salute uxoris mee cuius instinctu hoc opus aggressus sum et pro remedio animarum patris et matris et parentum eorum et ut me Deus meritis sancte Marie protegat et defendat et in presenti succurrat ad vitam eternam perducat.

Date: circa 1160–1170.

38

Cott. Galba E. ii, fol. 32 b.

Henricus rex Anglie et dux Normannie et Acquit' et comes Andagauie Willelmo de Bosco salutem. Precipio quod sine dilacione et iuste reddas abbati de Hulmo natiuos et fugitiuos suos cum catallis suis qui post mortem regis Henrici aui mei fugerunt de terra sua. Et ne feceris vicecomes de Northfolchie faciat ne quis eos iniuste detineat super forisfacturam meam. Teste Ricardo de Canuilla apud Windeser'.

Date: 1155–1176.

39
Cott. Galba E. ii, fol. 54.

Godricus dapifer et uxor eius Ingreda dederunt ecclesie Christi et Sancti Benedicti et fratribus de Hulmo terram de minori Medeltone pro animabus suis post quorum obitum. Radulfus filius Godrici ipsius suscepit eandem terram de Medeltone tenendam quamdiu vixerit inde reddens singulis annis x solidos ad mensam fratrum ecclesie Sancti Benedicti. Uxor quidem eiusdem Radulfi Letselina dedit curtinam ecclesie Sancti Benedicti eo tenore ut si Radulfum ipsa superuixerit habeat eandem terram de Medeltona eodem seruicio quo Radulfus quamdiu et ipsa uixerit. Si uero Radulfus habuerit heredem de muliere desponsata tenebit ipse heres ipsius Radulfi predictam terram de Medeltone reddens inde singulis annis xl solidos ad mensam fratrum. Si autem heredem non habuerit post amborum obitum remanebit eadem terra de Medeltone cum omni emendacione quam imposuerint quieta et libera Sancto Benedicto deo et fratribus de Hulmo. Hanc conuencionem ego Richerus abbas feci et concessi communi consensu fratrum in capitulo. Testimonio. Radulfi prioris. Aky. Wlfrici. Godwini. Gyomari. monachorum. Hermanni dapiferi. Meynardi militis. Bernardi magistri. Radulfi nepotis abbatis. Sirici. Goscelini. Willelmi presbiteri. Lisewy nepotis Radulfi. Willelmi de Hereford. et aliorum. Quicunque hanc conuencionem dissoluere presumpserit et auctoritate dei patris omnipotentis et Sancte Marie uirginis et sancti Benedicti omniumque sanctorum dei et sanctorum canonum ac nostri misterii perpetuo anathemate feriantur amen.

Date: 1101–1116.
Occurs also Dugdale Mon. Ang. iii, p. 87.

40
Cott. Galba E. ii, fol. 54.

Notum sit omnibus dei fidelibus quod ego Radulfus filius Godrici apud Norwycum ad monasterium Sancti Stephani deo et sancto Benedicto et Richero abbati et omnibus fratribus Holmensi ecclesie pertinentibus quietam clamo in perpetuum de me et meis heredibus scilicet terram de Hardelaie quam tenui de supradicta abbacia in firma ita firmiter ut nec ego ulterius nec aliquis heres meus in posteris

diebus inde calumpniam faciat. Et ipse supradictus Abbas et monachi
eiusdem ecclesie pro deliberacione terre supradicte mihi dederunt xxx
marcas argenti de substancia ecclesie. Et ego Radulfus hanc delibera-
cionem terre prefate feci coram duobus comitatibus videlicet Norfolchie
atque Suffolchie. Huius rei sunt testes Herbertus episcopus Norwy-
censis. et Richerus de Bealfo. et Osbertus et Walterus archidiaconi
Norwycenses. et Letselina uxor mea. et Radulfus dapifer meus. et
Eudo frater meus. et Lesewinus nepos meus. et ceteri.

Date : 1101–1121.

41
Cott. Galba E. ii, fol. 55.

Notum sit omnibus dei fidelibus quia ego Conradus abbas et nos
monachi sancti Benedicti Hulmensis ecclesie concessimus in communi
capitulo Willelmo de Curecun et suo heredi terram nostram de
Grenseuille in feodo et ad firmam reddentem unoquoque anno lx
sellos frumenti quamdiu inde nobis bene seruierint et predictam
firmam reddiderint. Ipse quoque Willelmus iurauit fidelitatem sancto
Benedicto et Abbati et fratribus et fortitudinem et auxilium in omnibus
que posset ad placita et ad hundredum et ubicunque necessarium
uideret et dedit nostre ecclesie duas partes decimarum eiusdem terre de
Blakeuurde et de Fridestone et de annona et de omnibus facultatibus.
Testimonio eorum qui affuerunt. Dompni Euradi episcopi. Rogeri
archidiaconi. Willelmi archidiaconi.[1] Rogeri de Lymefi capellani
Regis. Galfridi capellani Regis. Ingolphi presbiteri. Ade dapiferi. et
fratrum eius Willelmi et Richeri. Goscelini de Brumstede. Radulfi
et Hugonis filiorum Roberti. Thurstani filii Boyselyn. et ceterorum

Date : 1126–1127.
Occurs also Dugdale Mon. Ang. iii, p. 87.

42
Cott. Galba E. ii, fol. 55.

Conradus Dei gracia abbas sancti Benedicti de Hulmo omnibus suis
fidelibus per abbaciam. Sciatis me optulisse super altare sancti Benedicti terram et quicquid Egeluuardus et uxor illius Lefleda tenuerunt
in Houetone et Northwalsham ita videlicet ut sit amodo imperpetuum
ad uictum et ad firmam monachorum. Et sit una cultura et una
firma in dominio aule de Houetone nec inde unquam separetur.

Date : 1125–1127.
Occurs also Dugdale Mon. Ang. iii, p. 87.

[1] MS. repeats.

43

Cott. Galba E. ii, fol. 56.

Notum sit presentibus et futuris quod ego Anselmus abbas Holmensis ecclesie communi consensu fratrum concessi terram de Grengeuile Willelmo de Curecun et heredi suo in feudo et ad firmam reddentem lx sallops frumenti unoquoque anno ad mensuram ecclesie et sic distinctis terminis, ut prime xx mine reddite sint cum uentum fuerit ad festum Sancti Andree, secunde uero uiginti mine reddite sint cum uentum fuerit ad diem Pentecostes posteriores autem uiginti mine persolute sint cum uentum fuerit ad Natiuitatem sancte Marie. Huius rei testes sunt. Walterus Magister. Willelmus Brito. Robertus de Wals. Willelmus de Redham. Willelmus filius Hermanni. Ricardus filius Bondi. Odo balistarius. Ricardus filius Stannardi. Hegelot. Simundus. Rogerus. Ipse uero Willelmus cum recepit hanc terram a Richero abbate iurauit fidelitatem sancto Benedicto et abbati et fratribus et se redditurum supradictam firmam et dedit duas partes decime eiusdem terre et de Blakeuurde et de Fridestone in annona et aliis facultatibus. Testimonio eorum qui affuerunt. scilicet dompni prioris Wlmari et omnium fratrum. Hermanni dapiferi et filiorum eius. Roberti fratris Abbatis. Roberti balistarii et filii eius Odonis. Ricardi filii Stannardi. Walteri de Burch.

Date: 1133–1140.

44

Cott. Galba E. ii, fol. 56.

Sciant presentes et futuri quod ego Anselmus gracia dei abbas sancti Benedicti de Holm consilio fratrum eiusdem ecclesie concessi Radulfo filio Godrici terram de minori Medeltone quam pater eius Godricus dapifer cum uxore sua Ingreda donauit sancto Benedicto tenendam et habendam ipsi Radulfo ea condicione qua diffinitum est et confirmatum priuilegiis in communi capitulo presente abbate Richero scilicet quamdiu vixerit pro x solidis per annum ad mensam fratrum et post mortem eius rectus heres Radulphi dabit quadraginta solidos unoquoque anno monachis. Si uero heredem non habuerit eadem terra de Metheltone remanebit quieta et libera deo et sancto Benedicto et fratribus de Hulmo. Huius rei testes fuerunt. Hubertus filius eiusdem Godrici. Radulfus Kriketot. Alanus de Hechingham. Willelmus filius Asketilli. Willelmus presbiter de Redham. et ceteri.

Date: 1133–1140.
Original in Bodleian Library (Norfolk Ch. : No. 604).

45
Cott. Galba E. ii, fol. 56–56 b.

Notum sit fidelibus quod ego Anselmus gracia dei Abbas sancti Benedicti de Holm et omnis conuentus eiusdem ecclesie pari consilio et uoluntate concessimus huic Basilie uxori Radulfi filii Godrici terram nostram scilicet minorem Methelton' cum omnibus pertinentibus habendam et tenendam in omni uita sua pro una marca argenti de rente unoquoque anno pro omni seruicio et hiis terminis dimidium ad Pascha et dimidium ad Natale domini.

Date: 1133–1140.

46
Cott. Galba E. ii, fol. 56 b.

Notum sit fidelibus presentibus et futuris quod dompnus Anselmus gracia dei abbas ecclesie sancti Benedicti de Holm et totus conuentus monachorum eiusdem loci in capitulo suo communi consilio et uoluntate concesserunt et dederunt huic Osberno presbitero terram sancti Benedicti in Pastone cum omnibus pertinentibus habendam et tenendam ipsi in feodo et hereditate pro dimidia firma unius carruce sicut antecessores eius pro eadem terra reddere solebant.

Date: 1133–1140.

47
Cott. Galba E. ii, fol. 58 b.

Notum sit omnibus matris ecclesie filiis presentibus et futuris quod ego dei gratia Abbas Hugo sancti Benedicti de Holm communi consensu et concordi uoluntate tocius conuentus prefate ecclesie concessi et dedi Roberto de Ludham fratri Thurberti et suis heredibus in feudum et hereditatem totam terram liberam et quietam sine callumpniatore et calumpnia quam Walterus Tike tenuit in Northwalsham et Antigham in campo et in prato et in turbario et in omnibus locis cum filia predicti Walteri. Hec donatio facta est prece et petitione predicti Walteri et parentum suorum. Pro hac terra redditurus est Robertus abbati tres solidos per annum pro omni seruicio et pro omnibus consuetudinibus. Huius donacionis testes sunt. Willelmus de Hastingges. Willelmus archidiaconus. Thurbertus decanus. Osbertus de Thurgertona. Stephanus presbiter. Nicholaus clericus Abbatis. et ceteri.

Date: Circa 1150.

48
Cott. Galba E. ii, fol. 58 b.

Ricardus Basset Baldrico et Edwardo salutem. Sciatis quod clamo quietum monachis de sancto Benedicto de Hulmo omne rectum quod habebam in Hecham quam tenebam de eis in feodo ad firmam et eis reddo illud manerium solum et quietum. Ideo uolo et precipio ut reddatis illis omne instauramentum quod ibi habebam quia illud eis totum concedo et quicquid inde cepistis in blado et pecuniis et in aliis. Et cartam meam quam mihi inde confirmauerunt reddite. Ita ne inde clamorem audiam amplius. Et nisi fecistis vicecomes comitatus fieri faciat.

Date: before 1145, probably 1129.

49
Cott. Galba E. ii, fol. 60 b.

Uniuersis sancte matris ecclesie filiis Willemus dei gratia Abbas de Hulmo totusque conuentus eiusdem loci salutem. Sciatis nos concessisse et dedisse in feodo et hereditate Philippo capellano filio Galfridi de Fordham totam terram quam emimus in Bastwyk' ab Hugone de Wroxham filio Reginaldi et ab aliis heredibus illius terre pro octo denariis annuatim reddendis altari sancti Benedicti pro omni seruicio et consuetudine et omnem terram quam Galfridus pater suus tenuit in Hecham cum tota terra illa quam Odo filius Lequen et ea quam Sibaldus filius Brunstani tenuerunt in eadem uilla pro quatraginta denariis pro omni seruicio et consuetudine. Horum uero denariorum reddet idem Philippus quattuor altari Sancti Benedicti ad festum eiusdem in estate. Tres autem solidos reddet cantori ad restaurationem librorum ad Pascha. Preterea terram quam pater suus tenuit apud Suthwalsham de iure celarii nostri pro duodecim escheppes de ordeo ei concedimus. Has autem terras tenebit Philippus predictus libere et quiete cum omnibus pertinentibus eisdem terris. Et ut nostra donatio perpetuam firmitatem obtineat scripto nostro et munimine sigillorum nostrorum corroboramus. Sub horum etiam testimonio. Magistri Nicholai. Henrici Bolewyt. Thome de Ludham. Willelmi presbiteri. et ceterorum.

Date: 1153–1168.

50
Cott. Galba E. ii, fol. 65 b (in margin).

Sciant tam presentes quam futuri fideles dei quod ego Thomas dei gratia Abbas de Hulmo totusque conuentus eiusdem loci concessimus et dedimus in feodo et hereditate Nicholao de Asmanhae decem acras terre et dimidiam ante portam Wydonis Rufi in bruario quod iacet iuxta terram Ade de Houetona pro octodecim denariis de censu ad aulam eiusdem ville tribus terminis reddendo pro omnibus seruiciis et consuetudinibus. Terram autem habebit et tenebit predictus Nicholaus et heredes sui predictam bene et in pace libere et quiete pro prenominato seruicio. Huius rei sunt testes. Thomas de Waltone. Adam de Houetone. Gaufridus cementarius. Willelmus filius Petri. Hugo Cocus. et tota soka de Houetone.

    Date: 1175–1186.

51
Cott. Galba E. ii, fol. 56 b.

Notum sit presentibus et futuris fidelibus quod Walterus Halteyn dedit sancto Benedicto et monachis in ecclesia Holmensi eidem patri famulantibus in elemosina pro se et suis uiuis et defunctis unam acram de prato super ripam flumenis infra diuisionem de Heylesdone sole et quiete a se et suis heredibus in perpetuum ad faciendum et emendandum stangnum molendini monachorum de Hecham. Istamque donacionem ipse Walterus cum quodam cultello super altare sancti Benedicti optulit. Abbas autem predicti loci dompnus scilicet Anselmus et monachi dederunt Waltero sex marcas argenti per manum Simonis cognati sui. Quoddam et pratum pro quo Walterus reddebat ipsis xvi denarios per annum dederunt illi suisque heredibus sole et quiete in perpetuum. Conuenit etiam inter eos quod ipse Walterus haberet annuatim unam pelliciam et unas crepitas a camerario quales unus monachorum habere consueuit. Preterea susceptus est Walterus cum suis plenarie in fraternitatem loci. Ita ut si ibidem monachus fieri uoluerit suscipietur. Ubicumque autem defunctus fuerit tantumdem illi quantum uni ex ipsis a cunctis persoluetur in missis et psalmis et oracionibus. Hii sunt testes pacti et donacionis quam fecit Walterus super altare sancti Benedicti. Radulfus Kaniard. Robertus filius Thebaldi. Elebal. Willelmus de Burgo. Simon de Ludham. Willelmus Brito. Rogerus pincerna. Ubi terra diuisa est fuit dompnus Abbas Anselmus. Willelmus prior. Gerardus monachus Norwycie. Alfricus musard qui mensurauit terram. Willelmus presbiter. Godwinus filius Wlwan. Godwinus filius Ketel. et multi alii de Heylesdone. Et de Abbacia. Odo Albalistarius. Willelmus de Caletorp. Osbernus de Redham. et ceteri.

    Date: 1134–1140.
    Occurs also Dugdale Mon. Ang. iii, p. 92.

52

Cott. Vesp. F. xv, fol. 251.

Hec est conventio inter Osbertum decanum de Lewes et Radulphum de Kalli et fratres eius et Radulphum filium Goce. Radulphus de Kalli et Elias frater eius dederunt et concesserunt in liberam et perpetuam elemosinam deo et sancto Pancratio et monachis de Lewes ibidem deo servientibus totam terram que fuit patris eorum in Massingham quam Hugo frater eorum tenuit de Elia propter marcam argenti annuatim reddendam. Et Elias et Radulphus de Kally xii denarios annuatim reddendo et eam super altare de Hecham deo et sancto Pancratio optulerunt et cum istis Robertus de Kally et Ricardus frater eius et Willelmus filius Reinaldi cognatus eorum quicquid iuris in predicta terra ex iure successionis habere potuerunt deo et Sancto Pancratio super altare apud Hecham optulerunt et liberum et quietum imperpetuum clamauerunt. Omnes isti prenominati nec se nec alios per eos contra istam donacionem et concessionem esse venturos fide corporaliter prestita firmauerunt. Propter hanc donationem et concessionem ita factam Radulphus filius Goce de Luna dedit Elie de Kally x marcas argenti et Radulpho de Kally iiii solidos et Willelmo filio Reinaldi v solidos ita ut predictus Radulphus filius Goce predictum tenementum hereditario iure teneat de conventu de sancto Pancratio reddendo annuatim unam libram piperis et alteram cimini pro omni seruicio. Hec conventio facta est sub testimonio virorum subscriptorum. Galfridi et Alani de Snetesham. Ranulphi et Petri de Hunstaneston'. Willelmi clerici. et Alani de Thornham. Petri de Hecham. Willelmi de Repeham. Thome de Gerewode. Radulphi Barate. Ricardi filii Walteri. Reinaldi Buci. Rodberti Tutbien. et coram socha apud Hecham.

Date: late twelfth century.

53

Cott. Vesp. F. xv, fol. 284.

Notum sit presentibus et futuris quod hec est conuencio et concordia facta inter Eustachium Eliensem episcopum et Umbertum priorem de Lewes et eiusdem loci conuentum et Stephanum de marisco et Adam filium Ade et Ricardum de Medlers et Iuonem de Walsocha et Alanum de Hagebech' et Iohannem filium Gregorii et Willelmum Palmer et omnes participes et Galfridum de Belassis et Gocelinum de Walpol et Radulfum filium Ade et Adam filium Radulfi et Gosselinum de Walpol' et eius participes et Ricardum de Medleres et Thomam filium Remarii et Rogerum filium Semerdi et Petrum de Kailly et

Gilebertum filium Tomeri et Walterum filium Alani et omnes participes
et Willelmum Ruffum et omnes participes et Alanum filium Algeri
et Willelmum de Kailli et omnes participes et Herlewinum filium
Willelmi et omnes participes et Willelmum de Mustrol' et Radulfum
filium Gocelini et Radulfum de Betsted et Ricardum filium Gocelini
et eorum participes qui sunt de leta integra in Merslond. Et
Sampsonem abbatem de Sancto Edmundo et Rogerum de Scales et
Thomam de Ingaldesthorp' et Willelmum filium Alani de Remham
et Robertum de Sculham et Robertum de Cherewilla et Walterum
filium eius et Adam filium Alani et Godfridum filium Godwini et
Godefridum filium Arketel et Hugonem Strud' et Walterum filium
Radulfi et Walterum filium Galfridi et Ricardum filium Iohannis et
Petrum Delfred et Willelmum filium Stang' et Willelmum filium
Godefridi et eorum participes in uilla de Tilen' et Ilsington' et
Iohannem filium Willelmi de Wiginhal' et Matildam filiam Willelmi
de Len et Galgfridum filium Humberti de Len et Henricum filium
Eudonis et Adam Cholle et Petrum filium Alani de Clenchwarent' et
Alanum filium Hugonis et Hugonem filium Willelmi et fratres omnes
de contencione que fuit inter eos de tota pastura et turbaria que
uocatur Westfen et que fuit in communi a fossato cancellarii cum tota
longitudine et latitudine uersus occidentem in festo Sancti Iohannis
Baptiste anno nono regni domini regis Iohannis scilicet quod prefata
pastura et turbaria remanebit in communi in posterum et in perpetuum
prefato Episcopo Eliensi et eius successoribus et Priori et conuentui
de Lewes et Herlewino filio Willelmi et Willelmo de Mustrol' et eorum
participibus prenominatis in Walsocha et Walton cum suis partinenciis
scilicet Hagebech' et Walton et Tirington et eorum heredibus. Et
prefato Abbati Sancti Eadmundi et eius successoribus et Rogero
de Scales et Thoma de Ingaldestorp' et Iohanni filio Willelmi et eorum
participibus prenominatis in Tilen' et Ilsington et Clenchwarent'
et Len et eorum heredibus. Et si forte fuerit commune consilium
prefati episcopi uel successorum eius et prioris et conuentus de Lewes
et Herlewini filii Willelmi et Willelmi de Mustrol' et eorum participum
in tota [leta]¹ integra uel heredum suorum et prefati Abbatis Sancti
Edmundi uel omnium successorum et Rogeri de Scales et Thomae de
Ingaldestorp' et eorum participum prenominatorum in Tilen' et in
Ilsington uel heredum suorum quod prefata pastura et turbaria sit

---

¹ 'Tota' ends one line in the MS., 'integra' begins another. By
analogy with the earlier phrase 'leta' seems here to have been omitted,
and its insertion seems necessary to complete the sense.

partita inter ipsos. Quinta pars illius pasture et turbarie remanebit hominibus participantibus de Tilen' et Ilsington' prenominatis et heredibus eorum ad parciendum inter eos secundum quantitatem feudorum suorum sicut antiquitus solebat et debuit fieri. Et quattuor partes remanebunt domino Episcopo Eliensi uel eius successoribus et priori et conuentui de Lewes et Herlewino filio Willelmi et Willelmo de Mustrol' et eorum participibus prenominatis de Walsoche et Walton' cum pertinenciis suis scilicet Hagebech' et Walplo et Tirington' et heredibus eorum ad parciendum inter eos secundum quantitatem feudorum suorum sicut antiquitus solebat et debuit fieri. Et si forte contigerit quod plures oportent facere expensas et custamenta ad prefatam pasturam et turbariam tenendam et defendendam uersus homines de Wigenhal' uel aliquos alios prefatus Abbas Sancti Edmundi uel eius successores et Rogerus de Scales et Thomas de Ingaldestorp' et eorum participes prenominati in Tilen' et Ilsington' uel eorum heredes acquietabunt quintam partem omnium expensarum et custamentorum per singulam. Et dominus Episcopus Eliensis et predictus (prior de) Lewes et conuentus per suos senescallos affidauerunt et sigillis suis confirmauerunt. Et predictus abbas Sancti Edmundi similiter per suum senescallum affidauit et sigillo suo confirmauit et omnes ceteri partes affidauerunt et sigillis suis confirmauerunt. Hiis testibus. Symone de Insula. Galfrido de Swaddon'. Petro Pycot. Willelmo de Trumpington. Roberto de Laushille. Thoma de Heidon'. Simone camerario. Willelmo Britone. Willelmo filio Roberti. Alano filio Ricardi. Iohanne filio Godfridi. Petro Britone. Eustachio fratere suo. Thoma de Bec.

Date : 1207.

54

Cott. Vesp. F. xv, fol. 284 b.

Sciant presentes et futuri quod ego Alanus de Ingaldestorp' quando recepi Kenewi in firma a dominis meis monachis de Lewes huiusmodi convencionem cum eis feci et fideliter tenendam affidaui uidelicet quod quicquid propria industria vel de meo donando adquirere de feudo eorum potero post obitum meum dominis meis monachis remanebit. Ita tamen quod illud quod ex meo proprio pro terris donabo heredi meo reddatur. Iuratum est quod post decessum meum terra que vocatur Teldcroft monachis remanebit et ipsi reddent singulis annis ad festum sancti Michaelis heredibus meis iii solidos et iii denarios. Et sciendum quod ego Alanus dedi Willelmo de Sculham pro supra dicta terra xvi marcas et ix solidos ex quibus xi

marcae fuerunt monachorum et v (marcas) et ix solidos ex meo proprio.
Has v marcas et ix solidos reddent heredibus meis. Et ut hec
conventio posteris notificetur et rata habeatur cirographum meum feci
et unam partem munitam sigillo Osberti decani retinui et partem
illam quam monachis donaui meo proprio sigillo muniui. Facta est
hec conventio coram hiis testibus. Henrico priore de acra. M. sub-
priore. Gaufrido de Risinges. Lamberto de Cemest'. Alueredo et Gau-
fredo de Suenesham. Willelmo de Tirrington. Herveo de Brecham. Eadmundo de Gait'. Ricardo de Cheile. Petro filio Godeberti. Thoma de
Trumflet. Eustachio de Tatressei. Roberto de Caili. Ricardo de Eatun.
Herberto Hillington. et soca de Hecham.

Date : late twelfth century.

55
Cott. Vesp. F. xv, fol. 285.

Sciant presentes et futuri quod ego Albertus prior sancti Pancratii
de Lewes et eiusdem loci conventus dedimus et concessimus et hac
presenti carta nostra confirmauimus Thome filio Alani de Walpole pro
homagio et seruicio suo sextam partem unius tenmanloth in uilla de
Walpoll' que tenuit Alanus pater eiusdem Thome in eadem villa
illi et heredibus suis habendo et tenendo de nobis libere et quiete bene et
in pace. Reddendo inde annuatim pro omni seruicio consuetudine et
exaccione decem solidos bonorum et legalium sterlingorum ad tres
anni terminos videlicet ad festum sancti Michaelis quadraginta denarios
et ad purificationem beate Marie quadraginta denarios et ad penthe-
costen quadraginta denarios salvo nobis annuo redditu triginta unius
denariorum quod nobis idem Thomas debet pro alia sexta parte
alterius tenmanloth quam dedit magister Alexander eidem Thome in
libero maritagio cum Matilda sorore sua saluo eciam nobis alio redditu
annuo sex denariorum quod nobis debet sepedictus Thomas de
quinque acris terre et dimidia quas tenet de nobis in villa de Walpoll.
Teste universitate nostra.

Date : before 1244.

56
Add. MS. 28024, fol. 183.

Radulphus de Toeneio omnibus hominibus suis de soca de Neketoine
presentibus et futuris salutem. Sciant quod Ricardus de Portan'
(reddidit coram me Ricardo de Portan[1] reddidit coram me Ricardo

---

[1] Sic MS.

de Neketon' terram que fuit Bunde aui sui et Ade patris sui ipsi et
heredibus suis de se et heredibus suis hereditario iure tenendum per x
solido dando per annum pro omni seruicio. Quare volo et firmiter
precipio et hac carta mea confirmo ut prefatus Ricardus et heredes sui
eandem terram habeant et teneant tam bene et honorifice in bosco et
plano in prato et in pascuis ut aliquis predecessorum suorum illa
melius uel liberius habuit uel tenuit. Testes sunt Rogerus de Port'.
Rogerus de Hacot. Rogerus Malfras. Radulfus capellanus. Rogerus
de Kersyngham. Willelmus Blund'. Robertus Tusard. Petrus filius
Hahalwald'. Radulphus de Neketon'.

> *Date*: circa 1115.

57

Add. MS. 28024, fol. 183 b.

Radulfus de Toenio omnibus de soca Neketoine tam Francis quam
Anglis salutem. Concedo Guillelmo filio Estangrin' totum quod habeo
in soca Neketoine ita quod in quoque anno reddat $\overset{xx}{iiii}$ libras sicut suus
pater Estangrin' a meo patre nunquam melius habuit. In feofirma sibi
concedo et suo heredi. Ego et meus heres et mea uxor Aelicia
Pickeham autem mihi foris de firma retineo. Do uero sibi quoque
anno iiii capreos et sue uxori unum et extra siluam potero fugare
lepores et si uoluero capere aliquam uillam ut dem uel mutuem alicui
militi prout Gullielmus instaurauit ita accipiam quod dabo sibi quantum
alius dederit uel ponam sibi in dica sua. Et si quis uel instaurauit xx
solidos plus quam reddat ponam sibi quoque anno in dica sua. Et si
quis uoluerit mihi plus crescere in firma non auferam Gullielmo sed
teneat honorifice. Terra sua erit michi obses quod in meam firmam
reddat. Testes sunt G. Bland. G. de Port. Ricardus Grossus.
Nicholaus de Mammariis. Galfridus capellanus. Ricardus de Achi-
gneio. Tota socca Neketan' tam franci quam angli. G. de Lira.
Oliuerus sacerdos. Oliuerus de Fraunsat. Gullielmus suus socius.
Oliuerus de Neketon. Normannus. Oliuerus filius Tolguer. Bu-
smerus de Acra. Tosteus Sauer. Oliuerus de Ostona. Bondus de
Cressyngham. Gerham. Petrus de Crennis. Olfert de Catetona.
Godwinus diaconus. Iohannes sacerdos. Oliuerus de Acra. Valete.
Tribus terminis id est festum candeler' et pentecost' et sancti
Michaelis reddetur firma quoque termino xxvi librae et i marca argenti
et si uno defecerit aliquid secundo uel tertio termino totum reddetur.
Hec michi tenend' iurabitur.

> *Date*: circa 1115.

58

Add. MS. 28024, fol. 183 b.

Rogerus de Toenio omnibus suis hominibus tam Francis quam Anglis salutem. Notifico uobis me reddere et concedere Willelmo filio Estangrin' sibi et suo heredi in feodo et hereditate totam terram et homines et omnia illi terre pertinencia quam Estangrin' pater suus de meo Radulfo tenuit et quam idem Estangrin' et iste Willelmus de meo patre tenuerunt ita libere et quiete sicut isti ab hiis meis antecessoribus tenuerunt per seruitium 1 solidorum tantum (?) per annum et sicuti sua brevia testant. Testes sunt Ricardus Pontu filius Sampsonis. Andreas Gitonita. Normannus de Neketone. Aslond de Frousham. Rogerus de Lira'. Elemerus de Acra. Ricardus de Acra. Radulphus de Acra. et ad ultimum socca valens.

Date : circa 1125.

59

Add. MS. 28024, fol. 183 b.

Rogerus de Toenio toti socce de Neketan' salutem. Scitote quia concedo Guillelmo filio Estangrin totam firmam quam habuit a me et omnia sua feoda ex integre sicut unquam melius habuit et seruite ex inde sicut unquam melius servistis sibi uel patri suo. Testes G. de Port.' G. clemens. Ricardus Achigneyo. Fulco de Surtilinga sunt.

Date : circa 1125.

60

Ely Muniment Room, Liber ' M ', fol. 80.

Henricus Rex Anglorum Episcopo de Norwico et episcopo de Ely et vicecomitibus et omnibus baronibus et fidelibus suis francis et Anglis de Sudfolc salutem. Sciatis me dedisse et concessisse Oino episcopo Ebroicensi manerium meum de Brantford et xl solidatas in sochemannis in Claiendone hundredo et in Bosemere hundredo. Et uolo et firmiter precipio ut bene et in pace et quiete et honorifice teneat cum soca et saca et toll et team et infangenetheof et omnibus consuetudinibus suis sicut ego ipse tenui in meo dominio et cum omnibus quietancionibus quas idem manerium habuit in tempore meo de scyris et hundredis et geldis et danegeldis et placitis et auxiliis. Testibus. Galfrido Cancellario. et Roberto de Sigillo. et Gaufrido de Chindone. apud Londoniam.

Date : 1123–35.

61

Ely Muniment Room, Liber ' M ', fol. 91.

Ricardus dei gratia Rex Anglie Dux Normannie et Aquitanie Comes Andegauie omnibus iusticiariis suis vicecomitibus ministris et balliuis et fidelibus suis tocius Anglie salutem. Precipimus uobis quod firmiter et inviolabiliter faciatis obseruari racionabile divisam inter Tilneiam et Tyrrinton inter letam que est Episcopi Elyensis cancellarii nostri et Prioris de Lewes et Abbatis de Rameseya et Willelmi de Warenna et dimidiam letam que est Comitis de Clara et Abbatis Sancte Ædmundi et Godefridi de Lisewi' et Roberti de Cheruille et participancium eorum sicut facte sunt et perambulate per preceptum nostrum. Teste me ipso apud Touern' xxviii die Aprilis Regni nostri anno sexto.

Date: April 28, 1195.

62

Ely Muniment Room, Liber ' M ', fol. 113.

Henricus dei gratia Rex Anglie Dominus Hybernie Dux Normannie et Aquitanie et Comes Andegauie Archiepiscopis episcopis abbatibus prioribus comitibus baronibus iusticiis vicecomitibus prepositis ministris et omnibus balliuis et fidelibus suis salutem. Sciatis nos concessisse et hac carta nostra confirmasse venerabili in Christo patri Hugoni Eliensi episcopo et successoribus suis episcopis Eliensibus et ecclesie sue Eliensi in perpetuam elemosinam manerium de Branford in Suffolc cum omnibus pertinenciis suis et quadraginta solidos in sokmannis et in Claydone hundredo et in Bosemere hundredo quod Rex Henricus proauus noster dedit Oino quondam Ebroycensi episcopo et ecclesie Ebroicensi et quod manerium idem Episcopus Elyensis de licentia et uoluntate nostra emit de episcopo et capitulo Ebroicensis ecclesie ad opus suum et successorum suorum episcoporum Eliensium et ecclesie sue Eliensis. Quare uolumus et firmiter precipimus pro nobis et heredibus nostris quod predictus Episcopus et successores sui Episcopi Elyenses et ecclesia sua bene et in pace quiete et honorifice teneant manerium predictum de Branford in Suffolk cum omnibus pertinenciis suis et quadraginta solidos in sokemannis et in Claydone hundredo et in Bosemere hundredo cum socha et sacha et toll et team et infangentheof omnibus consuetudinibus suis sicut Henricus rex proauus noster illud unquam melius tenuit in dominico suo et cum omnibus libertatibus et quietanciis quas idem manerium habuit tem-

pore predicti Henrici Regis proaui nostri de scyris et hundredis et
geldis et danegeldis et placitis et auxiliis sicut carta predicti Henrici
Regis proaui nostri quam inde habet rationaliter testatur. Hiis testibus
uenerabilibus patribus. Roberto Lincolniense. Willelmo Wintonie.
Willelmo Saresburie. Rogero Bathoniense. Waltero Norwicense. et
Ricardo Roffense episcopis. Ricardo de Clare comite Gloucestrie et
Hertford. Rogero le Bigod comite Norfolcie et marescallo Anglie.
Humfrido de Boun comite Essex et Hereford. Hugone de Uer
comite Oxonie. Iohanne de Plesset comite Warewicie. Willelmo de
Cantilupo. Iohanne de Lexinton. Bartholomeo de Eryoyl. Petro Peyure.
Galfrido Dispenser. et aliis. Datum per manum nostram apud West-
monasterio. duodecim die Octobris anno regni nostri tricesimo primo.

Date: 1247.

63

Liber Niger Sancti Edmundi (Cambridge University Library) fol. 96.

Henricus Rex Anglorum Ebrardo Norwiciensi episcopo et Roberto
filio Walteri uicecomiti et omnibus baronibus et fidelibus suis de
Sudfolc salutem. Sciatis me concessisse deo et Sancto Ædmundo et
abbati et monachis Sancti Ædmundi terras illas quas Berardus eis
reddidit quas ei dederam de dominio ecclesie tam in dominio quam in
militibus et in sochemannis et uolo et precipio firmiter ut bene et in
pace et quiete et honorifice teneat ecclesia sancti Ædmundi et abbas
et monachi omnes predictas terras et homines in dominio sicut erant
in dominio die qua illas dedi predicto Berardo. Testibus Ranulpho
cancellario. et Nigello de Albini. et Mauricio de Windeshor.' apud
Windeshor'.

Date: 1121-1135.

64

Rylands Library, Registrum Eboracense ii, fol. 398.

Sciant presentes et futuri quod ego Swanus filius God' de Wybertona
concessi et dedi et hac mea presenti carta confirmaui Iohanni filio
Iordani de sancto Botulpho pro seruicio suo unum selionem terre in
Braac de Tittona in Northschiftyng' iacentem inter terram que fuit
Walteri Wyseman et terram que fuit Benedicti de Wybertona et
abutissat super Braac de Schirebec et draftam de Wybertona ei et
heredibus suis et cuicunque ipse vel heredes sui predictam terram dare
vel assignare voluerint. Habendum et tenendum de me et heredibus

meis in feodo et hereditate bene et in pace libere solute et quiete
reddendo inde annuatim michi et heredibus meis duos denarios ad
festum omnium sanctorum pro omni seruicio et pro omnibus demandis
ad terram pertinentibus. Et ego Swanus et heredes mei warantizabimus predicto Iohanni et heredibus suis et cuicunque ipse uel heredes
sui eam dare uel assignare uoluerint predictam terram per predictum
seruicium pro omni seruicio imperpetuum.   Hiis testibus Ricardo
Bacun. Willelmo filio suo. magistro Henrico de Conitona. Roberto filio
Reginaldi. Nicholao fratre suo. Thoma maleb.   Hamone de Fenna.
Iocio maureward. Rogero fratre suo. Hemerico de Tittona. Wacio filio
Haraldi. Adestanno ferratore. Iohanne Samuel. Rogero de Etham.
Willelmo filio Astoc. Willelmo filio Swani.

Date: Circa 1200.

65

Rylands Library, Registrum Eboracense ii, fol. 394 b.

Sciant presentes et futuri quod ego Swanus filius Siwall' de Scyrebec
concessi et dedi et hac mea carta confirmaui Iohanni filio Iordani de
Sancto Botulpho totum pratum meum in Folcringtoft quod iacet inter
terram que fuit Iordani filii Haldani de Scirbec et terram que fuit
Hospitaliorum in Huteredploghland in Middelschifting et abutissat
super Hilledyk uersus est et super communem uiam de Scirebec
versus west scilicet quantum octo bovatis terre in eodem loco pro
seruicio suo et heredibus suis et cuicunque et quibuscunque et quandocunque ipse et heredes sui eam dare vel assignare uoluerint. Habendum
et tenendum de me heredibus meis in feodo et hereditate bene et in
pace libere solute et quiete reddendo inde annuatim mihi et heredibus
duos denarios ad feriam Sancti Botulphi pro omni seruicio et pro
omnibus demandis ad terram pertinentibus.   Et ego Swanus et
heredes mei warantizabimus predictam terram predicto Iohanni et
heredibus suis et cuicunque et quibuscunque et quandocunque ipse
et heredes sui eam dare vel assignare voluerint per predictum seruicium
pro omni seruicio imperpetuum.   Hiis testibus Thoma de Muletona.
Bartholomeo de Muletona. Galfrido de Beningtona. Waltero filio
Stephani. Rogero filio Walteri. Gerardo filio suo. Alano rufo. Iocio
filio Iordani. Ada filio Reinuordi. Alexandro Gernun. Radulfo filio
Thome. Henrico filio Ricardi. Hamone de Fenna. Iohanne Samuele.
Thoma Malebranch. Roberto et Nicholao filiis Reginaldi. Gerardo et
Raumero filiis Iuthered.

Date: Circa 1200.

APPENDIX II

EXTRACTS FROM EXTENTS AND STATEMENTS OF SERVICES

I

The Extent of Walpole (Norfolk) in 1222

Cott. Tiber. B. ii, fol. 167 b.

De libere tenentibus.

Henricus de Walpol' tenet sexaginta et unam acras per seruicium militare. Idem tenet Holmum pro decem et tribus solidis et quattuor denariis cum Nordcroft et Radcroft.

Stephanus de marisco tenet unum mesagium pro sex denariis.

Radulphus de Walpol' tenet triginta acras pro duodecim solidis et sex denariis.

Alanus filius Alger tenet octociesuiginti acras pro uiginti et quattuor solidis et debet sectam comitatus et hundredi.

Thomas de Estcroftdich' tenet sexaginta et quinque acras pro nouem solidis et nouem denariis.

Willelmus Franceis et Thomas de Nordwold tenent dimidium tenmanloth scilicet sexaginta acras et quinquaginta et duas acras ex altera parte pro sex solidis et octo denariis.

Magister Stephanus persona tenet tres acras pro duodecim denariis.

Ricardus filius Hildebrond et Adam frater suus et Ricardus nepos eorum tenent sexaginta acras pro decem solidis. Idem tenet quadraginta acras et debet sectam comitatus et hundredi pro manerio.

De Consuetudinariis.

Galfridus de Cattestoue et participes tenent unam tenmanloth scilicet sexiesuiginti acras pro decem solidis et dant quatuor gallinas et uiginti oua et arabunt per tres dies si habeat octo boues uel per duos dies si habeat quatuor boues uel per unum diem si habeat duos boues uel per dimidium diem si habeat unum bouem et eodem modo. Arabunt omnes inferiores consuetudines et habebunt cibum suum et carriabunt fenum uel bladum domini per quatuor dies ad cibum domini et faciant aueragium inter duas aquas sine cibo cum equo et sacco et portabunt fenum per unum diem sine cibo.

Willelmus filius Christiane et participes tenent unum tenmanloth scilicet sexiesuiginti acras pro decem solidis et quatuor gallinis et uiginti oua et easdem consuetudines.

De Landlesmannis.

Adam filius Ricardi tenet decem et quinque acras pro duobus solidis et unam rodam pro sex denariis et Petrus West et socii tenent decem et quinque acras pro duobus solidis.

Hii omnes dabunt duas gallinas et decem oua et carriabunt per duos dies cum cibo et habebunt unam garbam et aueragium ut supra et fenum portabunt sine cibo.

Willelmus filius Petri tenet triginta acras pro duobus solidis et unam gallinam et quinque oua et carriabit per unum diem et easdem consuetudines.

Petrus filius Radulfi et Reginaldus frater suus tenent triginta acras pro duobus solidis et unam gallinam et quinque oua et unum carrietum et easdem consuetudines.

Alanus filius Decani et fratres eius tenent uiginti et quinque acras pro tribus solidis et quatuor denariis.

Euech et Radulfus tenent uiginti et quinque acras pro tribus solidis et quattuor denariis.

Euech ad ladam tenet decem acras pro decem et sex denariis et dant quattuor gallinas et uiginti oua et carriabunt per quattuor dies et easdem consuetudines.

Adam del Has et participes tenent triginta acras pro quattuor solidis et duabus gallinis et decem oua et duas carrietas et easdem consuetudines.

De Operariis.

Wido Palmer tenet triginta acras et dat de Wdefare duos denarios ad festum Sancti Andree et dat duas gallinas et decem oua et debet qualibet ebdomada per annum sex operaciones nisi festum impediat et si operet per totum diem habebit cibum suum uel usque ad horam nonam sine cibo et falcabit pratum domini cum participibus suis pro operacione et carriabit fenum et bladum pro operacione quousque totum carrietum fuerit. Et herciabit per unum diem sine cibo et sine operacione et dabit quadraginta garbas tegminis uel duos denarios et faciat tres quarteria brasii et ducet inter duas aquas. Et erit quietus de tribus operacionibus nisi duxerit super diem festiuum. Tunc non erit quietus. Et debet furnare panem operariorum secundum turnum uicinorum et facit aueragium et computabitur ei pro operatione, nisi fecerit aueragium super diem festiuum quia tunc non computabitur ei pro operacione. Et carriabit fimum domini cum quodam homine eunte ad plaustrum suum proprium cum bobus domini pro operacione. Et sciendum quod ibit ad carucam domini per dimidium diem sine cibo uel per diem integrum et habebit unum panem et quinque euntes ad carucam habebunt tres obolos in ebdomada et computabitur pro operatione.

Iosephus le Palmer tenet triginta acras eodem modo.
Galfridus le Lemmer tenet triginta acras eodem modo.
Walterus et Alanus tenent triginta acras eodem modo.
Ricardus Kideman et participes tenent triginta acras eodem modo.
Walterus Walbode et socii tenent triginta acras eodem modo.
Iohannes filius Ailwini et socii tenent triginta acras eodem modo.
Hildebrond filius Gode tenet triginta acras eodem modo.
Petrus filius Godwini tenet triginta acras eodem modo.
Willelmus filius Hugonis et socii tenent triginta acras eodem modo.
Alanus et socii.tenent triginta acras eodem modo.
Godwinus filius Ailwini tenet triginta acras eodem modo.

De Toftlandis.

Iohannes filius Algeri et Thomas frater suus tenet unam toftland scilicet decem acras et dat unam gallinam et quinque oua et debet qualibet ebdomada duas operaciones et dimidiam et non erit quietus propter aliquid festum nisi in ebdomada Natalis Pasche et Pentecosten et falcabit per unum diem pro una operacione et facit per annum unum quarterium brasii et ducet usque Wisebech' pro una operacione et furnabit et faciet aueragium pedes et dominus poterit capere pro manibus opus in autumpno ad tascandum dum carriat bladum et postea allocare ei. Idem tenet dimidiam acram pro duobus denariis.

Laurencius Folcard tenet decem acras eodem modo et dimidiam acram pro duobus denariis.

Willelmus filius Saine tenet decem acras eodem modo et dimidiam acram pro duobus denariis.

Willelmus et Rogerus de Ponte tenent decem acras eodem modo et dimidiam acram pro duobus denariis.

Euech' Carpentarius tenet decem acras eodem modo et dimidiam acram pro duobus denariis.

Galfridus Curteis tenet decem acras eodem modo et dimidiam acram pro duobus denariis.

Ricardus Caruer tenet decem acras eodem modo et dimidiam acram pro duobus denariis.

Robertus Bustardus tenet decem acras eodem modo et dimidiam acram pro duobus denariis.

Seinas filius Laurencii tenet decem acras eodem modo et dimidiam acram pro duobus denariis. Hii omnes tenent unam rodam pro uno denario. Et isti debent colligere gallinas et portare ad Wisebech' sine operacione nisi fuerit super diem operacionis quo scilicet die debeat operari.

Ricardus Wise tenet quattuor acras pro una gallina et tria oua et debet qualibet ebdomada per annum unam operacionem et dimidiam et facit aueragium pedes.

De Censuariis.

Goscellinus Marescallus tenet septem acras pro decem et quinque denariis et dat unam gallinam et tria oua et tres precarias in autumpno cum cibo et fenum leuabit sine cibo per unum diem.

Laurencius filius Ingelieth tenet septem acras pro decem et quinque denariis et dat unam gallinam et tria oua et easdem consuetudines.

Rogerus filius Walteri tenet decem et tres acras et dimidiam pro decem et octo denariis et dat unam gallinam et tria oua et easdem consuetudines.

Aldwinus tenet duas acras et dimidiam pro sex denariis et dimidiam gallinam et unum ouum et dimidium et easdem consuetudines.

Rogerus filius Godwini tenet duas acras et dimidiam pro sex denariis et dimidiam gallinam et unum ouum et dimidiam et easdem consuetudines.

Godwinus tenet tres acras et tres rodas pro duodecim denariis et dat unam gallinam et tria oua et easdem consuetudines.

Petrus filius Rogeri tenet octo acras pro decem et sex denariis et dat unam gallinam et tria oua et easdem consuetudines.

Ricardus capellanus et Reynerus et Godwinus prepositus et Willelmus filius Mayn' tenet nouem acras pro decem et octo denariis et dat unam gallinam et tria oua et easdem consuetudines.

Iohannes filius Radulfi tenet decem et sex acras pro duobus solidis et octo denariis et dat unam gallinam et quinque oua et easdem consuetudines.

Godwinus prepositus et Petrus clericus tenent quinque acras pro decem et sex denariis et dant unam gallinam et tria oua et easdem consuetudines.

Philippus Ruffus tenet unam acram pro sex denariis et tribus precariis.

Iohannes filius Mabille tenet duas acras pro octo denariis et dat unam gallinam et tria oua et easdem consuetudines.

Ricardus filius Hildebrond tenet tres acras pro duodecim denariis et dat unam gallinam et tria oua et easdem consuetudines.

Simon Cogge tenet duas acras et dimidiam pro sex denariis et dat unam gallinam et tria oua et easdem consuetudines.

Warinus frater eius tenet duas acras et dimidiam pro sex denariis et dat unam gallinam et tria oua et easdem consuetudines.

Rogerus filius Laurencii tenet tres acras pro octo denariis et dat unam gallinam et tria oua et easdem consuetudines.

Iosephus filius Ricardi tenet unam acram et dimidiam pro sex denariis et dat unam gallinam et tria oua et easdem consuetudines.

Iohannes filius Ailwini tenet quinque acras pro decem et sex denariis et dat unam gallinam et tria oua et easdem consuetudines.

Rogerus de Lathe tenet octo acras pro sexdecim denariis et una gallina et tribus ouis et sicut easdem consuetudines.

Reginaldus Pigge tenet tres acras pro duodecim denariis et dat unam gallinam et tria oua et easdem consuetudines.

Amicia uidua tenet tres acras pro sex denariis et dat unam gallinam et tria oua et easdem consuetudines.

Willelmus filius Gode tenet unam acram pro quattuor denariis.

Ketelbern tenet quinque acras pro decem denariis et unam gallinam et tribus precariis.

Petrus filius Ailmer tenet tres acras et dimidiam pro decem et quattuor denariis et dat dimidiam gallinam et tria oua et easdem consuetudines.

Warinus frater suus tenet duas acras et dimidiam pro decem denariis et dat dimidiam gallinam et tribus precariis.

Algerus et Walterus Bule tenent duas acras pro octo denariis et dat unam gallinam et tria oua et tribus precariis.

Euech' Bule tenet duas acras pro sex denariis et tribus precariis.

Edmundus et Iohannes tenent duas acras pro octo denariis et dant unam gallinam et tria oua et sex precarias.

Willelmus filius Petri tenet quattuor acras et dimidiam pro decem et tribus denariis et dat unam gallinam et quinque oua et quattuor precarias.

Petrus filius Radulfi tenet quattuor acras et dimidiam pro decem et tribus denariis et dat unam gallinam et quinque oua et duabus precariis.

Elstan tenet dimidiam acram pro duobus denariis et dat unam gallinam et duo oua et tribus precariis.

Walterus Walbode tenet duas acras pro octo denariis et dat unam gallinam et tria oua et tribus precariis.

Edmundus filius Widonis tenet nouem acras pro duobus solidis et quattuor denariis et obolo et dat unam gallinam et quinque oua et tribus precariis.

Alanus Brond tenet unam acram et dimidiam pro sex denariis et dat unam gallinam et tria oua et tribus precariis.

Willelmus filius Gode tenet duas acras pro octo denariis et unam gallinam et tria oua et tribus precariis.

Reynerus Legier tenet quinque acras pro decem et sex denariis et dat unam gallinam et tria oua et tribus precariis.

Laurencius prepositus tenet duodecim acras et dimidiam pro duobus solidis et duobus denariis et dat unam gallinam et quinque oua et tribus precariis. Idem tenet duas acras pro duodecim denariis.

Godwinus filius Algeri et socii tenent decem acras pro duobus solidis et duobus denariis et dat unam gallinam et quinque oua et sex precarias.

Wido Wth tenet tres acras pro octo denariis et dat unam gallinam et tria oua et tribus precariis.

Suewing et socii tenent quattuor acras pro duodecim denariis et dant unam gallinam et tria oua et tribus precariis.

Iohannes et socii tenent duodecim acras pro quattuor solidis.

Adam et Alanus filius Willelmi tenent decem et quinque acras pro tribus solidis et tribus denariis et obolo et dant unam gallinam et quinque oua et tribus precariis.

Hildebrond tenet decem acras et dimidiam pro decem et septem denariis et dimidiam gallinam et duo oua et dimidium et tribus precariis.

Galfridus filius Wlfrich' tenet decem acras et dimidiam pro decem et septem denariis et dimidiam gallinam et tria oua et dimidium et tribus precariis.

Laurencius et Hildebrond tenent septem acras pro uiginti denariis et unam gallinam et tria oua et sex precariis.

Ioscelinus filius Alani tenet quinque acras et dimidiam pro decem et tribus denariis et dat unam gallinam et tria oua et tribus precariis.

Adam de Ridermere et fratres tenent tres acras et dimidiam pro decem et quattuor denariis et unam gallinam et tria oua et tribus precariis.

Alanus et Wlfuod tenent quattuor acras et dimidiam pro nouem denariis et unam gallinam et tria oua et nouem precariis.

Petrus et Galfridus tenent quinque acras pro decem denariis et tribus precariis.

Gilbertus filius Euech' tenet quinque acras pro uiginti denariis et unam libram piperis.

Henricus filius Thomae tenet quinque acras pro uiginti denariis.

Galfridus Wlnod tenet septem acras pro duodecim denariis et unam gallinam et quinque oua.

Gilbertus filius Euech' tenet tres acras et unam rodam pro decem et tribus denariis et dimidiam gallinam et duo oua et dimidium et unam precariam et dimidiam.

Henricus filius Thomae tenet quattuor acras pro decem et sex denariis et dimidiam gallinam et duo oua et dimidium et unam precariam et dimidiam.

Petrus Pistor tenet octo acras et tres rodas pro duobus solidis et septem denariis et unam gallinam et tria oua et tribus precariis.

Welhee reddit per annum ad festum Sancti Michaelis sex denarios. Et de passagio [1] de Wellestrem ad festum sancti Andrei duos solidos. Et de pundscoth equaliter uiginti et sex [2] solidos et octo denarios.

2
Extent of Wiggenhall (Norfolk) in 1222
Cott. Tiber. B. ii, fol. 172 b.

Tilleneye et Wigenhale.

Petrus filius Ricardi tenet decem et octo acras cum pertinentiis in Wiggenhale pro duodecim denariis equaliter ad quattuor terminos et debet sectam curie de Walton et de Wisbech et est liber ita quod non dabit gersomam pro filia.

Iohannes filius Willelmi de Wiggehale tenet unum mesagium pro sex denariis ad festum Sancti Michaelis et est liber.[3]

Gufr' Eued' tenet decem et octo acras in Tillinheye pro septem solidis et quattuor denariis equaliter et debet sectam curie de Walton et Wisebech' et non potest maritare filiam sine licentia domini sed dabit gersomam et tallagium.

Godefridus Starling tenet decem et quinque acras pro quattuor solidis equaliter et dabit gersomam et debet sectam.

Willelmus Eued' tenet sex acras pro duobus solidis et debet sectam et gersomam.

[1] 'Sicut' erased.
[2] 'Denarios' erased.
[3] One line blank after this in MS.

Galfridus filius Godefridi tenet viginti acras pro quattuor solidis et duobus denariis et debet sectam et gersomam.

Herlewynus Bee tenet undecim acras pro tribus solidis et duobus denariis et debet sectam et gersomam.

Reyner Sleng tenet quindecim acras pro quattuor solidis et octo denariis et debet gersomam.

Filia Radulfi Testard' tenet sex acras pro uiginti et duobus denariis et debet sectam et gersomam.

Relicta Petri Starling tenet quattuordecim acras pro tribus solidis et quinque denariis et obolo et debet sectam et gersomam.

Willelmus et Thomas Dix falsi fratres tenent sexdecim acras pro quinque solidis et quattuor denariis et debet sectam et gersomam.

Willelmus Dix tenet sexdecim acras de terra que fuit Widonis pro quinque solidis et quattuor denariis et debet sectam et gersomam et Thomas Dix abstulit Ingelieth filiam predicti Widonis et ita sine waranto tenet terram illam.

Thomas Hors de Wiggenhale tenet uiginti acras pro uiginti denariis et debet sectam et gersomam.

Willelmus presbiter de Wigenhale tenet octo acras pro tribus solidis et quattuor denariis et debet sectam et gersomam.[1]

Memorandum quod Willelmus Dix de Tilneh' dedit de consuetudinaria terra episcopi quattuor acras abbacie de Derham sed nullum fructum ad hoc inde perceperunt.

3
Extent of Binham

This professes to date from the foundation of the Priory circa 1100 (see Introduction).

Cott. Claud. D. xiii, fol. 5 b.

Incipit tenura tenentium de Binham in prima fundatione per dominum Petrum de Valoniis.

Hec sunt consuetudines tenentium le mollond in Binham.

Rogerus Verer in primis xv solidos et iiii denarios in quattuor terminis anni. Et a festo sancti Michaelis usque ad festum Sancte Crucis in qualibet septimana mediam partem iugeris tenetur arare. Ita dico si ad opus suum in ebdomada bis aret nisi forte festum omnium sanctorum in die mercurii vel annunciatio Sancte Marie evenerit. Sin autem non. Et inter festum Sancte Crucis et festum sancti Martini tenetur adducere v quadrigatas lignorum. Et hoc totum ex propria faciet expensa. Et

---

[1] Two lines here blank in MS.

in autumpno cum tribus hominibus faciet tres precatas et quilibet homo ad nonam habebit unum panem et unam ferculum carnium cum caseo vel piscem et caseum et insero duos panes et quattuor alectia uel ualens quattuor alectum. Et si necesse priori de quarta precaria fuerit eum adiuuabit cum uno prandio. Et in tribus sabbatis autumpni cum suis sociis tenetur tres cariatas adducere ex propria expensa. In quarto vero sabbato a mane usque ad vesperam carriabit cum cibo prioris. Idem Rogerus nec uxorem ducere potest nec filiam alicui dare sine licentia prioris.

Rogerus Archer iii solidos annuatim in iiii terminis et ii cariatas ligni et alias consuetudines sicut Rogerus Verer. Sed faciet cum uno homine. In prima et hebdomada post festum Sancti Michaelis ducet fimum et vigilabit circa faudam ut mos est et recipiet quodcunque seruicium priori placuerit.

Robertus filius Sterger viii denarios in iiiior terminis anni et ii gallinas ad Natale et iii precarias in autumpno cum tali cibo ut Rogerus Verer et quartam precariam sicut Rogerus predictus.

Robertus filius Aldit xii denarios in iiiior terminis anni et omnes precariis ut predictus Rogerus cum uno homine.

Willelmus filius Aslac xviii denarios in iiiior terminis anni et unum carr. ligni et consuetudines ut Rogerus Archer.

Petronilla vidua iiii denarios in iiiior terminis anni et iiii precarias ut Rogerus Verer.

Richardus ultra Bec x solidos in iiiior terminis anni et omnes con-suetudines ut Rogerus Verer.

Robertus filius Hane xx denarios in iiiior terminis anni et unum carrietum ligni et arare et metere ut Rogerus Verer.

Rogerus Cochale similiter easdem debet consuetudines quas predictus Robertus debet.

Edmundus clericus easdem debet consuetudines ut Robertus predictus.

Walterus xii denarios in iiiior terminis anni.

Richardus Grom xx denarios in iiiior terminis anni et ii carrieta ligni et arare et metere ut Rogerus Verer.

Thurchillus filius Edmod xv denarios et obolum in iiiior terminis et omnes consuetudines ut Rogerus Verer et unam gallinam.

Thurstan ix denarios et obolum et iiii precarias tali more ut Rogerus Verer et unam gallinam ad Natale.

Luwine ii solidos in iiiior terminis anni et iiii precarias ut Rogerus Verer et semel in anno i auerage.

Symon macellarius xii denarios in iiii°r terminis anni.

Walterus nouus homo xvi denarios in iiii°r terminis anni et v precarias ut Rogerus Verer.

Alanus filius Radulfi xii denarios et iiii°r precarias eodem modo ut Rogerus Verer.

Willelmus Cunu' xvi denarios et iv precarias.

Adam Brazor xii denarios et iiii°r precarias.

Richardus Fader xii denarios et iiii°r precarias.

Edmundus Godines xii denarios et iiii°r precarias.

Iocelinus xii denarios et iiii°r precarias.

Edmundus Morlai xii denarios et iiii°r precarias et i chapon ad Natale.

Rogerus Berenger iii solidos et in ii annis iii carrieta ligni et iiii precarias annuatim et faudam seruare et fimum ducere.

Herbertus Boselin xiiii denarios et precarias.

Edmundus Kempe iii denarios in ii terminis in Natale et in die Iohannis.

Iohannes Faber xii denarios et iiii°r precarias.

Angerus Cocus iiii solidos et v precarias.

Willelmus frater eius xiiii denarios et ii precarias et i gallinam ad Natale.

Hugo cancellarius xiiii denarios et iiii precarias et unam gallinam ad Natale.

Willelmus Escofle xii denarios et iiii°r precarias et crassam gallinam in Natale.

Willelmus Mazon xii denarios.

Anna v solidos annuatim et ii carrieta et dimidium ligni et iii precarias cum ii hominibus et i precariam ut Rogerus Verer.

Rolandus et Hugo cum fratre suo tantumdem debent quantum predicta Anna.

Ricardus filius Alwal xlii denarios in iiii°r terminis anni et i carrietum ligni et iiii precarias ut Rogerus Verer.

Helewis et sorores eius xiii denarios in iiii terminis anni et iiii precarias more Rogeri Verer.

Edmundus filius Lewani i denarium.

Radulfus Subard vi solidos et c ova in pascha et ii carrieta ligni et dimidium et iii precarias cum ii hominibus et quartam ut Rogerus Verer.

Thomas Boselin xii denarios et iiii precarias.

Ywini faber iii solidos in iiii terminis anni de terra sua et xii denarios pro mareis et iiii precarias.

Anais del marais xxxiiii denarios et iiii precarias.

Mulieres del marais vi denarios et iiii precarias.

Iwin del marais ii solidos in iiii terminis et iiii precarias.

Akenild famula sacerdotis v solidos et iiii precarias.

Rogerus pistor xii denarios et iiii precarias.

Gilbertus pelliparius i denarium.

Thurchil carpentarius iiii solidos et iii precarias cum ii hominibus et quartam more Rogeri Verer et iii carrieta ligni.

Willelmus mercator iiii solidos in iiii terminis et ii carrieta ligni et iii precarias cum ii hominibus et quartam ut Rogerus Verer.

Odo xii denarios in iiii terminis.

Reginaldus cementarius iiii solidos et iii precarias et quartam sicut Rogerus Verer.

Willelmus le Grangier ii solidos et iiii precarias.

Nunne Beleset c ova.

Clemens iiii solidos et iii precarias cum duobus hominibus et quartam ut Rogerus Verer.

Rogerus Cocus xii denarios annuatim et iiii precarias.

Turgis xvi denarios et iiii precarias.

Asketel Ioud et Lune iiii solidos et iii carrieta ligni et iii precarias cum ii hominibus et quartam ut Rogerus Verer.

Leeuiue vidua xii denarios et iiii precarias.

Hakene sutor xii denarios et iiii precarias.

Togus xii denarios et iiii precarias.

Edmundus subulcus xii denarios et iiii precarias.

Odelina xiv denarios et iiii precarias.

Galfridus xii denarios et iiii precarias.

Hervicus corueiser xii denarios et iiii precarias.

Uluus pope xii denarios. Et Eluina xii denarios et iiii precarias inter hos duos.

Botild Bealmund xviii denarios.

Radulphus filius Lamberti iii denarios.

Iwim Archer xii denarios et iiii precarios.

Ulfus mercador xii denarios et iiii precarios.

Michael xii denarios.

Ailward Palle xii denarios et iiii precarias.

Rogerus Lente ii solidos et iiii precarias.

Galfridus Bernard xii denarios et iiii precarias.

Aliz filia Ricardi xiiii denarios et iiii precarias.

Thomas Kurn xii denarios et iiii precarias.

Habe filius Nicholai xii denarios et iiii precarias.

Symon Grene xii denarios et iiii precarias.

Edmundus filius Willelmi ii denarios.

Reginaldus filius Lamberti v solidos et iii precarias cum ii hominibus et quartam ut Rogerus Verer et iiii carrieta ligni.

Galfridus filius Ungolf xii denarios.

Tenentes xii acras et seruicia eorundem.

Mattheus pro xii acris a festo Sancti Michaelis usque ad uincula Sancti Petri semper in die Lune cuiuslibet septimane tenetur operari sed in Natali et Pascha et Pentecost cessat opere. Sed ita debet operari cum tribus hominibus ut habeat ii cumbos frumenti uel siliginis et i ordei cumbum et avene vi eskepes et tenetur properare ii cumbos brasii ad Natale et ii cumbos post et tam bene tentur facere quod bracista se teneat precatum. Et ad predictum brasium desiccandum habebit dimidiam acram stipuli et faciet average cum veniat ad illum per totam provinciam de Northfolch et ii careres ligni et omnes oues eius debent esse in fauda prioris exceptis matrialibus ouibus quas ipsemet habet in suo hospicio a Purificatione usque ad inventionem Sancte Crucis et omnes alie debent esse per totum annum in fauda predicta et omnia etiam eius animalia a festo Sancti Dunstani usque ad festum Sancti Martini iacebunt in fauda prioris nisi condonetur. Inter se et alium tenentur dare v careres in festo sancti Dunstani vel ualenciam et in illa ebdomina non operabitur nec nulla in qua auerabit et pro i ebdomada estatis falcabit dimidiam acram prati et a festo Sancti Petri ad uincula in qualibet ebdomada usque ad festum Sancti Michaelis metere et ligare tenetur i acram et dimidiam et hoc faciet in die lune et mercurie et in die veneris. Et si forte assumpcio Sancte Marie in aliquo horum dierum evenerit quietus erit a dimidia acra et faciet iii precarias cum tali cibo ut Rogerus Verer et quartam ebdomadam ut Rogerus Verer et carriabit insuper uel cum quadriga uel cum biga secundum morem Rogerus Verer.

Alanus Clogge tenetur easdem consuetudines facere quas predictus Matheus. Et Alanus filius Lewini easdem faciet consuetudines. Et Iordanus filius Seule faciet easdem consuetudines. Alanus Plome. et Galfridus Dole. Willelmus Brid. Rogerus Torele. Sirger arebois. Edmundus Kempe. Radulphus filius Ioni. Willelmus Stanardi filius. Elwinus Bincista. Rogerus filius Dom. Iohannes filius Toke. Iohannes filius Stanuine. Jordanus eiusdem filius. Isti omnes insimul predicti eadem debent consuetudines quas Matteus.

Willelmus Elfstani filius. Gilbertus pelliparius. Edmundus subulcus. Henrico palmerius. Radulfus carpentarius. Alanus carpenter. Radulfus Barrare. Edmundus filius Edeni. Sperefeke Bole. Godewinus Sift. Reginaldus filius Ulvi. Ouius. Terra Brostani. Omnes isti predicti a Matheo hucusque eandem debent consuetudinem quam ipse Matheus.

Tenentes xxiiii acras et seruicia eorundem.

Ranulphus prepositus in qualibet septimana a festo sancti Michaelis usque ad uincula sancti Petri bis tenetur operari preter in Natali et Pascha et Pentecosten scilicet in die Lune et in die Veneris. Preterea auerabit bis semper ubi Matheus operatur semel et iiii caries ligni et iiii cumbos tenetur properare ante Natale et iiii post et ad desiccandum brasium i acram stipuli habebit et omnes eius oves in fauda prioris per totum annum iacebunt exceptis matrionalibus ouibus quas in proprio suo hospicio a Purificatione usque ad Inventionem Sancte Crucis habebit et omnia sua animalia in fauda prioris iacebunt a festo Sancti Dunstani usque ad festum Sancti Martini nisi ei prior gratia condonet pro suo. Debet etiam in festum Sancti Dunstani v cleias vel precium et falcabit i acram prati et illud coadimabit et in illa ebdomada cessabit ab opere et in illa ebdomada in qua auerabit cessabit ab alio opere et metet et ligabit et coadimabit sicut Matheus et carriabit sicut Rogerus Verer et in precarias faciet cum ii hominibus et quartam sicut. Rogerus Verer et in proxima ebdomada post festum sancti Michaelis carriabit fimum secundum hoc quod habet in aratro et officium prioris recipiet ut ei continget. Warinus filius Leuine. Walterus Ricaldes. Alanus filius Willelmi. Radulfus Nouus homo. Adam filius Turka. Edmundus filius Lewini. Edmundus filius Willelmi. Isti omnes a Ranulfo hucusque eandem debent consuetudinem.

Tenentes vi acras et seruicia eorundem.

Alanus de Sugate in qualibet ebdomada a festo Sancti Michaelis usque ad uincula Sancti Petri semel tenetur operari scilicet in die Lune preter in Natali et Pascha et Pentecosten et i carreie ligni et i cumbum brasii ante Natale et i post et habebit i percatam stipule et oues eius cum animalibus more Mathei iacebunt in fauda prioris et in festo sancti Dunstani debet unam cleiam et falcabit dimidiam acram prati et coadimabit et a festo Sancti Petri ad uincula in qualibet ebdomada usque ad festum Sancti Michaelis bis tenetur operari scilicet in die Lune et in die Veneris et coadimabit et faciet iii precarias cum uno homine et quartam ut Rogerus Verer et carriabit sicut Rogerus Verer et in proxima ebdomada post festum sancti Michaelis secundum quod habet in aratro fimum carriabit et officium prioris recipiet ut ei continget. Ion filius Aileve et Arnulfus pelliparius easdem debent consuetudines quas Alanus facit.

Tenentes croft et seruicia eorum.

Matheus tenet unam croftam et in die Lune a festo sancti Iohannis usque ad uincula sancti Petri debet sarclere et a festo sancti Petri ad vincula usque ad festum sancti Michaelis in qualibet die Lune dimidiam acram tenetur metere et ligare et coadimare et quando veniet sarclere veniet sole oriente et serclabit usque pulsabitur ad altam missam et postquam monachi comederint sarclabit usque pulsatur ad vesperas et plantabit fabas ad inuitationem prioris. Ailmer Bigod easdem debet consuetudines quas Matheus et preterea omnes ei oves et animalia iacebunt in fauda prioris more Ranulfi prepositi.

4
Statement of the liability to suit at the Hundred Court of Mitford.

Taken from the extent of the manor of Shipdham made for the Bishop of Ely in 1277.

Cott. Claud. C. xi, fol. 225 b.

Istud manerium est in comitatu Norfolchie et in hundredo et dimidia de Mitford' quod spectant ad libertatem Elyensem et pertinent ad istud manerium et sunt libera in manu domini Elyensis. Ita quod dominus Elyensis et ballivi sui habere debent omnis attachiamenta et returna omnium brevium domini regis et placitare in eisdem hundredo et dimidio omnia placita que vicecomes potest placitare per brevem et sine brevi et de aueriis captis iniuste et contra uadium et plegios detentis tam de alienis feodis quam de suis propriis.

Nomina uillarum infra sedem predictorum hundredi et dimidii existencium scilicet. Schipedham capitale manerium. Derham. Lectona. Cranewrthe. Risinges. Bergh maior. Hardingham. Reymereston. Gerolfueston.' Thurston'. Mateshale. Bergh minor. Estwodeham. Northwodeham. Iakesham. Westfeld. Hokeringe. et Fyneberigge.

Isti subscripti debent sectas de hundredo in hundredum per annum scilicet

Schypedham.

Iohannes ate Kote et participes sui debent unam sectam.
Robertus ate Buk et participes sui unam sectam.

Rogerus de Verly unam sectam.
Symo Prudbern et participes sui unam sectam.
Homagium Friuill' unam sectam.
Alexander de la rode unam sectam.
Homagium de Caston' unam sectam.

Derham.

Hugo de Camera debet unam sectam.
Homagia in Morrawe unam sectam.
Ricardus Wlfketel et participes sui unam sectam.

Lectona.

Symon de Hecham et participes sui unam sectam.
Homagia in Morhawe unam sectam.
Ricardus filius War' et participes sui unam sectam.
Homagium Friuile unam sectam.
Willelmus filius Martini et participes sui unam sectam.
Robertus faber et participes sui unam sectam.

Kraneworthe.

Willelmus filius Rogeri de Suaffing' unam sectam.
Martinus filius Iohannis et participes sui unam sectam.

Risinges.

Willelmus de Buktone unam sectam.
Ricardus faber et participes sui unam sectam.

Bergh maior.

Brokefford' unam sectam.
Willelmus filius Walteri et participes sui unam sectam.
Rogerus de Oxelaie unam sectam.

Hardingeham.

Radulfus de Camais unam sectam.
Homagium suum unam aliam sectam.
Willelmus de Gurnay et homagium suum duas sectas.
Iohannes de Manceston' et participes sui unam sectam.
Benedictus de Brekles et participes sui unam sectam.

Reymereston.

Homagium comitis Warenne unam sectam.
Homagium Willelmi de Gurnay unam sectam.
Iohannes Gelram et participes sui unam sectam.
Homagium domini Willelmi Bardouf unam sectam.

Gerolueston'.

Willelmus filius Petri unam sectam.
Robertus filius Iohannis unam sectam.

Thurston.

Robertus filius Ricardi de Worthstede unam sectam.
Willelmus filius Roberti ad ecclesiam unam sectam.
Homagium Willelmi de Gurnay unam sectam.
Hermerus Wace et participes sui unam sectam.
Willelmus filius Philippi et participes sui unam sectam.
Robertus Oldeman et participes sui unam sectam.
Homagium domini Willelmi Bardulf unam sectam.

Mateshal'.

Robertus de Estfield unam sectam.
Rogerus Kyppe et participes sui unam sectam.
Manserus et participes sui unam sectam.
Ricardus Curneis et participes sui unam sectam.
Lucas del Wro et participes sui unam sectam.
Iohannes Wistan et participes sui unam sectam.
Homagium Roberti filius Ricardi de Worthested' unam sectam.

Bergh minor.

War' Horn et participes sui unam sectam.
Ricardus Ellured' et participes sui unam sectam.
Henricus de Bergh' unam sectam.
Thoroldus filius Benedicti et participes unam sectam.
Iohannes filius Gilberti et participes sui unam sectam.
Iohannes filius Nigelli et participes sui unam sectam.

Estwodeham.

Robertus de Kokefeld unam sectam.
Ricardus de Hakyslund dimidiam sectam.
Galfridus de Cattemere cum particibus suis unam sectam.
Homagium de Costesheye unam sectam.
Hugo Sailewastel et participes sui unam sectam.
Willelmus de Shotesham et participes sui unam sectam.
Willelmus ate Sclede unam sectam.
Magister Radulfus de Berri unam sectam.

Northwodeham.

Ricardus filius Willelmi unam sectam.
Rogerus de Seyncler unam sectam.
Thomas Thurford dimidiam sectam.
Ricardus de Bauaunt unam sectam.
Iohannes clericus et participes sui unam sectam.
Homagium constabularii unam sectam.
Willelmus de aqua et participes sui unam sectam.
Homagium de belhus in Northwodeham unam sectam.

Iakesham.

Robertus de Curcun unam sectam.
Iohannes filius Willelmi et participes sui unam sectam.
Rogerus de Brakefeld et participes sui unam sectam.
Andrea de Iakesham et participes sui unam sectam.
Homagium de Fineberge in Iakesham unam sectam.

Westfeld'.

Iohannes de Bretton' unam sectam.
Willelmus Wynter unam sectam.
Ricardus de Mora unam sectam.

Hokeringe.

Ricardus Thurubern et participes sui debent unam sectam.

Fyneberg'.

Est infra sedem ut supra sed non debet sectam.

5

Description of Soke of Bramford

Taken from extent of the Manor made in 1277.

Cott. Claud. C. xi, fol. 311.

De soka pertinente ad istud manerium.

Westrefield.

Aduocatio ecclesie et donatio in eadem uilla de Westrefield pertinet ad episcopum Elyensem ratione manerii de Bramford ut patet de supra. Persona eiusdem ecclesie tenet quoddam tenementum quod Augustinus de Westrefeld de eo tenet in eadem uilla pro duodecim denariis ad festum Sancti Michaelis per annum pro omnibus.

T 2

Thomas filius Alcheri tenet quadraginta acras terre pro nouem solidis et decem denariis equaliter et debet sectam curie et dominus habebit palefridum suum cum toto hernesio post mortem eius pro releuio uel meliorem bestiam domus si palefridum non habuit et si nullam habuit bestiam tunc habebit dominus quinque solidos et quattuor denarios tantum. Et post mortem eius filius et heres eius quietus erit de suo releuio propter predictum herietum et uxor eiusdem defuncti dotata erit de medietate illius terre.

Gundr' de Tudeham tenet duas acras terre pro duobus denariis per annum ad festum sancti Michaelis et per easdem consuetudines quas idem Thomas eo excepto quod non dabit eodem modo releuium nisi tantum quantum dat de annuo redditu quia non est residens.

Wyntenton'.

Aduocatio ecclesie eiusdem uille et donatio spectat ad episcopum Elyensem ratione manerii de Bramford ut patet de supra.

Persona eiusdem ecclesie tenet decem acras terre cum pertinenciis pro decem solidis per annum ad festum sancti Michaelis.

Radulfus Carbonel tenet duodecim acras pro sexdecim denariis equaliter et per easdem consuetudines quas predictus Thomas facit.

Brihtmerus Colle tenet duas acras et dimidiam pro tribus denariis equaliter et per easdem consuetudines quas predictus Thomas facit ut supra.

Ricardus Selote tenet duas acras et dimidiam pro tribus denariis et per easdem consuetudines quas predictus Thomas facit.

Heredes Ade de Blancheuilla tenent in Wytenton' et Thurleston' quinque acras pro octo denariis equaliter et facient tot et easdem consuetudines quas predictus Thomas facit.

Vincencius de Rubrok tenet unam acram pro duobus denariis equaliter et faciet tales consuetudines quas unus non residens facit.

Thurleston'.

Iohannes filius Alani Iohannes Ade Robertus le Tanner et Galfridus Ordmeri tenent septem acras pro uiginti denariis equaliter et unus quisque eorum faciet tot et easdem consuetudines quas predictus Thomas facit.

Willelmus de Pinton' senior et Willelmus iunior et Iuliana relicta Ædmundi et Brithmerus Colle tenent unam acram pro quattuor denariis equaliter et quilibet eorum faciet tot et easdem consuetudines quas predictus Thomas facit preter Brihtmerum Colle quia non est hic residens.

Walterus Gunter tenet unam acram pro quattuor denariis equaliter et facit tot et easdem consuetudines quas predictus Thomas facit.

Rogerus de marisco tenet duas acras pro octo denariis equaliter et facit tot et easdem consuetudines.

Alanus iustus tenet unam acram pro duodecim denariis equaliter et facit tot et easdem consuetudines.

Willelmus Colle tenet in Thurleston' et Wytenton' duas acras pro tribus denariis equaliter et per tot et easdem consuetudines quas predictus Thomas facit.

Charesfeld.

Prior de Letherinham tenet sex acras pro quinque denariis ad festum sancti Michaelis et debet sectam curie.

Cleydon'.

Petrus le barun et Gunnora Geynecrowe tenent unam acram et unam rodam et aliam rodam pro duobus denariis equaliter et per tales consuetudines quas unus non residens facit.

Robertus de Cleydon tenet in Cleidone et Hemingeston' septem acras pro uiginti denariis equaliter et per easdem consuetudines quas predictus Thomas facit.

Galfridus de molendina tenet duas acras pro tribus denariis in terminis sancti Andree Paschae et Natiuitatis sancti Iohannis equaliter et per tales consuetudines quas non residens facit.

Brianus molendinarius tenet unam acram pro uno denario ad festum sancti Michaelis et non est residens.

Willelmus de Cleidone tenet duas acras pro sex denariis equaliter et non est residens.

Prior sancti Trinitatis tenet in Cleidone et Helmigham uiginti acras pro quinque solidis et quattuor denariis equaliter et debet sectam curie.

Sumersham.

Heres Galfridi de Ambly tenet octo acras pro septem denariis ad festum sancti Michaelis et est residens sicut predictus Thomas.

Hemmingeston'.

Alexander Athelwine tenet quattuor acras pro quattuor denariis equaliter et non est hic residens.

Willelmus palmerus tenet octo acras pro octo denariis et non est residens.

Magister Iohannes de Eysh' tenet quattuor acras pro quattuor denariis equaliter nec residens est.

Iuliana de Bosemere tenet quattuordecim acras pro duobus solidis equaliter nec residens est.

Willelmus Lewine et eius participes tenent unam acram et dimidiam pro decem denariis equaliter et uterque eorum faciet tot et easdem consuetudines quas predictus Thomas.

Ada de Srubbelund tenet duodecim acras pro duobus solidis equaliter et non est residens.

Esk.

Egidius de Wechesham tenet triginta acras pro septem solidis sex denariis equaliter. Et faciet tot et easdem consuetudines quas Thomas facit.

Tudeham.

Margeria de Blancheuilla tenet uiginti acras pro tribus solidis et octo denariis equaliter et faciet tot et easdem consuetudines quas predictus Thomas facit.

Stanham.

Iohannes filius Roberti tenet duodecim acras pro duobus solidis et octo denariis in terminis sancti Michaelis et Paschae equaliter et est residens sicut predictus Thomas.

Ulenden'.

Robertus de Ulenden tenet triginta acras pro tribus solidis et sex denariis equaliter et est residens sicut predictus Thomas.

Blakenham.

Stephanus Tepekin tenet sex acras pro octodecim denariis equaliter et est residens sicut predictus Thomas.

Matildis Hert tenet sex acras pro octodecim denariis equaliter et est residens sicut predictus Thomas.

Ricardus Almar tenet dimidiam acram in Blakeham parua pro uno obolo ad festum sancti Michaelis et non est residens.

Batesford.

Margareta Potterere tenet unam acram pro uno denario in terminis sancti Michaelis et Paschae et non est residens.

Iohannes de Cruce tenet unam acram pro quattuor denariis equaliter et est residens sicut predictus Thomas.

Willelmus Margerie tenet unam acram pro quattuor denariis equaliter et est residens eodem modo.

Berkinge.

Hubertus de Berkinge tenet nouem acras scilicet Wymundeslond pro quinque denariis et obolo ad festum sancti Michaelis.

Iohannes Edus tenet duas acras pro quattuor denariis equaliter et est residens sicut predictus Thomas.

Hubertus del Hawet et idem Iohannes Edus tenent duas acras et unum mesuagium et unam grauam pro decem denariis equaliter.

Alicia Clunch tenet unam mesuagium pro uno denario ad festum sancti Michaelis et est residens sicut predictus Thomas.

6

Statement of the services of 'Reginaldus Clericus' (ante 1168.)

Marginal note in the Benet of Hulme Cartulary.

Cott. Galba E. ii, fol. 66.

Hec sunt consuetudines quas fecit Reginaldus clericus pro terra sua in tempore abbatis Thome et antea. De censu xxxi denarios et obolum ad tres terminos. Pro uno prato iiii denarios die sancti Benedicti in quadragesima. Pro faldagio iiii denarios die sancti Ethelberti. Ad multones v denarios. Ad commune auxilium iii denarios. Ipse debet iiii aueragia et dimidium de frumento, unam rucam ad festum omnium sanctorum. Unum quart' rasum de auene. Et debet arare ter in anno et excutere bladum semel in yeme. Unam gallinam ad Natale et oua ad Pascha. Et sarcler' i die. Et viii diebus debet operare in autumpno sine cibo. et i die ex piece cum cibo. Et gauelare i die et i die ad Hecham et carier' cum socio in autumpno. Hoc totum fecit Ethelstanus cuius fuit eadem terra ante eum.

INDEX